MYRNA KOSTASH was born in Edmonton and educated at the University of Alberta and at the University of Toronto, where she studied Slavic languages and literature before heading off to Europe for two years of hitch-hiking, doing odd jobs, and beginning a writer's life. She returned to Toronto in 1971 and spent four years as a freelance magazine writer – appearing mainly in *Saturday Night*, *Maclean's*, and *Chatelaine* – as well as teaching in the experimental women's studies programme at the University of Toronto. In 1975 she returned to Alberta to research and write her first book, *All of Baba's Children*, an account of the experiences of her parents' generation of Ukrainian-Canadians. In 1980 she published *Long Way From Home*, the story of the Sixties generation in Canada. She continues to write occasionally for magazines and for radio and television, and has had one stage play produced.

Myrna Kostash lives in Edmonton and spends her summers in a shack on a quarter section near Two Hills, Alberta.

MYRNA KOSTASH

No Kidding

Inside the World of Teenage Girls

An M&S Paperback from McClelland and Stewart

First printing January 1989

Copyright © 1987 by Myrna Kostash

Canadian Cataloguing in Publication Data

Kostash, Myrna
No Kidding: inside the world of teenage girls

(M&S paperbacks)
Includes bibliographical references.
ISBN 0-7710-4538-7

1. Teenage girls – Canada.   I. Title.

HQ799.C3K67 1989   305.2'35'0971   C88-094735-7

Cover design by Peter Maher
Cover photograph by Peter Paterson

Typesetting by Pickwick
Printed and bound in Canada by Ronalds Printing

Cloth edition printed 1987:

A Douglas Gibson Book
McClelland and Stewart
The Canadian Publishers
481 University Avenue
Toronto M5G 2E9

Contents

This book is for my sister, Janice

Introduction

I HAD TURNED forty and realized I was in danger of becoming an old fuddy-duddy – a grown-up pursing her lips at the sight of teenage girls with blue streaks in their hair and holding her hands over her ears at the sound of their music, not to mention turning grey before her time at the news that teenagers were having babies and snorting cocaine in the locker room and dropping out of school to get jobs as topless waitresses. I was getting close to the stage of asking the complaining question typical of adults confronting the arrival of a whole new generation after them: "*What is the world coming to?*" Sitting across the table from a fifteen-year-old, I did not want to be the complaining grown-up I mocked when I was that age: a passé, know-nothing stumblebum. But the question hung in the air, and I decided it was an honest one, and deserved an honest effort at a reply.

The fact is that I knew nothing about teenage girls. I didn't know any, didn't keep their company, never ran into them. As a childless woman (and one whose friends were only just starting to raise families), I realized that I had fallen victim to the fallacy that *my* generation was still at the cutting edge of youth, that we were still the *wunderkinder* of the post-war world, when in fact a whole new generation of people was growing up under my nose and seeing *me* as middle-aged. This was a shock. It would have been easy, even satisfying, to succumb to injured vanity and sneer at their naivety. I decided instead to go out of my everyday world (where everybody has a dusty copy of *Sergeant Pepper's Lonely Hearts Club Band*, reads *This Magazine*, and remembers the first time they saw an Italian art movie) and spend some time with girls who drool over Boy George, watch porn videos at birthday parties, and don't read a thing.

As a feminist, I was also very curious to see whether the revived women's movement, now some fifteen years old, had reproduced itself: in the lives of teenage girls, had we made any difference at all?

I had only three ideas with which to launch my project. One was to avoid the sensationalism of so many accounts of teenage lives. ("Adolescents are experiencing self-destructive, emotional, sexual and drug problems in ever-increasing numbers," as the *Vancouver Sun* reminded us in 1985.) Related to this was my second decision, to talk to adults only when absolutely necessary (some school counsellors, a couple of teachers, several youth workers), so as to keep the account focussed on what the girl herself had to say about her experience – what her life was like *from her point of view* – and avoid distorting it with the well-meaning interpretation, counsel, and moralizing of authority figures. Thirdly, I decided I would talk only to girls. For one thing, I couldn't imagine how I could get close enough to teenage boys to get to know them; for another, and more important, so much of what has been written about adolescence assumes that girls and boys live in the same teen culture, and that if you describe boys' experience in that culture you've described everybody's. No, I would write about girls.

And so I began. I began in my own city, Edmonton, by putting out the word among my friends that I wanted to meet teenage girls – did anyone know one? One friend shared an office with the mother of a fifteen-year-old; another friend knew of a colleague raising a sixteen-year-old; a third sang in a choir with some teenagers. And so on. I called the girls' parent(s), explained briefly what I wanted, and asked to speak to the girl herself. No one refused me an interview. (In fact, of all the contacts I made, only one girl decided against continuing past the first interview.) One thing led to another. A girl would tell me about her girlfriends, or a teacher or a counsellor would direct me to someone in particular, a girl living on her own, for instance, or a member of the Students' Council. Or I would look deliberately for them myself; I decided, for example, to try to meet non-white girls, a girl interested in computers, a Heavy Metal fan. I expanded my contacts to Vancouver, where I made a point of meeting girls who have dropped out of school, and to Toronto, where I "targeted" girls I could not readily meet in Edmonton – a girl from a private school, girls in the alternative schools, a girl in the peace movement.

Taped interviews – sometimes in my house, usually in the girl's bedroom – were the core of my research. With some girls, conversation was exhausted after a couple of hours; with others, an interview led to an on-going relationship in which I would see the girl intermittently over several months. In addition to the interviews, I kept a journal of impressions and reports or unrecorded conversations; I clipped newspapers and read literature in the field of adolescence. Above all, like an anthropologist, I did "field studies" – I went to discotheques, school dances, punk dances; to football and volleyball games; to dance and operetta rehearsals, a Christmas concert, and Grad Council meetings. I visited boutiques, Employment Canada offices, drop-in centres, dozens of classrooms and cafeterias. I hung out in shopping malls, and even went to rec room parties.

The conversations I had were remarkably candid. To my amazement (I have dealt with many a reticent adult in my work), my interviewees talked openly and at length about a great number of things without having to be coaxed or directed. They had, as we used to say, "the gift of the gab" and were wise beyond their years. (I am talking here about an *oral* sophistication that does not necessarily extend to their ability to read and write.) Only one parent attempted to intervene between her daughter and me – the distraught mother of a girl who had left home, who wanted me to tell her what was "wrong". I had to refuse. It was essential always that I saw a girl's situation only from her own point of view; I could not afford to identify with the parent's.

Before I went into the conversations I had no idea what I was going to hear. My tapes record my gasps, groans, and shrieks as I responded to particularly shocking or unexpected comments. I pride myself on my worldliness, but there were stories I heard – and that you will read – which were truly hair-raising and heart-breaking, and which I was hearing for the first time. Nobody else had ever asked, so the stories came tumbling out.

"Perhaps the most significant thing about adolescents in our culture," writes Sheila Kitzinger[1] in *Women's Experience of Sex*, "is that they are not taken seriously. Whatever the girl does, whatever she believes, someone will say, 'She'll grow out of it, it's just a phase.'" I like to think that the girls talked to me as openly as they did because they knew I *was* taking them seriously – listening carefully, asking questions, responding with genuine interest – and that, although I was an adult (and therefore "smarter" about some things than their girlfriends), I had no authority over them. They could disclose themselves to me *with impunity*: I would not lecture them, or turn them over to the cops, or insist they see a psychiatrist.

Besides, I'm sure they could tell I was enjoying myself enormously in their company.

"I would never want to change anything about me," said fifteen-year-old Sharon, "because then it wouldn't be me." I can't imagine myself having said that at her age, for I remember us girls as being, almost without exception, diffident, self-doubting, emotionally and sexually insecure, and all too ready to trade ourselves in for another model, as advertised in *Seventeen* magazine, for instance. But perhaps Sharon's assertion is grounded not so much on self-esteem as on an awareness that her generation is smaller than the one that preceded it, the ubiquitous Baby Boomers. She belongs to a minority and cannot count on her cohorts to challenge the distressing instability of the adult world and the deteriorating political and economic situation of the Western world; they are too few. Things are not going to get better. She has only herself to rely on.

There are other differences between us. Sharon and her girlfriends, without exception, had a vision of what they wanted to do in the world; it did not necessarily include marriage and family life. At her age, I and my friends, when we had such a worldly vision, always tacked it on to marriage; it was never as clearly outlined as the sunlit fantasy of ourselves in suburban kitchens. Sharon and her friends, in their hair-styles and clothing and language, present a whole bazaar of feminine types; when I look at my high school yearbook, I see girls cast from two moulds: the Cheerleader (the girl in the matching angora-wool sweater set) and the Frump (the girl whose own mother cut her hair). Among Sharon and her friends certain cherished assumptions – about monogamy, the nuclear family, chastity, heterosexuality – are assailable; what we took for granted in the early sixties – that good girls were virgins, that marriage was for keeps, that nobody *we* knew was gay – has been thoroughly undermined.

Some things haven't changed a bit. Girls still operate at a tremendous social and economic disadvantage compared to boys – they are paid less money at work, receive less attention at school, and are given fewer breaks at home. And they find themselves, for all the transformations of their own female culture, still locked in association with boys whose range of emotions, intellectual breadth, and sexual etiquette doesn't seem to have expanded a jot since the sixties. If anything, some things are worse. Now that the taboo against premarital sex has fallen, girls are receiving even less pleasure from sex, as cuddling and necking and petting are forgone in the rush for the joyless humping of teenagers on car seats.

It is not so easy, then, to make a definitive statement about the situation of teenage girls. What makes it even harder is the fact that adults' ideas about adolescence are so ambivalent. On the one hand, we seem to believe, despite all the evidence to the contrary, that youth is a "golden age" of unlimited enthusiasm, energy, and possibility; that, in spite of the fact that teenagers lack precisely the things that would help realize their fabulous potential – social power and economic security – they are somehow more "vital", more "intense", and happier than we grownups. We envy them their freshness and spontaneity and optimism, and, when we are defeated by our jaded palates and disappointed hopes, we see in youth the phenomenon that will save us: innocence and zest and raw emotion will carry the day. It is as though the teenager were a kind of Noble Savage, unlettered and bad-mannered, who nevertheless is closer than we are to unsullied human nature.

On the other hand, we assault, batter, and rape our children, abandon them to the streets, lose them to suicide, as though we cannot do what every simpler creature can: care for its young. We resent our children's "freedom". We complain about their lack of responsibility for family relationships and work routines, and grumble about their preoccupation with having a good time, without realizing, as culture critic Simon Frith[2] points out, that it is only people utterly without power who can "account for their lives in terms of play, focus their politics on leisure". We berate youth for its rebelliousness, its general lack of respect for us and our works, and its uppityness. But we produce, if studies are to be believed, our clones: young people who reflect back at us the imprint of our own values, prejudices, and opinions.

As for my own feelings, in the course of getting to know these girls, I was surprised by the strength of what I can only call the "parental" or "maternal" emotion I felt when a girl came close to getting into serious trouble, or told me about some psychic injury she had sustained, or day-dreamed out loud: I felt a strong surge of alarm and protectiveness and sympathy. I suppose I was remembering too what it had been like to be a teenage girl. Remembering that peculiar powerlessness of the dependant, the resentment of all the circumscriptions laid on me "because" I was a girl, the dreaminess of one who has everything still to do, the wonder and bewilderment of first friendships, first loves, first broken hearts, first recoveries. And I suppose I was thinking how I would not want to be her again for anything in the world, not even in the 1980s.

But I confess to holding out a small hope that the girls who come after me might embody in some way what I know about being a woman and making a life worth living. American scholar Patricia Meyer Spacks, in her very wise book, *The Adolescent Idea: Myths of Youth and the Adult Imagination*,[3] writes about "the longing of the adult world that their children should confirm their values – by living up to them even better than their parents have done or, at the very least, by paying lip service to them. . . . Seldom does one altogether reject an earlier self."

Because I grew up at a time when it seemed youth would make a revolution – cultural, sexual, spiritual, if not political – I have a special fondness for that earlier self, who seemed so brave and tough and free. And nothing would please me more than if, among "my" girls, there were those who said they believed in the revolution too and would fight. But that's the nostalgic "parent" talking. The writer, like the parent, has to let these girls go where they may. And wish them Godspeed.

M.K.
January 1987

I INTERVIEWED fifty or so girls in Edmonton, Vancouver, and Toronto. All their names, the names of the individuals they mention, and some identifying details have been changed. However, the assumed names remain constant throughout. Each of the twelve profile chapters represents a single individual; there are no "composite" portraits.

M.K.

ONE

Diary

From the author's high school diary, 1961, aged 16

JANUARY 17: "Dear sweet good loving understanding God – hear me, please. I'd love to go on a date with someone SOON."

February 1: "When E.'s gaze catches mine, he holds it intently and I give him a real soul-searching look. When I talk to him he gets a dazed look on his face. But I don't think he likes me really."

February 11: "I wrote an outline headed under 'Why E. Might Like Me' and 'Why E. Might Not Like Me'. I found that the latter much outnumbered the former, so I sort of collapsed inside, mentally gave up, and have felt much better ever since. Oh, God, he's got to be at the dance."

March 3: "E. has said so many sweet things to me. He said every song he hears reminds him of me, that my eyes could melt any man, that he'd be waiting for me with his everlovin' arms. Please, it's so wonderful, let it be true."

May 12: "E. was always afraid of losing me. He lost me tonight. We were at C's party and he ignored me completely. He never once spoke to me. He didn't ask me to dance and occupied his time cozily with R. He's been very mean to me and I won't forget it. I don't understand. Why must he prove he hates me? What have I done? He's so hard, so terrible, so cruel."

June 3: "I've been wondering whether I really want to get married, ever. Why get tied down? The life I've planned will be too exciting to end abruptly with a husband and the kitchen."

TWO

Judy

"I'm a very, very, very sentimental person."

FROM UNDERNEATH her bed she pulled out a large note-book, opened it, and, flipping through to the end, came to a poem she wanted me to hear. This was it:

> When I see you in the hallway
> My mind goes into flight!
> I don't know what I see in you
> That gives me such delight.
> People say I'm crazy,
> I tell them that it's true,
> But I guess they just don't realize
> How much that I love you!

She had not written this particular one – she has writ-ten others – but when a friend showed it to her she liked it so much she copied it out for her own collection, this large notebook of verses and jottings and sketches of flowers and glued-in newspaper photographs of Princess Diana. She shut it, sighed deeply, and said, in that unnervingly self-conscious manner of hers, "I'm a very, very, very sentimental person." She leapt up to pour me more tea, then dashed over to her closet, swung open its mirrored doors, and withdrew, for my delectation, one silk garment after another and several bolts of fabric, all of it brightly coloured and richly ornamented, gifts from an aunt who had been travelling to India for the express purpose, it would seem, of making appropriate purchases for her niece's dowry. (Judy stroked them with slender, appreciative fingers, but never in a million years would she wear any such thing to school.) The phone rang somewhere downstairs and she suddenly became very still, very alert. But no one called up to her and she resumed a chatty story about a slumber party she'd been invited to the last weekend, only to break off suddenly, race to the bedroom door, fling it open, and discover, to her considerable annoyance, her younger brother standing just outside.

"I can't stand it!" she shrieked and, grabbing her purse and a ski jacket, she pulled me with her, running down the staircase to the front hallway, where she shouted something at her mother and tugged me out the massive front door. I turned to have a glimpse of her mother, before the door closed on her, a small, dark-faced woman coming from the back of the house, clasping her hands in front of her breasts and looking at us with an expression of infinite misgiving. "I told her you wanted to visit my uncle's restaurant for your research," Judy explained, then directed me to the nearest shopping-mall McDonald's.

This is the way I will remember Judy: huddled into her jacket, her thick black bangs a kind of hood for her head, eyes moving frantically around while she sips Diet Coke at a Formica table at a shopping mall. I will meet her several times in just such a place, for precisely the same reason: Judy needs to get out of the house or she'll go nuts. She puffs gustily on More menthol cigarettes and taps them frenetically on the little aluminum ash tray, all the while nervously scanning the crowd for the faces of family friends, none of whom would be expected to understand what she's doing out of the house on a Sunday afternoon, smoking cigarettes. ("I want to look cool," she explains to me.)

That disconcerting self-consciousness: "I'm romantic. Romance is much, much more important than sex, don't you think? I'm still a virgin, but eighty per cent of the girls at school aren't. I write poetry. I'm madly in love with a boy. Do you swear you'll tell no one?" The story goes on for a full twenty minutes, a blow-by-blow account of in-conclusive conversations and aborted phone calls, of side-long glances, pregnant with meaning, of endless conjec-ture and speculation concerning the boy's intentions, of tormented doubts and wounding rumours and rapturous daydreams. For all the drama and excitement, however, Judy constantly interrupts her own story: "Do you think I'm pretty?" she asks, pushing her face forward, smiling brightly at me as though she knows I'm already con-vinced. Ten breaths later she sweeps her hair away from her face and wails, "I'm too dark!" only to forget this with another wave of her cigarette and an assured "I *am* pretty." There follows a fleeting reference to the time, a couple of years ago, when she was bulimic, vomiting after every meal; now, of course, she merely drinks Diet Coke and worries about getting fat.

She must hide her love away: the boy is a Pakistani and her father would kill him, if not her. Worse, she suspects that her father is arranging a marriage for her back home. There have been evasive references to an uncle's wedding at which the family's attendance is expected. For a second or two, I have an image of Judy gripping the edges of the Formica table, face down in the soiled napkins and empty cigarette package, while her parents haul at her ski jacket, trying to drag her all the way back home.

I will never understand her. She comes from a place I know nothing about, and just when I think I have under-stood her – Judy who loves Italian food and enjoys aero-bic exercise class and adores Madonna and struts her stuff in black high heels – she will abandon me and go off to that other place where she speaks Hindi and dreams of being a glamorous movie star in Delhi, walking about on the arm of a businessman, displaying around her throat the jewellery he has bought for her and feeding him the little cakes she has made in the conjugal kitchen. And then she will rejoin me, disclosing in urgent staccato that her father has openly threatened to move the whole family back to Bombay and has, indeed, struck her for receiving phone calls at home from a boy, and has since moved the phone into his own locked study. She has fled into her mother's arms, pleading not to be delivered without her consent into a marriage she is ill-prepared to endure (she is only sixteen), and is reassured that the only husband to whom her mother would promise her would be an Indian living in Canada: he would be kinder to her. Then the face is thrust close to mine, the hair swept back: "Would a white boy think I'm pretty?"

When I first met Judy's parents I felt like a suitor, on my best behaviour; as anxious to please as a boy, and as duplicitous. The occasion was a party which Judy was anxious to attend but to which she could not, of course, get her parents' consent; I, therefore, would serve as her excuse to get out of the house for the evening. It was a fairly elaborate deception: her parents had been told I was taking her to the theatre and then to a restaurant to interview her, which meant I had to be prepared in advance to discuss the plot of the play and its morality and to describe the restaurant, its location, its tone, and its menu. I arrived at their home, a very large and new structure on the southwestern edge of the city where other such families live (Judy's father is an engineer), and was greeted very solemnly by her parents and two young boys, big-eyed and speechless. While waiting for Judy to finish getting dressed, I sat with the family in the living room. This cavernous space, under a cathedral ceiling giving onto a solarium which housed one miserable plant, was sparsely furnished as though the moving van, dispatched a year ago, had still not arrived from the coast. The mother said nothing at all; the father asked me in a general way about my work and, about the evening, wished only to know what time I would bring Judy home. Nevertheless, I felt I had been intensely scrutinized, as Judy was when she finally made her appearance in very tight blue pants, black mps, and a large white jacket; I gamely assured her arents that it was perfectly all right to go to the theatre ressed just as she was.

To my amazement, this *was* Judy's idea of theatre dress, or, settled in my car, she pulled out from under the jacket er party outfit – a black off-the-shoulder blouse – together with a bottle of cologne, a little bag holding lipstick, blusher, and mascara, and a pack of menthol cigarettes. In several swift, deft movements, she switched the ar radio to the Top Forty station, lit a cigarette, slipped out of one costume into the other, twisted the rearview mirror into position to apply her make-up, and slathered on some scented "body cream". She laughed, she bounced around, she sang. She was going to a party.

Six months later it was exam week at the school and I picked her up in the school parking lot; the silent parking lot was empty and dead, and Judy, tapping her toe into the hot asphalt, waited impatiently. We had coffee in the mall cafeteria. "Notice that I've changed my brand?" and so she had, now smoking Benson and Hedges menthol because the boy she loves, Jason, hated her brand. She had something to show me, a picture; I thought it must be a photo of the beloved, but no, it was a picture, cut from a magazine, of his car, something sleek and red. She has told her parents, she said, that when she marries she'd like a car just like it. Don't bother with the Cuisinart and the crystal stemware and the designer shower curtain. This car, and the vision of herself careering about the city, hair blowing around her face while her lover's hand covers hers on the gearshift, is what she wants.

Suddenly: "I've told my parents to get me married right away. Listen, it's the only way to get out of the house. They'd *never* let me move out on my own. They want me to study, too, but they'd never let me study to be an actress, kissing and hugging strange men. My plan is to get married, stay a virgin for the first month, and, if I don't like him, leave him. Then I'd be a divorcee, wouldn't I? But I'd get to keep the car."

This was June. I had not heard from her for the two previous months. It was not like her, I told her, not to keep in touch. The story she told was from that place where I did not understand her; for all I knew it was a complete fabrication, so nonchalantly and imperturbably did she recount it. She had been failing her classes, she explained, and skipping out on most of them. This was so unexpected (she had been an Honours student) and so unacceptable to her parents, who had dreams of her working in her father's profession (as a married woman, of course), that, in agreement with a psychiatrist, she was signed into the "psych ward" at the university hospital: it was for her own good, because clearly something was very wrong with her. (It did not seem to occur to any of them, including Judy, that she may have been deliberately fouling her status at school so as to prolong her enrolment there and forestall any move back to India.) At first Judy treated the experience as a bit of a lark; she was out of the house, which was a relief, and she was pleasantly aware that a vague kind of Gothic glamour attaches itself to genteel women in madhouses. But twenty-four hours later she was genuinely upset, surrounded as she was by "loonies" and stuck in a room with an eight-year-old whose only "deviance" seemed to be that she was a bed-wetter and whose chastisement consisted of being denied candy. This broke Judy's heart and she phoned home and demanded to be released. She was, the next day.

What the hospital did not achieve, perhaps the school would: her parents and Judy visited the principal and it was agreed among them that she would be given another chance. She would be readmitted to her classes on condition that should she skip even one she would be expelled from school. She worked very hard for the next month, pushing her average back up into the 80s, and now everyone began breathing easier. What this meant for Judy, of course, was the chance to get away again: missing early-afternoon classes to have long, lazy breaks with Jason ("I lied to my teachers about not feeling well – I'm a good actress!") and bribing her kid brother – her only permitted companion on weekend evenings away from home – to go to the video arcade while she joined friends at the coffee shop.

There was, it seemed to me, one very simple thing to understand about Judy: the more she matured, the more terrified her parents became at the prospect of her unmanaged sexuality; the more they attempted to manage it, the more she sought to evade their authority. Of all the schoolgirls I interviewed, she was the only one for whom school life was an unequivocal good – "I love this school more than anything in the world" – because it provided her only means, for hours every weekday and occasionally on weekends, of living outside her parents' regime. Here she could dress as she liked (keeping a change of clothes and make-up in her locker), and talk with whomever she fancied. She could steal time away from classes to skip out to the mall or just to hang out in the washrooms and at the exits of the school, and, most important, she could rub up against peer culture: in school, in spite of her Indian face and her parents' schemes, Judy could become just another Canadian kid listening to Culture Club, reading love stories, and spending her allowance on French fries and plastic jewellery. The friendships she struck at school assumed an inordinate importance in terms of her self-esteem, a burden they could not always bear. She understood this: "Being a teenager is terrible sometimes; you get so fed up, you feel like killing yourself. Last year in grade ten I wanted to be popular and I tried too hard, I think. I tried to be friendly with everybody, smiled at everybody, acted cool, talked a lot, but it didn't work. This year I act like I couldn't care less about anybody and that's what makes me popular." So, at least, she would like to think.

Judy was hard on other girls. We strolled together

through the school halls one day at lunch hour and I pointed out a striking-looking girl, all dark of face and hair and eye, made up in pale purple lipstick and black punkish clothes; Judy commented that the girl had once dated Jason and who did I think was prettier, Judy or her? A girl in very tight blue jeans and a short black-leather jacket tapped her on the shoulder to say hello in the cafeteria; she was another of Jason's dates and was, of course, a "slut". We stopped by a washroom so that Judy could learn who was going with whom, dressed in what, to the next night's school dance. As she leaned over the sink, putting on lipstick, she heard that A. would be going with B., a piece of news that astonished her. *She* had heard, from B.'s brother, that B. "hates" A. She disclosed this bit of gossip to the gaggle around the sinks with obvious relish. I was not totally surprised to hear from her months later that a girl at school, to whom she had once confided her passion for Jason, threatened to tell Jason "everything" unless Judy paid her twenty dollars to shut up. Of such disingenuousness is so much girlish friendship made. Nevertheless, Judy did have one real friend, another Indian girl in her neighbourhood at whose house she would drop in after school for heart-to-heart talks.

"I have a different personality from my family," Judy said, pouring me more tea and offering a plate of confections she had baked herself. "I can't stay with them all the time. I have to get out, I have to party, I can't sit in the house all day. You kind of get sick of it after a while, you know what I mean? I *have* to get out, see the world, see what's happening." Because each moment of her independent leisure has been hard-won, her commitment to it is fierce. There is nothing casual about her enjoyment, so that even a holiday to the Rocky Mountains evoked in her only the melancholic reflection, "It's pretty here, but where's Southgate Mall?" She has spent whole days at the mall, her younger brother in tow, hoping to run into acquaintances from school with whom to see a movie or sit around a table in the ice-cream parlour. A wait at a bus stop has been the occasion for flirting with a boy from another school ("He was Lebanese, almost white"). An invitation to a party necessitated establishing an alibi – a girls' get-together – which in turn required the collaboration of friends in the deception. In the end her parents were suspicious and refused to allow her out of the house for the next two weeks, not even to go shopping, but it had all been worth it: Jason had shown up at the same party and, oh happiness, came in white pants, just like the ones she was wearing. Never mind that he didn't dance with Judy; he didn't dance with anyone else either, oh sweet relief.

On the pretext of having the chance to meet "all sorts of types" – punkers, preppies, heads, and Heavy Metal freaks – I was persuaded to buy a ticket to a hall party and accompany Judy there as a kind of chaperone. I had never heard of such a party – a group of teenagers pool their resources and rent the party room in an apartment building, arrange for a DJ and pizza, and charge six dollars per head for the privilege of attending – and was curious about it. As we pulled into the parking lot of a vast condominium complex south of the city limits, surrounded by the still-undeveloped fields of former farms, we could already make out the sounds of music from the party room. Kids were congregated outside the doors in little groups, chatting and sucking on bottles and reefers, while inside, in the large party room furnished with chairs and some tables, framed prints atilt on the walls, and carpeting on the floor, more kids were ranged around the periphery of the room swigging out of two-litre Coke bottles. It seemed like all teen parties of whatever time or place, and so there was a great deal of skittishness and whooping and running about, and not a little groping and nuzzling in dark corners. There was, in fact, a place called the "kissing wall" where the food counter opened onto the room from the kitchen. Lines of boys sat on the counter and girls stood, squeezed between their legs. Couples hugged and swayed all night, occasionally drifting off to dance, with the exception of one puny boy and his thin, blonde girl-child of a date in a mini-skirt who spent the entire evening leaning up against each other – not kissing, not talking, not embracing, just leaning, chest to chest.

But neither was there any disorder or mayhem. There was no dope that I could smell, no booze being sipped surreptitiously from paper cups, and only two drunk boys slumped like Raggedy-Andy dolls against the wall who now and then were escorted by friends to the washroom to puke. There were the fat girl, the fat boy; the skinny, runty boys in glasses, and the pimply, beardless ones; the dark-skinned "Pakis" (the generic name given all people from the Indian subcontinent) in smart sweaters; the gangs of girls seated in a tight huddle together, smoking furiously and laughing raucously as though to demonstrate their lack of interest in the boys strolling in and out the doors; the amorous couple on the dance floor undulating on one spot to the slow songs (the boy's hands resting on the small of the girl's back). I noticed that the girls were uncommonly aggressive, marching gamely up to the ranks of male wall-flowers to pluck one out as a dancing partner, cutting in on each other on the dance floor, even pinning their partner against a wall, arms on either side of his shoulders, to lean in for a kiss.

I was there to look after Judy. She was there to look out for Jason – she'd been told via the rumour mill that he would be there. He was not there when we arrived but he walked in an hour later and in a twinkling Judy was gone. Disappeared. She went off with him for a ride, she explained to me at 11:30, powdering her nose in the women's washroom with an insouciance I found infuriating. *Anything* could have happened, I remonstrated with her, imagining rape and abduction, and feeling, for the first time in my life, the bullying apprehension of the parent. But nothing like that had happened. What had happened was that, stopped at a red light in his sleek red car, Jason had kissed Judy. It was her very first kiss on the mouth from a boy and she was tremulous with happiness, particularly since he had promised to dance with her precisely at midnight. It was useless pointing out to her that curfew was at 11:30. I would not be getting her home before midnight.

11:45. Judy chatted with a number of different boys and accepted invitations to dance from every direction. This, of course, was designed to make Jason jealous but simply made it impossible for him to get anywhere near her. 12:00. Still no luck. 12:15. Jason sat with his back to the dance floor, chatting with friends, while Judy danced on, looking over her shoulder at Jason's back. 12:30. Jason turned around to face the dance floor, got up from his chair, walked over to the DJ, and requested a record. This had to be it: he would ask Judy to dance. She detached herself from her friends and made herself available, waiting. The song began, Jason walked right out of the room with a pack of male friends and into the night. I could not bear to look at Judy, but had no trouble convincing her it was time to go home.

Judy, however, was not easily discouraged. Her passion for Jason, which I first heard about at our first meeting, was just as keen ten months later, at our last. It did not, moreover, seem to depend for its nourishment on any sign of reciprocity from the beloved himself. No matter the degree of his indifference (the occasions he ignored her at school), his manipulativeness (the times he promised to phone and never did), his unkindness (the gossip he spread around about who he *really* loved; it was never Judy), Judy's devotion never wavered. The scanty news that "a boy" had phoned for her at home while she was out transported her: she grabbed her girlfriend's hand and put it to her heart so that her friend could feel its quickened beating. She even resorted to witchcraft, just that once betraying her doubt about the inevitability of destiny delivering Jason into her arms: before going to sleep she had recited his name backwards and, oh bliss, had *seen* him the next day at school, just as she had prayed.

There were times when the love affair seemed indeed to have an air of reality about it: Jason did manage to get through to her on the phone. "On Tuesday at two o'clock Jason phoned and I answered and he said he just wanted to wish me Merry Christmas. That was so sweet. I told him I wanted to give him a little present and he said he would try to get away for a couple of hours but then from Tuesday to Friday he was being such a shit with me that I decided I wouldn't see him. He said he'd call again, but when he did my brother answered and said I wasn't home. At 8:30 he called back. I said, 'Who is this?' He said, 'Come on, who do you think it is?' I said, 'I think it's some tall, dark, average-handsome guy.' I acted like I couldn't care less. He said, 'I called because I thought you might be expecting me to call.' I said, 'What do you think, that I'm going to sit by the phone all day?' After that he didn't call for a while."

But the substance of the relationship (such as it was) struck me as based on such fundamental bad faith that it was all I could do not to shake her in the middle of one of her tedious recitations: how he had flirted in front of her with an old girlfriend, called and hung up on her, lured her into the stairwell of the mall only to whisper, "Let's just be friends," taken her out in the car for a tête-à-tête ("I *do* have feelings for you") only to ignore, later that same day, the kisses she blew at him across the cafeteria, and to chew her out for bumping into him, "accidentally on purpose" as she put it, in the hallway. Her only defence against this sort of cruelty was to say, whenever she sensed his withdrawal, that she hated him.

But when he pressed his suit in a directly sexual manner, she had only the flimsiest defence: "He would never seduce me," she explained to me one afternoon as I drove her back to school from the mall. "He respects me too much." She leaned back against the seat with a dreamy look on her face – so open, that face! – and recounted the details of the last time she had been with Jason, alone in his apartment, when he challenged her to play Truth or Dare, daring her to pull down his pants, and, pressing up against her on his couch, the hump of his erection making her squeal, wrestled her down to the floor. "I was straddling him and he dared me to kiss him five times in five different places, and so I kissed his mouth and his eyelids and on each side of his mouth but he said that didn't count so I kissed him on the neck. He put his hand up under my blouse but I told him to take it away so he slid it around to my back and stroked me there, and he asked me what my feeling was for him and I said, 'No,' and he said, 'C'mon, tell me,' and I said, 'It begins with L and ends with E and has O and V in the middle.' I asked him what *he* was feeling but he said he wouldn't tell me."

The last time I saw Judy we drove miles away from the school to a small pizza restaurant to have coffee. She swore me to secrecy, as she had done at our first meeting, about her parents' plans for her. For two years they had been talking about moving back to India and now it seemed they were prepared to do so, or at least to take the whole family back for the uncle's wedding. Judy was aware that the purpose of the trip was to display her before potential husbands; after all, at sixteen, she was about to come into "full feminine bloom", as her father put it, and in a few more years she would have faded, and who would want her then? Her mother, she noticed, had been out on several shopping trips buying expensive clothes Judy was not allowed to wear before arriving in India. From behind a cloud of cigarette smoke she acknowledged, casually, that she may very well return to Canada with a husband.

Her expression was composed, her tone less girlish than usual; for a few seconds I could see the emerging woman behind the frank, unblinking eyes and relaxed mouth. She was gone again, to that place where a girl sits, hands folded decorously in her lap, while her parents scrutinize the son of friends of the father's cousin, a twenty-five-year-old chartered accountant with good prospects in a bank in Vancouver; they determine his genealogy, his social cachet, and his prospects, and pronounce him worthy, or not. Judy's mother's marriage had been arranged in this way: she had been pretty, and reluctant to go to university, but neither could she be left to her own devices, "having fun and partying". So she was married at seventeen, and tells Judy she does not regret it.

When the subject of an arranged marriage had first come up between us, Judy had railed impressively against it. She was *not* marriageable, she insisted; after all these years in Canada she would be taken for a "slut", which is to say unmanageable, with ideas of her own about marriage. She had told me: "I'm not going to treat my husband like he's some kind of god. I'm not going to be a housewife. No way. Never. Why should I sit at home all day long, cooking for some guy, just to please him? We're going to be equal."

No such brave words came from her now. But as she kept on talking, the virgin with the love poems under her bed, the high school girl with the thousand dreams, the daughter beginning to imagine, chaotically, her own freedom, slowly re-emerged. She disclosed her fantasy of running away with Jason. Alternatively, she might submit to a marriage but only to go out every night with her friends, driving them around in her red car from bar to bar, disco to disco, no longer under her parents' supervision or, according to this fantasy, under a husband's: "If he complained, I'd divorce him! And I'd never ever have sex with him." Or, a third possibility, she'd become a famous movie star, fabulously rich and adored by multitudes. Judy: she was so young.

For months afterward, I rang her home but no one ever answered. According to some girls who knew her at school, there was some vague information that she had "gone back" to India. No one really expected to see her again.

THREE

Best Friends

"We were always together. Always, always, always."

THE FIERCE, proprietary affection that teenage girls have for one another – or, more often, for one special other – is a phenomenon of a particular moment in their lives. At that moment they hover apprehensively on the frontier of heterosexual commitment; one, two steps forward and they will have entered that territory where the culture of heterosexual desire swallows up all other relations and where female friendship becomes merely a momentary refuge from the unremitting negotiations of male-female co-existence. At seventeen most girls have already crossed over into heterosexuality. Around fifteen and sixteen, however, they are still virginal (sentimentally if not technically), committing the best of themselves, their loyalty and affection and honesty, to another girl.

This is the time of the "best friend". Never mind that within months, or even weeks, best friends will have a falling out and a new girl will be chosen to take the place of the rejected or alienated one: the complex of feelings remains consistent. The best friend is she who has the right to your time and attention and the privilege of hearing your confession. Never again in life will there be someone quite so unambiguously interested in you.

"In grade nine, me and Mary and Karen were all good

friends. In grade ten, me and Mary paired up and Karen was out of it. We were always together. Always, always, always. After school we went out. She was either at my place or I was over at her place. Weekends we were always together. Inseparable. But we split apart. So when I went to grade eleven I felt really insecure. I hung around with a group, but it was a long time before I let anyone get really close. Now I've totally opened up to friends again and it feels really good."

Friendship can mean something as simple as the enjoyment of someone's company, the three or four girls you always think of when you think about going to a movie or out for pizza or putting together a game of Trivial Pursuit, the three or four who know how to kid each other without getting their noses out of joint and who also know when to be serious, to hear you out when you've got something on your mind. "We all love each other for how we are and we know each other for how we are," says Terry, speaking of the friends she'll be taking leave of as they all graduate and disperse. The thought makes her pensive but hopeful: how can you fear loneliness when the whole wide world is full of people you may befriend?

A friend may be waiting for you just around the corner: the one who walks into the classroom, on the first day of school, in baggy trousers and a big sweater and bobbed hair – *all* the other girls are in jeans and T-shirts and ski jackets – and she's so *bizarre* you've just got to meet her, you with the skirt and the ponytail, and you sit down beside her in the cafeteria and you ride your bikes home together and, what do you know, you're friends. A friend doesn't *have* to be just like you. And your two best friends don't have to be like each other: Kelly has a close friend in the school band who never says anything, and another in drama class who's simply outrageous, will go up to perfect strangers and ask them *questions* ("Where'd you get that ice cream?" "How do you spell your last name?"). But mainly a real, true, good friend is someone you *earn*, a girl you've known for years and who's seen the worst of you (the tantrums, the jealousy, the dissimulation) and who still likes you and wants to be close. She knows everything about you because there is nothing you could say that would disappoint her: she has no illusions about you and does not sit in judgement. (Friends, unlike parents, do not live according to infallible codes.) Such a person, says Nina, is not so much a friend as a "touchstone". Even if they part as they grow older, she will have the memory of this intimacy – and this deep satisfaction at having been understood – as a reminder of what is possible between women.

"I prefer my own company," says Rea, "or my girl-friends'. It's more relaxed than with boys. You don't have to put on a front." She was speaking of boyfriends, that category of male intimate in whom you have a romantic interest and before whom you must feign indifference, but other girls talked to me of friends who are boys: male companions, buddies, even confidants. The advantage of a male friend, as opposed to a boyfriend, is that you can take the initiative, call him up, say, suggest a hockey game (you have an extra ticket), and have a good time together, no questions asked, no claims staked. "You don't have to kiss him good-night, or anything else," says Nina, who'd rather be "single and happy" than with a boyfriend whom she keeps around just to drop his name at the lunch table. Vera can "pal around" with guys who – maybe because they're kind of insensitive, you know? – don't go all "weird" on you like girls do, demanding you have lunch with *them* and what have you been saying to so-and-so and how come you don't want to go with *us* to the mall after school on Fridays any more? Vera gets some of the best grades in her class, and having a male friend, as opposed to a boyfriend, means not having to apologize for being so smart: "It's not like in my mum's day when girls were supposed to be just dumb chicks." Unfortunately, she goes on to say, most girls feel constrained to behave exactly as though they *were* dumb chicks, clucking over stupid things like somebody's haircut or some guy's baby blues and worrying all the time about silly things like not having their homework done on time or not having a date for the school dance or not wearing precisely the right shade of pullover. Who cares? Boys don't care about such unimportant things, and that's why Vera seeks them out: they don't waste her time.

Given the volatility of adolescent emotions, it is not surprising that friendships, even the most constant, are forever under threat from other irresistible emotions, and that friends are engaged in the knotty enterprise of working out an *ethic* of friendship: Which rules are to govern their behaviour with each other? What is right and what is wrong in this territory that's been staked out as a kind of autonomous republic within the realm of adult mores? What, for example, is the etiquette governing the situation Kelly found herself in one Friday night when, in the company of five old friends from junior high, she walked into a restaurant where she saw another group of friends from school she has been wanting to get to know better? She decided to keep company with those with whom she'd arrived; it was only polite. What do you do when one of your friends hates another of your friends, is jealous of the time you spend with her, demands an accounting of your weekend, for all the world like a suspicious boyfriend? For a long time Barbara listened patiently to Sonia's complaints and accusations, trying to reassure her that her closeness with Pat didn't mean she couldn't be close to Sonia too, etc., etc., to no avail. Sonia was inconsolable and Barbara finally had to tell her, "It's your problem." Carol almost lost her friend Sherry when she told her that the people she was hanging around with were bad news – ordering Sherry around, making her feel stupid, a truth Sherry didn't want to hear just then.

Friends have a way of changing their habits, their minds, even their lives, leaving you to figure out how you'll continue to fit in, if at all. Rea's nineteen-year-old best friend is going to have a baby and suddenly it's as though she's travelled to another world, one into which Rea cannot follow her. There is a great mystery unfolding there, with its own language and tales and blushing confidences, unintelligible to Rea, who's still trying to decide what courses to take in grade thirteen and who feels "kind of left behind". Michelle is in a "friend crisis": she now feels she's leaving behind her friend of three years. "I'm going places and she's not," she explains, having described her realizable dream of working in New York as a hairdresser. "She doesn't know what she's doing with her life but I know what I'm doing with mine. I still talk to her, but she doesn't realize yet that I don't consider us best friends any more." What do you owe your old friends at the parting of the ways? Arden was sure, in leaving the town she'd grown up in, that she'd taken leave forever of the friends she'd known all her life. And, in fact, on going back for Christmas, she ran into some who wondered what had happened to her, she'd changed so much. But with her two best friends it was as though she'd never left – "It's like you're still living here," they told her, except for this: it was from their *separation* that they all realized how fond they were of each other. "We got into a real deep talk about that," says Arden, a little awestruck.

In the heat of their friendship with one another, girls will reject the possibility that attraction to a boy – a manifestly inferior species in any case, incapable of real speech and lacking abysmally in self-knowledge – could threaten the special status of their *mutual* affection. But inevitably the status will be challenged as girls are drawn in, by lust and anxiety and curiosity, to the heterosexual world of the couple. Contrary to what the girls would like to believe, the two "cultures" – that of the couple and that of the friendship – are mutually exclusive: you cannot, unless you're socially and psychologically very adept, enjoy both at the same time. Unless, like Mandy, who had once been deeply hurt by a friend who had "drifted off", away from her, on the arm of a boyfriend, you make sure that you and your new boyfriend socialize with your old girlfriends from time to time, doing the things you always liked to do as a gang of girls (going out for dinner, to a movie, to a disco): "When my boyfriend went away to university, I found that I still had all my friends, and they were really supportive of me." Much more common is Nina's experience: her best friend has had a boyfriend for two years, a situation that almost broke the friends up. She understands now that, because she was so busy with her own activities, she simply wasn't "there" for her friend in the way the new boyfriend was: "When she was upset, I was never at home, and so she turned to Jim." But at the time it was a very distressing experience to be supplanted by a boyfriend. "I felt very offended that she'd choose Jim over me, and so I got really mad one day and told her I felt totally left out, and I yelled and I cried and finally she understood what I was feeling." They came up with a compromise – that they'd reserve time each week just for each other – and now Nina defends her friend's love affair with alacrity: "She loves him, I'm sure she loves him, she *does* love him, and if anybody tells me that a sixteen-year-old isn't capable of loving someone, well, I'll just disagree with all my might."

This is not, however, the whole story about the relationships girls strike among themselves. Through much of the language they use in talking about each other runs a streak of unmitigated nastiness, a shrill and cold-hearted aggression designed to wound. At the very least a vague and free-floating anxiety seems to charge the air when more than two or three are gathered together, as though something unpleasant were about to happen, but from which quarter no one is quite sure. One girl described it as not being able to "trust" your friends fully, fearing that, when your back is turned, they will "put you down"; or fearing that something is being planned from which you are to be excluded, or that the other two "know" something you do not. More extremely, girls hurl obscene epithets at and about each other – slut, bitch, sleaze – and cruelly disparage each other's bodies – so-and-so's tits hang down to here, man, and so-and-so's thighs are gross, and check that hairdo, a rat's nest, no kidding. They pass along damaging and probably spurious tales about each other's sexual behaviour and reputation (who does "it", with whom, and how many times). That fact that all such mortifications have as their source sexual insult, and that the nature of the insult seems to have been borrowed and learned from male sexual hostility towards women, would suggest that female solidarity – that touching inseparability of young "best friends" – is broken in the transition to heterosexual social codes. Girls wanting to live among males are learning who it is they have to please and flatter and cultivate, in order to live in a socially successful manner, and it is no longer each other. By the age of sixteen and seventeen, it is already obvious that males control social power (in the sense of who has authority in a group), and a girl's identification with female friends is at best profitless and at worst prejudicial to her best interests. She is right, then, to wonder just which one of them she can trust to keep her secrets and to defend her affections from the mockery of boys.

By 1980, according to sociological surveys, friends had replaced parents as the most influential people in a teenager's life.[1] This phenomenon was regarded by some observers as not particularly alarming, since "peer culture", constructed primarily of trivialities, ephemera, and "nonessentials", implies no permanent rejection of adult-related values. It was seen by others, however, as a sign that the "moral authority" of parents over their growing children had "collapsed". In fact, the conclusion need be neither so sanguine nor so lugubrious. Teenagers may *seem* wild and alienated. But their flamboyant subculture obscures the essential conservatism of their values (their hedonistic goals for their personal future, for example, or their petit bourgeois political attitudes), all of which are highly derivative of their parents' own. In terms of the teenager's view of adult culture, though, girls may very

well have a more optimistic perspective than that of boys;
female adulthood, in an era of spreading feminist culture
and of the politicization of women's labour, holds more of
an attraction for today's adolescent girl than in earlier
generations. She looks forward to her maturity: financial
independence, adventure, sexual pleasure.

But neither is "peer culture" merely a transitory phenomenon of little consequence to the emerging adult. For
working-class girls in particular, for whom the culture and
relationships of the school environment will soon be a
thing of the past, not to be extended into university, peer-
group attachments become proportionately significant: it
is within friendships and romances that they learn those
"life and death" skills of interpersonal negotiation that
will form the ballast of their mature relations, especially
since they will have so little collective political or social
clout to rely on. But there are ways in which, for *all* girls,
their friendships and love affairs carry an identical promise: it is among a girl's own generation, not the soon-to-
be-superseded parental generation, that she will discover
if she is worthwhile and desirable and deft, if her ideas
bear examination, if her fears and doubts are shared, if
she is capable of making her own decisions. It is here that
she will discover if she is going to overcome the perilous
loneliness of the fledgling human suspended between family and fellowship.

FOUR

Carla and Sharon

"We can go anywhere boring and Carla and I will make it fun."

CARLA AND Sharon want you to understand that they're unique. Everybody else they know in school is the same, but they're unique. Which isn't the same as weird. Weird is what everybody else is – snobs, fakes, sluts, geeks – but Carla and Sharon are not like that. It's true Carla has been classified as "weird", but that's a misunderstanding; Carla is *serious*, quiet, which, in a zoo, makes her seem different, weird. Sharon understands this. Even before she'd met Carla she'd heard about her – that she'd been at a party which she had to leave early because she was "blasted off her ass", drunk – but the girl she met in typing class was a serious person, with a lot on her mind. They began talking. They discovered that they agreed with each other about a lot of things, particularly about what they liked and didn't like in other people. Take Lorraine, for instance, who they agree just doesn't know how to be serious, who walks down the hall in her perfect clothes and greets *everyone* with a simpering little "Hi . . .". Like get a-*way*, says Sharon. They discovered right at the beginning that they could state their minds to each other.

SHARON: We can read each other perfect.

CARLA: She's always in a good mood.

SHARON: *She's* never in a good mood.

CARLA: I'm just a quiet person. . . . I like Sharon's spinni-ness.

Can you believe this? Sharon, spinny? Well, she "does" spinny but she's no airhead. Spinny is when you giggle a lot or you don't know what's going on. Sharon knows what's going on. "You're a mature spinny," says Carla. What intrigued Carla right from the beginning was Sharon's accent. Sharon comes from Akron, Ohio – this is something important about her she wants you to know right from the top – and she and Carla talk a lot about the difference between teenagers in Edmonton and in Akron, so much so that Carla is getting sick of it: "I don't like the way you dwell on the past," she says. So they talk about the kids in school and the goofy teachers. They sit in the back of the class, tip their chairs back, and have a good giggle. It drives the teachers crazy but they can't do any-thing about it because Carla and Sharon are good stu-dents and had their homework done a week ago. Sharon's average is 83 and she types 43 words per minute. If she has trouble in French class, say, Carla will yell out the right word to help her. But no one breaks them up. They're *friends*. Sharon: "Carla is neat."

When I met Sharon, in her divorced mother's apartment in downtown Edmonton, she'd been in Canada only a couple of months. New city, new school, new faces, new way of doing things. She'd never taken a bus to school before (let alone transferred from one bus to another) and on her first day at Harry Ainlay Composite High School she was late. She'd transferred to the wrong bus, dropped her books and papers while scrambling to get off, and then wandered through the look-alike corridors of the school in a vain effort to find her classroom. She ate lunch by herself and got lost going home. But a month later she had friends, and things to do and places to go. She is, after all, from Akron, Ohio.

In Ohio she had lived with her father while her mother had set herself up in Edmonton as the business manager of a psychiatrist. With her father she had lived as independently as she could, speaking to him only when necessary, paying him back any money he lent her. With her mother she's more relaxed and enjoys staying around the apartment. She gets home by 4:30, does her homework, helps out with supper (her best dish is broiled sole fillets), and, for the first time since she was a kid, watches a lot of TV, because she lives miles away from her school friends. She's on the phone a lot, mainly with Carla, plotting things to do over the weekend. In Akron she'd be hanging around the malls playing "Galaga" or "Galaxian" video games or she'd be skating and tobogganing; in Edmonton she lounges on the rug and watches the Green Bay Packers battle the New York Jets but what the hell. . . . On Monday she'll be back in school, in the thick of things.

When Sharon first got to Ainlay, she hated it. It's a hard school to love – a low-slung, windowless, modernist bunker sprawled on expensive real estate bordering the boom-time suburbs in the south end of the city. Brookside, Riverbend, Aspen Gardens, Westbrooke, the very names bespeak the pretensions of an upwardly mobile middle class requiring the services of the nearby golf course and country club, the shopping malls, and the city's biggest high school (an enrolment of 2291 students in the fall of 1986), with a "high profile" as an academic school that is also capable of fielding large football and basketball teams: the quintessential projection of the aspirations of the parent-clientele.

To be sure, inserted among these ostentatious neighbourhoods are smaller ones of subsidized-rental townhouses and the tract housing of the suburbanized working class. Even *within* the households of the prosperous there are individuals suffering failure: Carla's father, for example, was for many months an unemployed computer systems manager. But Harry Ainlay C.H.C. has a "rep". A disc jockey on a local AM pop station encapsulated it with a salute to the city bus driver who "has to drive all those poor little Ainlay kids around who haven't had their sixteenth birthday yet and gotten their Mercedes Benz."

This is perhaps unfair, but even the principal, George Nicholson, admits "you walk the halls and the kids seem happy." At the same time he confesses to being mystified by these same students at a school dance punching the air with their fists as they rapturously intone the verses to Twisted Sister's "We're Not Gonna Take It", a paean to the rebellion of a boy, nagged beyond endurance by his father, who forces the tyrant out of a window. There are no windows in Harry Ainlay, only miles of featureless corridors, sealed in from the street, and explained in a floor plan you pick up from the Main Office. "If your goal is as an institution," Nicholson points out, "maybe you should look like one."

Carla and Sharon are thriving in the bunker. They're pleased to be Ainlay students, even at grade-ten level: it's in a good part of town, the hot part, the rich part, with a higher class of people – well, not *really* higher class in the sense of higher than lower, but in the sense of "okay" people – than some other schools they could mention. There's not a lot of drugs floating around, and there aren't any stabbings like in the tough part of the west end, and you don't get a lot of those disgusting preppies like at that snooty school, Ross Sheppard, on the other side of the river. Ainlay is punk or rock, football and wrestling.

But, even in Ainlay, not everybody is cool. Take that handful of Heavy Metal kids in their Rush T-shirts: Sharon would *never* party with them. At the other end of the social scale are the "richies", the seventeen-year-olds on to their third car: you love them, you hate them. Some of them will accept you whether you have money or not. On the other hand, who wants to be judged by how much money your parents have? Sharon gets teased about living in a posh apartment building and she *hates* that; she gets seriously upset, even when Carla says it, says she's a "richie". Okay, maybe she and her mother don't have to worry about money or about affording things, but the truth is she was happier back then when she still *wished* for things: "It was a good feeling, always longing for something and then finally getting it, like getting presents at Christmas. You wait and wait and wait and finally you get them; and it doesn't mean that much, not so much as *hoping* for them." As for Carla, the first car *she'll* get she'll pay for herself, and it'll be a Datsun.

They hate fake people, people who come up to you so very friendly, "Hello, how *are* you?" and you don't know if they're just saying it to get you to vote for them in the Student Council election or if they really want to be your friend. Or the super-jocks, the people who look down on you if you like to party, to drink. Or the Pakis. Not that Carla and Sharon are exactly racist – Carla doesn't think there's prejudice in the "teen world" at all – but, on the other hand, she'd *never* go out with one. Black guys are okay, even if her father wouldn't approve, but she believes that "the East Indians have just come over into our world and taken over most of our economy." "Tell me about it, man," says Sharon. But, hey, all these different groups of people make the world go 'round. What would life at school be like if everybody was the same? What would you learn? When you criticize people it's not to put them down, it's to find out what *you* don't want to do or be like.

Definitely you do not want to be a slut. Not that you should be preoccupied with your "rep" – that fear of someone (someone *male*) looking at you the wrong way, seeing you as either a slut or a prude – but you should be very, very careful about the statement you are making about yourself as you teeter down the hallway on your high heels, swaying your little bum in the spandex toreador pants on your way to the cafeteria and a tableful of hooting boys.

CARLA: One day when Sharon was sick, I was talking to her on the phone at lunch break and I could see into the cafeteria and I counted the guys around Penny's table – *eight* guys. She's a slut, man, a real easy rider.

SHARON: She'll give it.

CARLA: To any guy.

SHARON: Her virginity. Over and over again.

CARLA: She's dying for attention. She's probably very insecure and that's her way of hiding it.

But what is Joan's problem, the slut who does it three
times every weekend? Or, even worse, Karen, who gives
head in the gym bleachers, no kidding. And the guys don't
even *like* her. That's how desperate she is. When a guy
wants to get his rocks off, he calls her, but that doesn't
mean he likes her. But she's popular, if that makes any
sense. With the boys, anyway.

Other girls are merely dippy, dizzy, bubbleheads. They
just *sit* there, looking attractive (they hope), like Penny,
who's just "there" at the cafeteria table, "like a tick on a
dog", says Sharon. And what she doesn't know about
make-up Carla could blow her out of the water with.
Some girls are treacherous; they'll hang around you and
you'll pour out your heart to them and then they'll turn
their back on you and tell their friends everything you
said. Jealous and two-faced, that's what girls are like.

Carla likes kindness in girls, and honesty, and respects
those who are happy and pleasant people. But they're thin
on the ground and so she's closer to guys. Even though on
the whole they tend to be "geeks, pricks, and horny bastards", she's hung out with them since she was a kid,
played soccer and football with them, sat in on their conversations about cars and stereos. Girls, on the other
hand, just want to talk about boys. What a bore. Sharon
is closer to guys too. It's easier to talk to them or even
safer; a girl wants to know too much about you, but a guy
doesn't ask too many questions.

Carla and Sharon have friends whose company they
enjoy, but on the whole they're rather disappointed in
their peers. "They try to be like everyone else," they say.
"They try to 'fit in' all the time." Whatever happened to
standing up and being counted, standing up for what you
want, even making a decision unacceptable to "the

group"? Most kids won't take the chance. Carla, on the other hand, has been standing up for herself since she was in grade seven.

I met Carla when she accosted me in the school hallway between classes: "I hear you're doing a book about teen-age girls. You should talk to me. I've had an interesting life." She was all of fifteen but who's to say. . . ? We dropped by the canteen for a can of Diet Coke (she said she was addicted to aspartame) and met later in the after-noon in a quiet cafeteria. We only had a few moments between classes and it all came out in a dramatic rush: the unemployed father, the executive secretary mother ("I'm real proud of her"), the lawyer uncle, the immigrant grandparents. The litany of catastrophes: the suicide at-tempt in junior high school, the undiagnosed anorexia, the school suspension for possession of tranquillizers, the punk hairdo and clothes, the ulcers and ligament prob-lems, and the arthritis in the fine, small hands laid out in front of us on the table. Then the bell sounded and she was off.

Carla and Sharon met in typing class. I sit in on it with them one morning at 8:15. The objectives of the class that day are to type at least 110 words in four minutes with no more than five errors, and to type a short, personal busi-ness letter. Nothing much happens for the rest of the pe-riod apart from the clatter of IBM and the occasional query. How much space do I leave between the province and the postal code? How do you include an apartment number in an address and still use only three lines? In spite of the fact that the teacher is an enthusiast of the discipline – "If you don't know how to type when you go into computers, you'll be illiterate" – Carla and Sharon are not impressed. "It's a basket-weaving course." If you can't get an A you're in real trouble.

Carla's best subject is English. She likes poems; she likes their "vagueness" and the fact you have to think about them. It's a challenge. Analysing *anything* is a challenge; movies, for instance. The sci-fi flick *2010*? No problem. She just "picks up" on mysteriousness. She likes to write, too. Not direct things, like newspaper stories, but poems. Writing about vague things like feelings.

Chemistry is Sharon's best subject. Girls aren't supposed to be good at it? Am I serious? Sharon *loves* science.

Chemistry 10, at 9:45 in the morning. The teacher, a man in a three-piece suit, begins the period with a joke about Reagan, Trudeau, a priest, a hippie, and three knapsacks on a plane about to crash. The class groans. Behind him on the wall are admonitory slogans: "Only Nerds Litter", "Time Will Pass, Will You?", alongside "The Periodic Table of the Elements", "The International System of Units", and several Travel Alberta posters. The teacher administers a test. Limestone ($CaCO_3$) is heated to give. . . ? What is the formula for the reaction of hydrochloric acid with calcium carbonate? Sharon is good at this sort of thing – she had eighty-six per cent on the last test – but is having trouble figuring out the hydrogen combustion formula. She collaborates on the answers with the girl at the next desk – a "nice" preppie, as she puts it – a vision in pink: pink sweater and pink scarf and pink ankle socks, with waves of blonde hair, and mauve eyeshadow, pale-pink fingernails, and, oh preciousness, a clear plastic pencil case decorated with little blue hearts.

What's a good teacher? Someone who can "relate" to you, not just hand out orders. On the other hand, not someone who tries to talk like teenagers talk and who laughs at stupid things. Sharon: "He can crack a joke but he can't want too much to be treated like a kid and he can't want to be too powerful. Something in between." She likes her math teacher, for instance, even though she's a "terrible" student. Carla (disdainfully): "That's because you talk all the time to *Kevin*." Sharon claims to pay no attention to the teacher, to laugh and giggle and disrupt the class, but she also knows when to be serious. She claims the teacher understands this about her. "We're straightforward with each other."

Math 10 at 1:56 in the afternoon. The windowless room is lit rather gloomily by fluorescent lights. "Charlie Brown" and more Travel Alberta posters. The teacher is in her twenties, dressed in blue sneakers and denims and a cotton smock. Animatedly she is covering the board with algebraic equations. A girl with a calculator gripped in one hand holds forth on the problem of determining the formula for the perimeter of a rectangle. Sharon gives it a shot: "Why can't $x + y$ equal 10? Or why can't xy equal 10? . . . You mean it has to work *all* the time?" Someone else has an idea but it's not right either. The girl with the calculator makes a stab . . . and the discussion goes on for some time. There's another problem, about quotients. The answer is: $x = 7y + 5$. "I got it!" a girl wheezes in disbelief. Soon most of the class is yelling out solutions and suggestions to the whole boardful of problems.

Sharon considers herself smart. As smart as the guys. But, then, it's hard to tell whether the guys are so smart, says Carla: they're too horny. Carla considers herself to be creative. She enjoys looking in fashion magazines for ideas and is *always* thinking about how her friends could do their hair and make-up differently. Sharon would rather analyse a painting. But that's because she's more interested in objects; Carla is interested in people. That's what makes the first ten minutes of any class the worst part of the day: you're not allowed to talk to anybody. The absolute best part is the breaks between classes when you can finally talk your head off to your friend, letting out all the anxiety that's built up during the class. Especially during those last ten minutes when you're watching the clock and it seems, you could swear, that the hands have stuck.

Carla's weekend began on Friday morning at the doctor's being treated for black-outs. (Is she still not eating?) That

evening she took her medicine and called Sharon. They
decided to go see a movie with Carla's brother and some
of his friends. After the movie they ended up, predictably,
at Earl's downtown – a franchise restaurant much favoured by teenagers because the staff treats them like
grown-ups – for something to eat, and they all went dutch.
Then the group went to Sharon's place to watch a dirty
movie on TV until 2 a.m. It wasn't so much dirty as funny,
they admit. A movie made in the sixties: a guy wearing
horn-rimmed glasses, girls in mini-skirts, a teacher direct-
ing students' sexual fantasies . . . weird. On Saturday
morning Carla went Christmas shopping with her mother
downtown and later, with both parents, to Food For Less.
She stayed at home that evening but talked to Sharon on
the phone. They watched a TV movie "together": they call
each other up, each turns on her TV to the same movie,
and they comment on it over the phone as it plays. Sharon
spent the day shopping with her mother as well, at West
Edmonton Mall. She came home with a new Prince album and spent Saturday afternoon listening to it. On
Sunday they both got up late, cleaned up around the
house a bit, and did their homework.

CARLA: This was a boring weekend.

SHARON: On a not-boring weekend we'd party on Friday *and*
Saturday nights. We'd go to someone's place but it could
also mean just going to a movie and then hitting Earl's. We
can go anywhere boring and Carla and I will make it fun.

On the Sunday evening they are together at Sharon's
sitting at the foot of Sharon's mother's brass bed, talking
to me. They sprawl, they flop, up and down on one arm;
they sit cross-legged, leaning into each other, brushing
against each other, laughing, nudging, squealing, even
briefly falling silent in quiet consideration of some idea or
other. The puffy, duvet-covered bed, the enormous white
pillows, the soft colours of walls and floor, the floral print
in the gold frame, the two girls in tête-à-tête (Sharon
holding for examination a bottle of Estée Lauder Age-
Smoothing Cream) – the little tableau is one of endearing

femaleness. They are, in the best of female traditions, "best friends".

They're loyal, they swear to me. Each knows the other well enough to know just how far to go before they get on each other's nerves and then to pull back; which is another way of saying they'd never betray the other for a boyfriend. Carla had asked Sharon, when Sharon was seeing Bobby, if she was still going to "do stuff" with her, and Sharon had said, of course, I won't forget you. The question has come up again, because now Sharon is seeing Mark and last Friday she did a not-nice thing: she had felt tired and begged off going out with Carla when she got an invitation to go out with Mark. She phoned Carla right away to tell her what was up and that she was going out after all. Carla hung up on her – and called back in half an hour to apologize. Nevertheless, Sharon reassures her that from now on, if she has a date with Carla, that's it. She'll turn Mark down.

They're virtually inseparable. The evenings they're stuck in their respective homes, their long late-night phone calls take the place of hanging out together and give them a chance to fill each other in on what's happened that day since they last saw each other. After all, they never run into each other after lunch; they don't even have classes on the same side of the school. Nothing very important comes out of these calls, just items to "file" for future reference.

How to dress, what to wear. Sharon says it's hard work being a girl – would a boy stand staring into his closet wondering what to wear every morning? She plans ahead the night before. Right after her prayers she lies in bed mentally ransacking her closet and putting together her outfit for the next day. Or she'll have phoned Carla for advice. They agree Carla has excellent "fashion sense" and practises what she preaches: her own look is "casual New Wave", hair with a slight body wave in short layers and slicked with a light gel, make-up in creamy brown and soft pink shades (or "radiances", as Sharon calls them), loose pants and baggy shirts tucked in at the waist. Sharon's look is "sporty": Nike sweat pants and an oversize white shirt – which her mother pays for, unless Sharon wants something her mother really dislikes, in which case they go "halfies". She confesses that her clothes "rack up a bill", but it's important not to wear the same pants twice in the same week. Her mother nags her about this silliness – as if anyone is keeping track of Sharon's wardrobe! – but *Sharon* keeps track. Neither Carla nor Sharon ever wears a skirt – Sharon has never seen Carla past her ankles, never – although Sharon used to wear one once a week, until she made the humiliating mistake of wearing a red-and-green-plaid number and Carla didn't *tell* her, God, how disgustingly *preppie* she looked; if only Carla had *told* her she'd have gone home at lunchtime and changed.

Femininity is something you have, or you haven't; it's natural, it's just there, within you, without your having to worry about it, at least not at age fifteen. Maybe, they feel, when you're twenty-five and don't have a man you have to worry about it. . . . "Sexy" is a look. You put it together, like the girls in designer clothes from expensive boutiques and designer haircuts. Sexy is also a certain kind of body: a bust that's not too big, slender torso and waist, a compact bum. Bony is not sexy. Carla's anorectic body is not a turn-on but neither, on the other hand, are Sharon's "thunder thighs". What Sharon likes about her body is everything from the shoulders up: "I like my head. My head's perfect."

Sharon has only two requirements of a boy's physical make-up: that he be taller than her when she's wearing heels, because she likes to slow-dance, and nothing could be more awful than swaying around the dance floor looking down at the top of some guy's head; and that he have a nice butt. That's the one thing she always looks at on a guy – his tush. Carla, for her part, is more interested in cars and stereos. She goes to car lots and stares at *cars*.

But, seriously, what does it matter if the guy is cute or

handsome and well-built if he's a nerd? He should be smart, too, be able to carry on an intelligent conversation – if you can't talk to him, what's the point of spending time with him? – and want to make something of his life. The way it usually happens is this: the guy and you are friends first, and then he makes a pass at you and you become boyfriend-girlfriend. The important thing is the friendship first; that way, you treat him as an equal and you don't have to waste your time trying to *impress* him.

In Carla's opinion, however, boys are too possessive. She has two friends who've been going out together for two years and the guy does not like it at all when his girlfriend even *looks* at another guy, or if she goes out at night without him. Well, Sharon wouldn't put up with that: "If he doesn't like it, that's his problem. Seriously." She speaks from experience, from a relationship in which her boyfriend was in "total control" – she was always following him around, and when she wasn't with him she didn't know what to do with herself – and when it broke up it was like a ton of bricks had been lifted off her back. Never again, man. Just once Carla had a steady boyfriend and didn't particularly "like" it. She wants a boyfriend, she doesn't want one. It all depends on her mood, and in any case she's got to "straighten out" her life before she goes out again. Sharon, however, is always falling in love; she loves that special nervousness, the skittishness, the butterflies in her stomach at the sight of the beloved. If only, just once, he could be perfect: "I want a guy who can be soft but he's got to be able to take control, too."

For a couple of months she thought Mark might be the one. She saw him in the hallway, hanging out with the dozen other black guys in the school, and she was smitten. Mark reminded her instantly of Akron and her black friends there; she wanted him. She arranged to meet him through a mutual friend, and, what do you know, they began "seeing" each other. "Seeing" a guy means you're allowed to "see" other guys at the same time; "going with" means neither of you is allowed to see anybody else.

So Sharon was seeing Mark, hoping, maybe, to go with him soon.

SHARON: So he asked me out. We went to a movie.

CARLA: Did you watch it?

SHARON: Yes, we *watched* it.

CARLA: Who picked the movie?

SHARON: He did. We picked the place where he works so we could get in for free. Then we went out and I had an OJ.

A month later she was no longer seeing him. They were still good friends, she assured me, but he was in love with somebody else, an eighteen-year-old from Toronto who he'd met last summer and who'd come west to work. Mark said when he got things straightened out with this girl he'd definitely come back to Sharon. But he didn't want to hold her back. "Don't worry," she told him, "if another guy asks me out I'm not going to sit around getting over you." And a month after that he had another girlfriend altogether. "She's barf city, man. A friend of his told me they go out because she'll do 'it'. I don't do 'it'. Too bad."

Hey, Carla, you want to come over to Sharon's place and watch *Miami Vice* tonight?

FIVE

Schools

"Where was everybody for Crazy Hat Day?"

LIKE MAYORS and council members of small towns, the principals and vice-principals and department heads of big city high schools are boosters, members of a kind of Chamber of Commerce of pedagogy. Authoritative with the trappings of office – the phalanx of secretaries in the General Office, the swivel-seated leather chair, the command over the p.a. system – they impress upon the visitor the high seriousness of their business. Now that students are no longer obliged to attend their neighbourhood high school but can "shop around" for the one that best suits them, principals, like mayors, are in the position of having to attract custom. And so we get the expansive gestures in the direction of the teeming corridors, the statistics, the guided tour through the carpeted Learning Resources Centre (formerly known as "library").

Francis-Xavier Separate School, for instance: 800 students, of whom eighty-five per cent are enrolled in the university-directed program, many in the Fine Arts department or in one of the eleven French classes. (These data are not unrelated to the fact that the school's feeder areas are upper middle class.) McNally Composite High School: population some 1100, many bussed in from the suburbs. Students hunkered down in the Computing

Science program and the chess and computer clubs or whooping it up at the football and volleyball games (all the teams are called Tigers). "The kids have a sense of belonging here," says the veep. "It's *their* school." Down south in the suburbs of Millwoods, J. Percy Page C.H.S. is a very new entrant in the marketplace, open for business only since the fall of 1984. Although its timetables offer no spares (those blanks in a student's timetable giving licence to goof off), its Student Adviser program, its Self-Aware-ness and Study Habits and Vocational Guidance units, and very low teacher-student ratio (1:20) are intended to attract those students who desire a lot of personal contact with teachers and administration. In the inner city, on the other hand, a school that has seen better days has lost more than a thousand students since the upwardly mobile working-class and immigrant population made their trek to the new housing tracts on the rim of the city. This school once boasted some of the city's best athletes, drama students, and academic achievers (future architects and aldermen and off-Broadway actors graduated from here); then it serviced a rather transient population of diligent Asian immigrants, mixed in with drop-outs, re-peaters, and drop-ins on the Academic Occupation (for-merly Trades and Service) program, the English-as-a-sec-ond-language program, and the Business Education courses. Now it has tripled its grade ten enrolment by offering a Performing Arts program – electronic music, stagecraft, ballet, among other courses – and attracting students from across the province.

No principal would be so disingenuous, of course, as to deny that the complex society over which he maintains authority is threatened from time to time by crisis and disorder: the syringe found in the boys' washroom, the absenteeism, the girl fainting in Physical Education class because she hadn't eaten for two days, the black eyes and bloody noses among both sexes ("The bitch stole my boy-friend!"). "We have our share of vandalism," says one principal, "and we have the amorous couples groping in the halls – which does terrible things to the girl's reputation, by the way – and a girl who consistently skipped her English class we discovered was being beaten at home by her stepmother." A counsellor at an inner-city school deplores the high rate of drop-outs from grades nine and ten (many return to school when they discover how boring life in the video arcade can be). He speaks of the "faddishness" of single mothers keeping their babies, even bringing them to school to show them off; the "shocking" nonchalance towards the prospect of unemployment; and he mentions the bad eating habits: "I can't believe how many French fries with gravy we sell in the cafeteria in a week."

There is perhaps no clearer point of view of the relationship between authority and this intricate society of teenagers than that of the school cop. Doug B. was weary, after four years on the street, of the "negative" aspects of police work: picking up drunks, handing out speeding tickets, hassling hookers. So he signed up for the School Resource Officer Program in the city of Edmonton's police department and was assigned to an inner-city high school. He's twenty-six years old, he's blond and slim and attractive, and he loves his work.

"You want to see the other side of a policeman?" he challenges. Okay, so the first two months on this job he walked around in his uniform – he's not in the school to skulk about, and when he comes up to some kid and asks what's in the bag, it's important that the kid knows who's asking – but now it's blue jeans and a nice sweater. Fully half his time is spent in classrooms lecturing on drug and alcohol abuse, weapons offences, and sexual-assault prevention, or in the auto mechanics shop diddling with some machinery, or in the food-prep lab making chili. No kidding. The point is you'd never get the respect of these kids if you marched up and down the halls in uniform all day handing out tickets. They aren't stupid. But they do need to get good information. There's always some guy who thinks there's a law that lets him walk around with a knife if the blade is less than eight inches long or some girl who says she can carry marijuana as long as she isn't selling it. How many kids in the shop classes are making weapons that could get them ten years? Doug has a bagful of these things he's confiscated: knuckle-dusters, a chained club, a jagged-edged, perfectly lethal Chinese star.

He tells me this story: he was walking the hallway one day when a kid called him a "pig" in a loud and obnoxious voice. The kid was immediately throttled and pinned up against the wall by another guy who asked him what his "fucking problem" was. Listen: he coaches a floor-hockey team and *half* his team he charged with criminal offences last year and still they play for him! Girls hang around his door or lounge invitingly on his furniture – he has pictures of his wife all over the office – eating their heart out. He keeps his office door open, when he isn't patrolling the halls, to answer questions about a kid's criminal charge or a parent's plea: Can't *you* talk to her?

They test him. They test him physically in the floor-hockey game: everybody's up in the stands, watching, as some meathead takes a swing at him with the stick and Doug dumps him on his butt real quick and the challenge is over. Everybody has seen it. They test him with suspicious-looking roll-your-owns that turn out to be tobacco. Girls who've been ticketed in the parking lot come to see him, batting their eyelashes; they still get the ticket. His creed is to be "fair, firm, and honest" and absolutely consistent with his charges. Everybody has the idea that as far as the law is concerned you're treated differently if you're rich than if you're poor. In this school, in these hallways, in his office, there's no difference.

Doug's boss is the Chief of Police, not the school principal. He doesn't answer to the school bureaucracy, nor is he bound to contact parents. Maybe this is why kids seek him out: the confidentiality, the no-nonsense advice. He's not so old he can't remember what it was like to be seventeen and under terrific pressure from peers to do this or that outrageous thing. Problems he can't answer right away he makes sure he finds out about from among the fifty-five social service agents he knows. If you draw a blank on *one* kid's problems, there will be fifty who'll hear about it, and that means fifty who won't come near your office.

Everybody dumps on this school – kids from other schools, the media, ex-teachers. A thuggish, dope-crazed, gang-ridden school. Gangs? "You *show* me a gang," Doug challenges. Watch these kids come up to him – Hello, Constable B! Hi, Doug! – and you tell him that's a gang. The school has not had one rumble since he arrived. Who makes up these stories, anyway? He, too, had a "preconceived notion" about this school: that it was going to be hell. But two guys squaring off in the hall and knocking each other in the head a few times, that's *normal*, that's high school. It happens everywhere. And drugs, too. It's just that some principals won't say anything about it, so their schools won't look bad. Any problem that takes place in this school takes place in every other school in the system, he can guarantee it. The difference is in the degree. This is an inner-city school, it's downtown, all kinds of people drop in. If *you* had something to sell, where would you go? And you've got to consider the upbringing these kids have had, what their lives have been like at home, what kind of lives their *parents* have had, what their social standing is. But it doesn't mean they don't know right from wrong.

Girls can get into anything boys do, you bet they can. Doug can show you girls downtown he wouldn't turn his back to. There are girls in the school who assault each other in the washroom or in the hallway with others watching. (Girls don't jump in on each other's fights.) He catches as many girls as guys with drugs, and he's had to charge some with being a "party to an offence" – sitting in a car getting loaded while the boyfriend does a break and enter. He knows some girls with strong moral values who got involved with riffraff and were totally turned around, but he's also seen girls change guys who have a criminal record into what he'd call respectable citizens, out of sheer force of affection and sexual favour.

Girls have their very own problems, some minor (the mother wants them home by nine o'clock and they're sixteen and don't want to listen), some major (the father is beating them up). Girls are constantly coming to see him because they're looking to move out of home, or the girl's already moved out and the parent is on the phone, asking him to send her back. He tells the girl that legally he can't force her to go back home, but what's right and what's wrong is another thing. And he tells the parent that he can't force her to stop living with this guy she just met, even if mentally and emotionally she is still a child. His role is to decide who needs help most – the immature girl or the obdurate parent.

Girls get beaten up by their boyfriends. Some boyfriend. A couple of weeks ago he laid a charge on an ex-boyfriend. He had been in jail, got out, went to see his old girlfriend, entered her house, with her permission (he says), without her permission (she says), and assaulted her. Doug saw her in the hallway with an ugly welt on her face and asked her to come and see him about it. (Assault is a criminal offence.) She agreed she wanted a warrant issued against the bastard right away. Girls get harassed by boys in school. The guy has taken the girl out, got a crush on her, doesn't want to see her hanging around with other guys, so he roughs her up a bit. We're talking growing-pains. A girl comes in to see Doug, tells him she's in love with so-and-so, gave him "everything", and now he's dumped her. What's going on? Doug can explain this, show her the guy's point of view: once you've got "everything" from a girl, what are you going to hang around for? Doug doesn't approve of this sort of thing any more than the broken-hearted girl does, but attitudes are hard to change overnight. He's got a neighbour who has two kids: the boy, when he turns sixteen, he's going to fix up with a hooker; the girl he's going to lock up until she's twenty-six. What are you going to do?

"We're trying to reinforce positive feelings in young people about the police department. We don't want them to stereotype the police because of one bad officer on the street. Just like I don't want to say that because one student is a little maggot in the corner they *all* are."

Hey, that's great. The cop's doing some good work. But a girl from the school tells me Constable B. took her aside and asked her to be a "narc" for him, slipping a note discreetly under his door if she ever saw a kid doing dope. She told him to take a walk.

Like products with brand-names, schools have "reps", and the student takes this into consideration: you wouldn't want to go to Jasper Place C.H.S., only headbangers go there; McNally has awful school colours (brown and orange; gross!); Old Scona is just so brainy; the kids at Ross Shep are all into bragging, or lying, about how much money they have; so-and-so's friend quit Vic Comp after she got roughed up in the Jamaican students' hallway; and so on. Forget the fancy computer sciences programs, the video libraries, the student advisor teams; the reasons the *students* have for picking a particular school are not necessarily pedagogical, and if Ainlay has a good drama program but Caroline's friends don't go there, then Caroline won't go either. In a marketplace where, in spite of superficial packaging differences, the public high school is a *generic* institution, the meaningful differences among schools come down to the question, What kind of kids go there?

If they had power, they'd change a few things around. McNally is no fun: in the past you were not even allowed to eat your lunch in the hallways. (In other schools, this is quite a sight: kids sprawled out on the concrete floors, leaning back against their lockers, eating, doing their homework, visiting. Officially, the cafeteria is the designated eating area. Unofficially, the hallway – a featureless and functional space reclaimed by the students for their own social purposes – has taken over the role.) At Ross Shep, the lockers are – quel drag! – assigned, which means you aren't necessarily going to be positioned close to your friends. (This is a vital issue. The most important part of the school day is the breaks between classes, and because it's necessary to go to your locker to switch books for the next class, this is the best time to visit with your friends, whose lockers, if you are lucky, are alongside yours.) As for J. Percy Page, the school that wants to be *close* to its students with its Student Advisor program and its award-winning interior design, a student complains that, because of the Student Advisor, she can't skip classes any more without her parents' being told ("He's only there to pry into your life, and it's none of his business"), and because of the openness of the interior she feels she's constantly under surveillance. The washrooms, for instance, are not enclosed spaces (the toilet cabinets, with doors from floor to ceiling, are situated off a hallway, and the sinks and mirrors are open to view), and this effectively eliminates an important social space for girls: the girls' washroom, a place to have a smoke, put on lipstick, and gossip, away from adult supervision.

Perhaps when adults (or their stand-ins, the Students' Council) complain about student "apathy" towards the school, they mean in fact that the students fail to care about what adults care about: discipline, respect for property, and "good clean fun". The student newspaper at Harry Ainlay C.H.S., The *Titanic*, editorializes on the woeful state of school spirit: Where was everybody for Crazy Hat Day? Why isn't anybody joining clubs? Where are the fans for the football games? Why is it more fun to sit in the rotunda "making garbage"? This is to miss the point: activity that one chooses, even just making garbage, is the only free activity.

In fact, there are any number of things students care about. The Social Studies 30 trip to Europe, for example.

Collecting cans for the Food Bank and school supplies for Nicaragua. Buying doughnuts for a Grad Council fund. Playing in the school band. Auditioning for the school play. Writing poems for the school literary magazine. Competing in a wrestling match. Which is to say, there are points in official school society where students' and management's interests coincide.

Outside the concrete bunker that is the high school a chill March wind is blowing around the scraps of paper and sand left behind by the retreating snow. Pale-faced pedestrians are slogging their way through the slush across the roadway to Southgate Shopping Mall. It is that time of year, so the folklore goes, when most Albertans think of committing suicide. Winter is simply never going to end. You are never going to be warm again.

Inside the school, however, at Harry Ainlay C.H.S. (Surf City, Alberta), March 12–15 has been declared Tropical Days Week.

11:45. The school bursts into its hallways as social life resumes at the lockers, in the cafeteria line-up, in the rotunda. Groups of buddies stake out their various positions on the low-rising steps and around the pillars of the rotunda while teachers patrol the area, pointing admonitory fingers at empty pop cans and discarded cellophane wrap. There are gaggles of girls together, hugging cans of Diet Coke, like these three: blonde-streaked curls and blushed cheeks and blue eyeshadow, white lacy blouses, little white earrings. Clones. Andrea from the Students' Council takes a mike, walks into the centre of the rotunda, and says something. It is inaudible. Presently, just to get things going, she and a boy from Council take up position with a limbo pole. "Hey, what happened to the Ainlay school spirit? We had *forty* people do this last year. Come *on*!" she bellows, while claques of boys standing at the periphery jeer. The music comes on. The Beach Boys. (I can't believe this; this music is twenty years old.) Three boys and five girls approach the pole. Strut their way under. This provokes some hooting from their friends, but they carry on gamely. More join them. The pole is lowered. There are disqualifications: a boy falls over, so does the next boy, then a girl, as the onlookers groan in sympathy. Knees spread wide, feet resting on the inner arch, head thrown far back, they hang suspended in the air under the pole, and fall backwards. Now there are three girls left, two. The rotunda is packed. A single girl, emerging from under the pole, falls on her knees and is declared the winner. Teddy from the Grad Council joins me. "It's dying, all this stuff. You see the same old faces here – these are the same kids who showed up for the dance marathon. And will show up for the grape-throwing contest." The problem, it seems, is so many kids leave the school during lunch hour, rev up their engines, and head for the mall.

Next day is Tacky Tourist Day. Some kids give it a try. In the cafeteria line-up are lots of girls in pastel-coloured pants and shirts, but these look like everyday preppie wear. More fanciful is the guy in the burnoose, the girl in pink shorts and coral beads. The winner, clearly, is the boy in the straw hat and the Hawaiian shirt and shorts with a plastic lei and a camera hung around his neck, Noxzema on his nose, and a coconut held aloft in one hand. Here are fantasies of collegiate California from the TV shows – bright, splashy clothes, slim legs and narrow hips and flat bellies – but the flesh is white and the hair unbleached and it's snowing outside the windowless walls.

Finally, it's Friday night, and the dance. Sports attendance at Harry Ainlay has been dropping off, while dances become more and more popular, to the point where advance ticket sales provoke mob scenes in the rotunda, and forgers and scalpers can make a small killing.

The rotunda is jumping, the energy from the dancers could raise the roof. They are, undoubtedly, fuelled: they drink at private parties before they get here or tank up in cars in the parking lot, chugalugging Strawberry Wine Cooler, leaving the empty bottle on the curb. They'll dance to anything. Girls are dancing in twos and threes together while the usual line-up of guys, leaning up against a wall, are looking cool. It's okay to cut in on another girl's dancing partner; it's *not* cool to get upset about it. (Carla: "I wanted to dance with Duane but Karen told me to fuck off." Sharon: "I would've decked her.") If you see a guy you like and you already know him, it's okay to go right up to him, say hello, and ask for a dance. If you don't know him (have never talked to him), it becomes necessary to sidle up with your entire gang of girlfriends in the direction of *his* gang and to signal flirtatious interest, to which he may choose to respond. It's okay to arrive with girlfriends and leave with a boy (in fact, your friends, if they're real friends, will encourage this); it's semi-okay to leave with another girlfriend altogether; it is *not* okay to arrive with one boy and leave with another.

The teacher-cum-chaperone goes on patrol. She's looking for passed-out drunks in the washroom, but only finds a sink clogged with cigarette butts. If she patrolled a little later, she'd see the girls popping pills, vomiting, shrieking only half-convincingly about their horrid hallucinations. Outside in the hallway a girl leans against the wall, weeping, and explaining to her friend, between gulps, that her boyfriend has dumped her, right in the middle of the dance, gone off with that bitch Lorraine. Around them are kids racing up and down the corridor, squealing and screaming, or clinging to each other in passionate embraces by the water fountain, or just sitting on the floor, smoking. Two girls excitedly recount a scandal: "Did you hear, Larry wants to break up with Diane?" "Wow. She's always had a guy, what's she gonna do?" "They got into a fight. She put her hand through the wall."

A cop and a teacher haul a very drunk girl into the staff room. They want to phone her mother, but she can't remember her mother's phone number. There's no point, anyway, she sputters repeatedly. Her mother is out with her boyfriend. Her parents are divorcing. "I'm sorry, I'm sorry, it's all my fault, what do you expect me to do?" she says over and over again. The teachers pay her not the least attention (have they heard it all before?), but a girl-friend puts her arm around her, they bend their heads together and croon in soft voices. . . . The cop will drive her home.

Carla: "I didn't like that dance. . . . I was kind of drunk. I started at 6:30, beer and wine. And then a bunch of people came over after the hockey game. I was totally loaded. So I left the dance early. Anyway, the music sucked."

As the sociologists have discerned, alongside the official school – the institution managed by the school authorities – there is the unofficial school[1] constructed by the students themselves, a social and cultural complex that exists in the gaps and crannies of the other. Here is where peer-group life, its rituals and values, is acted out: where girls learn about fashion, and punkers hook up with each other, and conspiracies are hatched by the lockers, and lovers meet up in the cafeteria, and kids are initiated into drugs.

Most city schools, like large towns, are too big for the individual student to know everyone else. It becomes necessary, in order to defend oneself against loneliness and exclusion, to find a compatible group to hang out with. To the outsider, the group is a clique, to the insider it is a warm nest. Teddy, who belongs to a rather formidable group of grade twelve preppies, admits that "to someone outside our group we look scary, we seem, well, unapproachable, but actually we're quite open and friendly. At least we talk to a lot of other people compared to that other group around the rotunda who are really stuck-up." Nevertheless, hers is the group that sets the standards for those who care about pleasing them. They drive smart little sporty cars, the keys dangling from their fingers as they lounge around the Grad Council office at the end of the day. They go to Hawaii with their parents at Easter, and rent chalets together at Banff, and shop in designer boutiques at West Edmonton Mall. They even have their own territory: at the corner of the rotunda between the bookstore and the General Office. (The corner by the cafeteria, on the other hand, is the black girls' turf.) For kids who live in subsidized housing or even in trailer parks, yet go to school alongside these princesses, the social nexus can be cruel. Imagine, too, the social trauma when Daddy loses his job and they take away the big house with the swimming pool on Westbrooke Drive and later even the condo. . . .

A counsellor: "The peer-group pressure and exclusiveness are fierce. If you're in a clique, you don't dare let in an outsider; your own status and sense of belonging are too fragile. I've had to start a 'new students' group for kids whose families came into Alberta during the boom and who experience this school as the cliquiest, coldest, and unfriendliest place they've ever been. I've arranged for a room where new students can eat lunch so they don't have to sit alone in the cafeteria, being ignored by all the others."

Arden came straight into grade twelve in Ainlay from the junior-senior high school (population: 481) in Gimli, Manitoba, and has resented the move bitterly. (Her father works for the CN and was transferred to Edmonton.) In Gimli, she lived in a neighbourhood where people talked to each other and went to a school where everybody hung out with each other (the only really distinct groups were those who liked to party and those who stayed at home), and nobody was bugged for coming from the farm, and you didn't call each other names for tastes in music.

Ainlay is very different. They call Arden a "headbanger" and snicker behind her back and pretend they don't see her at the mall. She wears jeans, a black leather motorcycle jacket, and concert T-shirts, like the one she's got on right now – black, with the imprint of a Rush album cover – which she inherited from another head-

banger girl who wanted to get rid of it. Somebody had
made fun of it, somebody in green fluorescent socks, for
God's sake. So she likes Heavy Metal. So? She does *not*
worship Satan, she does *not* listen to Judas Priest all day
long, she does not even hang out at any particular exit in
the school. She knows six people at Ainlay; they're all
from out of town.

Corry at Vic is another kind of outsider, a white girl in
a multi-ethnic school. It used to drive her to tears, listening to all the inscrutable languages being babbled in the
hallways, making her feel as if she had wandered into
some strange world miles away from her own, especially
when she stood at the bus stop, rearing up like a giraffe
above all the diminutive Chinese and Vietnamese bodies
(she still can't tell them apart) around her. But it doesn't
bother her any more. In fact, she appreciates the chance to
meet so many different kinds of people. "Once you're out
of school," she has the feeling, "you're always going to be
divided into whatever spectrum of society you belong to; I
mean, society just puts you there and you stay there, in
one place." In school, in this school, you mix it up, to a
point.

When she first got there she was told: upstairs is white
people, downstairs is the United Nations. And you
watched your step: Blacks dominated the lockers around
the store. The Vietnamese, the Chinese, the Filipinos,
each staked out a quiet corner for themselves. Even the
whites were divided up: the Ukrainians, affectionately
known as "dumb bastards", hung around together and
were left alone.

But you still run into each other all the time, in classes,
in the cafeteria, at your locker. The kid who has his locker
next to Corry's is half white, half Chinese, very quiet, a
real brain, which she doesn't hold against him. She
doesn't mind getting to know him but she keeps her distance; in this school, if you're seen hanging around the
"coloured people" too much, you'll get a reputation for
being "like" them – weird, sneaky, frowzy somehow. It

happens in all social circles, this business of prejudices. At the Christmas Lit, for example, a group of black kids came out on stage to do some break-dancing and were booed off.

Barbara is a Jamaican in a predominantly white, middle-class school. She'd never been more scared in her whole life than during the first two months, before she had any friends. She'd walk into the cafeteria, buy lunch, sit down, and feel as if the whole place was staring at her, making her feel as if she was the only Black on the entire planet. There were other Blacks, but she didn't see them; all she could see was white. She was so nervous she couldn't eat, just went home and cried.

Now she has some friends – Blacks and a Japanese girl and a Paki girl. When the Jamaicans are all together they talk their own lingo. Real fast. They'll slow down a bit when whites are around but basically whites aren't *supposed* to understand. This embarrasses her black friend Jackie very much. Jackie hates patois, she thinks it's too loud, uncouth. Jackie's problem is she wants to be white, and rich. There's a rich guy she's trying to impress but he'll never notice her. He's white. Wouldn't matter if Jackie was the richest girl in the school. . . . Barbara's not embarrassed.

On the other hand, the fact that there are only twenty black kids in the school suits her fine. All her life before she came to Canada she was surrounded by black people and it began to get on her nerves. People watching each other real careful, and if you dress better than them, for instance, they'll be thinking, Who does she think she is? Just because you dress nice you're a show-off? That's stupid. So Barbara figures she's better off surrounded by white people. The black guys call her an Oreo cookie – black on the outside but white on the inside – but it's not true! Maybe she just *likes* white people.

Well, not *everything* about them. She thinks they dance weird. When they dance to hard rock, they jump around and shake their heads so hard it makes her tired just

watching them. It's crazy. There's no rhythm to it. Just
listen to the music, find the beat. When she can't stand it
any more, she hops a bus and goes to a break-dancing
competition.

There is no single teen culture; there are several cultures,
or what one girl has called the "multiculturalism of teenagers".² She singles out Mods (elsewhere known as New
Wavers), arty types who favour The Clash and baggy
pants; Punkers, with their celebrated Mohawk-style hair-
dos, slam-dancing, and self-defined anarchism ("Apathy
sucks!"); Headbangers, or aficionados of Heavy Metal
bands and very tight jeans, the last of the greasers; Preppies, who are clothes-horses especially fond of Ralph
Lauren designs, are fans of Duran Duran, and are the
group most liked by adults. There are also, perennially,
those most basic of subcultures, passed from one generation to the next: Brains and Jocks.

Not every subculture is represented in every school; in
fact, schools will be known as havens of one or another
subculture. At the middle-class schools, preppie is de ri-
gueur, this being the subculture most congenial to the
sons and daughters of the affluent: the girls' pin-ups on
their locker doors feature male models in Calvin Klein
clothes. Preppie, of course, not to mention New Wave, is
banished from Vic, the boys belonging to these cultures
being viewed as "faggots".

The school cop takes me on a patrol of Vic, scene of a
near riot recently between headbangers and breakers, to
prove to me that this school is "normal". Sure enough,
here is the requisite "head" section in the old wing, dope
smokers who share "their" space with Heavy Metal boys
and girls splendid in spike-heeled boots and black leather.
Relatively speaking, the kids are more dressed up in the
new wing, which is known as the "academic" territory. . . .
Hi! Hi there! He stops to talk to a girl in very tight jeans
wrapped around stick-like legs (are they *all* anorectic?)

and asks her why she's been skipping. "I haven't. I was in Calgary." "That's skipping." "I got in late last night. Slept in." "I still call that skipping." He points out a guy leaning up against a wall, holding an unlit cigarette, who spent the summer in jail, after being busted holding forty hits of acid. And that girl over there had a baby last year. And . . . oh-oh. He sprints off. A crowd has gathered at one of the exits and is getting very excited: two guys are outside, rolling around on the pavement, bloodying each other's noses. He comes back, clutching their IDs. "They're hot," he says. I'm not sure whether he means their tempers or their documents.

Tour number two. Jodi, a grade twelve student at Strathcona C.H.S., knows the place intimately. Like an amateur anthropologist, she has identified the pecking order of its unofficial society and learned to recognize the distinguishing features of its subgroups. She agrees to take me on a tour of the school's social zones and to characterize them; to draw me a highly coloured social map, in other words, from the point of view of a seventeen-year-old who is herself "heavily into" the arts and drama and obscure German synthesizer music, and certain bistros downtown. Her opinions are blunt, even scathing.

It's lunch hour and all the various social territories have been claimed by their denizens. Here's the "head" hallway, near the main doors; they listen to Heavy Metal and smoke dope and Jodi says it's dangerous to walk alone around here. We do a fast turn and scurry on. At another doorway we'll see the "rejects" from their group: they cluster in the vestibule playing cards and doing each other's make-up and stepping outside to have a smoke, kids who couldn't even make it into the heads' group, that's what kind of losers they are. The main hallway is one of the places where the preppies congregate. Check the Polo shirts, the penny loafers, the shirts hanging artfully below sweaters; check the Social Convenor of the Student Council. That's preppie.

Up the stairs, through a door, around the corner: this is the Mod hallway. These are kids who listen to Ska music, The Who, The Jam, and some are even musicians in alternative bands. They're into being outrageous. Yesterday they posted handmade anti-nuke posters in their hallway but the teachers tore them down. This is a very pretentious hallway, says Jodi. They all think they're intellectuals. We sit down on the floor. The chubby girl with the spiky black hair over there on the windowsill is the local bisexual slut who hangs out at the Boiling Point restaurant lounge. All her lovers fool around too. There's Rafael, the "Riverbend punk", who's got all kinds of money and is protesting God knows what. You've got to watch out for that very interesting Oriental girl in the baggy striped pants and oversized man's jacket: she's a gossip, and vicious.

We reach Jodi's hallway, the Drama hallway, in the school's Art wing. The principal once tried to disperse this crowd by locking up the lockers, but the social life was too intense for her to get away with that. So they're still here, playing frisbee and laying out potluck buffet lunches on the windowsills. A pale, slender, close-cropped Polish boy is a member, and weird Gloria, who likes to drop her French fries and ketchup into a glass of water ("I *love* blood") and drink it. Jodi points out that her hair is a mess, her clothes are gross: "She looks like she came out of a garbage can." Jill spent some time in Toronto, following a gay singer around. She once spent a night sleeping in the street on a sidewalk grating. She's never got over it. Val is the ultimate Valley Girl: she's dumb and she messes around and nobody can figure out how she gets good marks. Gillian boasts about being in analysis, diagnosed as manic-depressive and addicted to Valium. Jodi's been called a lesbian for holding hands with her girlfriends and "alternative" for wearing ripped shirts. Anything that isn't tight jeans and pink sweatshirts is "alternative" to some people.

The Drama hallway has radical politics. They want to save the world. Some are even socialists: they think everyone should have and live the same. The *real* radicals, like the girl who always wears a red armband, think Russia is paradise. Their hallway used to be festooned with underground newspapers from Vancouver and Sandinista T-shirts and a *Time* magazine article about the Americans' mining of Managua harbour, but the principal took it all down, saying, "You're here to learn, not fight." Fight? Who's fighting? Ask *one* question that isn't in the books and immediately they think you're a raving revolutionary.

Last year no one on the Students' Council ran for president, so the administration hand-picked a brainy kid who's the ultimate in school spirit: goes to all the games, sock hops, and bake sales, and all that stuff. The only other true believers are the grade tens (the darlings), who live to go to the school dances and get drunk and sick so they can show up on Monday morning looking wasted. Big deal.

We make our way back to the main hallway, peeking into the library and the cafeteria. These are spaces given over, uncontested, to the kids utterly without cachet. The Chinese kids having "intellectual discussions" in the library. The Pakis carrying computer games to the cafeteria. In the cafeteria, in the back-left corner, the acid rock crowd listening to their ghetto-blasters; at the front, the airheads, the Farrah Fawcett-lookalikes who get banged at parties; and between them, hovering in the middle of this no man's land, the detritus of teen society – the kids in dumb clothes, with bad skin and goofy haircuts, the kids with no friends, the geeks.

The unofficial school has appropriated its own spaces from the official institution; it has also appropriated its own time. From the designated computerized timetable, it has snatched the spares, those periods of time ostensibly given over to homework and library work; more subversively, it has created "skipping" out of classes altogether. In both cases, this is time to goof off with your friends in the hallway (playing with water pistols, exchanging audio tapes, throwing around birthday streamers) or to hang out in washrooms smoking cigarettes and examining your make-up. This is the time to score some dope, at certain well-known exits or outside on the avenue, under the Daniel Hechter billboard. The breaks between classes are likewise claimed. Boyfriends holding their girlfriends around the hips, rubbing noses. Girls making plans for lunch hour. Weekend gossip passed on. Hairdos retouched. Recent purchases displayed. Whole and complex social transactions negotiated in the few minutes left before the bell sounds . . . to be continued at lunch-time in the cafeteria.

The cafeteria is a large, functional, noisy place with orderly rows of wood-and-metal tables and metal chairs under low fluorescent lights: it becomes a distinctive space from the sheer impress of teenage gestures and activities. The group with the ghetto-blaster. The kids at the chessboard. The girls doing homework. The boy holding court with six adoring fans. The kid sprawled on the tabletop, and the one, in dignified solitude, picking at his lunch and nodding his head to the beat of the Walkman in his ears. Girls huddle in the queue – sweatpants, Flashdance tops, sneakers, shoulder bags, earrings, mascara – to buy chocolate milk and French fries with gravy and to wave and shriek at a friend standing in the doorway. A teacher walks by and a boy steps out of the line-up to try to sell her a ballpoint pen for a dollar. She opens her purse. "What's the money for?" "Drugs, Mrs. Lyons. Drugs." She looks appalled. "Lots of them. For one dollar."

Tara loves her school. It's her life. She's there from eight in the morning until three in the afternoon, all her friends are there, she has a ball. Besides classes, *everything* goes on at school, everything you can dream of. You have – skipping! That's the best part; she's very good at it. She simply doesn't go to class. You can always forge a note, make up an excuse. She's a terrific bullshitter. She prides herself on it. Last year she had 154 absences; a very bad girl. It got to the point where one more absence and they would have kicked her out of school. But it was worth it.

When you skip you can do all kinds of things. Go to the mall to shop or have a coffee. Just sit at a table for four people and soon there will be six or seven around it and some will leave and others will take their place. Hi! How's it going? Come sit down with us! You buy a plate of fries and you only get one out of it for yourself. Or you can get in a car with a friend and just drive around town, looking for boys you know. . . . Or you can stay at school. There's all kinds of things you can do at school. Go to the weight room. Stand at an exit to smoke and meet your friends. Her exits are numbers 11 and 12. There's other exits for punks and heads. And another for the cool dudes – the one beside the gym – and the one by the parking lot for the guys with cars. They you can go to the bathrooms and see who's there. Her bathroom is the one beside the chip store. She goes to all of them but that's the one where she *hangs out*. Sits there and talks. Meets the same people there every Monday morning. They do their make-up and gossip. Like, this Monday she knows she's going to go straight there at 7:30 and tell whoever is there what happened to her on Friday night. Maybe they'll decide to skip the first class. Go to the mall. . . .

Five storeys above College Street near Fran's restaurant, in the rooms of a nondescript Toronto office building. Kids sprawl on the vintage furniture of the "lounge" or lie on cushions. One lies in the corner, his head under a camera tripod. On the receptionist's desk is an electric soup kettle emitting savoury steam. They yawn, stretch, sip black coffee; this is noon on a Monday and they're finally waking up.

This is a general meeting at SEED school. All cigarettes out, please. Marge, the Director: Who's interested in working with handicapped kids? Or in free tickets from the Italian consulate to the new show at the Art Gallery? Kid: Marge's first grandchild was born last night. Kids: Yeah! Claps and whistles. Teacher: I have videos of two of Lina Wertmüller's early films, two of the greatest made since the beginning of time. Anybody interested? Another teacher introduces a bright-eyed student teacher who is a singer and pianist and is thinking of doing a historical survey of music styles. Students and student teacher regard each other with hesitant interest.

Now comes the gist of the meeting. Representatives from the Krishna Temple would like to come to SEED to lecture about vegetarianism and serve some food. Marge has misgivings: would every other cult demand equal time? On the other hand, the food is a great idea; too many people around here aren't eating properly. Student: What if the Scientologists want to come and give IQ tests? Another objects to the use of the word "cult" and says the administration should credit the students with more "insight" into how to handle their own affairs. A vote is taken, hands are raised, looks like a "yes". Teacher: You yes-voters, how many of you are actually going to show up for the lecture?

This is an alternative school, a full-time accredited school within the Toronto Board of Education with a program and organization "co-operatively" managed by students, staff, the occasional parent, and "catalysts" (adults from the community at large who come to the school to give special lectures). It is a school for refugees from the secondary schools.

The place is poor. In the sixties such schools were called "free" or "experimental", and their poverty was consistent with their ideological repudiation of educational bureaucracies. Now the place just looks shabby, as though it were being punished by deficit-ridden Boards for being so doggedly marginal. The art classes, for instance, serve only two or three students at a time. (I pass the clay heads from the sculpture class on a table in the hallway.) They

are very badly supplied, although the photography dark-
room is reasonably equipped, and the library, I am informed by the student who is showing me around, is "stupid". There's nothing of value in it, apparently; the Board
is very stingy. A workroom known as the Old Dada Room
has a piano, and the "computer sciences lab" has three
training terminals; in a cubbyhole-cum-study sits a lone
Olympia Selectric, broken.

Students manifestly do not come to SEED for its facilities. They come for the *idea* of it, for its promotion of a
certain idea of education in which teacher and student
collaborate in the process of instruction. Students, for
example, interview would-be teachers, and no teacher can
be dismissed without the unanimous vote of a general
meeting. There is a functioning race-relations committee.
Upset by a new influx of students wearing swastikas (who
argued it was a Hindu peace symbol), it instituted, pro-
vocatively, a dress code. In the winter/spring of 1984–85,
160 students were officially enrolled, but only 60 will show
up on a regular basis. Three-quarters of the students are
living alone, on Student Welfare; if a parent phones the
school, the office will inform her or him only that the child
is enrolled; if the student is sixteen years old or older,
teachers will not even talk to parents without the student's
permission. "We don't want to be police."

Seven female students sit in a circle in the library (temporarily creating a women-only zone, vigorously de-
fended) and tell me what kind of people, or SEEDlings
(their word), they are. A little shell-shocked, says one: "I
went through a whole year of going to classes and loving it
but not being able to *write*. I just wasn't used to it, the
independence." Another had heard that SEEDlings stayed
in the same grade for eight years because they were never
expected or forced to be in class, and so they spent their
days in the lounge, smoking cigarettes and nursing hangovers and the effects of a weekend on MDA. This is true for
some, but it's important that this be a place where you can
come just because you *are* fucked-up and hurt. "The per-

sonal lives of people are affected here," says one girl approvingly. And right away you notice how SEEDlings like way-out characters. They take eccentricities seriously; some people get away with an awful lot of attention.

"But this school is not a joke. I came here expecting ha-ha-ha. But I read a novel a week, I write an essay a week." They've come from conventional classrooms, forty structured minutes of sitting at the back and never saying a word and maybe getting two minutes of the teacher's time in a week, of learning to regurgitate the teacher's opinions and kiss ass, to this place. Here they find a French class with only one other student for a whole hour; ten-page essays; an hour-and-a-half-long seminar on physiology; teachers who love their work. They also find community "catalysts" who want to share their enthusiasms: the stockbroker who reads Shakespeare, the lawyer who's fighting pornography, the comparative-religion professor who simply loves to teach. And if you work well in spurts, you don't even have to show up every day, just "in spurts".

From casual observation at a few alternative schools, I had gathered the impression that they draw more female than male students, which was confirmed by Myra Novogorodsky, Women's Studies co-ordinator for the Toronto Board of Education. She pointed out that, with a grant of $2000 per student from the Department of Education, alternative schools are simply unable to finance expensive science and computer labs. Because of the "gender distinction" between arts and sciences, boys are drawn to the big secondary schools offering math and science programs, and girls to the more "humanistic" environments of the alternative schools. "Softness and touchy-feelyness is part of the environment, and these are traditionally labelled feminine. Macho behaviour is actively discouraged. And in this environment with smaller numbers of students certain skills, which girls miss out on in the large schools, are developed: skills in meetings, in dealing with adults, in handling mistakes."

The circle of seven girls in the SEED library have horror

stories of their earlier schooling. Forest Hill school, very straight, very preppie, where everyone hung around in cliques and ostracized anyone who did not "fit". This sounds familiar: "I had the same experience. It was horrible. They taunted me. They were all rich preppie princesses driving their brand-new cars and that wasn't me. I don't come from a rich family, my mother's an artist, they thought I was a total nut case." At Eastern Commerce for four years, surrounded by Beauty Queens whose goal in life was to get picked up by some hunk in a car. Impossible to talk to such girls *intellectually*. Try to say something serious and they'd look at you as if you were speaking a foreign language. It was so *alienating*, you know? They knew all about how to apply make-up and get a haircut and put clothes together, just like in the magazines, and the awful thing, the terrible thing, is it *works*. Boys chase after them and the other girls are driven insanely jealous.

Competition and pressure and cliques. Wanting to be accepted, *needing* to be, with no sense of self at all. North Toronto, an upper-middle-class school. Fashion and cliques. Being trained for the role of society wife. . . . She had to get out of there, she was so goddamn miserable. Emotions were scary, being on your own was scary. She came to SEED to explore herself, and now when she runs into old classmates from North Toronto they gape at her and say, "Oh my God, is it true what's happened to you?"

"I was having a discussion the other night about how women's bodies are untouchable even to themselves. There's no way you can touch your own boob!" (Peals of laughter) "And I had this image from my old school of all these girls walking down the hallway with their books clasped in front of their bosom. You don't see us standing around here like that."

It is mid-February, and outside the leaded panes of the window large, wet snowflakes are floating down into the courtyard. I am sitting on the faded chintz covering of an old but solid chesterfield, under a vaulted stone ceiling, and admiring the extravagance of a large basket of fresh daffodils in front of me. The shriek of girls' voices floats in from some distance. Elsewhere someone is playing a piano. I am enchanted, as though I'd been set down in a tableau drawn from one of those novels I used to love to read as a girl: the Ukrainian-Canadian girl from the prairies spellbound by stories of fragile but plucky English girls growing up, with such airs and such melancholy, in boarding schools. For this is Havergal College, a private school for young women in Toronto, and I am waiting to see the Headmistress. I want her permission to hang about the college and get to know a "typical" Havergal girl.

I am called in to the office and served tea in a mug while a white terrier runs about underfoot and over the furniture. Our conversation is pleasant: about Miss Dennys's recent trip abroad on behalf of the college, and about her retirement plans and her apprehension about her replacement's unfamiliarity with the "Havergal community". Miss Dennys is short and plump, with white hair and glasses, and an accent that sounds faintly of Ireland, or perhaps of Newfoundland. I tell her about my research project and what I'd like from her. She seems interested, even intrigued. We talk briefly about her charges – how pressured they are, unfortunately, to "get going" on their professional lives, in their cases on medicine, law, and business – and I leave it up to her to call me back with the name of someone who would like to be interviewed. She never does. Nor does she return my calls.

So, I still don't know who they are, these WASP and would-be WASP princesses floating serenely and confidently through the neo-Gothic halls of privilege, or what it's like to be them. I have only a copy of the college paper, *Behind the Ivy*. Here I read of the antics of the boarders – "room hopping, food fighting, pizza partying and radio blasting" – and the concern of the editor that Havergalians have lost days and days of school through Games Day and the Christmas recording sessions and the Pope's visit. I read about fashion counsel re the "high tech" look ("electrifying details of bright neon colours") and ethics counsel ("Your parents can afford to send either you or your sister to Greece this March break. Do you. . . ?"). There is news of bazaars and Old Girls' teas and semi-formals. And it is like being back again, fourteen years old, nose buried in a book about those incomparable girls in their boarding schools on the moors.

Mandy says she has no idea how much money her father makes (he never discusses it), but she guesses she's a pretty typical St. Clement's private school girl. Her father is a management consultant and a partner in the firm and her mother is a homemaker. One of the things that attracted her parents to the school was that, as these things go, it wasn't very expensive. Last year the tuition went up by $300 to $4000 and her class lost two girls just like that, which Mandy regrets: the higher the tuition, the less likely the school will have anything but the most middle-class kids. It's not as bad as Upper Canada College (for boys), where every other name you read is the son of the chairman of the board or of the president of something important. At St. Clement's everybody has the same chance to accomplish things. Of course, they won't have quite the same chance as UCC boys, like her brothers. They are taking courses St. Clement's couldn't dream of offering: economics, an art program, lots of sports in up-to-date facilities.

But still, she says, she's ahead of kids in the public schools. Her parents made her come here, in grade nine, because of what was happening in the schools. She reports with satisfaction that the private school can set its own curriculum, hire and fire its own teachers, enforce discipline. As a result, Mandy, who never used to work at school, now works and is "motivated". St. Clement's suits her. If she were the rebellious type she'd be totally fed up with the place by now, skipping classes and failing to do her homework, just dying to get out, but Mandy, who didn't come in until she was fifteen, arrived an "already well-rounded person" and already sick of boys: she submitted to the school's code without protest.

At nineteen, Mandy is an extraordinarily self-possessed young woman, bright and emphatic, with very good manners and not the least bit of awkwardness in my company; the sort of girl who used to be called "well brought up". We sit in the sun porch on cheery patio furniture, sipping tea from china cups; her mother served and then vanished. Mandy sits cross-legged in the chair, her tunic hiked up mid-thigh. She looks disarmingly girlish: school tie coming loose, long straight hair falling about her shoulders. At her age, I was travelling to Europe for the first time and falling in love with a French boy and about to fall into the mid-sixties. What, I wondered, was about to happen to a girl like Mandy?

She wears a uniform of navy-blue tunic belted (in grade thirteen only) with a yellow rope, or "curtain cord", as she refers to it; on her legs, navy-blue knee socks, and oxfords on her feet; the uniform is completed by a plain white shirt and a blue tie with the school's crest, a very literal cross and anchor, for the school's motto is "The Cross is my Anchor". No make-up is tolerated and no necklaces, but gold studs or pearls in the ears are permitted (quite illegally she's wearing diamond studs), and only the school ring and one other, without gems, may decorate the fingers. Only a beret may be worn on the head, only a navy-blue V-neck pullover over the shirt, and all coats must be longer than the tunic. She agrees to it all. She's in school to learn, not to strut about in a fashion parade. The Havergal girls, by contrast, give her a good giggle: they arrive at school just *so*. As though looking perfect were important.

Because the school has a reputation for academic excellence (within its limits of arts and humanities) and because the girls compete ferociously for grades, the St. Clement's girl has a "rep" among private-school kids as the bookish type who fancies herself intellectually superior. Of course, it's not the school that's important, it's the person, but school can mould you none the less. Those Havergal girls, for instance: so rich and so preppie, so image-conscious and snotty and stand-offish. The Bishop Strachan girls are even worse. Word has it that they're even wealthier than the Havergal bunch and so *intense*. Mandy noticed this while playing tennis with them. They were out to *win*. Win! Who cares? On the soccer field, the St. Clement's girls would be casually kicking the ball around while the Bishop Strachan girls were doing *laps*.

Socially, St. Clement's has just about the worst rep – that stereotype of the brainy, dowdy girl always comes to mind. Only other private schools are invited to school dances – there is very little chance to get to know anyone from a public school through the school – and you can imagine how interested the UCC boys are in St. Clement's girls when they can hang out with the fashion-plates from Havergal. The dances at St. Clement's can be positively embarrassing. This year the Headmistress stood at the door and examined everyone's school ID – one boy even brought his report card! But it's important to have contacts with boys, Mandy feels, even in these ridiculous circumstances. Otherwise, you grow up thinking boys are God.

But academically it's no loss not having boys around. Girls end up competing with each other, anyway, and you can lose status even just among girls. Mandy gets laughed at when she asks a stupid question in math. It's not a very good idea at all to let down the group. Say you're running after some boy instead of doing your share of the research for a class presentation; well, it's just not nice. Everybody hides their marks from each other. Mandy doesn't care. She got 30 in calculus once and told everybody about it, but a friend who got only 70 on a history test threatened to drop the course, she was so mortified. St. Clement's can do that to you.

The St. Clement's girl is highly motivated to do well in life, says Mandy, which means to go to university, get a good job, and make (or marry) lots of money. When the Headmistress gives her speech at the end of the year about the future, she always stresses job opportunities, and now there's an effort to establish a network of Old Girls. If you're from UCC you can go anywhere in Canada and the States and run into Old Boys and you help each other out. But the St. Clement's network is still very weak; the most famous person who went there, as a little kid, is Carling Bassett, and what good is that to most girls? Mandy has her own network – the high-spirited group of girls she's got to know at the school, and these friendships are what she'll take away with her when she leaves.

Who knows what she'll go on to do with her life? She's already shocked parents and friends by announcing that she doesn't know if she'll go to university. She will be going to Grad, however. She's bought a dress that looks as if it was sewn from Christmas tree tinsel; it's very narrow, with big padded shoulders and a deep V in the back. Shocking. Everyone else, needless to say, is going in taffeta.

SIX

Kelly and Connie

"Oh well, there's always tomorrow's game."

WEARING the number six sweater (a dark-blue shirt with a white collar), with grey shorts and blue knee-pads, Kelly is warming up for this afternoon's game against the Salisbury Sabres. She's in grade eleven at Ross Sheppard, a classic "all-rounded" student who does well in chemistry and French, plays the clarinet in the school band, works on weekends at a boutique in a shopping mall, and plays on the school's junior girls' Thunderbirds volleyball team. She loves sports best of all.

The junior girls play in the small gym (the boys' teams work out in the large one), and so, because there are no bleachers, those of us who've come to watch the game – a handful of girls, a sprinkling of teachers, one or two boy-friends – sit on the floor, slouching against the wall. This is an important game: if the Shep girls lose it, they're out for the season. Still, no one is particularly keyed-up. The Salisbury team (from a lower-middle-class suburb) arrives, looking somehow meaner (bulkier, grimmer) than the Shep girls. As it does its warm-up stretches, a Shep player drives a sudden spike ball into the midst of them. It is the first challenge the Shep girls will offer Salisbury.

Sadly, it is also the last. Shep plays badly. Balls hit the ceiling, are fired at the players' bench, and fall inconse-

quentially wide of the court. For all that, the players exhibit a lot of energy and enthusiasm, accompanying their
lacklustre performance with much jumping up and down
and a great deal of hand-clapping and shrieking. Whenever a Shep server scores a point, the rest of her team rush
around her, giddily congratulating her and reaching out
their hands to touch her as though she were a talisman of
luck. But it is in vain. In spite of the occasional plucky
yelp – "Go, T-Birds!" – and Kelly's own swift, clean serves
across the net, ten minutes into the third game they are
trailing 8 to 1 and are visibly wilting. They trip over their
feet and fall over each other. "That's girls' sports for you –
hysteria," grumbles a male coach who's wandered in from
the other gym to watch. "They're more concerned about
how they look than with saving the ball." With all due
respect to his professional's eye, I don't think that is the
problem here: in their efforts to keep the ball in play they
dive and slide along the floor, without effect. They lose.

Kelly will explain to me later that the T-Birds lost to
the Sabres not because their opponents were much superior but because "when we started to get beaten some
people thought, 'Why even try?' Once you start losing, it's
really hard to get yourself back up." "Why even try" is a
long way from the sort of distilled blood-lust one asso-
ciates with the (male) athlete, and with the ardent labour
of the body exerting itself at all costs to win. Why should
women's games be so different? The shallow observation
that young women are anxious about their appearance is
hardly an explanation. What is at issue here is their relationship to their *body*: even to the inexpert eye, most
teenage girls seem to inhabit it somewhat gingerly, as
though to wield it forcefully would be to damage or
hurt it.

At this game and elsewhere – in physical education
classes, at games of badminton and volleyball – I watch
fifteen- and sixteen-year-olds move with minimal exertion,
as though their bodies were already ponderous and somehow disabled. It is interesting that a 1986 McMaster Uni-

versity study found that among fourteen- to sixteen-year-olds in Ontario more girls than boys smoke tobacco, drink alcohol, and sniff inhalants such as glue and gasoline. A recent Participaction report that teenage girls are the least fit people in Canada raises the question whether this lack of fitness is the cause of the sluggishness or its consequence. Is it possible that girls avoid fitness in some misguided pursuit of feminine tenderness? Alongside the occasional images in magazines and on television of young women in neon-bright outfits lifting weights in post-modern spa interiors, a much older, much more deeply rooted image competes for the identity of girls: the woman at leisure, languid upon her chaise longue, gazing into a mirror, absorbed in the passivity of her own useless flesh, her body awaiting the quickening touch of a lover. *This* is femininity. To be lithe and quick, rambunctious and on the move, is to be a kid, a sexless kid. Kids run around whacking balls. *Women* lean back, striking poses.

Kelly, though, is not like this. Her coach calls her a "fine athlete": she has a strong body, good hand and eye co-ordination, and an acute sense of timing. "She's receptive, is able to translate an instruction immediately through her body." She's weakest as a sprinter, strongest as a long-distance runner and in the water. It's a question now of maturing into a disciplined *artist* whose body performs no more, and no less, than what it is instructed to do. Kelly doubts that she will get to that point: she sees herself as a competent athlete, good at many sports – soccer, track, volleyball – but not outstanding at any particular game. She accepts this. She plays for the love of it.

This, more than any other reason, is probably why Kelly will never be a star athlete. For it is not love but aggressive, single-minded competitiveness that wins games, and while Kelly will try her hardest, she feels that "it's not the worst thing in the world to lose." She finds it hard to train for track, for instance; rather than submit to the grinding routine of training, she prefers to get out and *run*, flying into the wind. It doesn't even have to be a race.

It isn't personal glory she's after: for her, one of the keen-
est satisfactions of sport is to play with a team, to connect
and share with others, and, of course, once you have the
sense of connection with fellow players it becomes impossible *not* to worry what you're prepared to do to win.
"Usually we won't ever show feelings of anger towards
each other during a game. You just can't let that happen.
Everyone is going to make a few mistakes and that's to be
expected. Like in a soccer game, you're playing for an
hour and a half and nobody thinks that every time you
approach the ball you're going to do something perfect
with it." It feels good to win, she won't deny it, but that
isn't half the pleasure of the great, gulping relief to be
finished a race, a game. To have done it, period.

But girl athletes pay a penalty for their femininity. According to a report in the *Globe and Mail* ("Girls Winning
the Sports War Against Shutouts"), male-run sports organizations do not promote female athletes, pay them very
little, and seem to hope that from sheer inattention they'll
go away. To give one example, the Ontario Lacrosse Association spends a total of $160,000, of which its women's
team receives $5000. The Supreme Court of Ontario has
ruled that girls may not play with boys in the minor
hockey leagues, but a twelve-year-old girl has initiated a
discrimination complaint with the Ontario Human Rights
Commission all the same. Her persistence is remarkable;
by the time they reach high school, most girls have become sufficiently discouraged by the hostility of the male-
dominated athletic milieu, and by the visible impoverish-
ment of the female sector, not to mention the innuendoes
regarding female jocks, that they avoid physical assertive-
ness wherever they can, taking physical education classes
only if they have to, and dragging their laggard bodies
along with them. It is not, to put it mildly, the stuff of
which champion volleyball teams are built.

Kelly acknowledges all of this: that girl teams don't
have fans, that even the most sports-minded boy will
rarely make a point of watching a girls' game, that the

interest is so tepid because the girls' "skill level" is so much lower; if the senior girls' basketball team, for instance, were to play the senior boys', they'd be slaughtered. She understands why it would seem to a male athlete that girl athletes are not *serious*: she remembers in phys ed class how many girls objected to the instruction to *squat down* to be ready for the ball; they said they felt "stupid" in that position, especially if a boy were watching: "ladies" don't squat. But she rejects the notion that any female player she knows would "let a ball drop on the floor just to look good. Everyone else would wonder how you got on the team."

No, the difference goes much deeper than that: girls simply aren't as competitive as boys. All his life, Kelly argues, a boy has been told he can get somewhere in sports: win an athletic scholarship, be a big hero. But girls do not have this incentive, for the simple reason that girls' sports do not "go" anywhere. Where is professional women's basketball, soccer, hockey? Towards which goal, exactly, is a woman athlete called on to compete? Unsurprisingly, girls have different *feelings* from boys when they play. "Boys withdraw into themselves when they're upset in games," Kelly has observed. "They become very moody, but girls will yell and scream and try to boost each other up. When guys lose, they blame it on themselves and it's the end of the world. When we girls lose, we say, 'Oh well, there's always tomorrow's game, it's no big deal. We all did the best we could. What else could be done?'"

It's a matter of some debate whether these feelings are "natural" to women and to female culture, and ought, in fact, to be encouraged in the name of co-operativeness and tolerance and uncorrupted playfulness. The other possibility is that they reflect physical timorousness and a certain feminine lack of gumption, as though to be very strong and very talented were to invite some kind of punishment. "Sometimes," says Kelly, "I think a girl is afraid of doing too well. You kind of want to be average, you don't want to stand out."

But Kelly is not losing any sleep over it. What *she* knows is that she's got muscled legs but weak forearms, that she's terrible at baseball but pretty good at hurdles, that she looks good – she's not just skin and bones – and feels good and loves to horse around with her team-mates and call some of them her friends, all of it the gift of her enthusiasm.

It is a conceit of adults raised before the installation of a television set in every Canadian home that no young person since that watershed event has known how to amuse herself. The function of the imagination, so the argument goes, once an idiosyncratic instrument harboured in the memory and dreams of the person, has now been transferred to the solid-state mechanisms of the "box", relieving us all of the obligation to generate our own pleasures. Of whom could this be more true than the current generation of teenagers, who have been relieved not only of this onerous task, but of countless others? They are no longer obliged to read, for instance, learning speech and the collective wisdom of their culture from *conversation* and the electronic media; they need not write but only *tell* us what's on their mind; the skill of banging out popular tunes on the piano has been made redundant by the one-button marvels of the synthesizer. Meanwhile, the convivial group around the radio has shrivelled to an audience of one, her Walkman plugs in her ears, absorbed in the very private pleasure of a song shared with no one. Given the pervasiveness of all these modes of entertainment, and the passivity with which they are consumed, it has been assumed of post-sixties young people that they are creatures in whom imagination (and, therefore, self-generated pleasure) lies desiccated and puny, like a vestigial digit.

This may very well be true at the level of some broad and scientific sociometric investigation, but it is certainly not true at the level of the individual and anecdotal experience: Kelly practises swinging her arm like a pendulum so that the arc of its sweep will send the volleyball in flight just so, and Connie lifts weights because a strong arm and shoulder is a beautiful thing that works as it was meant to, and Nina, whom we will meet later, stretches out in splits in the air because she imagines herself a free being inhabiting space where before there was only vacancy. The wonder of it all is that, in spite of the tyrannical presence of the entertainment media and their capacity to fill in every leftover space with sound and fury, in spite of the unchallenged assumptions of mass culture that no one should be left for a moment alone with her own thoughts, and in spite of the terrific pressures from teen society that bear down and flatten individual peculiarities (oddities of manner, speech, aspiration), these girls have managed to appropriate some activity, name it, and imprint it with their own fantasy.

To pursue *her* enthusiasm, Connie had to invade a male sanctuary, the weight-training room in the basement of her school. She had never thought of herself as someone who would want to lift fifty pounds with one arm, but when she heard over the school intercom that a weight-training instructor was available, she nudged a couple of girlfriends and said, let's go for it. She'll admit now that there was an element of "faddishness" in what they wanted to do and something "intriguing" about their pioneering effort – three girls in a roomful of guys pumping iron who curled their lips and snorted at their arrival. She was at first repelled by the fetid and grimy atmosphere in the small room: "When there's a bunch of guys in there it really stinks, you can almost smell the dampness on their bodies. It's gross, like a guys' locker-room." But as more girls arrived to train, the air improved considerably (deodorant, baby powder, "Charlie" cologne), and the bodybuilders, accepting the new status quo, went back to their single-minded concentration on the bench press and the barbells. Eventually, Connie found her own reasons to be there after the excitement of shocking male peers had worn off. As she puts it, "I'm not doing it just to be cool."

"It", however, is not the awesome effort of the young men at the chin-bars and the leg presses, rhythmically repeating the exercise with a glazed look on their faces as though hypnotized by the staggering monotony of their labours, or the boy lifting fifty pounds, just like that, from floor to chest, over and over and over again, the slabs of his muscles appearing and disappearing beneath his skin in a weird choreography of the flesh. What Connie is doing is more leisurely: a few bench-press repetitions and a brief workout with the hamstring curls and the thigh extenders (ten pounds), with pauses in between during which she drapes herself over the equipment, and chats with a friend who is flexing her arm and proudly displaying a bulge of bicep. The instructor, herself a competitive body-builder who trains three hours every day, says there's "no difference" between the training men and women do on this equipment, and that Connie (who doesn't "think she can do anything more") could be working a lot harder.

But it is obviously not Connie's ambition to be a body-builder, to become (in the eye of some beholders) a grotesque caricature of the male physique: she is here to improve her "body tone", to keep the fat off, to banish the softness and mushiness (as she perceives them) of her too-feminine body, which still, to her disgust, cannot move very heavy objects, obliging her to call upon the aid of a male. What she *enjoys* about this workout, it seems to me, is the revelation of the stamina and accumulating power and comeliness of her very own body – not of some idealized Wonder Woman, challenging the muscular pre-eminence of men in their own shape. There she lies – long and slender legs astride a bench, her boyish buttocks pressed down against it, and the spheres of her breasts wrapped under the T-shirt which is riding up her flat and narrow midriff – triumphantly pushing twenty pounds of lead.

SEVEN

Classrooms

"How do you define the root of an equation, Shelly?"

THE POSTERS of the Lamborghini racing car and of a sci-fi fantasy don't fool anybody. This is a Math 13 class, and the kids hate it. The teacher, in a pale-grey suit, her hair swept up into a hair clip, gently admonishes the class to get down to work, but Susie mutters, "What a bitch!" Tammy, leaning back against the wall, mentions a friend who finally succeeded in killing himself over the weekend (with a plastic bag), and two boys in opposite corners exchange paper darts. The teacher says "Shhhh" from time to time over the general hubbub, while a kid with Walkman earphones pulled down over his Wheat Pool cap struggles alone with "Simplify $(x - 5)(x - 2) - 1$".

Half an hour into the class a statuesque girl in fishnet stockings saunters in, blowing bubblegum. Susie tells me that if the teacher asks the girl where the hell she's been, she can say she had a call from her mother in the office, she was throwing up in the can, or she was at the doctor's for a pregnancy test. She herself has used all three of these excuses with good results. But the teacher asks no questions of the latecomer. Susie combs her hair. Her friend busies herself applying lipstick. Two others pass notes. Three students, with unopened books and feet up on the desk, lean back against the wall, whistling.

On to a new class. Math 23. If 2 lines L1 and L2 have slopes of m1 and m2, and if etc., etc., what is the product of. . . ? God, who cares? "How do you define the root of an equation, Shelly?" Long, long silence. The teacher has to answer his own question. Show that the root of $3x + 2 = x$ is -1. . . . Everybody bangs away at their calculators. This whole section will be tossed out of the Math 23 curriculum, the teacher says, because calculators can do the work. He's mild-mannered and wears a mustache, a tieless brown shirt, and a leisure jacket. Linda rolls her pencil up and down the top of her desk and yawns. Her neighbours are drooping over their books or, seated sideways, are staring out of the window. Karen is doodling, Shelly looks petulant, and Linda finally drops her head on her forearms. Everything in this room is a conspiracy of drabness – the pale-green walls, the fluorescent lighting, the brownish-grey linoleum, the Fire Exit sign, and the world map and the Alberta Wheat Pool calendar on the walls. There are no noises, no disturbances. No one speaks unless directly addressed. No one volunteers a thing. "I was really disappointed," the teacher says mildly, "to see how many of you goofed on this one." God, who cares.

Math 20. The teacher, in his forties and wearing the school sweater, has a profusion of geraniums and cactuses on his desk. He bounces around the front of the room, chatting away. "Dave, I know it's fashionable but you are *late*! . . . What's the problem over there, you guys? . . . How many x's to the ones, can you keep track? . . . Have I written the dividend in polynomial form? . . . Notice the lag in your answer? That's the difference between you and a computer." The class is reviewing a quarter-final exam in Math 20; Kelly scored 22 out of 25. It wasn't very hard, she explains. Kids chew gum, fiddle with their shoes, play with their calculators, even read novels (*Flowers for Algernon*, in one case), but they are only apparently inattentive. This class is on its way to university.

The girls. Long red fingernails, gold bangles. Bright-pink shoulder bag, frosty-pink lipstick. Punk hairdo. Frosted hair. Blue smears encircling the eyes, oversize red shirt, black suede ankle boots. Blushing pink face blooming above a pearl on a silver chain. "I can't see that far. I don't have my glasses." Miss Preppie – streaked blonde hair, a big pale-yellow sweater, and an arm ringed with gold bangles – is the most enthusiastic student in the class. She's got all the answers. It's the boys in the corner behind her who whisper and giggle through the entire period.

A conference sponsored by the Science Council of Canada in 1981 on the science education of women in Canada[1] revealed this: among grade eleven students in Ottawa, 40 per cent of boys and 76 per cent of girls were studying no physics or chemistry; in New Brunswick only 39 per cent of grade twelve girls, as compared to 53.5 per cent of the boys, were enrolled in a math class; Nova Scotia reported 1440 boys and 787 girls studying physics in grade twelve in 1979–80. Overall, more girls than boys study biology, a science perceived as "easy" – or, more astutely, as "interesting" or "not so abstract."

For anyone concerned about the minuscule number of women working professionally in the sciences (there is only one female full professor of physics in Canada), these statistics reveal a continuing problem. For the science subjects most frequently avoided by girls – math and physics – are also the ones often required for admission to postsecondary education. "By opting out of physics and mathematics early in school," the Science Council report warns, "a student eliminates any possibility of being seriously involved in any branch of science." That student is most often a girl and what she is doing has a name: math (or science) avoidance. The social consequences are dramatic. In 1976 in Canada the percentage of doctoral candidates receiving degrees in engineering, mathematics, and the physical sciences who were women was too small to be measured. In 1983, of 220 Ph.D.s awarded in engineering and applied sciences, ten went to women, or 4.5 per cent; of 340 degrees in math and the physical sciences, women earned 44 degrees (12.9 per cent).

Why do girls hate and fear math and science?[2] (Perhaps the question is loaded. If we were to ask why *boys* hate and fear English and French, we would perceive another sort of social crisis altogether. But what males avoid is not, apparently, a problem for anyone but themselves.) The answers are various. Girls have few role models, female math teachers and female scientists. Boys don't like girls who beat them at "their" subjects. Girls don't see what "use" the sciences are. Sciences and math are "cold" and "theoretical"; girls like "people-oriented" subjects, or at least animal-oriented, hence the interest in biology. Little girls are given dolls, not model spaceships, to play with. Parents and teachers like girls who are quiet and dependent and follow directions, a recipe for lack of confidence in the girl: she can no longer "imagine" being able to do something difficult. A study by a University of Winnipeg psychologist[3] revealed that, even when women rated their level of ability as "high", they still avoided math and the sciences. The disciplines were simply unimportant in terms of how the women saw themselves.

The problem is familiar. Femininity, defined socially, conspires against those traits of the girl's personality that would produce a science student: love of intellectual challenge, pleasure in solitude, satisfaction from theoretical problem-solving, fantasies of inspired break-throughs, and, perhaps, of power and money. There is nothing to be gained, in labour or in love, from having a "good mind" in chemistry; in fact, there is much to be lost if one values the appreciation of men. What on earth do math and science have to do with being a successful woman?

The question is almost subversive, implying scepticism of a male value system that sanctions the pursuit of abstract and absolute perfection, the retreat into "pure mind", and the fascination with how *things* work – with gizmos more or less lethal. If these are the only ways and means of "science", then girls are not interested. They have better things to think about.

This is a Chemistry 20 class. On my desk top, these graffiti: "Rush sucks"; "Break-dancing sucks dog shit!". After a brief stint at the board, explaining the formulae for the "enes", the "anes", and the "ynes" (question from Connie: "Why did chemists make up such dumb names?"), the teacher returns to his desk to correct papers. This seems to be a signal to the class to shut their books and visit with their buddies.

Perhaps girls avoid the sciences because they are not as smart as boys? This explanation is offered from time to time from quite respectable quarters but is elsewhere discounted: whatever may be the gender-related difference in *achievement* in math, say, is too small to explain the very large difference in girls' and boys' *participation* in the discipline. In any case biological research has failed to establish conclusively that there are innate gender differences in mathematical ability.[4]

The question of girls' performance in math and the sciences must be understood, first of all, historically. It has been only relatively recently that advanced (secondary) education has been accepted as appropriate for females. At best, such education was seen as of little or no use to girls whose adult lives were to be devoted to housekeeping and child care. At worst, it was regarded as decidedly pernicious in terms of their psycho-sexual vulnerability. In other words, women have only a brief experience, culturally and socially, as students of higher education undertaken for its own sake. Is it much wonder that even today girls fail to take themselves completely seriously as mathematicians?

The students are seated on tall blue stools at long lab tables while the Science 11 teacher, bushy-bearded and in

blue jeans, lectures on breathing, its process and apparatus. Without using notes, he lectures in a vividly conversa-
tional style, about the trachea, about cilia and mucus.
"Yecch," says a girl behind me. He turns to the board and
draws a schematic representation of the esophagus and
throat lined with cilia. Susie blurts out, "It looks like
Tracy's hairdo!" Tracy punches Susie in the arm. Now the
teacher directs everyone to put her hand over her throat
and to swallow, feeling what is happening to the larynx.
"I can't find it!" The teacher finds it, gently squeezing her
throat, which makes her giggle. "You guys know the Ma-
mas and Papas?" Some do, or at least know that Mama
Cass died of a choking fit. Susie is no longer paying attention. With the help of the girl next to her, she's madly
writing in the answers to last week's assignment (she's late
as usual): What is cartilage? What is the structure of
bone?

In a grade eleven psychology class in a Catholic high
school, the majority of students are girls and the subject
under discussion is child development between six and
eight years of age. The subject and the classroom population are not unconnected: psychology, inasmuch as it is
concerned with "people", is one of those classically "feminine" subjects. Girls, they tell me themselves, are interested in people, not things. They are, apparently, especially interested in children.

"How should you handle a kid who steals?" asks the
teacher, consulting her notes. "What is moral development dependent on?" There is a lot of rustling of notebook pages while students look for the answers, but the
teacher wants a *discussion*. She herself tells a number of
anecdotes, and encourages the same of her class. So we
hear not only her claim that "we have the right to leave
twenty dollars lying around without having to worry
about it, or the right to have a place for *our* records in the
record case," but also the story from the boy who built

himself a fort which his sister contrived to decorate with flowers and curtains, an intervention that so enraged him he took an axe to his own creation. "Who is more exclusionary?" asks the teacher. And the whole class answers, "Girls!" "Girls," says the teacher, "you are so mean to each other."

The discussion turns to the question of television violence, of *Hill Street Blues, The A-Team, Magnum P.I.*, which inspires one girl to confess: "I *like* that. It's a good show!" They discuss the films *Hallowe'en*, which everyone has seen, and *The Terminator*, which everyone agrees is pretty gross and dumb but which everyone has gone to see, regardless. The teacher raises a faint objection to *Indiana Jones* but is shouted down. The class is extraordinarily animated; everyone, it seems, has a point to make, a question to ask. "Why don't parents want their kids to watch soap operas?" "Why is it so bad to be old and grey and wrinkled and fat?" "Why is our society so competitive?" At this point, the teacher tells the story of an anthropologist who attempted to teach some Inuit people to play basketball. They never got the hang of it, insisting on *helping* each other shoot a basket. "But everybody was happy." The class loves this story.

That class was mainly female, and the fact that they loved a story about Inuit who failed to "play the game" speaks perhaps to their identification with people alienated by or excluded from competition. For many girls find their daily experience in the classroom is alienating: they do not "belong". Much is made of the fact that the "feminine" person – all docility and passivity and compliance – is the ideal student much beloved of authoritarian teachers. But research indicates that "teachers praise boys more than girls, give boys more academic help, and are more likely to accept boys' comments during classroom discussions."[5] Boys are louder, talk more, and shout out answers, while girls raise their hand and wait to be noticed. In the intellectually competitive arena of the classroom, rarely a co-operative setting committed to the principle of mutual aid, girls are poorly prepared to survive, let alone flourish. Girls receive approval not so much for meeting an intellectual challenge as for being neat, polite, and studious. A female student who wants to please her teacher, then, is going to "play it safe". In an American research study[6] reported in 1974, the ideal female student was perceived by teachers to be "appreciative, considerate, efficient, obliging, calm, co-operative, mannerly, poised, thorough, conscientious, dependable, mature, sensitive". The ideal male student, by contrast, was described as "active, assertive, frank, adventurous, curious, independent, inventive, aggressive, energetic, enterprising."

Perhaps in a culture of girls' own making, such feminine characteristics would be broadly appreciated, but girls live in a boys' culture in the classroom, dominated by male discourse, and here they are sabotaged by their own girlish niceness, modesty, and agreeableness. One could argue that, by the time a girl is in high school, she is in a position to make her own choices in education – she could *choose* to study physics – but in a sense the choice is not in fact available to her. What boys learn as they toss footballs around, play with chemistry sets, and hammer away at video games is, arguably, related to certain mathematical, chemical, and physical laws regarding space, motion, trajectory, and combustion. But what does a girl learn of such things when playing with dolls, helping Mummy set the table, and staying close to home? What she learns is helplessness and dependence and expecting no more of herself than do the adults around her. Bad mark in math? Never mind, sweetie, it's not important.

We had a math teacher who had a Ph.D. He was really really quiet: he looked like he was afraid of the class. He was terrible. In the last month he remembered that he'd forgotten to go through about four units. He didn't interest you in anything; you couldn't read his writing. It was the worst class. But when I studied by myself, I did fine.

What she is telling us confirms what "motivation research"[7] has isolated: that there are two kinds of motivation arising from two different environments – "extrinsic", from controlling environments, and "intrinsic", from environments that "support autonomy". In other words, we learn best in a situation where we are in charge of our own process. Good teachers know this and encourage it. But, in spite of good intentions, teachers are often obliged to be authoritarian or controlling: the school administration, school boards, parents, departments of education, are all breathing down their necks demanding "results".

And some teachers are sexist, and reserve the best of themselves for their male students.

These are strong words. But a Canadian study[8] has underscored how, in science classes, girls are often the object of their teachers' teasing and how, in the labs, the teachers address their observations and questions to the boys, effectively marginalizing the girls' experience. Teachers give boys more attention, encourage extended conversation with them, are more likely to give them detailed instructions, and react with precise and often laudatory remarks to their answers. By contrast, they tend to tell girls not to interrupt, provide only bland and vague responses to their answers ("Okay", "Uh-huh"), do not engage in conversations with them, and tend to *do* an assignment for them when they get stuck.

Consider the fact that, in Newfoundland for example, the ratio of women teachers to female students in high school is 1:75, while in elementary school it is 1:12. Since the percentage of women teachers in high schools across Canada is only 31.5 per cent *and declining*, girls are in danger of deeper and deeper alienation as the schools become progressively masculinized.[9] There is, for example, a body of literature showing that girls in co-educational schools are both more likely to be *offered* physics, and less likely to take it, than girls in all-girl schools! Is it any wonder that girls perceive themselves to be, in "male" environments like the chemistry lab or the computer centre, inappropriate and unwelcome participants?

The aging teacher population is a factor here. A thirty-

eight-year-old teacher is one of the youngest in her Toronto school, one of the few to have been formed as an
adult in the sixties, not the fifties. In any case, she says, for
most people the political and social radicalism of the sixties was a superficial phenomenon, a dalliance with pot
and love-ins; as for the tumult of the women's liberation
movement in the seventies, this has touched her colleagues
not at all. That so many of them should put up a resistance, active and passive, to the introduction of formal
Women's Studies to the curriculum is disappointing, but
not surprising.

Myra Novogorodsky is an assistant co-ordinator in the
combined program of Women's Studies and Labour Studies within the Social Studies department of the Toronto
Board of Education. Some of her duties are to monitor
books for sexism, to teach teachers how to criticize sexist
materials, and to introduce them to Women's Studies
teaching materials. There is a twelve-lesson course of
study in the history of female suffrage movements, for
instance, which grade eight teachers are *supposed* to
teach. "It's not supposed to be a choice," she says, "but in
fact some teachers don't 'get around' to it. My job is to
take the materials to teachers and make them comfortable
using it, make it feel safe." So, suffrage is "safe", as are the
questions of sex bias and sex-role stereotyping and putting girls on soccer teams – safe, after ten years of agitation. This is what is called an "equality of opportunity"
approach, Novogorodsky claims, "not a women's liberation approach, but even that not everyone accepts."

Teachers resist. Because the program is not compulsory, some simply refuse to teach it, period. Only three
schools in the Toronto public system have approved a
year-long Women's Studies curriculum. Other schools
make excuses: "We already cover it." Others are aggressive: "Women have all the power already." "Women are
breaking up the family." More sympathetic teachers manage to introduce feminist content simply by posing questions about what's being studied: Where are the women in

this story? How would this event have been different for women? "I do believe," says Novogorodsky, "that putting Women's Studies into the schools is going to make a difference to girls. I don't pretend that it will make feminists out of the men and women who teach it and study it, but I hope it's the beginning of some kind of critical thinking of the society in general."

The drama teacher, plump and round, demonstrates the three parts of falling down on stage (collapse at the knees, roll over on the hip, lie down on the shoulders), a demonstration that provokes a great deal of good-natured laughter at the sight of her girth tumbling down. The kids enjoy this class. They learn how to pull hair, pull ears, and choke an enemy on stage, and the room is filled with their squawks and squeals as they haul each other around by hair and ear, and let loose with ferocious growls and grimaces, or roll on the floor in the mock-agony of being clubbed to death. The teacher assigns a task – to create a little scene with a beginning, a middle, and an end, in which someone gets slapped and falls down. The first group up "tells" the story of a magazine photographer who asks a girl to pose for him. She's flattered and accepts, but when she learns he wants to send the photographs to *Playboy*, she goes berserk. To the enthusiastic applause of the rest of the class, she slaps him around, throws him to the ground, and beats him up. She exits to great cheers.

Compared to the girl who gets the top marks in the French class, Lorraine takes it easy. She "spreads herself around" in a variety of extracurricular activities. The other girl is always studying, *always*; she's in the library at lunch-time, she goes straight home after school to do her homework, you never see her just hanging around. You'd be surprised who are the good students. At the Awards

Night last year, a bunch of preppies lined up for the prizes. Preppies! The kids who are otherwise so clothes-conscious and who even skip classes to socialize in the cafeteria, the guys who've been goofing off since grade seven, suddenly blossom in grade eleven. Lorraine's friends who used to copy her notes are honours students this year. In grade eleven something happens after the January report card: students drop out of the school band or off the volleyball team. "It's hell on wheels at home," is the explanation. The pressure is on to upgrade marks. The consequences are material, for mediocre grades may very well mean the student will not be able eventually to enter the university or faculty of her choice.

We're talking about middle-class girls, the girls who have benefited most from the liberal ideology of the public school: that both sexes have the right to the same education. Never mind that, as we have seen, girls do not in fact pursue the same education; the point is that they have the potential to do so and, individually, are competitive for top math marks, do enroll in optional Computer Science programs, and have a vision of themselves winning a Nobel Prize one day. More typically, they are in English and French classes, working tidily at the verbal tasks at which they apparently excel, and taking seriously the intellectual assumption of the lesson: that it is important to know the answers to certain (prescribed) questions, to know how to find the answers, and to know the correct procedure in fulfilling assignments. This is what they're in school "for": to learn to think for themselves within a carefully defined situation.

And so an English 20 class will concern itself with a reading and an analysis of the stage version of Ken Kesey's *One Flew Over the Cuckoo's Nest*, or an interpretation of scenes from the film *The Great Santini* (whatever happened, I wonder, to reading *books* in English class?). In this way the class studies socially and psychologically "relevant" material which contains useful instructions in how to get along in the adult world. Questions and discussions. Not just any answer will do. Why is stuttering such a big deal? Do we have any responsibility for what's going on in the "cuckoo's nest"? When was the last time you were called a name you hated? What does he mean: "I think I understand you now, Dad"? ("Um, okay, this is only what I think, okay? If you love someone, like, you're going to be mushy.") Ben says his father had to die for him to become free; did he?

The teachers, attentive to the answers and responses, manifestly have a commitment to the lesson at hand. There is no indication that they think or feel the girls in the class are an anomaly. (The majority of the students in the English classes do seem to be girls.) This is a middle-class classroom in a middle-class school: boys and girls alike learn that it's important to understand an instruction, to understand what you're reading, and to express yourself when called upon to do so. Even the girls seem to believe this. Certainly there seems to be no awareness that, in spite of the overt ideology of the school, girls are streamed into programs of study (arts, humanities, and social sciences) that often have no obvious vocational application, express work aspirations inconsistent with their scholastic achievement (the girl with the honours marks in biology wants to be a stewardess), and assume that they are eventually going to have to choose between working full-time and rearing a family. The school never actually says any of these things to its female students, but neither does it explicitly challenge them. The public school is, in fact, an arena of considerable ambivalence about the education of the daughters of the middle class, as though to educate them fully would be to lose forever the ideal of the happy, stay-at-home wife and mother of the bourgeois family.

No such ambivalence attaches to the education of the daughters of the working class.

Susie came to the physical education class without her

gym gear ("I forgot") and was made to sit out the class in an empty classroom writing out one hundred lines of "I will be more responsible in the future" ("Can you believe that?") before going to her Period Two class, Beauty Culture. Here the assignment is to braid a Fishtail (a braid across the back of the head) on a mannequin. Hands shaking – she's been sick, she says, with a strep throat and a bladder infection – she tries to hold three strands of hair separately in one hand while plaiting them with her right ("Such a bitch!"), but the strands get tangled and won't lie flat. The girl next to her is concentrating very hard on just combing and combing, but others are chatting up a storm while lackadaisically threading hanks of hair this way and that. They're comparing the number of classes they've skipped so far this year – 150, 250, and (the record) Susie's 283 – and complaining bitterly about the school: "This school sucks!" You can get kicked out after a couple of days' absence from classes even if you have a perfectly good excuse, and you can get a detention for misbehaving, and there's this one teacher who calls the students "children", as in: "I slap children's hands who touch expensive things." They would all love to transfer to another school where you can skip five classes in a row without your parents' being told.

Fifteen minutes late, Pam arrives and throws her books onto the counter next to Susie's work area. She's been held up at the office, called to account for all her recent absences. Barely coherent, she rages against the counsellor: "Does she think I'm the only seventeen-year-old who ever got pregnant?" In her blue jeans, T-shirt, and sneakers she looks like such a kid, so girlish, she should still be climbing trees and falling off her bike. With one hand holding a braid and tears coursing down her chubby face, she explains to the sympathetic group of girls gathered around that she's had to miss so many classes because she's been in the goddamn court trying to get custody of her baby, but the fuckin' school doesn't care about that, oh no, and now they want to throw her out even when she's showed up for classes again for the first time in weeks, I mean she *wants* to be in school and *they* want to throw her out, oh shit. . . . The bell goes. Susie will finish the braid tomorrow. And Pam will quit school.

According to a 1985 report from the Canadian Advisory Council on the Status of Women,[10] there is "some evidence" that students from working class backgrounds are channelled into non-academic or vocational programs by well-meaning or "class-biased" teachers and counsellors. In spite of a girl's demonstrated intellectual capacity, they will encourage her to take up typing, accounting, beauty culture, and domestic science as the most "appropriate" course of study for someone with her probable future: waged work in a female job ghetto, and marriage and children at an early age. Never mind that the prophecy is self-fulfilling. The "streams" of instruction in a typical composite high school – general diploma, business diploma, senior matriculation, say – are as neatly divided between the social classes as are the arts and sciences between the sexes.

Here, for example, is the way their teachers talk about them. At a high school in Edmonton specializing in students with a history of academic failure, only forty per cent of whom will finish grade eleven (and only half of them will finish grade twelve), the teachers complain that the "vast majority" of students don't bother to work hard. In spite of the fact that the girls tend to be enrolled in beauty culture, business education, health care, and food preparation, it's been a long time since a mere high school diploma counted for anything. They haven't, however, aimed their sights any higher: they don't want to be pushed in class and show no interest in learning for its own sake. Very little in the academic curriculum "turns them on", and there's absolutely no status in studying, or in speaking up in class. The chronic "low self-esteem" which characterizes a student who has been identified for years as a problem learner is debilitating: she avoids further failure simply by not trying. Compared to this by-now-inevitable pattern of disappointment, the achievement of holding down a job and earning her own money is a palpable success. Even the most ghettoized or exploitative job, in the fast-food industry or in a boutique or at a hair-dressing salon, holds out this possibility. "I'm absolutely shocked," said one teacher to me, "that these kids don't show more concern about their future prospects. They're blasé. They don't seem to care about building themselves up. They don't have plans."

Plans? Let's talk about plans. The girl is sixteen; she could drop out of school if she wanted. What's to hold her there? At home she lives with adults who made their own way in life without benefit of higher education, who do not, ever, read books, and who view education professionals with, at best, a benign contempt. The girl, in short, finds it difficult if not impossible to visualize an educated future for herself.[11] She does not "see" herself making a commitment to hours, months, years of book-work, respecting big words and orderliness where previously in her life there had been neither. She cannot imagine herself caring for a high grade in social studies in order to qualify for entry to a university she will never think of attending. Her own non-verbal skills – applying make-up, cake-decorating, funk dancing – are held in low regard, and the school-related skills she's learned, such as typing or bookkeeping or hairdressing, can be easily transferred to the labour market, a transfer she is under some pressure to make, from parents who have grown weary of supporting her, from friends now working and with money to spend, and from her own desire to be independent of adult authority. Nothing in her world would support the idea that, through her own academic effort, she could get more than she thinks she deserves. Women, even high school graduates, work at dead-end jobs, their only hope of advancement being an attachment to a man with a steady job. So, beauty culture it is. You don't have to read any books, and you can talk as much as you want to while doing a manicure. English 30? What for?

English 13 is a non-academic course for students who will do no other English courses in high school, and is taught by a social studies teacher who doesn't expect anyone to read anything more than a page at a time. I look through Susie's notebook. She's made notes from a lecture about "heroes" ("epic heroes were the models for the ways soldiers should behave in battle") and written her own account of a contemporary hero: "Indiana Jones has got to be the greatest hero around. I went to see his movie and I thought it was great." Out of a possible forty marks on an exam about the "varieties of heroes and the societies that produce them", she earned fourteen. You see, she explains, she wasn't at school the day the teacher talked about this. Halfway through the class, she asks for permission to "go to the washroom". In fact, she goes out for a smoke and doesn't come back.

Such students, said one of their teachers, "don't feel they have any control over their lives, nor that anything they do matters". Their contemptuous disregard of scholarship, their inattentiveness, restlessness, and sly insubordination in the classroom, their pleasure at ignoring regulations, all form a reaction to their perceived and real powerlessness. Who is the system trying to kid, claiming that good grades and orderly behaviour will make a difference to what happens to *them*? In defiance of an institution that separates their destiny from that of their middle-class peers, they create a kind of sub-institution and culture all their own: they goof off in class, sneak out for smokes, skip whole days with abandon, "forget" their books at home, and concentrate their energies on what really matters, their clothes and their friends. Whether or not this is a "culture of resistance" is debatable. By indulging in rude behaviour in the classroom and refusing to be instructed in such "boring" and "useless" subjects as math and English, and by quitting school altogether to go out and work, working-class girls only reinforce their class disadvantage – illiteracy, inarticulateness, and indecorous behaviour – and their vulnerability to the crises of the labour market, where the well-paid trades, such as carpentry and plumbing, are still male preserves. And, unlike boys' resistance, which, in its swaggering vulgarity, confirms masculinity, girls' resistance is decidedly unladylike (swearing, cat-fighting, hanging-out in the street) and gains them no favour. This may, in fact, be more a case of resistance to femininity than to school,[12] but in either case it's self-defeating. The working-class girl at school can't win.

EIGHT

Susie

"When the bills are coming in and there isn't the money to pay them, love don't mean shit."

SHE WAS sixteen, and in a crisis. Tired, so tired, of everything (of school, of banging her head against a learning she didn't give two hoots about, of a hermetic little society of teachers and kiddies whose company she did not want to keep), she quit grade ten and went home to sit down and think. Where was she going? What did she want to do? Maybe she wanted to work, to have a change of scenery so to speak, to have some money. And so she went to the real estate office where her mother worked and for a while was paid for pulling listings off the computer, and then she did telephone soliciting for the local newspaper, hustling subscriptions, and then she worked at the front counter of a dry-cleaning plant, but still she would come home and twist her hands and cry. Her boyfriend, Cal, was no help. He'd been out of work for months, twiddling his thumbs in the living room of his father's house, drapes drawn and television on in the middle of the afternoon, his father's snores coming from the next room as he slept off the whisky. Cal was no help at all. Susie was so upset in those days. "Cal," she said, "what are we going to do? We've gotta figure something out. I've gotta do something. I can't just sit around for the rest of my life."

Susie is not without ambitions, or talents even. She likes to draw in a sketch-pad and colour in posters and take pictures with her Instamatic. She has a bit of a green thumb: all the flowering violets in her mother's living room, in December, are her achievement. But mainly Susie is a genius around animals: her idea of a good time when she was a kid was to go to the zoo and cuddle all the baby animals, even the snakes. Her dream, even as she was cleaning up after her own pet doves and budgies and gold-fish, was some day to have a baby cougar or grizzly bear all to herself. Then the girl next door, who had a beautiful white jumper called Beauty, invited Susie to learn how to ride her. The horse – this beast that could take her flying through blue heaven – became her favorite animal, and Susie decided that she would grow up to be a horse veteri-narian.

To be a horse veterinarian, of course, means that first you have to acquire an education.

Getting her high school diploma will be the bane and curse of her existence. A modest enough acquisition, it hovers mockingly between her fatigue and her ambition. She hates school, she quits it, weeps, goes back, slips, flounders, and so on.

Susie has been told – by teachers, by her mother, by Cal – that she has brains, yes! but doesn't use them. To herself, she doesn't feel "extra special", just normal, average. The ninety-six per cent she once earned on a math test, how-ever, still makes her exceedingly proud of herself: she in-troduces the mark into a conversation like a badminton trophy onto a mantelpiece. But the truth is she has not had even "normal" success at school. Even when she re-turned to school after her crisis, impelled there by the dreaded dead-endedness she saw yawning in front of her, she could make no success of it. She was kicked out just before exams, for arguing with the English teacher, who said she'd been sleeping in class, not paying the least attention or showing the least interest, but Susie said she'd just put her head down on her arms: she hadn't been feeling well. Asleep or awake, however, her marks had been low. Well, what do you expect when the "bag" of a teacher, no matter how many hours Susie worked on an essay, would never give her more than fifty per cent?

The following fall, Susie tried again. She transferred to another school and began grade ten for the third time, studying Math 13 (algebra), English 13 (Heroes in Literature), Social Studies 10, Science 11 (Basic), Beauty Culture 12 (Introductory), and Physical Education (compulsory). In October things were still "pretty good", she was keeping on top of the material, although she had missed a few days because of the flu. ("I have allergies.") She was still hoping to finish the year. But by December she was slipping badly. She had a report card she was afraid to show Cal. Rightly so, for when she did show it he went nuts. "What are all these skips?" he cried. Twenty-one in phys ed alone! "You're supposed to be in school. If you skip another day, that's it." She guessed that he meant it – that he'd break off with her, he was so mad. Contrite, she promised him she wouldn't skip any more. But really it was no use.

"I've never been serious about school," she had admitted, but it was more than just a question of her attitude. She had grievances. What's the point of doing something you don't like? You have to enjoy what you're doing in order to do it well. And she couldn't stand the Social Studies class, or Accounting ("boring!"), or track and field exercises. She thinks high schools should have a whole array of courses so that you can pick and choose – Photography and Beauty Culture, say, and to hell with math and English. It's good to have the basics, of course; everybody needs to know how to multiply and divide, but who needs *algebra*? You need to know the metric measurements but you don't need "x times x, and x to the

power of, and shit like that." Maybe architects need to
know, but a horse vet, a child-care worker, a real estate
agent?

It was no help to Susie that she was two years older
than her classmates. She'd take her place at the back of
the classroom and with measureless disdain attempt to
ignore the yapping and hooting of the "assholes" around
her. How was she supposed to work among people like
that? And why did the teacher put up with it? "I think a
good teacher should be strict at times," Susie offered,
when asked her opinion. "Like, if you've been screwing
around for half an hour and she's already told you to lay
off and do your work, I think they're right to bawl you
out, but not to be a bag. I think a good teacher is someone
who is easy to get along with, is willing to help you and
isn't a real jackass. Good teachers are hard to come by."

In March, Susie quit school before they could throw her
out. She had been missing classes again and the school
had been phoning her mother about it and she figured if it
was going to be that much of a hassle, she'd bloody well
quit and get a job. To propitiate her mother and Cal in
their disappointment and disapproval – Cal would have
been so proud of her at her graduation, eighteen-year-old
Cal who had quit school in grade eleven to work in his
dad's repair shop, who had held her hands and pleaded,
"Don't quit school. We'll work things out so we can still
see each other, but don't quit!" – she promised she'd try
again another year.

What a job can give you, and school cannot, is money.
Susie's and Cal's needs are not extravagant – for instance,
they date only on weekends, when they like to go out to a
movie and a pizza restaurant – but money is required all
the same. When you go to a friend's house to play cards,
you bring along the fixings for screwdrivers, and you pitch
in to pay for the rented videos your good buddy plays on
the VCR he got for his birthday, and you save up for the

staff Christmas party where Cal works, and one of these days very soon Cal is going to need to buy a half-ton with a canopy on the back so he can hook up his trailer and put his trail bike on it and go out into the mountains for his summer holiday. Christmas is a killer. He bought Susie musk-oil perfume, lingerie, a pink T-shirt, a suede jacket, and a ten-carat gold bracelet, not to mention a diamond engagement ring, but he can manage this, bringing home a grand a month from his general labourer's job at a sheet-metal factory. But Susie does not make this kind of money. She paid for Christmas presents – a blue velours bath-robe, an automobile vacuum-cleaner, a twenty-four-carat gold-plated tire gauge, a Playboy-bunny keychain, and a Playboy-bunny mirror, all for Cal – out of babysitting money earned at the rate of two dollars an hour.

At the time of her crisis, when she had quit school and Cal was out of work, Susie was worried sick that their poverty and frustration would undermine their love. Mindful of what had happened to other couples – men or women, without jobs, yelling obscenities at each other, sick and tired of each other's nagging company, depressed and restless and resentful all at once – she was nevertheless reluctant to accept a friend's advice to "make sure the money's going to be coming in" before deciding to move out of home and in with Cal. "Geez," she told her friend, "that's not love." "But, Susie," the friend replied, "when the bills are coming in and there isn't the money to pay them, love don't mean shit."

When Cal found work at the sheet-metal company, making refrigerators, stoves, and gas-station canopies, he was a happy man again. He worked hard and thought about apprenticing in the trade, where he would eventu-ally become a journeyman, earning seventeen to twenty-one dollars an hour, enough to support a family. Well, that is the dream, the vision, the possibility. In the mean-time he was spending all he earned on the trail bike, the half-ton, a VCR, and Susie's engagement ring.

Having quit school, Susie looked for work for six

weeks. She applied at the local all-night grocery, the gas
station, the video rental shop, a little café, but they all
wanted an eighteen-year-old, or someone with more experience than she had. At the point of discouragement she
heard through a friend of a friend that a day-care centre
had recently fired two staff members; on a Friday at three
o'clock Susie applied for a position and at four o'clock
they phoned her to tell her to come in on Monday at eight.
She was elated. Her working situation was far from ideal –
four dollars an hour for an eight-hour day with a raise of
fifty cents after two months, sixty children (play-schoolers
to nine-year-olds) to look after in less than pristine surroundings ("the nursery stinks like hell," she reported) –
but she was eager to work: she likes kids. Her job was to
pack lunches and put children down for naps and to take
them for walks to the park, to vacuum and tidy up, all of
which she found easy and enjoyable.

But the boss was not the easiest person to get along
with: one day she was nice to Susie, the next day she was
mean and cold, and complaining about her to the owner.
Hey, it's just not fair. Susie's co-workers were real back-
stabbers too, real bitches, ready to get you into trouble if
you didn't do everything according to the rule book, ready
to go tattling to the boss the day Susie answered a phone
she wasn't supposed to. So Susie tried just to do her job,
mind her own business, and leave. She had enough on her
hands looking after unhappy and lonely kids weeping and
pissing their pants and throwing food around without having to worry about how the staff were going to screw her
up.

Two weeks into the job, Susie was fired. The boss told
her she didn't have enough experience, fired her, and then
hired a fifteen-year-old with no experience whatever. Susie figures what happened is that her immediate supervisor, who was a "real bag", and with whom she did not get
along, complained to the boss about Susie's "attitude"
and put it to the boss: either she goes or I go. So Susie
went. There would be no point in taking a grievance to the

Labour Relations Board: "The supervisor would just deny everything." So Susie walked.

On December 27 Susie and Cal first met and on December 29 he asked her to go steady. On their first anniversary, last Christmas, they got engaged. She opened the little box and there it was: five diamonds in a setting of fourteen-carat gold. He put it on her finger and said she was now his fiancée. She moved her hand around this way and that in the light, admiring the fine shape of the stone and its glinting ostentation, but would not let anyone else try it on; that's bad luck. Cal had also bought a wedding band to match it but she could not see it until the wedding day. Ask her when that will be and she laughs a high, horsy laugh. Susie's in no hurry to be married.

But Susie enjoys being a fiancée, enjoys her responsibilities and obligations. When Cal works night shift and Susie is back at school, it's her job to call him at noon to wake him up. When Cal is working night shift, Susie does not go to the Hallowe'en or Christmas dance, she babysits. When Cal gets off work at three in the afternoon, she waits for him to pick her up at school. There is not, then, a lot of time for friends. In fact her best friend, Lola, a model, whose picture from the newspaper ad she proudly shows around – a long-haired blonde in a black ten-gallon hat, a cowboy shirt, cowboy boots, and short shorts – she hasn't seen for several weeks.

At thirteen, fourteen, fifteen, Susie learned from her mistakes, learned what kind of jerks there are hanging around the bars, the bars she called her territory. And so you get the impression that Susie at seventeen would rather, thank you very much, be a fiancée.

Susie was born in St. John's, Newfoundland, of an eighteen-year-old mother deserted by the father of her child during the pregnancy. Susie was left in her grandmother's care while her mother waitressed and went to school, then married a man who legally adopted Susie and fathered Susie's stepbrother. But, as Susie says, you know how it is when two people just don't get along; Susie's mother left the marriage to live again with Susie's father and get pregnant a second time by him with Susie's sister. The man wanted to marry her, but she turned him down for the same reason he'd walked out on her in the first place: he was a trucker, and he screwed around with women all along his route. Susie's mother moved out west to Calgary, taking all her children with her. Susie has not seen her father since, or heard a word from him. As far as she's concerned, "Dad" is her stepbrother's father; of all the men in her mother's life, this guy really qualifies. "I think he's a right-on person."

Being a kid – a tomboy, a brat – in St. John's, being independent, with no one hovering over her supervising, monitoring, hectoring, was the best time of Susie's life. She'd go back instantly to being that kid if she had the chance: a kid with a bow and arrow shooting birds out of the trees, playing with trucks and tractors, sailing through the salty fog on the white back of Beauty. "No way was anybody going to put a dress on me!" At twelve, thirteen, she began to change, began to like boys and staying out late and flirting in the bars; curfew was when she got home. She hated wearing a brassiere, though, and the first time she got her period – she went to pee, pulled down her panties, and saw blood, pow! bang! that was it – she went hysterical, screamed, freaked; her mother had more or less explained it all to her, but the first time it happens it's still a bit of a shock. Susie was not pleased. She asked her mother if there was any way she could stop having periods, and when her mother made cautious reference to a certain kind of "operation", Susie bugged her for months to let her have a hysterectomy, unimpressed that the surgery would leave her incapable of bearing children.

At seventeen, however, Susie is reconciled to her femaleness. Enjoys it, even celebrates it, as she walks down the street in tight sweaters and jeans, the shapely flare of her buttocks and the plump swell of her breasts a kind of achievement all her own. Susie is looking forward to having babies.

But she's no fool. She found out early on that there are a lot of guys out there who want to go out with you for one reason only, and if you get pregnant, it's "Sorry, babe, see you later." Real assholes. Not for her the heat of the moment, the imprudent embrace, the pill or condom left behind in the drawer: as soon as Susie planned to have sex with boys, she told her mother, and her mother put her on the pill. "It takes two to tango," says Susie, "and if you can't handle the responsibility of a relationship and a pregnancy, then stay out of the sack." Susie does not approve of abortions to take care of "mistakes."

"I once thought I was pregnant and my mother wanted me to get an abortion. I said, no, but I think I would have, because the guy wasn't the type to stick around. But I would have regretted it for the rest of my life, because I'd always be looking behind me. The child never had a chance to live a life and it was my fault. I'm not saying it's wrong to have an abortion; if you're anything up to eighteen years old and the guy with you isn't responsible, then I think that's okay if that's your choice. But I don't think it's right for the doctor or your mother or your girlfriend or even your boyfriend to tell you you should have one.

"I don't care what plans a girl has. I figure if you're going to get pregnant, you have that child; you carry it through, that's your responsibility. Once you have a baby inside you. . . ." Once Susie's pregnant, she's pregnant. The determinism of her position would be alarming if she weren't herself so prepared to be a mother.

She wants two kids, a boy and a girl, and she wants them before she's twenty-five so that she won't make the mistake of having them out of "loneliness" when she's older. While she sympathizes with a girlfriend's decision not to have children because the world is so "fucked up" – with child abuse and rape and molestation – Susie accepts the challenge of doing it right, which means, specifically, getting married first. This is an anomalous position to take, considering her mother never married her father but raised Susie with "love and attention" all the same, and gave Susie a family life, albeit of women and children. Perhaps, however, this was only second-best, for Susie feels strongly that kids should be able to talk about "Mum and Dad", and that a family isn't a "real" family unless Mum and Dad are married.

She wants to be at home with her children at least until they go to school. This is not just because she doesn't want to miss out on their first steps, their first words, but because, from her own observations at day-care centres, she sees that so many child-care workers "don't know how to handle kids" and that so many day-care-centre operators "just piss around" or, to be more specific, operate "real holes, filthy, smelly, gross places where cockroaches will be running around one of these days."

Susie sat down with Cal one night to discuss how they'd share the labour of their household. She said the responsibilities should be shared, and he did not disagree as she went through the list: they would do the dishes together, clean up the bedroom together, vacuum the house together; she wouldn't mind doing the cooking if he'd clean off the table; he would hold and feed the baby if she was washing the floor. He would bathe the baby too, wouldn't he? And change its diapers? Here Cal finally protested: that is a "lady's" job. Susie: "But you'll do it, though." Cal: "No, I won't." Susie: "Yes, you will." Cal: "No, I won't." Susie: "If I'm up to my arms in dishes and can't get to the baby, too bad, sucker."

Out of school, out of work, Susie's been checking the newspaper to see what's available for a seventeen-year-old who's dropped out of grade ten and been fired from her last job: cashier, waitressing, cook's assistant. . . . She wants something, anything, full-time until she can make up her mind about going back to school one more time in an effort to graduate. She's sure she can get a job; all the concern about youth unemployment is a "lot of crap", in her opinion, brought on by kids who will only take jobs that pay seven, eight dollars an hour. Well, dream on. Of course, she needs to make at least three hundred a month if she's ever going to be able to support herself outside her mother's house. Perhaps she could find a part-time job and combine it with babysitting at twenty dollars a day: think of all those parents out there who don't want to send their kids to day-care or can't afford it. They can afford Susie.

For the moment, Cal is satisfied where he is, but he has no desire to work in sheet metal the rest of his life. He can also do stucco and drywall – maybe he can open up his own little business one day. But last week he bought a brand-new Chevette – a real deal with AM-FM radio, cassette player, rust-inhibitor spray, and perma-shine for $7115 – and now he's got to keep his sheet-metal job, like it or not.

Susie has a friend, the daughter of a Baptist church minister, raised in the strictest correctness, who's run away from home and is working as a stripper when she isn't on the street. That will never happen to Susie. Maybe her attitude isn't the greatest – easy come, easy go, one day in school, the next day out – but she has no doubt she will be able in the end to take care of herself and even her babies. After all, there's always a job of one sort or an-other out there, and everybody, even Susie, is good at something. She sure can jump a horse, or did once, on the back of white Beauty, swooping down the foggy slopes of St. John's.

NINE

Boys

"With boys you have to make a special effort."

LEARNING boys. Learning seduction and sex and the double standard. Learning love and loss. It begins with flirting in the cafeteria – a sidelong glance from under half-raised eyelids, a smile, an embarrassed giggle – and ends with a broken heart and a vow never to be so vulnerable again. There is not, at this stage of life, much of a sense that boys are on your side. For all the excitement and thrilled anticipation and delicious speculation provoked by burgeoning desire, heterosexuality among adolescents is a culture of afflictions: shyness, self-doubt, discomposure, heartache. Boys can do all this to you – and take you to heaven.

The game. The first thing a girl understands about being with boys is that they're different from girls. According to one nineteen-year-old: "With boys you have to make a special effort. You can't talk to them the way you talk to girls. They have different interests, they're easily distracted, you never know what's going to upset them." In order not to be misunderstood, a girl must take on a kind of protective colouring. Hence the coy innuendoes of her speech, the dissembling self-confidence, and the noncommittal sexual suggestion, all of them observed, disdainfully, by her girlfriends as "total personality change".

Her self-consciousness is acute: her whole being is a receptor, registering not only her own anxiety and desire but also the tones and moods and nuances expressed by those around her – she *knows* she's being watched, being talked about.

Sometimes the consciousness of this interest will force her hand, as was the case with Connie, who, one glorious spring, found herself the object of four boys' attention. Four! She'd been thinking she'd like to make a commitment to someone (the last time she'd had a boyfriend was in grade six, and she was now in grade eleven) and here was one, offering a movie on Friday night, and another with an invitation to a party, and two more just hanging around her at school, making each other jealous. This was great fun – the attention, the courting, the suspense – and she began to reconsider her previous decision to see just one guy at a time. But then her girlfriends intervened, pointing out that "everybody" was talking about her situation and that she'd better choose one boy; it didn't look "right" otherwise. *Guys* can fool around with a bunch of girls at once, but for a girl it's different. She looks, you know, sluttish. Although Connie understood herself to be someone who really does enjoy a lot of male company but no one's in particular, she accepted this interpretation of her situation, and chose the boy with the invitation to the football party. . . . There's no getting around it, really. If you're seen *twice* with the same person, your friends assume you're "seeing" each other. Presto, you're a couple, named as such by your little community. "It was my friend's birthday, so I took him a card and the next night I took him my chemistry notes and we watched TV. His ex-girlfriend arrived with her birthday card and when I ran into her the next day she said, 'So, you're seeing him, eh?'"

Boyfriends can be a serious proposition, or not so serious. Arden met a guy on a bus ("It was really wild") who pressed her about where she worked. Of course she wouldn't tell him anything except that it was at a certain mall, and he said, "I'll look for you in every shop until I find you," which is exactly what he did. They went to a movie and talked about motorcycles and Heavy Metal bands, and he's been calling her every night since. "He's really nice but it's not serious." She could just *tell*. Barbara, on the other hand, is only interested in "going out", which is to say, seeing one guy at a time until they break up, which could happen within days; if you're interested in seeing two different people on two different weekends, well, then, you do not "go out", you date. There's no rule, she says, about how many dates you have to have with the same guy before you're considered to be "going out" with him. If you're lucky, he'll ask you "Do you want to go out with me?" before everybody starts gossiping. If he's black, he'll say, "Do you want to be my woman?" And that's what you'll be, "his" woman. It was precisely this aura of male proprietorship around "going out" or "going together" that discouraged Lorna about the one serious relationship she's had. It lasted three weeks, long enough for her to learn that her boyfriend was seeing other girls, while forbidding her to enjoy any other boy's company. Forget it. It is probably not an unrelated phenomenon that the boys at her school, she reports, are hanging around *junior* high school girls in the effort to get laid.

While for most girls it is the approval or the disapproval of the peer group that controls so much of their dating activity, for the daughters of immigrant parents it is the family that intervenes most decisively. Parents from Mediterranean and Asian cultures have still not ceded their right to exercise authority over their children's sexual and marital behaviour to any state apparatus or "peer group". It is in the interests of the family as a whole to regulate the choices of the still-unmarried, for upon those choices rests the welfare of dozens of individuals, at least until, under pressure of the forces of Canadianization, the extended family breaks down. The struggle between Canadian-born daughters, who live already in the culture of individual self-determination and female emancipation ("the free-

dom to choose"), and their parents is real, and very pain-
ful. Teresa has twice been caught by her parents, alerted
by neighbours in the Italian neighbourhood, sneaking out
of the house to meet her Oriental boyfriend. Then they
found her diary. There has been a lot of "yelling and
screaming" in the house as a result, but, Teresa reasons,
"they can't be any madder than they were the first time,"
and she sneaks out again. Her only other chance to see
him is at school, and she can only speak to him on the
phone when her parents are out. She will not be deterred.
The alternative is to acquiesce in the traditional arrangements, which decree that it is simply not acceptable to
have a boyfriend, ever. One has only a fiancé and then a
husband. Until her parents select a suitable fiancé (and
they have gone as far as to investigate the possibilities in
their native Calabrian town), she is a child, to be bawled
out and embarrassed in public for unladylike behaviour,
to be supervised without relief, to be gossiped about, and
to be subjected to petty regulations. If her parents carry
out their scheme to travel back to Italy to betroth her, she
will simply run away.

There are many ways of offending one's parents. The
emerging sexuality of a child is a disturbing event in most
households, and heterosexual culture has evolved the
means by which the disturbance can be contained and the
development directed along prescribed channels; and all
of this is very much in the air, carried by all media. But
when Frances came home, radiant with her new love, to
tell her mother that she was involved with another
woman, there were no means and channels that her
mother could employ to assimilate the news. All she knew
was that it was intolerable that her daughter and her
daughter's lover should ever be together under the roof of
her house. Frances moved out, amid accusations and
counter-accusations that she needed to see a "shrink",
and went on welfare, a double blow to a working-class
woman of German stock: how could she answer why her
daughter wasn't living at home? If Frances's lover had

been male, Frances thinks, there would still have been a family scandal. But it could at least have been talked about, fretted over, and analysed this way and that, and her mother could have been consoled, and eventually Frances and the lover would have been invited over for dinner; but there is no handy scenario of reconciliation with a lesbian daughter. Her mother has refused all invitations to come and visit Frances in her new digs, explaining that, once she had seen with her own eyes what was what, she could no longer deny it, her only comfort now.

Over the millennia, a mother's warning to her daughter that "men are only after one thing" (and each dating situation, then, is fraught with the possibility of seduction or rape) is a tacit acknowledgement of our culture's assumption that sex is something that women "have" and that men "want", and that, denied it by a woman's refusal to "grant him the favour", a man can be expected to take it by force. As the Canadian sociologist Edward Herold writes,[1] this view of heterosexual exchange theorizes that women don't enjoy sex for its own sake, but use it as an instrument of negotiation to get what they *really* want: love. Similarly, men will use any means at their disposal, including protestations of love and gestures of affection, to get as much sex as possible. This is a somewhat bleak view of heterosexual courtship, but obviously the point can be made that, where femaleness is primarily valued as an object of carnal possession, a girl must be very subtle to hold out always the *possibility* of such possession without in fact indulging it; once he's "had" her, the theory goes, a man need no longer court her, let alone love her.

Whether or not teenage women share this view of their sexuality is the subject of another chapter. Let it only be noted here that the same sociologist quoted to such dismal effect above has also observed, in a study of young women attending birth-control clinics, that women with "high self-esteem" were much likelier than those suffering from low self-esteem to be free of sexual guilt, to make the first move in sexual relations, and to agree to premarital sex in a "love relationship". On the face of it, these do not sound like women held in thrall by patriarchal "Thou shalt nots", but rather like women who assert their right to dispose of themselves as they see fit. Such a one is Lorna, who first made love with a boyfriend she had for some months and does not regret it, even though the relationship was short-lived (she broke it off): "I felt a lot closer to him afterwards, it was a lot easier to communicate." She has no trouble with the idea of "casual" sex (making love with someone you're not in love with), because she sees it as an act of sharing – not forever, granted, but for the pleasure and delight of the moment. "I don't see why you should deprive yourself of such feelings just because you're not in love with him."

But Lorna is, at sixteen, uncommonly mature and self-possessed. The capacity to distinguish between needs and wants, to stand up for yourself, to know how to separate lust from love, to detect manipulation and insincerity – these are all the gift of experience, acquired, unfortunately, all too often at the hands of some man not worthy of a virgin's confidence.

My conversations with teenage girls about their boyfriends yielded virtually nothing but complaints about these relationships; make of this what you will. There were a few well-considered remarks about a certain boyfriend's "gentleness" and his "caring", another's capacity for friendship and conversation ("We're really interested in what each other is doing, which is rare, I think"). One girl appreciated the fact her boyfriend had been easy to get along with, and another that he wasn't jealous of her academic achievements and ambitions, and a third that he "didn't mind" her going out with her own friends. There was even a reflective moment when seventeen-year-old Liz, who had obviously given some thought to the question of one's own responsibility for one's well-being, said that "to be happy with another person you have to be happy with yourself first, because if you don't *have* yourself, you can't really have anybody else." Even from such cryptic evidence, it is clear what young women want from intimate relationships: courtesy, camaraderie, and elbowroom. That their grievances are legion would suggest that they are not getting what they want.

At one end of the scale of relationships that didn't work out are the ones that were merely boring. The guy was cute but conceited and, having nothing to be conceited about – he was unbelievably dumb – was a crashing bore; in retrospect, the relationship had been a complete waste of time. . . . He had been her true love for two years, but then she moved away, and when she saw him again, at Christmas, she realized she had drifted away from him, body and soul, and there was nothing to be done about it: she had changed and she didn't want him any more. . . . They had been very happy together – he was her first boyfriend – but it just got to be too much of a good thing, seeing each other every day, and she wanted out, wanted independence and excitement again. . . . She had a boyfriend for a month or so and it was handy having someone to dance with at the clubs, but quickly enough she noticed she wasn't seeing that much of him, and when she did they didn't have much to talk about; she broke it off with minimal fuss and remains unconvinced that she's at any disadvantage being single.

It gets nastier. He hated Blacks, he hated Pakis, bohunks, and punkers, he hated the pink streak in her hair, and he hated her friends; she broke it off without regret. . . . The Captain – immature and not very bright – couldn't stand anything about her. *She* just wanted to have fun, but he was constantly nagging her, telling her what to wear and how to cut her hair and what were her best colours, mocking her taste in music, and referring to her ideas as "stupid". Ha. All *he* was interested in was sports, so there she was, watching hockey games on TV, a pastime she despises, and going alone to the theatre. It lasted three weeks, long enough for her to regret it still and to feel bad about herself, and to recoil (gross! bleah!) at the thought of his touch. . . . For two years they fought, often quite violently, unable to say, "Look, I was wrong, I'm sorry. Peace." Their jealousy of each other got the better of them and she knew it was over when she couldn't bear to have him anywhere near her.

The truly unbearable thing is not having room to breathe. The boyfriend is constantly *there*, in her space, taking up her time and demanding her attention when she wants some of both for herself. He acts as if they're married, interrogating her about where she's been and with whom and why (he, of course, goes off without explanation), flying into rages at her insistence on her independence not just for now but for the future, too. Conversely, he can't bear to be away from her, is no longer interested in seeing his old friends, wants only to hold onto her like a clam on a rock; she wants to pry him loose. It's in the very concept of the word "girlfriend": being some*one's* girlfriend, which means no one else is allowed to look, to touch, to speak, and you are not available to anyone else. "It's just the worst," says Nina, who likes her old self, single and unattached, much better than the girl who was not allowed to flirt at parties, to speak with everybody who was there, male and female, hugging some and sitting in others' laps. "What's wrong with that? Why can't I do it if that's how I feel? Who says it's 'unacceptable'?"

But some hearts are truly broken, egos humiliated, self-possession tattered, and the girl-in-love, who had been all aflutter with exquisite sensation and fervent expectation at the approach of the beloved, is now haunted by his withdrawal. This is the oldest and simplest complaint of them all: *Why has he changed so much*? Where there had once been a moon-struck cavalier, offering his devotion to the end of time, there is now a cold and taciturn male unmoved by her sorrow and interrogation ("What's happening to you?"). Once he had loved her; now he ignores her when his friends are around. Once he had loved her; now he discusses, *in front of her*, which of her friends he'd like to go to bed with, and she swears to break it off. But even in her miserable loneliness he can still reach her ("I really want you") and she tries it again, only to be dumped at a party because he's mad at her for some offence she has no idea she has committed, and so they fight, and she weeps, and they make love, and so it goes, with her crying noisily into the pillow while he, cursing, pulls on his boots and stomps out.

All the apparent power of the girl – to judge what a boy is worth, to decide what will develop between them and where to stop it, to draw him to her with sexual allure and to hold him at bay while she decides whether or not to satisfy him – is compromised in the actual commitment she makes to him. The power is reversed in the process of the relationship, for a relationship is highly visible, involving manifestly public behaviour (couples are social entities), and it is in public that the codes of the sexual double standard are enforced. Her attachment must be seen to be monogamous, her affection demonstrable and unconditional, her need greater. Suddenly it is he who has something *she* wants: a fondness for her that is not only sexual. If he refuses to give it, that is the sign of his power to satisfy *his* need without ceding an inch of his self-containment to the claims of love.

I was walking behind them on Harbord Street. His hands were in his pockets as he walked briskly along, facing straight ahead. Both of her arms were threaded through one of his and she was turned sideways, face tilted up towards his noncommittal profile. She scampered along, keeping up with his pace. She was shaking him. "Listen to me!" she said. "*Listen to me!*"

Almost everyone I spoke to had a vision of heterosexual bliss, which she invariably labelled "romantic", a word (accompanied by a sigh, a wry grimace, a roll of the eyes) clearly freighted with apology and resignation, as though she were well aware of the depreciated value of that vision, and of her own hapless investment in it none the less. To be "romantic" means, in the first place, to love flowers and love songs and Valentine's Day cards, picnics in October, and phone calls just to say good-night – all the trivia of a relationship meant to signal that one is treasured. It is a signal, too, that the boyfriend is not afraid of his own affectionate impulses: "I knew a guy who was romantic. He was constantly sending me letters, even though we lived in the same city, because he *felt* like it. I think a lot of people are afraid to do that." This is a kind of courage required a hundredfold in the grown-up male or lover who, so the romantic fantasy goes, will be "soft, kind, and gentle", gentlemanly, good-humoured, and ardent, and eager to open up his mind and heart to his partner.

That such a man should be acknowledged, hopelessly, as a "fantasy" attests to the fact that the majority of males that a teenage girl actually meets are the antithesis of the romantic lover. They are uncouth and artless, mean and contemptuous, running together in packs where the style is one of studied machismo: indifference to and aloofness from females. They are not, however, to be held altogether responsible for this insensibility. A girl who confessed to having "romantic ideas" about boys also admitted to having no idea how to get along with them ("I don't know what to say to them"), a perplexity multiplied by every rebuffed overture made to a girl by a hopeful, bashful swain. Some girls will also acknowledge the bewilderment provoked in young men by the new feminist culture. Tara, astonishingly empathetic, can imagine how that feels: "A guy knows how his father treats his mother and how men treat other men, but how does he know to treat this woman who's saying, 'I can do anything you can' *and* 'I'm a woman too'? She wants to be treated like a woman but she doesn't want to be treated like that means she's some low thing. So what's he to do?"

This is crucial: a young woman is nurturing dreams of

connubial harmony and solicitude precisely at the time of a young man's most violent need to establish his independence from "feminine" or womanly or motherly values (softness, kindness, gentleness) and to align himself with the culture of his kind, which tells him that all things feminine are held in contempt, including of course "romance". In American writer Sharon Thompson's vivid phrase (in an essay about adolescent sexuality),[2] he wants to "get under the skin of a woman without feeling a thing, without ceding a single fresh cell of memory, without crossing a single synapse back toward infancy, without losing an iota of self, of manhood." That girls persist in their fantasies despite all this must mean that some need, far greater than any discouragement from male resistance, is clamouring to be met.

While boys in their own milieu are learning that "if you express yourself you're weak and you'll get hurt," girls in theirs learn how to manipulate this "natural" male impulse to evade commitment. They learn from songs, for instance (lover haunts neighbourhood of tantalizingly unavailable female), and from movies (heroine has affair with married man, they quarrel, she leaves, he stops her, in the nick of time, at the airport). They learn from magazines like *True Story*. Barbara: "I liked this one: 'Come Back To My Loving Arms'; it's a true story. Some guy left her, then came back. I like love stories. Tragedies. Anything about the life of a teenager. Here's a good one: 'My Boyfriend Says I'm All Bones But My Mirror Tells Me I'm Fat'. And: 'Love Memories Aren't Enough For Me', about divorce. This girl and her brothers have been with their dad since their mum left. He marries another lady and the lady treats the girl real bad. She has to work all day in a laundry and then the lady kicks her out of the house. Her father is a real weakling. She goes to live with her boyfriend, so it turns out happy." And they learn from books like Harlequin romances, and current best-sellers – "I read it because I think it's good to sit down and dream about stuff like that, even if it's only one chance in a million that it can happen to you" – although girls who read anything at all are a distinct minority.

Not to take anyone's word for it, I did some of this reading myself, asking myself if there were a discernible archetypal romantic scenario. From one issue of *True Story* I read a story pitched at teenage readers ("The Date I'd Prayed For Since I Was Thirteen"), the tale of a high school student in love with the school's hero, a football star, who miraculously invites her to a dance and who shortly afterwards reveals his true colours: he's a cocaine addict. All is not lost, for the boy looks so miserable and so contrite in his abasement that the girl dedicates herself to his rehabilitation: "Tim and I have faith in each other. Together, we can lick any problem that comes along!" Far more baneful is the story of Pam, in "No Matter What Anyone Says, My Heart Won't Listen: We're Right For Each Other", who recounts the tumultuous events of her love affair with and marriage to Mike, a seemingly tender-hearted and devoted mate who cannot, however, overcome a criminal streak in his nature. Their love turns hellish, but Pam extricates herself in time to accept the new love offered by a soft-spoken, thoughtful, and impassioned co-worker (in the town library!) who has been willing to wait for her attention.

The classic romance novel, typified by Harlequin books, has devotees numbering in the millions, not a few of whom are teenagers. Picked at random, *Illyrian Summer* by Iris Danbury (first published in 1965 and reissued in 1975 and 1982) tells the story of Sarah, a typist-cum-scriptgirl on a film shoot in Yugoslavia, who is in love with Adam Thorne, a British engineer working in the vicinity. The plot hinges on the uncertainty of Adam's feelings for her. Told from Sarah's point of view, the drama, such as it is, deals entirely with her overwhelming anxiety about his state of mind and heart: her minute dissections of his glances, his off-hand remarks, and even the tone of his voice, the motivations of his every coming and going. They have no conversation to speak of and do not, of course, even touch, yet she "loves" him. No matter. In the last one and a half pages, he reveals that he loves her too, and they plan their wedding and discuss the glamorous future that lies ahead (he's being posted to South America).

Such fiction has spawned a racier version (for the more "modern", liberated reader of the eighties), such as the Silhouette Desire book *Make No Promises* by Sherry Dee, published in 1982. Here the terrain of love's contention is decidedly more ambiguous: a casino, for example; a gambling cad for a fiancé; a "mysterious force" drawing the strikingly beautiful heroine to the "dangerous, magnetic" centre of the "unbelievably handsome" but jealous, possessive, and malevolent-eyed hero, known as Steele. They meet when she stumbles and falls on his yacht, a misfortune that results in a rent in her shirt and the revelation of her "full, jutting breasts". They proceed by alternately chilly and steamy degrees (her "kiss-bruised lips, flushed face, passion-glazed eyes", his "rock-hard frame") to an encounter of considerable abandon; and culminate in a climactic sex act in which it is revealed that the heroine has "kept herself" for true love after all:" 'A virgin!' Steele said with awe."

Certain elements are common to almost all romantic fantasies. The heroine is young, modestly employed, and without relations, all of which make her socially vulnerable to the hero, who is invariably older, wealthier, and more powerful (his name, as in Thorne and Steele above, gives this away). There is very little female friendship depicted, the only other woman of interest being the sluttish rival – older and more sexually experienced than the heroine – for the hero's affections. The plot concerns the heroine's inappropriate and hopeless longing, the hero's arrogant and angry spurning of her mute appeals for love, her sexual wakening in spite of her resolve to resist, his internal struggle between loving her and leaving her, a penultimate crisis during which all seems lost, and then the final clearing up of the misunderstanding and the resolution in marriage or at least in true love.

Not surprisingly, given the number of women readers of romance (over fifty million copies sold worldwide each year), feminist critics have paid the subject considerable attention. Without much difficulty, some have argued that it represents "soft-core" pornography for women. In an important essay in *New Republic* magazine in 1980,[3] the American academic Ann Douglas isolated a number of elements that were also to be found in pornography: female vulnerability enthralled by male authority; the heroine's terror of the hero's coldness, silence, and aloofness, and her simultaneous yearning for his presence; his physical brutality and her rapturous submission; and his power to dictate the terms of their relations even as fond husband-to-be. Douglas writes: "The timing of the Harlequins' prodigious success has coincided exactly with the appearance and spread of the women's movement and much of its increasingly anti-feminist content reflects this symbiotic relationship. . . . As in hard porn, female identities are obligingly so much tinder in the crucible in which the male ego is to be reforged."

But other critics would not agree, or at least would argue that, for all its anti-feminist content, the romantic narrative can be and is appropriated by female readers for their own purposes: a "utopian wish-fulfillment fantasy" (in the words of Janice Radway, who has written a book about the readers of romance fiction)[4] in which, unlike in real life, hardness, indifference, and emotional cruelty yield to tenderness and love. This is what all the romantic heroines want – tenderness, passion, sexual responsiveness, and pleasure rooted in the security of being loved – and because it is a fantasy they do get it all.

The Canadian sociologist Angela Miles[5] goes as far as to argue that the romantic fantasy isn't about male-female relations at all. In its preoccupation with love and nurturing and protectiveness (*not* sex and arousal and dominance), in its details of tender male behaviour (the hero cuddles the heroine during a thunderstorm, he tucks her into bed), in its narrative structure of resistance-love-rejection-reconciliation, the romantic fantasy is a story about *mother*-love. Like Mother, the romantic hero is strong, self-sufficient, and in charge; like her, he is, alternately, domineering and punishing, and loving and protecting. He/she is the source of all emotional nourishment and, just like the child she was, the woman reader gives herself over to his/her care. "The heroine will live happily ever after," Miles writes, "in the womb provided by the hero. In romantic fantasy loving is mothering; to be loved is to find a mother." Not since puberty, at which point attachment to a male becomes her primary interest and she takes on "mothering" responsibilities, has a woman the opportunity in our culture to be *taken care of* physically, emotionally, spiritually, sensually: her fantasy about being carried off by the knight in shining armour is her displaced longing to be babied again.

This is all the more clearly seen in lives of girls and women where good feelings and personal pleasure are not present in their everyday world: in these cases they must seek them out vicariously. Faced with futures of dull work and little pay and slow promotion, if any at all, young women fantasize the romantic hero and scenario by means of which they'll evade their destiny. It is in the realm of the imaginary, where she is a free being, that a girl dreams up the lover who will bring happiness, the love that will confirm her desirability, the wealth and power that will banish the meanness of her life forever. Even for middle-class girls, the romantic scenario is one in which, unlike real life, the lover is sensual and sensitive, eschewing genital sex and his orgasm for caresses and avowals of love. Girls' investment in romance means, according to two British analysts of female subcultures,[6] that "they can demand that boys go through at least some of its motions to prove their commitment and this in turn works as a kind of lever in the power game in which in every other way they are disadvantaged from the start."

The adolescent woman, of course, possesses almost no social or economic power. She spends money, but it is earned from the most menial tasks, or comes from her parents; her intellectual skills are still crudely fashioned; she has no notion yet of how liberating good work can be, or any experience of her sexuality except what is reflected back to her from male fantasies; she is expected to be helpful to others, "unselfish", obedient, and well-behaved. Where, in this life, is her opportunity to have an adventure? How, in the midst of tedium, can she learn about taking risks, being brave and resolute, overcoming obstacles and disappointments, and winning in the end? This, then, is a purpose of the romantic daydream: to set off on a quest for love, *the* female adventure par excellence, the "primary vocation for girls who live dangerously".[7]

In the romantic fantasy, the brutishness of the male is softened by the appealing vulnerability of the woman-in-love. But in real life this same feminine susceptibility seems only to infuriate him: he lashes out at her, he humiliates her, he beats her, and, finally, to spend himself, he "makes love" to her. "He" is very often the boyfriend of a teenage girl. And this is no romance.

For example. At eighteen, she met a twenty-two-year-old "hunk", a big and gruff and menacing logger with a collection of knives, whose smouldering violence attracted her: it made her feel protected. She moved in with him the second week of knowing him. Then the heavy drinking began, and the fights. He accused her of seeing other men and warned her he would kill her if he found out; he railed at her for not getting pregnant, and cursed her in his drunkenness for "making" him impotent. Always, in his beer-sodden rages, he would want to have sex, and it was there, in bed, that he first assaulted her: he tried to stran-

gle her, stopped, and said he was sorry. In the next assault, triggered by the information that she had had other
lovers, he broke down the bedroom door behind which
she was cowering, pushed her up against the wall, pulled
out a knife, and pressing it against her throat, told her that
he hated her and was going to kill her. She fought him off
and, naked and screaming, ran to a neighbour's to call the
police. When they arrived, they told her she was being
hysterical and turned to have a friendly chat with the
boyfriend, who had wandered over to find out what was
going on. It was obvious that they, police and assailant,
knew one another, and at that moment of realization she
felt "devastated" and unspeakably alone. She went back
to live with him. A few weeks later, in spite of her numb-
ness, her guilt (she really was a "whore"), and her love,
she left him – the last straw had been the news that he had
raped another woman. Convinced that she truly was a
"shit", a piece of meat, and, loathing the idea of ever
being close to a man again, she began hooking, and is
hooking still.

The story (slightly altered here) was told to Jean Bennet
and Jeny Evans as one of a series of interviews they held
with battered teenage women. Until they undertook the
research on behalf of Battered Women's Support Services
in Vancouver, there was not a "single shred of solid documentation" available from Canadian sources.[8] Now they
are collecting it, hours and hours and hours of haunted
teenage autobiography; gradually, in the listening to the
scarcely supportable details (the loss, the anguish, the
grieving that will not come), it sinks in that one is hearing
these stories for the very first time.

"B. saw me in the bar with another guy. He told me to
leave. He was yelling at me all the way home. Calling me a
bitch and other names. I tried to stay out of his way when
we got back but he kept arguing and slapping me. My
nose started bleeding. I said I'd had enough. He hit me on
the side of the head and my head slammed against the
wall. I passed out."

At one end of this spectrum, where a man calls a woman "fat" or a "bitch" or a "slut", the abuse is hardly registered, not even by the woman herself, so accustomed are women to hearing this language addressed to them. But every such exchange diminishes her self-esteem; if she no longer protests, it can only mean that she believes it to be true. The verbal assaults progress: she is bellowed at with obscenities if she comes home five minutes late, if she's spending "too much" time with her girlfriends, if she got her hair cut (or didn't get it cut). At the other end of the spectrum, he threatens her life, knife at her throat, gun in her ribs, baseball bat across her skull, and sometimes he succeeds in killing her. Should she survive these assaults, she becomes a kind of zombie, going through the motions of a life, no longer even thinking of saving herself: what is there to save? Her silence is absolute.

We have not heard these voices because they belong to people to whom we have not been accustomed to lend an ear: young, female, frightened, demoralized, often poor, and on their own. Who will succour them? One can begin by listening.

Battered girlfriends, like battered wives, come from diverse backgrounds. Upper-middle-class: divorced parents, mother's rich but violent new man, runaway daughter slicing herself up in the bathroom of a group home, fixing MDA on the street. Or a civilized family with only the occasional swat across the face from Mum and Dad. Or divorced parents, and a daughter perennially afraid of being left, abandoned. The boyfriend could be anybody: an intellectual university student introduced by a friend; a dope dealer living down the hall in an inner-city hotel; a bouncer in a bar; a neighbour met in the community centre; a married pharmacist. Frequently he's good-looking, has nice manners, drives a car, has money to spend. The girl is impressed, excited, flattered. Then she's in love. And the abuse begins.

They had a fight one night because she showed up at the tavern where he was drinking with his buddies – he didn't like to be "spied on", he told her. He hauled her outside, yelling "slut" and "nobody disobeys me" at her, and told her to get lost. She waited for him at his place, but on his return he said he never wanted to see her again. It was only after her promise that she would never disobey him again, and her vow that she loved him, that he forgave her and let her stay. Two weeks later, on a double date at a nightclub, she got up to dance with her girlfriend, a provocation. Back home, her boyfriend accused her of "slutting it up" and threw her across the couch and smacked her across the face, breaking his own ring in the process. This provoked another smack. "Somehow I got him to forgive me. I did it by saying I knew it was all my fault."

He called her stupid, fat, and lazy. When she tried to talk, he demanded sex. He took sex. It hurt her to walk around the next morning. She didn't like it, but she thought it was *her* problem; her boyfriend agreed, told her to see a therapist. "I felt that if I could just be nicer or tried harder to please him it would all be okay." When she menstruated, he called her "gross", but she "made up for it" by giving him head until her face hurt.

Some of these relationships last only a couple of weeks, others continue for years. Unavoidably, one must ask, why are these girls – thirteen-, fifteen-, eighteen-year-olds – with these men? Why don't they fight back? Why, in God's name, don't they leave and save themselves?

The short answer is that of course they would leave if they felt they were free to do so. But they do not feel free. They feel trapped and immobilized, suffering a paralysis of will and imagination that begins with their very real isolation within the relationship. The boyfriend has long ago forbidden her to hang out with her old friends, he never takes her anywhere outside his own territory, she's lucky to see *him*, he's so busy; her parents, who hate him, are unavailable; and her girlfriends, who've noticed the bruises and welts, disapprove. It's true he batters her, but other people who know him – his buddies, his mother, his boss – all think he's a great guy; he's fun, he's sexy, he's bright, so it must be something about *her* that brings out the nastiness in him. Hasn't he called her a bitch, and seen her flirting with the guys she works with, and warned her not to make him mad? If only she could get it right (if only she were prettier, thinner, richer, smarter, better-dressed, more easy-going), he'd stop hurting her.

It's all very confusing. She got a promotion to a full-time position, which she thought would please him. Instead, he demanded dinner be ready every night at exactly the same time. When she was promoted to head cashier, it was the last straw: he accused her of screwing her way to the top. He would never tell her he loved her except when they fought; the more they fought, the more she thought he loved her. He never touched her in public, not even to kiss hello, and when they made love she'd feel so empty she wanted to weep. Forget the sex. If just once he'd held her and told her he loved her, without wanting to hit or fuck her, she'd have been a happy woman. After a while, a woman forgets what drew her to this man in the first place; after a while, she stays because she's simply too afraid to leave. She knows he's capable of carrying out his threats against her – "I'll kill you!" "I'll beat you to hell and back!" "Wherever you are, I'll always find you!" – and she lives on the edge: one false move and he'll attack. She's looking over her shoulder to see if he's following her in his truck; she's scared to answer her phone; whenever he gets mad, her knees shake. "I literally could shit my pants. It must be like the feeling you get just before you know you're going to die." One girl would always sleep on her stomach, her arms folded protectively around her breasts.

Doubting themselves and their capacity to alter their situation, they accept it, justifying their boyfriends' behaviour. "He was fantastic when he wasn't being violent." She would stick around for the nice times, hoping that her love for him would soothe his troubled soul. He'd had such a terrible life, after all: an alcoholic father, a mother who beat him with an electric cord, a brother in jail, a sister on the streets – it would make her weep in sympathy to think of the utter lovelessness of this man's life. *She*, feeling his pain, would stick around, *she* would not abandon him. Torment her as he would, she would deliver him from his anguish.

Why is this happening to teenagers?[9] The virtually irresistible pressure from peer culture – the "childhood sweetheart myth" that Bennet and Evans identify – to be coupled with a male and to stay by him no matter what, to be seen in public as "worthy" of his attention, to take upon yourself the responsibility of managing the emotions in the relationship, and to offer yourself up, like a romantic heroine, to the frenzy of his sexual passion, moves a girl into the dubious area where her unhappiness and humiliation are "deserved". She, in the meantime, is caught in a vortex of guilt, confusion, terror, and self-disgust, with no one to talk to. At worst, her girlfriends ("catty bitches") are not to be trusted; at best, they are helpless, with too little life experience of their own to know how to support her. She may have burned her bridges to her parents, having stormed out of their home in an act of rebellion: "It's either us or him," they said, and she chose him. The resources available to her that would allow her to sustain her independence are pathetically limited. A sixteen-year-old who wants to flee her abusive boyfriend and who cannot return home has no alternative but to live in a group home, where she may or may not be eligible for social assistance, or to work for minimum wage or less in some grossly exploitative situation ("working for two dollars an hour, ten hours a day, as glorified babysitters in the two-career homes of the middle-class," as Jeny Evans puts it). No wonder, then, that the larger experience of the boyfriend, his cash, his car keys, his social ease at the nightclubs and bars, are infinitely more desirable than her dependence on, and patronization by, family and social services.

At the heart of her experience, however, is her utter

lack of belief that she has the right to dispose of her body, her self, as she sees fit. Where on earth would she have acquired such a belief? Social messages regarding her sexuality are contradictory, to say the least. On the one hand, educators and parents alike conspire to withhold any but the most rudimentary and clinical data from teenagers, as though their developing sexuality and the associated emotions were no more problematic than the details of the menstrual cycle, and no less taboo. Evidently sex is either so awesome, or so repelling, that it cannot be discussed with any kind of candour with adults. On the other hand, this cloak of silence covering the *experience* of sex is lifted to allow the broadcast of pornography, soft-core and hard-core, as though the only sexual display our society is comfortable with is that of rape or seduction. Alternative images of female self-reliance and independence compete unequally with popular fears that a feminist is a lonely workaholic, hostile to men and excluded, therefore, from the consolations of marriage. *Who would want to be like that?* A teenage girl wants very much to be loved. And so, ignorant of her own psychosexual processes and of what is "okay" and "not okay" in sex, knowing only that sex is "about" love and here she is having sex so this thing that's happening to her must be love, she lies down with her tormentor.

I told Carla and Sharon and Arden that this is what had happened to a girl from their school: she met a boy she knew at a party and accepted a ride home with him and his friends. She was seated in the back seat with the boy; they were cuddling. He pressed further, she drew back, he grew angry, she struggled to release his grip, he pinned her down and attempted to rape her. She was far too tight for him to penetrate but he would not be thwarted; he beat her about the face and breasts as though the blows would unlock her. His friend at the wheel said nothing, did nothing. Dumped at her home, she discovered to her relief that her parents were asleep. Her sister helped her bathe and got rid of the torn and bloodied clothes. She has told no one about this incident except the school counsellor, who has told me, and now I was telling her schoolmates.

Outrageous! they cried in indignation. They would never succumb to such assault. If a man hit *her*, said one, she'd walk out on him in two seconds flat; if he beats you once, he'll beat you again, and if you keep forgiving him or even if you just keep silent, he will never stop beating you. Even if she had twenty kids and no way of supporting them, said another, she'd still walk away. She'd seen her father strike her mother and she could never understand why her mother "stayed around for all that shit". Well, said the third, their mothers belong to another generation, where being wife and mother is everything, where being "woman" means sticking it out with your husband, but today's generation of young women knows "we're important as individuals, not as *wives*, and we don't have to put up with any of that crap."

Brave new words. But the fact is that the most independent, self-reliant, and confident girls I met tended to be those without steady boyfriends, just as in the "bad old days" when women were counselled that they could not have "everything": freedom, and love. And not every girl is susceptible to feminism's vocabulary and imagination. There are thousands of others to whom the vision is impossibly remote, and probably not even desirable. Their peers mock these "man-haters" who hate babies, make-up, and chivalry. They harbour grave suspicions about women who exercise personal authority, and share the widespread ignorance of the niceties of a girl's civil and personal rights. From where in her being is she to find the means to tell the lover who's beating her, "You do not have the right!"? Instead, she defends herself as best she can by always being as "good" as possible, by trying desperately to please her guy and keep him in a good mood; or, says Jean Bennet, "they retreat inside themselves, go-

ing into a place where they can't be touched or hurt."
Later, when they've escaped the relationship, some will
become feminists, join battered women's support groups,
and spread the word about their suffering and the reasons
for it. Others will want only to forget. Many are afraid
ever to be alone with a man again, while others lose themselves in promiscuity, "degrading-type jobs", drug and
alcohol addiction. Some take pride in their new independence – "It felt good and powerful to leave him" – refusing to see any other man for more than a month at a time,
fearing the dependency of attachment. Cracking the shell
of their own stupor, they come to life again in hate, the
purgative rage of a woman coming to her own rescue.

One woman looks back on herself as the seventeen-
year-old in a married man's hotel room, posturing ob-
scenely on his bed, and sees only a figure in a pornographic tableau. She works now at a rape crisis centre and
joins anti-pornography pickets outside video "boutiques".
"I feel," she says, "like I need to atone for it." As though
the expiation were hers.

Ruth

"Tell her please to come back!"

A BAG OF rice, some tinned food, a number of wooden chopsticks and blue Chinese bowls, two towels, and a pair of bedsheets were stacked neatly in her bedroom closet. She had accumulated them, item by item, on her shopping forays into Toronto's Chinatown – the cheapest neighbourhood she knew of – and had carefully put them away, taking out the bowls from time to time to admire them in the window light and to reassure herself that soon, soon, she would be packing them into boxes and taking them away with her. She hadn't found an apartment yet but she was looking. She knew exactly what she wanted: a roomy, sunny, white-walled, old-fashioned flat down around Queen and Bathurst, big enough to give her the feeling she was finally in charge of her own space. Her own walls, where friends could drop by any time they liked to do anything that pleased them, and she herself would not have to worry about being found, at three in the morning, stumbling, stoned, against the furniture or having to deal with the family circle around the dining-room table at breakfast, all of them pretending they didn't feel the indignation that was written on their faces. Ruth dreamed of moving out of home.

She felt she hadn't had a real home to live in for years

anyway, so why prolong this polite masquerade of family life? Her parents had split up when she was seven and her sister four. Her mother had left them behind to go set herself up in the city, leaving them in the care of a father who was, to put it bluntly, a mess, a man at the end of his tether, weeping into his whisky, inconsolable as he contemplated his future. With two kids in the back of his car, he drove hither and yon about the country from Winnipeg to Prince Edward Island, looking for a job (he was clever, he was educated), one beat-up jalopy after another parked in motel parking lots, the three of them down to their last dollar, and little Ruth trying to cheer him up – and so inevitably he gave the children over to their mother in Toronto. What Ruth did not truly appreciate at the time was that their mother had remarried.

The man, the new husband, is loathsome. In the beginning, she tried a couple of times to be his "daughter"; he'd introduce her to his friends as such, and she liked that. But as she got to know him she withdrew: he was a prudish, tight-ass Brit, a man who had grown up in boarding schools and had apparently learned there never to express any feeling more profound than civility, so that she's never seen him smile, she says, or cry. He is just not a human being, really (and those kids he has from his first marriage, well, they must have been conceived by means of artificial insemination!), and so she has nothing to do with him. He disapproves of her totally – he goes through her mail, pokes around in her room when she's out, unplugs the phone when he considers she's on it too long, and locks up the television set in his own room – but she couldn't care less. She doesn't talk to him, she doesn't look at him, she does her best to pretend he simply isn't there.

Mother is a more complicated case. She's a smart woman with a good job in the media and lots of interesting friends, she's independent and strong-willed and self-sufficient, and that's just the problem: she doesn't need Ruth. How is Ruth to make any difference in her life? Her

father she can help – extend him sympathy and kindness –
but her mother doesn't need any of this. And even if she
did need something of what Ruth could give her, she'd
never let Ruth know, and so Ruth has stopped talking
with her about anything important: there's no "information" her mother has that Ruth wants, or any information
Ruth has that she wants to give her, and so, she says, she
doesn't really feel part of her mother's life, or even part of
her, and she doesn't "see" her mother in her future. Her
mother says she loves her, but Ruth isn't sure she believes
her. How can you love someone you don't deep down
know? And Ruth has made sure her mother doesn't know
her.

She talked about this with her good friend Laurie, sitting shoulder to shoulder in the booth of a diner on Yonge
Street, sipping from cups of weak tea cloudy with milk.
They admitted that they had privileged lives, living in big
houses with parents or step-parents with plenty of money,
and that they could come and go pretty much as they
pleased. Ruth didn't even have to come home at night any
more, just as long as she telephoned to tell her parents her
plans. "I've gained my freedom, too," said Laurie, a personal triumph after a year of running away every week or
two until her mother realized she couldn't keep her from
doing what she wanted to do. But none of this was the
point, really. The point was to be away, out, gone. As long
as you live at home, there are rules: you can't bring certain
friends over, you're not allowed to smoke, you can't make
noise, you can't play as loud as you want that "ghastly"
music of yours, and so on. It's very boring and stupid.
Ruth has only been wanting to do her own thing. What's
the big deal?

Once, three years ago, when she was thirteen, she'd
stayed out all night, and you know what her parents did?
They called the cops! A cop was waiting in the house
when she arrived in the morning and he sat her down and
gave a very heavy philosophic talk while her parents
looked on, saying nothing, just nodding their heads in

smug approval. As the cop went on and on – "I'm going to tell you a little story and I want you to listen carefully" – Ruth wanted to giggle (he was trying so hard), even though the "little story" had to do with a girl who had disappeared from her home and not been found for days – raped and murdered and stuffed into a freezer. "For two weeks I was out in the cold looking for her," the cop said with unimpeachable solemnity, "and all the time that little girl was colder than I was!" Ruth recounts this, and it still makes her shriek derisively.

A year later she was talking to cops again, this time after a six-day flight all the way to Thunder Bay. Her boyfriend, Alan, had phoned her late one night to tell her he was still in love with his old girlfriend, Molly, and wanted to go out with her again, and Ruth freaked out and said, "Fine, go ahead, but I'm leaving." Trembling from head to foot, heartsick and dangerously "tempted" by the subway trains hurtling out of the tunnels towards her, she made her way downtown to the bus depot, where she bought a ticket for Thunder Bay and cried all the way there. Her friend Tony picked her up and drove her to Rainbow's house – Rainbow had harboured runaways before – and there she hid (peeking out through the curtains to see if the cops were parked outside) while her mother, who had talked to Alan, negotiated with Tony: "Tell her please to come back!" Rainbow said she shouldn't do it but Tony said she should, and when she thought about it – that she was hungry and broke and weary from crying, and that she couldn't do anything about Alan from Thunder Bay – she decided she would go back. The cops were waiting at home again and gave her another talking-to, about how "irresponsible" she had been, etc., etc., just a lot of blah, blah, blah.

She was dragged off then to a family counsellor, who told her she was seriously disturbing the family and they'd be much better off without her; she was a rotten, rotten kid. Okay. So that was her role in life, to be her family's rotten kid. But she's not a rebel any more. If you rebel against something, you're acknowledging that it's there and that it's bugging you. She doesn't do that any more. She thinks she can live her life the way she wants to live it without having to pay attention to what's going on around her. She keeps her mouth shut unless she has something to say or unless she's asked for her opinion, in which case she'll say she thinks everybody is full of shit. But she doesn't feel obligated to elaborate.

She has few friends. They come in and go out of her life like stray cats. She has to flip through her ragged address book to be reminded of those she once befriended before they vanished: lots of Alan's friends, a nice guy from her old high school, a brother and sister couple who hung out at the same clubs as she and Alan did, and a hairdresser who was into picking up chicks and talking about finding the "ultimate truth" (she got sick of that and put him on hold). She feels lonely, she admits, utterly without self-pity, but having a lot of people around doesn't protect you from loneliness either. She was surrounded by "friends" in high school who, when they weren't being clingy (passing her notes full of hurt feelings about the fact she had had lunch with so-and-so and not with them), were being bitchy and dippy, gossiping unpleasantly about one another's sex lives (if you could call it sex) and giggling like perfect babies about boys: "Oh, *he* called me last night, ooooh, and you know what he *said*? He said, 'Hi, how are you?' Can you believe it? How *are* you? Ooooh." Ruth and Laurie (her friend these days) like to talk about drugs.

Ruth's relationships with boys have been protracted and difficult: it is here that her character has been put thoroughly to the test. Some, of course, she's let pass, and so has emerged relatively unscathed from the encounter. Ultimate Truth, for instance. They met when he cut her hair at a Rosedale salon, called her up and invited her to his place, but she was fourteen, he was twenty-four, and she decided she didn't want to find "ultimate truth" at this point and told him, "See you later." Then she went around with his friend Jamie but dropped it (he had a very bad temper), refusing to take his calls, which came five and six times a day.

But Alan was another story, Alan the alien, funny-looking and blond-white and so skinny he "dripped" toes and fingers, Alan the bone-rack she met at a friend's house when they were both fourteen and knew at once that he was unlike anyone she had ever known. He was the school outcast, the guy who wore mismatched socks and drooled, who skipped his way home from school like a perfect imbecile, but his *mind*, his mind was very interesting, he was at least several steps ahead of Ruth.

He taught her two things. The first was that not all men are pigs. She was reading *The Female Eunuch* and was angry the whole time she was reading it; she said to him, "You're a man and all men are shits." But he wouldn't accept that. He said, "Some men are, some aren't. You've got to get to know us as people." That was one thing. The other thing he taught her was how to pee. As a kid living out in the country, she'd always been terrified of sitting in the outdoor toilet, afraid that something was going to rear up and grab her from below and pull her down. So she started holding it, refusing to go to the toilet. She could hold her urine for three days. But Alan told her, "When you have to go, go!" She thinks it was the most valuable thing she got from the relationship.

It lasted a year but it was difficult. They were together constantly and never saw other people except those they ran into in the clubs; she neglected her friends to be in his company. They fought. He started drinking a lot, which she paid for with bits of Christmas-shopping money. And then, unknown to her, he began seeing Molly and telling her, just like he was telling Ruth, that he loved her. They broke up, then Molly dumped Alan for some Italian guy with a mustache, and Alan and Ruth were a number for another six months, until Molly dumped the Italian and Alan started hanging around her yet again. He phoned Ruth and told her, and she fled to Thunder Bay.

It took two months to get over the loss of Alan and the jealousy towards Molly that was eating her up. When she did get over it, she felt more independent and stronger as a woman. She "cooled out" towards men, figuring that her closeness with Alan was as close as a man and woman get, and if she couldn't have that kind of closeness again she'd settle for independence. Then she met Damien.

They were a striking couple. They sat in the south-facing window of a funky Queen Street café, eyes half shut against the wintry light and the cigarette smoke coiling up from their fingers, like two cats on a window ledge. Both wore broad-shouldered black coats from second-hand shops, and huddled down inside them as though to fall asleep there. Ruth's skin was as translucent and bloodless as bone china and her features were diminutive and lovely. She looked out from clear, unblinking, hazel-coloured eyes and sipped cup after cup of coffee with small, arched, peach-coloured lips. Since she wears only black and grey, the hennaed red of her matted mop of hair kindled, as it were, her whole appearance. By contrast, Damien was wan as chalk, with a long, pale face and long, thick white hair. Round tinted glasses obscured his bright, red-rimmed eyes, and even his jewellery – several rings and several studs, and a tiny dangling crucifix in each ear – was cool and colourless. He was an art student, or had been, and was living on welfare while waiting for unemployment insurance cheques (he had been briefly employed as a waiter). He paints and draws, and was thinking of entering an Experimental Art program at a Toronto college. He spoke very softly and with a certain sweetness. Ruth was in love with him and was very happy.

They listened to Billie Holiday records together and The Velvet Underground, Iggy Pop, and Bauhaus, and found only one club that played alternate music, *their* music, both of them disdaining the "electrobeat shit" favoured by the rest of their generation and the funk-dancing in the pick-up bars. They preferred the jazz clubs or staying at Damien's place, listening to records and getting stoned. They read the same books: William Burroughs, Andy Warhol, and Fran Leibowitz. They spent their money on records, foreign movies, coffee, cigarettes, and drugs. At eighty dollars a gram, MDA, snorted or injected, was their drug of choice. Ruth calls it the "love drug" and says with conviction that she can "handle" it, drugs being dangerous only if you use them "to escape a bad life". Her life, their life, was not bad.

At thirteen, Ruth was smoking pot. She doesn't smoke it any more because it makes her paranoid. Booze usually makes her throw up. She had her fill of it when she was with Alan, drinking every night at the clubs with him and his friends, and now hates to be around drunks. Drunks are "stupid", and Ruth dos not like feeling stupid. She's done Valium and Benzedrine; she hates bennies now – they're basically caffeine, so it's like drinking too much coffee and getting hyper, and she doesn't like feeling hyper. With cocaine she feels good for about ten minutes and then she wants more. She doesn't know about heroin; it sounds "boring" to her, even though she carries Burroughs' *Junky* in her bag and consults it like an almanac. Really the only drug she bothers with now is MDA.

Twice she has injected it, the second time only three days earlier and she was still a little unnerved from the experience, finding it difficult, for instance, to put lighted match to cigarette, cup to saucer. Among the four of them – Damien, Laurie, Laurie's friend Gregory, and herself – they had had a gram of the stuff. She lay down in the bathtub and Laurie "did" her with the needle and she felt the rush – the tingly feeling all over and the ether in her throat – and then she went a little berserk. She wanted to scream, to throw up. She was flailing about and screaming but Damien was shooting up just then and Gregory was smoking and all cooled out and Laurie told her she was going to be all right. She turned the hot-water tap on hard, burning herself before the others noticed what was happening – she pulled her sleeve up to her shoulder and peeled back the bandage and there it was, a big red welt of a burn – and then, finally, she could hear Damien talking to her. He was saying, "Relax," but it was echoing or "strobing", so that what she heard was "RELAXrelaxrelaxrelax, ITSOKAYitsokayitsokay," very freaky, but that's the kind of drug it is (mescaline, Demerol, and amphetamine), up and down, and soon she was up: she was kissing Gregory, she was kissing Damien, Damien and Gregory were kissing, she was kissing Laurie, they took their clothes off, she touched Laurie's breast; she was feeling good about everybody. The next day, though, she was down again. She took a bath and it all came back to her and she began to weep while her body floated out beyond her like some bloated, featureless thing, and the songs coming off the Patti Smith album, all about needles, were terrifying and she couldn't remember, had she or hadn't she been banging at her sister's bedroom door, screaming for Gregory? It would be six months at least before she injected MDA again. She simply did not like that feeling of being so out of control and unable to think in a straight line. She wants always to know exactly what she's doing.

In any case, it isn't the drugs themselves that are so intriguing to her; it's the culture surrounding them, the "danse macabre" of the needles – she finds needles *interesting* – and the street life of the Burroughs novels and the cadaverous, austere faces of artists like Patti Smith and Lou Reed, the life having retreated from their eyes as from the blinded saints on desecrated icons. But there's a difference between finding something intriguing and actually wanting to live it. Living it is about being desperate, about being a junkie, a bum, an outcast; once a junkie, Ruth says, always a junkie, one hit and you're a junkie again. Ruth doesn't like desperation. She had her little experience of it, the desperation of looking for money for MDA, knowing a party was coming up, wanting to do "DA", gotta have some, want some, really really want some, want a good time, and then not finding the money – fuck! – and scrounging it off her kid sister. She wants to be able to walk away from it; maybe it was a blessing that she had such a bad experience with it. She could have got into it but now she can move on. The mystique, the allure held her for a while, the pure theatre of rolling up her sleeve on the bus, taking out her needle, banging it for air bubbles . . . it was all an act, but at least she was being noticed. It's getting harder and harder to be noticed, Ruth says, but when she saw the real thing the other day, two real junkies, she was nauseated. That's not what drugs should be about. They should be about love, and finding a place for yourself.

Shortly after the MDA episode, Damien and Ruth broke up. He went back to live with the girl he was with when he had met Ruth: he told Ruth that he felt he had been "cheating" her because he was still in love with Anna. Ruth had known something wasn't quite right all along and had been "freaking out" around Damien, which freaked *him* out because he knew that she was freaked out, but didn't know why. They decided to stay friends, but shortly after that he visited her in her room and they made love and he freaked out all over again, Ruth said. But she at least was clear about what was going on: she had to leave him to do what he had to do with Anna, and she had to get on with her own life.

She's been a "love junkie", looking and looking for it, thinking she's found it now here, now there. She took her first lover at thirteen. He was twice her age, a musician in a rock band, and they had a "kind of" relationship. He would take her out, showing her off to his buddies, boasting she was twelve, driving her around in a big car and taking her to cocaine parties and getting laid, not just with her but with waitresses, models, the receptionist at a tanning studio. She got sick of it and moved on.

If she had the chance to go back and sit with that thirteen-year-old self, she'd probably despise her. She wanted to fall in love, has always wanted to, and settled instead for anything else that came close to it, usually sex. For the longest time she thought fucking was the same as falling in love, that that was as good as it got. Life without a man scared her; call it sick or weak or twisted or dependent, but when Alan broke up with her it was like the cosmos came crashing down around her. She was harrowed with loneliness.

Now she at least has an image of herself – an internal movie she can play before her mind's eye – as someone who enjoys being alone, in her very own place, reading and listening to music, and she tries to focus on that girl and take strength from her. But, to tell the truth, she's happier when she's in love and close to someone, and she knows that the next few months will drive her crazy, knowing that Damien is out there and she can't have him, knowing that she's missing what she never had – which is stupid, really stupid, and Ruth does not like feeling stupid.

Seven months later Ruth moved out of home. Those who called for her at her parents' house were told by her kid sister that Ruth had left home and gone she knew not where – no address, no phone that she knew of. By her mother they were told that Ruth had gone to live in a commune with a bunch of "dogs", which is to say a number of young men who hadn't the first idea about how to keep house, and that she was no doubt already sick of the place and, if you should see her, please tell her to call home. How is it, her mother wanted to know, that someone as bright and gifted and beautiful as Ruth could be so unhappy?

It was not, in truth, the happiest household in the world, this degenerated "anarchist commune" in one of Toronto's working-class immigrant neighbourhoods. To reach Ruth, you walked right through the wide-open front door, turned right from the front room (stuffed with foam mattresses, bits of clothing, old comic books, and empty orange juice jars), and climbed the staircase, stepping over small piles of trash, to the third floor. Her room was also disorderly, but Ruth's touches were obvious: her collection of black-and-white postcards on the wall, a charming wall cabinet lined with small pots of herbs, a pair of brass earrings scattered on a piece of blue silk. At four o'clock in the afternoon she was just waking, struggling out of a sleeping-bag to reach for a cigarette, her skin is pellucid and bloodless as ever but showing some bruises (she had a "mystery disease", she said, and nonchalantly wondered if it could be AIDS). She was pleased to be living there, if only because the rent was less than a hundred dollars a month, but the decision to move in had not been calculated – her boyfriend at the time had taken a room there – and she was still unsure how it all was going to work out. With her, she had brought some clothes, her bed, a small carpet, her books and records, and, of course, the blue Chinese bowls; these she kept in her room, refusing to give them over to the communal kitchen, where they would only get "scummy" and broken. Every three days she assaulted the "disgusting" kitchen with a rag and Lysol. She was the only one in the house to be bothered by stacks of mucked-up dishes in the sink, and mouldy and rancid food stinking up the fridge, and cockroaches skittering behind the cupboards. She had tried the tactic of posting friendly little reminders on the fridge door, but had been told this was "fascistic" – just as her desire to lock her bedroom door betrayed her failure to trust her housemates.

She will write a book about this one day, about these people with whom she has lived in considerable intimacy, knowing their habits and sounds and smells without being quite sure that she liked them. There were two girls, Gillian and Joan, whom she characterized only as "nice"; a third girl in the household, a WASP princess whom she rarely saw, but who had been busted for trying to forge a counter-signature on a cheque lifted from the glove compartment of her daddy's BMW. Other household members seemed also to have brushed up against the arm of the law; the two who defaced political campaign posters with anarchist graffiti, for instance, and the one who had been repeatedly stopped and searched while walking down the street, just minding his own business, or so he said.

The others were just bizarre. Brian, who had slept with every girl in his alternative school (except the two lesbians), in the commune, and at the local nightclub (including the stripper). He was tall and skinny, no longer quite the geek he had been in high school, and with a come-on to women that was evidently efficacious: "I have to show you," he would croon, "the duality – the pleasure and the pain – of Zen." Jack, who cut off his pink Mohawk hairdo because Ruth, among others, could not talk to him and keep a straight face, and who was one of the messiest people in the house, using his mattress as an ashtray. And Simon, Ruth's friend, quiet, artistic, happy alone in his room playing his flute whose silvery, glinty notes would wake her up in the next room and make her smile and snuggle into her sheets.

Her first responsibility to her new life was to pay for her independence: along with four others in her commune, she was living on student welfare. She was receiving $342 a month and a stipend for school supplies. From this she had to pay rent, utilities, telephone bills, and food (her mother continued to give her money for a bus and subway pass), an obligation that had not yet defeated her. She knew how to find cheap food in the ethnic markets, and her everyday pastimes were modest – reading poetry, scrounging for interesting old clothes in flea markets, nursing a cup of coffee while scribbling in her journal – although she did indulge in the occasional extravagance, buying a hit of MDA or a hand-dipped chocolate or a book of Edward Gorey sketches out of her slim earnings from odd jobs. She had been known to babysit to earn money for MDA and had lasted a few days at a frozen-yogurt emporium a summer ago, but then the need for employment had become serious if she was ever to save the mo-

ney that would release her from living at home. She found
a waitressing job in a small café near her school and
worked so hard there that her tips on the weekend (sometimes as much as one hundred dollars) soon outweighed
any reason she could think of to stay in school. And so she
quit, unconvinced in any case that the place was doing her
any good (she had been told not to read Camus, he wasn't
on the curriculum). A few months later, now living on her
own, she had a job in a trendy café in the Annex, the area
near the University of Toronto, bussing and washing
dishes and floors in ten-hour shifts for five dollars an hour,
money that went mainly to discharging old debts to
friends and to paying the rent, her own and others', in the
commune – there was always someone who was short at
the end of the month.

Ruth was never a great success in school. At fourteen,
she was pulled out of secondary school, where she had
been known as "weird" and "depressing", shunned by
those whose society was "catty and cliquey and full of
gossip". She was put into a private school for girls, where
she was even more isolated as the "weirdo" – the girl who
wore white-face, and many earrings all at once, and hair
that stood straight up, and, over her uniform, a jacket that
said (a friend had penned it on): "Viva la Nicaragua Li-
bre!" She was prepared to put up with the place for a
while – after all, her parents were spending five thousand
dollars to keep her there and she was learning rather interesting material, the poems of T.S. Eliot, for instance, and
the Russian alphabet, but not even the sonnets of Shakespeare could keep her long among the innocent little rich
girls with long, straight hair whose fathers were doctors
and lawyers, and had gone through the sixties with their
crew-cuts intact. Never in her life had Ruth been confronted by people who, en masse, thought exactly the
same thing about everything: "Freedom before peace", for
example, or "Better dead than Red". And so she quit, and
would not go back.

Her next school could not have been more different, an

"alternative school" that was, in fact, patronized mainly by the kids living in a nearby housing estate who were in school only because the law said they had to be, but would rather have been "doing" Lysol and peddling reefers. Ruth went there because she had run away from home to live with Alan, who was enrolled there, but it was one of the most depressing episodes of her life, hanging out with skinheads and glue-sniffers, and, like them, not having more than fifty cents to rub together and being unable to pay for anything to amuse herself with. She transferred to another alternative school, where, she was pleased to discover, ordinary classes were not held – a student simply consulted with her teacher-tutors and went home to do the work. Furthermore, she was under no compulsion to socialize with any of the other students; coming into the school only to see her teachers, she paid none of the others the least attention. It was great. She was a good student for as long as she took it seriously. But when she met Damien *and* took on the café job, she dropped out of school: she couldn't, of course, do everything. Six months later she was enrolled in yet another alternative school, where she was allowed to take grade thirteen courses (even though she had credit for nothing past grade nine) and for some weeks engrossed herself in the required reading for Philosophy and Logic, the Nineteenth-Century Novel, Twentieth-Century Poetry, and Play-Reading, although she had already read most of the books on her own. But now she wasn't feeling well and was already falling behind and was finding it difficult, in that screwy household, to be left alone to do her work. Who was to say if Ruth would ever finish school?

It might not be the most important thing, anyway. Ruth wants to learn how to write, to *be* a writer, perhaps, too. It scares her a little, the thought of putting her work forward for criticism and having it torn to pieces; this is perhaps the reason why she tends to write with flippancy and sarcasm, as though to signal to her putative critic that she herself doesn't care for her work. Ruth can "do" deep and meaningful, as she puts it, and keeps a diary where she does precisely that, mainly to keep track of what happens to her, to record it before she forgets, but this is not the sort of writing – "scathing poems about my last broken love affair" – she wants to publicize. Who cares? She wants to write about things that have nothing to do with her except that she, Ruth, created them. Ruth wants to be an artist.

She doesn't know what sort of an artist she's going to be. She could finish grade thirteen and study further – communications or philosophy, say – or become a drummer in a rock band, or get into some line of work that would yield the "millions" she would like with which to buy good clothes and travel and feed her friends smoked salmon and champagne. Or she could neglect to finish school. She could party all night and sleep all day, forgetting to go to classes. She could go to nightclubs that open at midnight, looking for a tall, blond, green-eyed beauty, and follow him home. Or she could just drift away, moving from house to house, abandoning at each move one more artifact from her earlier lives so that, finally, she had only what was in her pockets, a china-doll waif in an enormous coat who, when last seen, was turning a corner and disappearing just as someone turned to look again at her, thinking he knew her.

Families

"Hey, what's a normal family anyway?"

T HE DAUGHTER, who has decided to move out, calls the break-up with her parents "torrid". Her grievances are deeply felt if ambivalent. How can she fail to admire parents who have their own successful computer-programming business in Ottawa, to which they devote sixteen hours of every day and from which they extract a living that supports life in a big house on The Driveway, two cars, fur coats? On her own now in Toronto, living hazardously on student welfare, she sometimes accepts money from them: "I got traded in for computers somewhere around the age of twelve, so I don't feel guilty taking their cash now."

The break-up was a drama of mutually inflicted pain – "I love my parents intensely but we also hate each other very intensely" – and if it occasioned torrents of tears and lengthy, acrimonious argument, it was also, she perceives, accepted with a certain relief. The household, reduced to adults and pets, could reassemble itself in tranquillity and maybe even with some admiration for the spunky daughter who had "stood up" to them in order to pursue her own project. That the parents themselves disapproved of this project, the daughter acknowledges: "What do you mean you want to write poems, act in plays, sculpt?" She imitates their harsh, censorious voices. "What kind of practicality is that?" The fact is, while chasing after these ambitions, she wreaked havoc on the household, stumbling in the door at five in the morning, sleeping until noon, getting up only to wash and dress and go out again, to join God knows whose company. This was, of course, her way of saying, "I want to do and learn and create, to *breathe*, and I can't do it here among your goddamn computers and Italian furniture." But they could only see her as irresponsible, disorderly, and gratuitously bad-mannered. She is convinced that they are convinced that she is a "terrible human being".

Yet they all wept when she left and she wishes, yes she wishes, there could have been "some other way" to go.

Behind them, many adolescents see a Golden Age when the family was close and its members were amiable and solicitous of one another, when the child was unequivocally taken care of and the parents had no higher purpose than to nurture their young, and each other. Then, suddenly, parents have become unreasonably demanding, hectoring, peremptory. They're nosy, bossy, and unpredictable. How is one to live with such people?

"I didn't get in until midnight and my dad was waiting up for me and he goes, 'Where the hell were you?' And I go, 'I went to a movie.' And he goes, 'I didn't know that.' I *had* told him. So I got into massive crap about that. Then he said my room was a mess and my clothes have to be put away just so and he went through my drawers, *really* messing them up, and he's giving me shit and I agree to everything, just to get it over with."

In their survey of Canadian teenagers, Bibby and Posterski write that "only 65% of teenagers report that the family is 'very important' to them." Yet 90 per cent say that they "highly value" friendship and love, a statistic that leads to the conclusion that large numbers of teenagers must be looking for intimacy and affection in some relationship other than with their families. Why are their families "unavailable"?

In a word, they are living under extraordinary stress. Hundreds of thousands of adults are unemployed, unemployable, or marginally employed and live with their children in poverty. As various regions of the country move in and out of boom-and-bust cycles, whole communities flourish and then wither, and families uproot themselves and move on. Children are raised in apartment complexes or suburban tracts where their parents cast about in vain for a sense of neighbourhood. Parents quarrel, become drunk and violent, and divorce.[1] Single mothers, confined to female job ghettoes, pay disproportionate amounts of money for child care and struggle at home with housekeeping, regret, and loneliness. Meanwhile, divorced fathers may or may not pay support, may or may not have the time on Saturday to take the kids to the zoo. Like barometers of the domestic climate, children register their distress in the face of such difficulties. They run away, attempt suicide, become bulimic and anorectic; some doctors report that they even exhibit symptoms of stress-related diseases: headaches, stomach aches, high blood pressure, and high blood-cholesterol levels.

For all its obvious inadequacies, the family remains the institution where the most fundamental issues of relationship are negotiated: trust and loyalty, power and independence. A young ego can be constructed or destroyed here. Whatever the ostensible reason for conflict (curfew, allowance, dating rules), what is at stake is the teenager's struggle for the right (as acted out in relationship with others) to dispose of his or her own being. Small wonder, then, that the family, in all its various constitutions, can be the site of the most intensely felt exchanges.

The perplexed fifteen-year-old who says that when she was thirteen her parents "didn't mean anything" to her, but now she's "confused" because surely the fact that they *are* her parents must "mean something", is working out what one is owed in family relations. She "hates" her father, she says, but she hates to say it because it brings no relieving guilt. Somehow, she confesses, she "has to" live with the fact that he is her father and she is struggling to find the means to respect him, because, after all, he gives her food and shelter and education, without which she'd be condemned to be a "bum". *Why* must you forgive your parents *because* they're your parents? What does that *mean*? 'Round and 'round she goes, answering her own perplexed questions with the admission that, in spite of all their problems, they live together with great, great love, "like the Mob", doing crazy and violent things to each other but, after the dust has settled, forgiving.

Many family problems have been laid at the door of the women's liberation movement, including the withdrawal of the mother from her traditional role as full-time house-keeper and child-minder into the "selfish" pursuit of career or simple job; thus, the argument goes, she risks rearing a generation of traumatized children, not to mention destroying the family altogether. There are several things wrong with this argument. The women's movement didn't "make" women enter the post-war labour force; the expansion of the western economies in the late fifties and the ensuing inflation rate and depression of the seventies and eighties exerted pressures on the family that could only be relieved by sending out both adults to work. In the second place, it has never been established that a mother who works outside the home damages her children *by that alone*. In fact, it can be argued that the mother who works outside the home for wages is an invaluable role model for her daughter and an effective proponent of women's rights inside the home; the job may be boring and badly paid, but it brings money, and power, into the household and ultimately subverts the traditional subordination of the housekeeper-wife to worker-husband, which is not a bad lesson for any girl to learn! Finally, there was nothing in the narratives I heard from girls that would suggest that the mother, working at home or outside, is anything but the single most influential person in her daughter's life.

Most daughters are deeply divided in that relationship, even those most positively disposed to their mothers, like the girl who speaks of "respect", not love, for a mother who married immediately after high school graduation and raised three children before divorcing and going to university to get a degree: "I admire that and take my hat off to her." Or the girl who would not, under any circumstances, want to have her mother's life – a full-time housewife with only one child left at home and an alcoholic husband – but who would take her mother's side in any argument or confrontation.

But many mother-daughter relationships are troubled, even unhappy; and they are every bit as formative as the happy ones. Sometimes the daughter's grievances are petty, based on the daily irritants of curfew and house rules. Sometimes the daughter cannot even articulate her grievance: "It isn't anything Mum *does*, really, it's just the fact of her *presence* that bothers me. I want to say, 'Get away! Get away! I don't *want* to talk with you, look at you, be in the same room with you.'" And in other cases the daughter's sense of injury is palpable and hints at a still deeper wounding. In all these narratives, the capacity for empathy has been distorted by the competing claims of authority: you cannot *afford* to love this woman and to understand her when your own ego is under threat of absorption into hers. Mothers get trashed precisely *because* they are mothers – the caring, tending, obliging person you must separate from in order to grow up.

Eighteen-year-old Barbara has lived with her mother, a laundress at a hospital, for only two years. Before that she lived in Jamaica with her brother and her aunt. When the children came to Canada, Barbara acknowledges, her mother was suddenly "saddled with" two teenagers. Her reaction to her new responsibility was to be very strict. No dating. No girlfriends until mother had "checked out" the family. No white people around the house. No bus trips on her own to see her grandmother. No going anywhere on the weekend until the house had been cleaned. (This did not, however, apply to the brother, who was assigned no chores.) When Barbara turned eighteen, the rules were eased somewhat. On weekend nights she can stay out until two in the morning and her mother asks no questions. Barbara will volunteer the information about where she's going, but not with whom and *never* that she is, in fact, meeting her (white) boyfriend. "If she knows about him, she knows. I don't really care. That's her problem." The fact is, she simply does not discuss "personal" things with her mother: "I don't relate to her. I never did." It's a stand-off, of sorts, a compromise until she can leave home. ("Go, go!" says the mother.)

Carla on the other hand, knows that most teenagers would be happy to live in her home – it's big and full of nice things – but she herself is desperately unhappy there. For as long as she can remember, she has known that her mother doesn't "truly love" her father. She knows that both, in their chagrin and disappointment in each other, have turned on her. They pick on her, constantly carp and criticize, and let her know she's let them down. It scares her. She's *scared* to live at home. She *knows* her mother didn't really want her (after all, she didn't want the marriage) and remembers vividly how she wasn't allowed to make any noise when playing about the house. Remembers, and will never forgive, how her mother, drinking with women friends in the afternoon, laughingly told them all the funny things Carla had confided to her – really private, *personal* things – and they all had a good giggle. No, this is not a woman she can deep down love, nor is she someone Carla wants to be known by. Carla is just waiting to grow up and get away – to travel around the world and never, ever, marry.

Penny asks, How do you trust a woman who sent you to a shrink? A whole battery of shrinks, in fact. The typical middle-class family's strategy of coping with disturbance: you don't, because she's been *bad*, beat your child or throw her out on the street, you send her to a shrink, because she's *sick*. The process begins with something

trivial, Penny's coming home very late, for example, pro-
voking her mother into having a "spontaneous aneurism"
and wondering, aloud and at the top of her voice, wanting
to know and not wanting to know, what Penny is up to. It
soon escalates to a heart-stopping confrontation about
Penny's friends. Is her mother really prepared to hear this
– that Penny is a "bouncing bisexual" who's hanging out
with a bunch of artsy-fartsy intellectuals who have no
money but lots of drugs? This can only mean one thing:
that Penny hates her mother. Thus begins the succession
of visits to the shrinks until Penny finally just leaves town.

In comparison with the passionate and hurtful exchanges
in which mother and daughter actually engage, the relations between daughters and fathers are considerably
cooler, even remote, as though the father has succeeded in
not wounding his child through the simple expedient of
having little or nothing to do with her. Some examples:
the father who deserted the mother when the daughter
was six weeks old and from whom the girl has heard
nothing since, except, once, to receive a gift of, yes, roller
skates; the father who never ate meals with his family,
never went on vacations with them, never even touched
them, preferring his own company in a basement room;
the father whose conversation is limited to "How was
school? Did you have any tests? That's good."
    The father who is more involved may be a figure of
some severity – strict and reproachful, disparaging of his
daughter's friends and jealous of her time with them – or,
on the other hand, may be too "soft" and yielding and
imperturbable, as if it were all the same to him how his
daughter was behaving and what spiteful things she was
saying to him: "My dad and I will have a big fight and
then he'll forgive me. He'll forgive me for anything. I
forgive him for two days and then I hate him again."
There is something in these men that is curiously uncommitted to the emotional drama of parenting, which with-

holds anger and judgement and petition, as though the only way to win the allegiance of one's child is to be endlessly agreeable. From the daughter's point of view, this is infuriating evasion.

"So I come home an hour after my curfew, all psyched up to get yelled at. I'm clenching my fists and looking at my feet. Oh, God, he's going to hit me, I know it. And you know what he does? He asks me how my day was! I tell him, 'Fine,' and go to bed. On the verge of tears. Dad, I *know* you want to yell at me; you are *supposed* to be mad. At least give me the benefit of feeling guilty."

Other fathers and daughters lost each other long ago; there have been years and years of non-communication, slights and offences accumulated, false pride sustained. Now how does one begin to open up to this stranger? To say one is sorry for all the years of estrangement means to take the lid off the hurt feelings and the bitter resentment. As one girl said: "It's too much work."

Two adult actors, four student actors, three teenage hosts, and an invited audience of ten teenagers: Catalyst Theatre of Edmonton is in rehearsal with a show about the family life of teenagers. A scenario from a documented life is presented and the audience is invited to respond. For example:

Melanie's parents have separated, which wasn't altogether a surprise to her. Her problem now is that *she* has become the mother to her brothers and sisters because her mother, enjoying her new freedom, parties every night and won't even take the time to talk with Melanie. What should Melanie do? Audience: "Leave her mother and go live with her father."

Second scenario: Melanie is living with her father. It is the weekend and she is preparing to spend it out of town with a friend when she gets a call from her mother. Her mother would like to see her. Melanie, wanting both to visit her friend and to see her mother, is torn about what to do but finally decides to see her mother and cancel her other plans. In the event, her mother fails to show up at the arranged time and place, and when Melanie phones her on Monday, she explains simply that she "forgot". Did Melanie do the right thing? Audience: "Her mother takes her for granted and Melanie should stop hanging on to her. She should have gone ahead with her original plans. Everybody's lying to everybody else, and parents are always saying the wrong thing."

Third scenario: This is only the third time Elizabeth has seen her father since her parents' divorce. They are both a little uncomfortable. He mentions that he's moving to Toronto, and, by the way, how did she like the dress he sent her? He mentions that he's getting remarried and would like her to come to the wedding, and, here, please take these pearls, they're for you. Elizabeth balks at the invitation. She wouldn't feel right, she'd feel disloyal to her mother. Her father remains obtuse: he's not asking that much. And so on. His obtuseness escalates to pig-headedness, her diffidence to resentment. She gives back the pearls: "I love you, Dad, but you're a jerk." Is Elizabeth being too hard on her father? Audience: "He was trying to bribe her. He should be more sensitive to her situation, but maybe this is the only way he knows of showing his love."

Three scenarios are hardly conclusive data, but they were evidently sufficiently provocative to elicit the confident judgements of the audience. There seemed to me to be remarkably little sympathy expressed for the mothers in the stories and a corresponding quickness to support the least ambiguous solution to the dilemmas: simple desertion of the terrain of conflict. Resolutions do not seem available through negotiation and compromise. And adults, for all their maturity and social power, are seen as untrustworthy and self-centred, people whose motivations are embarrassingly intelligible. Perhaps there is no way for a child to find her way to a compromise in such shifting territory where it is no longer obvious what is required of her: dependence or independence, loyalty or neutrality, empathy or judgement; and if she decides to save her own psychic skin first, who can blame her? If her parents, in splitting up, put her interests at risk, then she'd better look after them herself.

"I can remember before they separated everything was so tense. There were so many feelings that hadn't been opened up, you could cut the air with a knife, and I just hated coming home. I didn't feel any love from them; they were so caught up with the tension between them that they didn't have any time for their kids. This went on for a year. I remember my sister yelling, 'I hate this house! Talk to each other, do something!' Finally, my dad left. After he had moved out, things started to happen. My mother let out her feelings of anger, she was crying, my dad started crying. . . . He wanted someone to talk to but I was really uncomfortable and very busy. I didn't see much of him in that period. When he moved back after eight months, it was such a big improvement. I was happy to have them together, but that was a time in my life when I wanted my parents to keep away from me and I didn't need them. . . . I didn't want to uproot myself because *they* were having problems. I told myself it was their problem, they were working it out, I wasn't involved with it, I might be affected by it but I was going to stay out of it.

"I cried one night and after that I didn't cry again."

Where, among these fragments of families, these re-alignments of relationships, these lurches in daily routine, is the safe place where the child will be cared for? Small wonder that the child's first reaction to divorce or separation is terror.[2] *What is going to happen to me?* She witnesses the dissolution of adult management – the household is in turmoil – and of adult personality: all is acrimony and accusation, recrimination, insult and obscenity, or, perhaps worse, icy correctness. She perceives herself, in the midst of all this agitation, suddenly and utterly on her own; larger issues than her daily welfare are under negotiation, and, for the moment, nobody takes much notice of her. Other, more authoritative adults, such as lawyers, accountants, and psychiatrists, move onto the domestic landscape, taking over where there once was a parent, now gone; the melancholy, the yearning for the absent one, are intense. The parent who is still on the scene, most often the mother, is forced to be both parents at once, the one who holds down a full-time job and the one who comforts and lends an ear. In practice this means, of course, that she is more the one than the other (first things first), and her daughter discovers she has less access to her than ever before: "Go to bed, honey. Mummy's tired." Unless, however, the mother, needing more than ever someone to do for her what she is doing for her children, turns her daughter into a sixteen-year-old "confidante", in a thoroughly unnatural reversal of expertise. In sum, the parents have abandoned the act of parenting. Once the child has her sea legs in the new domestic regime, she effectively raises herself.

I cannot think of any other explanation of why, in spite of the fact that the divorce rate in Canada has multiplied ten times since 1960, once the drama of separation is concluded and the new arrangement settled into, the children of divorced parents are not much different from kids growing up in conventional households. This point is made by Bibby and Posterski: "Teenagers from environments where divorce, separation and death are involved differ negligibly from other Canadian young people in the importance they give to themes such as honesty, hard work, politeness and cleanliness. . . . Once removed from the limbo of separation, children of divorced parents . . . hold attitudes about the future that are not dampened by their situations at home. Their feelings about getting married, having children and family life generally remain undaunted." Their point is that what children cannot endure is not so much the loss of a parent as the instability of living in that no man's land between one kind of family and another. It is not surprising that the young girl "grows up fast", having found the means, in other words, to mother herself. A school counsellor has noticed that children of divorced parents take up relatively little of her time, that they have "adjusted", they "cope"; they even handle the bizarre new arrangements – weekdays in one house, weekends in another, two Christmas Day dinners – with "composure". It's the best thing that could have happened, they might even say; now they are shared by two happy parents instead of one antagonistic couple. "Kids are more realistic nowadays," says the counsellor. In other words, they no longer have the expectation that Mum and Dad, sis and kid brother, Fluffy the cat and Rover the dog, are going to live happily ever after together like some kind of advertisement for breakfast cereal. "Hey," asks fifteen-year-old Sharon, "what's a normal family anyway?" Speaking for herself, she doesn't know a single one.

Kelly, for example, whose parents have both remarried, and who alternates weekly between living in the one household and living in the other, has, besides her own "real" brother, two stepbrothers and one stepsister (from her mother's second husband's first marriage) and two half-brothers (the babies produced in the two remarriages). For her summer holidays she travelled with her mother and her stepfather, stepbrother, and half-brother. She describes the varying family components with the utmost matter-of-factness; she is not, clearly, to be pitied. If anything, she is to be envied her multiplicity of familial relations, the web of caring and attentiveness woven around her by all her relatives. It's a contemporary version of the extended family, and all of it a far cry from the niggardly affiliations of the nuclear family, which has excluded, by definition, any members other than what Germaine Greer[3] calls the "copulating couple" and its progeny, which increasingly tends to be just one child.

Sharon and her mother constitute another kind of family. They display all the feelings and realize all the gestures of a much more complex household: love, admiration, loyalty, intimacy; sharing responsibilities, looking out for the other's welfare, opening the home to friends. Her parents' divorce seems to have been the best thing that happened to Sharon. When the divorce papers finally came through, Sharon liked the idea that now her mother has "sole custody of me and all my possessions" and that she is free of any legal or formal obligations to her father. Under no circumstances would she want them back together. But she remembers the break-up.

"It was the summer between sixth and seventh grade. I didn't see it coming. They just sat us [Sharon and her older brother] down in the living room and told us, straightforward, they were getting divorced. They didn't say they didn't love each other any more, they just said they didn't want to live together. It made sense to me but I was upset. I called up my best friend, I cried, and then I went to bed. I *cared*, but I didn't let it ruin my life; I had exams coming up. I went away for the summer and when I got back my mum had already moved out and the house was only half-full. I cried then because I missed her. I never cried because of the divorce – it didn't mean anything to me; I wasn't affected by it. Sometimes that makes me feel guilty, but divorce is so common you almost expect it to happen."

For his book *The Myth of Delinquency*,[4] the Canadian writer Elliott Leyton observed at very close range the circumstances of delinquent children committed by the courts to living in a "training school" somewhere in the Maritimes. He asked himself what could account for the fact that their parents, mostly working-class or on welfare, had washed their hands of them. "What are the pressures placed on those at the bottom of society that make many of them seem to despise their own children? What are the constraints that lead them, alone in society, to conspire with the social agencies to jail their own flesh?" The phenomenon he has singled out – that the middle-class parent, mindful of her or his social and economic position, is bound to re-embrace the delinquent child, but no such

compulsion directs the behaviour of the socially and economically powerless parent – leads him to the conclusion
that we ought to speak not of delinquent children but of
delinquent *families*. For a child who runs away from
home, preferring to take her chances on the street, who
carves up her arms with an X-Acto knife, who boozes it
up and pops handfuls of pills and fucks four guys in a row
from the tavern up the street, has been *created*: she did
not spontaneously "become" this person on her own. A
family reared her.

Everybody yells at everybody else. There are no civil
verbal exchanges. When the adults drink, the yelling turns
into punches, cuffs, kicks, swipes. A father may go after
his sons with fists, belts, bottles, and two-by-fours; his
daughters he may even rape, while the mother says to
them, "Wait till you get married. Then you'll understand."
The daughter persists in running away; returned by the
authorities, she's chained to her bed. Money for the kids'
clothes, for their breakfast or school lunch, is gone by the
middle of the week, drunk up at the bar. Insults, threats,
obscenities are routine.

This is a family at the end of its tether, but it would be a
misrepresentation of the "delinquent family" to locate it
only among the "underclass". The pressures of unemployment, poverty, and hopelessness may be most intensely
felt there – as though the "underclass" family were the
organ into which the body politic discharged all its toxins
– but the statistics gathered over the last decade relating to
family violence, especially sexual violence, have revealed
how women and children are assaulted in all the classes of
society. According to the police of Vancouver, fifty-two
per cent of the city's sexual attacks take place in the home
("You could almost say it's safer on the streets than inside,
when it comes to sex offences," said Sergeant Gordon
Howland).[5] In that simple statistic there is no complacent
suggestion that the home in question is necessarily "underclass". It was the counsellor in a middle-class suburban
high school who told me of a girl who came to her with

the story of her father beating her mother, and with the question, "Do *all* husbands beat up their wives?" She wasn't sure, you see, if it was normal. Another student from the same school has witnessed her unemployed engineer father get drunk and beat her mother, an act he claims not to remember when he's sober. "I've built a wall around me," she says, "that's ten feet thick, to keep him away from me."

A girl who's been assaulted by each one of her mother's boyfriends now says, at seventeen, that she's "hostile" to men, a reaction that at least incorporates an element of self-defence. But some girls are beyond defending themselves. It's hard for us to imagine the utter confusion they are thrown into by the father who provides for, protects, loves, and rapes them. How to comprehend the terror at his approach, *and* the terror that he will abandon them; or their blank despondency when the mother, the teacher, the police, the court, will not believe them, when the psychiatrist, wagging a knowing finger at them, says he's onto their "tricks".

According to the Report of the Committee on Sexual Offences Against Children and Youths (or the "Badgley Report", after its chairman), published in 1984,[6] about one in two females and one in three males in Canada have been victims of "sexual offences". These are, to say the least, alarming figures and have been challenged, but no one denies that young people are disproportionately at risk: four in five victims of "unwanted sexual acts" were under the age of twenty-one when the offences were first committed.

Of these, three out of four are girls. And, again according to the 1981 National Population Survey on which the report was based, 29 per cent of these girls were between the ages of seven and eleven at the time of first assault, and 36 per cent between fourteen and fifteen. No fewer than 48 per cent of their assailants were "friends and acquaintances", 9.9 per cent "incest relationship", 8.4 per cent "other blood relative", and so on. The Report refers to sexual offences as "endemic" and takes note of the fact that it is extremely difficult to be more precise about the nature and extent of the abuse because of the silence of the victims. "Telling others those closely-guarded secrets requires considerable personal courage since doing so invokes stigma, may result in the condemnation by family members or by persons who are responsible for their care and may lead to an external professional scrutiny of intensely personal concerns."

Not all family assault is sexual. Sherry's father beat her up once when she was in grade nine: she had brought home a desperately bad report card and he attacked her, first yelling at her and slapping her face, then hitting her once across the face so hard that she fell sprawling on the floor, where he began kicking her and wouldn't stop. She struggled to her knees, grabbed a hammer out of a cupboard, stood up, and told him if he touched her again she would kill him. Sherry's friend Jodi has been assaulted by her brother. He's a man with a short fuse and she grew afraid to be alone in the house with him. He's thrown furniture at her, barricaded her in the bathroom and punched her face as she tried to push her way out, slapped her face, punched her stomach. She was seventeen and felt defenceless: to call the police would have "killed" her mother.

Such violence in middle-class families cannot be explained by the socio-economic degradation of its members. Perhaps the more conventional models of psychodrama can help:

Consider, for example, the description of mother-daughter conflict given by a Toronto-area psychiatrist who has specialized in the treatment of the child and the adolescent and their families. "The relationship between mother and daughter is historical," he told me. "As a teenager starts asserting her independence and becomes a sexual being, you get mother and daughter competing for father. This is ubiquitous. What is *abnormal* is the degree to which it occurs; for example, when it becomes incest."

There is no such thing as an untraumatized person, he argues; everyone who has worked out the Oedipal relationship, who has developed a strong super-ego, who has learned to think abstractly, has been through the traumatic experience of growing up. Not everyone will make it. When a boy doesn't, or stumbles, he comes to the attention of the courts. When a girl fails – she is anorectic, suicidal, depressed – she comes to the attention of the shrinks.

Elsa's not sick or weird or crippled, she's merely in a rage. It's not she who is "dysfunctional", it's her family: divorced parents who cannot or will not care for her. Dr. P. is the sixth psychiatrist she's seen in her fifteen years – she refused to speak to the other five because, she reasoned, there was nothing wrong with her. Fair enough. But Dr. P. has told her that she still has to "work through" her anger at her emotionally absent parents. All the acting out in the world – spitting at her mother, throwing food around, urinating and defecating in her mother's bedroom – won't bring them back together.

Placed in a foster home during a period when she was particularly intractable, Elsa was a model child with her foster parents. But her own parents are far from model. What do they expect from her? Her mother, trying to finish her university education, had supported her father through law school. When he was established, he moved out of the home – "an indulged, pampered and narcissistic personality" – and asked for a divorce. Give him credit for keeping up with the support payments (so mother and child can live in a home in the suburbs), but, now preoccupied with a new girlfriend, he manages to see Elsa only once a month and "forgets" his appointments with Dr. P. Her mother, in the meantime, spends much of the day and night in lecture halls and libraries, her fridge is often empty, and Elsa is "screwing around" with boys, doing drugs (grass, hashish, cold remedies), and running away to live on the streets.

If the street doesn't get her first, she'll do all right, once she realizes that what she can't get from her family she can get from within herself or, if she's really lucky, from some friends.

Whether Jane will ever unlearn the lessons of a five-year-long incestuous relationship with her stepfather (it began when she was nine and ended when she was placed in a group home) is, according to Dr. P., debatable. What she has learned from having been sexually assaulted as a child is that all significant or intimate relationships have the potential to be sexualized; that is, not only may they be sexual, they may also be exploitative and manipulative. This after all was the nature of the "special thing" she and her stepfather "shared", an act that was carried on with a great deal of deception and veiled threat, and practised furtively against the fear of disclosure. When Jane learned at school that incest is a crime not only in the legal sense but against her person as well, she informed her teacher of her situation. The mother promptly denied it, not wanting, in Dr. P.'s view, to be forced to choose between her daughter and her husband. The stepfather likewise denied it, and Jane was taken out of the family altogether.

In a sense, this removal was too late to be of any help to Jane. She had already learned that she had some "special power" over her stepfather, something he wanted that she had, and that she could manipulate this power in her negotiations with him and her mother. For such a young and socially powerless person, she had a great deal of control over her interpersonal relations. What she did not have, though, were friendships with people her own age. It was as though she had been held enchanted in some kingdom of the wicked stepfather, confined within a dark and stultifying chamber, where not even her mother came to look for her. In the group home where she lived for two years, the other residents found her to be a "little bitch" and a "snake in the grass" – power-hungry, controlling, and aggressive.

In family therapy her mother continued to deny the incest had taken place, and Jane raged at her for this denial, and for having "allowed" the assault to happen in the first place. As for rage at the stepfather, this has yet to take root in her. Like her mother, Jane is unwilling or unable to take the risk of expressing open anger at her seducer: the wicked stepfather, after all, is still the head of the family. What would happen to them all, what would happen to *her*, if she drove him away?

In some families, the remedy for intolerable pain or unhappiness is that the daughter takes herself away – she kills herself, or tries to. In 1983 in Canada, 250 teenage boys and 39 girls committed suicide, a rate that has risen four hundred per cent in the last fifteen years.[7] Suicide is the second leading cause of death, after accidents, among young people aged fifteen to twenty-four. (Quebec, for some reason, has the highest teenage suicide rate in the industrialized world.) It is estimated that for every completed suicide there are between thirty and one hundred attempts. And, if girls are less successful at it, it is because they use less violent means – they will slash their wrists or take an overdose of pills rather than shoot themselves – which also, happily, gives them time to change their minds or to be found, and to ask for help.

As the 1985 CHUM radio documentary *Walking in the Rain* pointed out,[8] any *medical* disorder attacking young people on this scale would be promptly attended to: research teams and funds and publicity would be deployed in an effort to protect the young from unseasonable death. But suicide, like incest and battery, takes place within families, and there it hides, disguised and ultimately even denied by all concerned, because families are *private* assemblies of individuals whose dealings with each other, for better or worse, are none of anybody else's business. There is a dreadful irony in the possibility that the very thing that binds the members of a family together in a protective, mutually supportive, and intimate allegiance is also, when exaggerated into defensive and exclusive relations, the thing that obscures the individual agony played out within.

But increasingly, far from being muffled by parental zealousness, adolescent anguish is endured in great loneliness: over and over, the testimony on the subject speaks of teenagers' feelings of isolation, solitariness, abandonment, as if they'd been set adrift from the traditional points of succour – relatives, neighbourhood, church – but given no alternative alliances. Of course, this loneliness in itself is not likely to provoke suicide, although it may provoke depression and suicide attempts; but added to other factors it could be devastating. No one single factor "makes" a girl kill herself, but, put together, neglect and abuse, addiction, alcoholism and exhaustion, self-disgust and self-pity, can be overwhelming. Why should she believe that she can pull out of it? Where could she ever have learned that she has power over her life, or at least over what happens next?

Consider these girls. Her family flatly declared that Diane[9] could not see her boyfriend any more, period. This was the final straw; she was sixteen and was *always* being told what she could do and could not do: go out, make certain friends, see certain movies, buy this dress, that coat, enroll in this course and not that one. And so on. Now it was: you cannot see that boy again. She swallowed a bottle of pain killers. . . . Carla was tired. At fourteen she was exhausted, and everyone around her was telling her, hey, shape up. They had been telling her this all her life. If something went wrong, blame it on Carla. If she stepped out of line, everybody yell at Carla. Such high standards! Carla could never meet them, could never be as smart and disciplined and sweet-tempered and pretty as she knew they wanted her to be. She took uppers, she took downers, she swallowed seven tranquillizers and a bottle of rubbing alcohol. All that happened was that she fell asleep, and when she woke up she was still exhausted. . . . One girl's sister, raped repeatedly by her father, committed suicide.[10] The surviving sister tried it, too. Another girl, loathing and fearing her father for his incestuous assault on the stepsister in the bed next to hers, ran away from home and took an overdose of pills. She was admitted to hospital, released, overdosed, was re-admitted, re-released, and so on.

All of them survived. Did they really want to die? Yes, if to "die" means finally to sleep in peace, to float in oblivion freed from the pain of consciousness, to "be" in some place where the helplessness and disabled rage and loneliness are only a bad dream. Today is unbearable, tomorrow is more of the same, let there be an end to it. Did they really want to die? Perhaps not, if somehow they had been able to believe that they had the will, the force, the authority, the confidence, to change their hellish little world, that the pain could end without their having to kill themselves to stop it. But convincing a girl that most personal failures and losses and humiliations can be overcome, by the future adult if not by the adolescent, that the bleakness is not necessarily permanent, that "crisis counselling" for six hours a day, five days a week, for six months, can pull her out of her depression is not the same thing as giving her power. As long as young people (and young women even more than young men) have only the economic power to work at minimum wage and to consume; have no power to affect the decisions of their parents, not even the decision to live together as a family; have no political power in the mainstream of electoral politics, no legal power to live independently of guardianship or to seek medical care on their own authority or even to stop going to school, it is stupid to argue that it is "unnecessary" that they kill themselves. It is worse than unnecessary. But, to them, at the end of their limited options, there is precious little else that will empower them. In death, they will make their mark.

It came as a considerable surprise to me that my "Families" file – of interviewees' accounts of their family lives –

was relatively thin. They had, it seemed, not very much to say about their families, compared to the fat accounts of their friendships and their school lives. It is normal, of course, that adolescents begin to extricate themselves from the domestic web as they form the relationships that will mark their adulthood: friends and mates. But the interviewees' reticence was too often an afflicted one – uncomfortable with the things left unsaid or punctuated with bitterness – for me to accept it as merely normal. It seemed to me that these girls had simply ceased to live, emotionally if not physically, in their families. Nothing, or very little, "happened" to them there any more. At best, the other members of the family were registered as benign, neutral presences of little account to the girl's "real" life with friends and boyfriends. At worst, of course, the reticence represented a contained and papered-over anguish. Good, bad, or indifferent, family life was not a subject that inspired these teenagers' conversation.

That some individuals do live happy family lives is not the point I wish to make here. Rather, the collective pain of women and children in particular is audible and palpable and must be accounted for. What this usually means is that someone must be blamed for it – the working mother, the unemployed (or workaholic) father, the self-centred, grasping child – although this is argued in a quite sophisticated way. Neil Postman, for instance, in *The Disappearance of Childhood*,[11] isolates the phenomenon of the "childified adult", the grown-up who does not want to assume the responsibilities of adulthood, namely the rearing of children and the care of the elderly, preferring the permanent adolescent condition of living unmated and childless. Even more extremely, Herbert Hendin argues in *The Age of Sensation*[12] that parents "program" their children to commit suicide: because parents seek their own self-gratification and psychological well-being before they look after the sustenance of their children, children "get the message" and do away with themselves as inconveniences. Divorce, which only recently has come to be viewed as an acceptable, even desirable, resolution to destructive marital relations, is now viewed in some quarters as an evasion of the need to look after children's welfare, the argument being that divorce is undertaken for the *parents'* benefit; in Germaine Greer's *Sex and Destiny*,[13] divorce is the mechanism by which middle-aged men, succumbing to the western notion that repeated sexual excitement is the sine qua non of human happiness, get rid of their menopausal wives.

Though the disease or disorder may be obvious – immaturity, irresponsibility, narcissism – the cure is not. Greer makes the case for the extended family – as though we could all choose to live like Iranian shepherds or Sicilian *capos* and not be bothered by the sacrifice of female sexuality and education and labour on the altar of male prerogative. As for the legions of young adults who do not want to parent or even to marry, preferring to make money and relieve the stress of doing so at aerobics class, this is a middle-class scenario and has nothing to do with the "lifestyles" of the poor and the working class, who, under terrific strain, *do* raise children while keeping the wolf from the door. In any case, *how* is society to herd the unmarried and the childless back into nuclear families when the glue that kept the component parts stuck together – the forty-hour-a-week working dad, the full-time housekeeper mum, and the economically dependent children – has dried up over the last fifteen years?

It remains to be seen what people will recommit themselves to, if not the revived nuclear family. Time was, not so long ago, when young people talked about "intentional communities" and co-ops and communes, about smashing monogamy and reinventing the tribe, of be-ins and love-ins practised en masse, and of "family" which embraced everyone they had ever loved. No one talks like that any more. No one, apparently, even believes it. Pity the children growing up and provided with only their young and unrelated selves as a place to call home.

TWELVE

George

"I don't think I'm old enough to deal with this shit."

IN THE LATE sixties several hundred hippies and political dissenters settled on small farms, singly and collectively, in the Slocan Valley of the West Kootenays in British Columbia. They had come from far and near in a deliberate emigration from urban centres of compromised bourgeois institutions and corrupting capitalist exchange, and they settled down to raise not only marijuana, corn, and goats, but babies too.

Fifteen years later some of these babies are teenaged girls. One is George, eighteen, whom I met one wet and dark September afternoon in Vancouver in a tumbledown east-end house where she was waiting for me, a coffee pot and the fixings for Player's roll-your-owns laid out on the table. George is large and round and dusky with fine golden-brown hair that sweeps her shoulders as she talks. George loves a good talk.

She remembers a lot of moving around, the journeying of her parents in search of a place they could refashion as home. They began in California, in San Francisco's legendary Haight Ashbury district, where they lived at the time of George's birth shortly before moving to a commune near Mount Shasta, and from there to the Slocan Valley. Or was there a journey first to Morocco? She has a vague memory from her fourth year, of a long, plastered outbuilding on some land near Tangier, of herself as a little blonde girl hiding behind the dark-haired, long-haired, slender, skirted mummy who did not wear a veil but walked proudly in self-assigned freedom. In any case, Mum and Dad and George (there would later be two brothers) were off to the Slocan, like so many others she knew as she grew up, hitting the roads in their funky buses and wheezy cars, renouncing work routines and marriage, to find a whole new life in deepest Canada.

George's parents found it in Vallican, on a farm purchased from a longtime resident, with a big garden, a cow, a horse, and poultry. There her father, with long hair and beard, did the gardening and her mother the baking. They worked also to make some money, the Slocan, for all its bucolic appeal, being well integrated into the surrounding cash economy. Mother was a singer in a local rock band, Father an occasional chef and tailor (and landlord, collecting rent from an inherited property in the States). George went to school in the Valley, the butt of hippie jokes from kids who "ate white bread, believed in Santa Claus, and didn't know where babies come from," as she describes them. It used to bother George that she was a hippie, i.e. unassimilable, but now she would not exchange that childhood for another. She remembers the very first toke she had, at seven, and the houseful of Valley neighbours, their low chuckles and the songs of Fleetwood Mac and Neil Young and Cat Stevens her lullabies as she lay tucked in bed warmed by the communal cordiality in the rooms below. Even now, when she hears one of these songs, it all comes back and, as she says, "puts a peace in her mind."

Her parents split up in 1972. It was not a particularly traumatic event, just another variation in the numerous households George had already lived in and would live in. Her father took the older boy to Hawaii, while George stayed behind with her younger brother, her mother, and her mother's boyfriend. Then the shifts became complex;

her parents shuttled separately back and forth between Vancouver and California, Vancouver and the Slocan, the Slocan and California. Finally, when she was thirteen, George and her two brothers moved in with their mother and her new boyfriend (eventually husband) and his two daughters; George was in grade eight and here she more or less stayed put for the next three years.

Because her parents had never lived conventionally as a couple – she cannot recall seeing them together in the same bed, for instance – George claims not to have been affected by their divorce at all: *other* violences would hurt her, but not this routine domestic mutation. Her father, she learned later, was gay, had been so even before his marriage, was drunk a lot during one period, and "freaked out" at his kids, so that it was a kind of relief to be introduced to "Uncle Leonard" and to be told not to feel too weird if Dad and Uncle Leonard kissed each other from time to time. George did not feel weird; she already knew all about gayness from other Valley kids and stuck up for her dad one hundred per cent. Her mother's boy-friends, on the other hand, were unqualified jerks, and, although George has always been proud of her mother – has taken great pleasure in seeing her name up on posters on telephone poles – she decidedly disapproved of her taste in men, most particularly the man who beat her and who, in reply to George's protests, threw a television set at the girl.

George tells me her mother regrets many things about the part she played as a mother – that she wasn't often available to her children, that she neglected them while she pursued her disorderly career as a rock'n'roll musi-cian, and that she didn't teach them how to live in the world, so that George walked out of her house not know-ing anything about how to earn and manage money, for instance. But George regrets nothing. She wishes it was the sixties again, this time for *her*, so that she could hitch-hike around, happy somewhere, anywhere, under the sun, enjoying good dope and sex and good talk on the shores of far-flung seas, and dreaming, when she needs the comfort of it, of the one place she still has for home, a farm in the Slocan Valley.

George screwed up in grade eight. The year before, when she was living with her father, she did a lot of dope in his company. That was how she preferred to spend her time, in fact: skipping classes to sit in the park, get stoned, go to McDonald's, and then home to watch TV under the lenient supervision of her father, who did not take the admonitory phone calls from the school very seriously. The school transferred her to an alternative school, and there, in an environment arranged for "difficult" students, she had the most satisfying intellectual and social experience of her life. The curriculum was close to that of the mainstream schools, but, with a ratio of twenty students to three teachers, she became close to her teachers and discovered she was very smart in science and English. More than that, she discovered that she could be smart, and excited about her classes, and yet still party: she could come to school with a hangover and the teachers would make jokes about her holding her eyelids open with toothpicks. She could swear and smoke in class, and did not have to put on an act, which in her terms meant no having to pretend she was "nice".

The program went no further than grade ten. In grade eleven she was failing again, every subject but English. She hated school. She would sleep until noon, having stayed up very late, and would go only to those classes that appealed to her, Social Studies and English, and failed Social anyway. The teacher hated her, oh how she hated George. She hated the kids she hung out with, the jean-jacketed crowd, lippy and surly. But who was she to tell George who her friends should be – George would pick her own; it was *her* life. This was her life: rushing to school five minutes before the bell, rushing out to meet the gang in the park, maybe twenty of them, or at the Britan-

nia Community Centre, just sitting around talking, jok-
ing, arm-wrestling, shooting some pool, spending hours
and hours like this, until it was too late and she was too
tired to do homework or get up in the morning. She still
likes to hang out like that, doing what kids like to do.
She's just a bigger kid.

She quit school at seventeen and got a job as a cashier
in a small neighbourhood grocery, starting at $4.50 an
hour and getting raises, over six months, to $5.00 and then
to $5.25. She cleared eight hundred dollars a month, the
most money she'd ever had in her life, but she worked
hard for it, the hardest she'd ever done. She checked stock,
stacked the shelves, washed them and the cooler cases
down, washed the produce, and operated the computerized cash register – all of which she learned to do within a
month of her employment. She loved working in the
neighbourhood, and walking down the avenue to the
store, waving at friends and customers who would always
have a "hello" for her and a snippet from the story of their
lives, and maybe an invitation to a party. She was always
more than an employee. As far as her boss Teresa was
concerned, she was like a daughter, a member of the family who worked together in the store.

It was lovely while it lasted. But, if George was like a
daughter, then Teresa of necessity was like a mother.
Teresa would advise George, urge her to move out of
home, console her when she wept over the cash register
after a bad scene with her boyfriend, and cheer her up
with ice-cream cones. But the initial warmth chilled as
George resisted Teresa's increasingly pressing maternal
demands: it *felt* as if George was constantly under surveillance and it seemed to her that Teresa enjoyed yelling at
her, finding fault with all she did and said, and arguing
with her decisions. Finally, on her birthday, she phoned in
"sick" so she could spend the day partying with friends,
and the next day came to work only to be greeted with a
blast from Teresa – "You think that's all there is to life,
partying?" – and fired on the spot. George knew Teresa

wanted her to plead for her job, to ask forgiveness and throw herself on Teresa's charity, but George would do no such thing. She just smiled and walked out. Weeks later, when George dropped by to buy a snack at the store, the staff told her they weren't allowed to serve her.

For those few months, George had money. Every two weeks she took her pay cheque to the credit union (she had learned to bank, and never to write a bad cheque) and put some into savings, but the largest part of it was spending-money. She gave her mother a hundred dollars from every cheque for room and board and then, when she had moved out, spent at least five hundred dollars out of eight hundred on rent, utilities, and food. She'd buy second-hand furniture, cassette tapes, and cotton sweats, she'd buy posters and dope and cheap restaurant meals: spending money was its own entertainment. But there was always just enough to last between pay cheques.

George, you see, loves to party. She'd go to a couple of favourite bars, spend $4.50 on a rye and Seven, buy her friends drinks, buy the DJ and the bouncer a drink, get drunk – she was happy in those days. Night after night after night it was the same: the same big party at the same bars and then, after hours, a party at someone's house. If she ate, she almost didn't notice, grabbing bags of chips and hamburgers on the run between parties. It was a gas.

She had moved out of her mother's house and into an apartment with a girlfriend and the friend's brother but was rarely there, "way up at Nanaimo and Twenty-second". Mainly she was out partying or, on her days off, sleeping all day. But, to tell the truth, she was also afraid of the brother, a big, weird guy who yelled a lot. One day, in one of his weird moods, he taunted her about her breasts ("Still growing, eh?") and she told him to shut up, and he came up to her, flashing the fish-cutting knife, and in one swoop slit open her shirt and said that any time she wanted to leave was fine with him: she was gone. She moved into her own apartment closer to work and to her favourite bar, but the two months she was living there she slept alone exactly three times. Her boyfriend hung around a lot and so did her friends – she always had a bottle of Jack Daniels on hand. She was taking it easy, going to the bars, to the beach, then back to the house with friends to keep her company.

When she moved in with her brother, the partying got even wilder. She had lost her job but still had some savings until the welfare cheques would start to come in ($340 a month), and, as for her brother, she didn't even want to know where *his* money was coming from: all she wanted to know was, would there be the money *this* day to party? At six o'clock, friends, mainly boys, would start to arrive, and the drinking and the toking and the craziness would go on until two, three, four in the morning. There was a fight once and George, not even knowing what it had been about, mopped up the blood in the hallway. There had been a hilarious night with George giving all the guys Mohawk hair-cuts. And there was another night in the park with three girlfriends, four double hits of acid, two twenty-six-ouncers of Southern Comfort and one of coconut liqueur among them. George fried her brain that night; the next day she noticed the shattered mirror and the shredded jumpsuit in her bedroom and could not, for love or money, recall what on earth had happened. It had been fun, though.

At first, living on welfare didn't seem to cramp her style ("I did as much partying as ever"), but eventually it began to get her down, not having enough money to pay for more than her rent and a bottle of Jack Daniels, borrowing money, hanging around her mother's house to watch TV. Her brother started to bug her about her friends – "You are all becoming such bitches!" – and she seriously considered moving out. Who needed the aggravation? The constant partying – the boozing and the hangovers, the fooling around, and the fact that she did all the cleaning up – was making her tired, believe it or not, and so she moved in with a girlfriend and her mother, where, to judge from the religious paraphernalia scattered about the kitchen shelves and walls, partying is not on the agenda. This is where I meet her: under the crucifixes, drinking coffee. She's into reading now (Stephen King and C.S. Lewis) and collecting pictures of James Dean and meeting friends, the "Brit bums", over the pool tables at the Britannia teen centre.

She has no boyfriend at the moment. Boyfriends, on the whole, just cause George a lot of grief; take, as examples, her very first one and her latest. She was thirteen, he was fourteen, they were both brand-new to sex and, to her infinite surprise, she got pregnant. She had been using a cervical cap, but it was less than one-hundred-per-cent effective, obviously, and she sought an abortion. The fact that, even when you try to prevent it, you can sometimes get pregnant makes her pro-abortion in her views. That, and the prospect of herself at thirteen raising a child alone (the boyfriend split) and on welfare (how could she work *and* raise a baby?): "There was *nothing* in my mind that wanted me to keep that baby." Some dope dealers she knows paid for the abortion. As for her latest boyfriend, she loved him and loves him still; he's sweet and handsome and sulky. But since he finds it hard to stay with just one girl and since George is the kind of girl who likes one guy at a time, she realized after weeks of heartbreak it just wasn't going to work out and they parted company. He immediately started going with her best friend. George totally hates her friend now, but for Danny, the ex-boyfriend, she can still summon a wistful half-smile and a faraway look of troubled remembrance.

She met him through the girlfriend: he was gorgeous. Although he was only half Filipino, he called himself a Filipino and was very, very proud of it. He was living on welfare and would go fishing from time to time, bringing back to George the fruit of these occasional labours, but mainly he liked to get stoned, to drink, to run around with women. She had heard he was bad news but it didn't matter; she was in love. Even when he slept with one of her friends a week before her birthday (had he no conscience?) and still showed up at her place as though nothing had happened, arms full of flowers, she could only weep from confusion and relief. Even when she heard that he'd beaten up every one of his previous girlfriends, she could take pride in the fact that he'd never beaten her. He slammed her up against a wall once, but he never hit her. Even after she'd told him to get lost, she would cry and cry for all the love she'd wasted on him. He still calls her, sometimes at four in the morning, drunk and weeping, just to talk. It's very confusing for George. She still has feelings but he doesn't want her the way she wants him. "I don't think I'm old enough to deal with this shit," she said to me. "I don't think anybody is old enough."

Now she's trying to figure things out about her whole life. It feels overwhelming – "I don't even know sometimes what it is I'm supposed to be figuring out" – but she's sure she can think her way through it. She needs to find another job, but one in which she doesn't feel she has to stay on just because she needs the money too badly. (Thank God, she says, that she's never learned to type.) She wants to finish high school, which means going to night school, a schedule that would eat up all her time. She'd like to go to art school, to travel. "I'm good at painting. I like dancing. I'd like to go to aerobics classes. I want a career, like Commercial Design, that I have to go to school for, that pays well, that I go nine-to-five for and retire from at sixty-five."

This is what it's come down to then, the great hippie experiment of the Slocan Valley, circa 1969 – aerobics classes, and worrying about the pension plan in the year 2032?

THIRTEEN

Outsiders

"You'll have to forgive me. I didn't know anybody gave a good goddamn."

Living Successfully at STOP *86: For A Pleasant and Relaxed Atmosphere: 1) One chore a day is required to be done by each resident. 2) Be responsible for all your own belongings. 3) We are* NOT *responsible for stolen goods. 4) Mice and bugs are* PESTS, NO *food stored in rooms. 5) No smoking upstairs or in the kitchen!!!*

IN THE LATE sixties, with the flotsam and jetsam of the youth movements bobbing visibly in the public spaces of Canadian cities – abandoned by family and bereft of home – the YWCA on McGill Street in Toronto opened its basement to kids who needed a place to crash for the night. Later they moved this operation over to Spadina into a house leased from the city, offering shelter for some twelve or fifteen street kids and a program that spoke of the degeneration of the counter-cultural project from optimistic self-organization (hippies taking care of each other in communes and on "hog farms") to demoralized dependency (runaways and drop-outs lining up hungry and sick and cold at soup kitchens). Besides shelter, the house staff offered counselling regarding health care, job search, and social assistance. When the operation, now aimed at sixteen- to twenty-five-year-old women, moved to Madison Avenue as STOP 86 ("a women's crisis and planning centre"), it kept all these services and added others (nutrition and educational and vocational counselling and organized recreation), testifying to the desperation of young women without home or money or friend, the dream of the gypsy life lived in fellowship and supported by communal industry now blown away in the wind.

The house rouses itself at seven o'clock, bustling around in the rooms making beds (four, five, six women share a room) and flitting to and from the bathrooms, sitting down to breakfast at 7:30, checking in with staff at 8:30 (going over the day's timetable of job search and interviews, apartment-hunting, appointments to keep at this and that agency) and picking up bag lunches and bus tickets and sanitary napkins, and running or sidling out the door by 9:30. But if a girl has arrived overnight (at 4 a.m., say, having been locked out of her apartment by her lover or her mother or her mother's lover), or is emotionally incapable of making appointments and keeping them, or is in a crisis, she will stay in the house and talk to Sharon.

From ten in the morning to four in the afternoon on a Friday, Sharon sits in the staff room and listens. The first story comes from a sixteen-year-old who arrived at the house the day the man she was living with had threatened her with a gun. It's a story that goes back through several episodes of assault and battery to an incestuous rape at the age of nine, and culminates in an anguished confession to Sharon that she isn't "attracted" to men.

Sharon's next appointment, with a weeping, pregnant seventeen-year-old abandoned by the father of her child, is inconclusive: the girl is in the second trimester of her pregnancy. Should she want to have an abortion, she will have to move fast on it before all legal possibilities close down to her, but Sharon is unable to determine, from behind the tears and long, inarticulate moans, what she wants to do. Finally, just before four o'clock, Sharon has the deli- cate task of teaching a girl, about whose odour her room- mates have complained, how to take a bath. Armed with a bottle of bubblebath, she takes her by the hand to one of the bathtubs and constructs of this pathetic event a "treat": the girl, marginally retarded, splashing gleefully in the water and sending bubbles into the air while Sharon curses the parents (foster or otherwise) to whom this child was not even worth the time to be shown how to bathe.

This is who comes to the house: girls who've run away from home or from a group home or who've hit Toronto from a small town, dreaming of setting themselves up in a cosy little pad and in a groovy job, only to spend their last cent on a roach-infested basement room that's costing them seventy-five dollars a week, and on the bus fare for one more fruitless visit to a Canada Employment office. Pregnant girls from out of town waiting to get into hospi- tal for an abortion or into a maternity home to deliver. Girls just released from hospital or from psychiatric care (depression, schizophrenia, attempted suicide) or from jail (forging cheques, forging doctors' signatures on prescrip- tions, theft, assault, attempted murder) who've looked up "YWCA" in the phone book or run into somebody on the street who tells them about the house. Rape and incest victims, battered lovers, battered daughters, girls without allies, whose mothers acknowledge nothing. Daughters of fathers who, having beaten them half to death, demand an apology for the attempt to run away. Runaways who are going to "teach him a lesson" and are never reclaimed. Street kids who spend a few days just to get warm and eat three squares a day. Hookers on the lam from their pimps.

At thirteen she told her mother, "If Dad fucks me one more time, I'm leaving," and her mother replied, "Well, he's going to, so you might as well leave right now," and so she did, with ten dollars in her pocket and a bus ticket to

Toronto. A friend had once told her that the place to hang
out in Toronto, if you're a runaway and have no money, is
the Eaton Centre, around the fountain, and she remembered this. With the ten dollars gone on cigarettes and hamburgers, she headed for the Centre, hoping to meet up with
someone with ideas about what she should do next, or at
least about where to go to party. Two days, and nothing.
On the third day, getting a little scared, very hungry and
miserably lonely, she moved over on her bench to make
room for a guy who said she looked like she could use some
company. A kind word, a friendly face, somebody to tell
her story to, and so she spilled it out, over the hamburger
and chips and shake he bought her, and at the end of the
story he said she could crash at his place until she was back
on her feet. She took him up on the offer and for the first
two weeks it was as he promised her: he kept his hands to
himself, and she kept the place tidy. Then one day he
brought her flowers and took her out to a real restaurant
and to a party with all his glamorous friends – real dudes in
Italian suits and dark glasses, foxy ladies on their arms, all
of them stoned on mysterious substances – and then he
brought her home and made love to her. She was thirteen
years old and thought she had died and gone to heaven. She
moved from the couch to his bed.

The next thing he said to her, after "I love you," was, "If
you love me, you'll love my friends, too," meaning she could
do him this little favour of screwing his buddies. She refused, and he seemed to accept this and took her to a party.
The party consisted of six men and they raped her for three
days. At the end of it, her boyfriend said if she didn't go out
now and work the streets, he'd kill her. She believed him. It
took her five years to escape: four years of being terror-
struck by the examples of prostitutes who had tried and
failed – a woman who'd had acid thrown in her face, a girl
called Ring because her face had been pressed down on a
red-hot electric burner and held there – and one year of
waiting for an unsupervised moment. She escaped to STOP
86 and there she stayed, hiding out inside, knowing she was

being looked for. If *one* hooker goes free, unpunished, then the whole system of the pimps' awesome psychological power will be in jeopardy. In the end the staff was able to get some money together and send her off to start over again in another city. She made it.

For A Pleasant and Relaxed Atmosphere: 6) Stealing, fights (physical and verbal) are not nice. PLEASE BE CAREFUL. *This is not tolerated. 7) Definitely no drugs and/or alcohol in the house. 8) No boyfriends or girlfriends hanging around on the front porch. 9) Prescription and non-prescription drugs must be kept in the office. 10) All women living here must be in by curfew or you will lose your space in the house.*

The announcement board is full; there are notices concerning the Charter of Rights and Freedoms, Handling Unemployment, sexual harassment and abortion, a poster advertising a Caribbean Calypso Festival, and a scribbled recommendation: Pot is good for menstrual cramps.

There are twenty-five women at any one time in the house, in various stages of crisis, and the girl who thinks she's going to be given her own outfitted bedroom with a door she can shut and withdraw behind into her private fantasy of the Lady of the Camellias had better think again. It's not quiet in this house; girls can arrive around the clock, ringing the bell at 3 a.m. for help; you don't know who's going to be in the bed next to yours when you wake up because its former occupant might have failed to show up at curfew and forfeited it to a stranger; there are no locks on the bathroom doors because girls have tried to kill themselves within bolted bathrooms. On the other hand, the staff will never turn down a hug, or tea for two, and there's a whole bunch of other girls up to their necks in it too and one of them, you never can tell, could become a friend and you could combine your welfare cheques and get out of here into a home of your own.

At four o'clock the residents start filing back from their daily rounds, some having accomplished what they set out to do and got themselves a job interview or a dental appointment or help from Legal Aid. Others, however, are crushed and despondent and bewildered, and now Sharon must deal with these, the rejected and helpless ones, the girl who's failed, for the thirtieth time, to get a job even as a chambermaid, and the black girl turned away by the umpteenth landlord, and the girl who spent the afternoon with four guys she met while sitting on a curb, all bored by the prospect of schlepping over to Canada Employment, who invited her to an apartment to listen to some music and have a toke; they all had sex with her and let her go with three dollars so she could buy herself a pack of cigarettes and arranged to see her again the next day to do it all over again. And she said, sure. She's telling Sharon all this and Sharon is asking her what she's getting out of it besides the cigarettes, and she's twirling her hair around her finger, saying, "Oh, well, you know," and she begins to cry and cry and cry, and can't be stopped. "You'll have to forgive me," she says at last. "I didn't know anybody gave a good goddamn." She's sixteen.

Coming through the house are women who have had to give up their children to institutional care because they could not find affordable accommodation as single mothers or who have put their names down on two-year-long waiting lists for subsidized housing. While waiting, they've made do in mean little rooms they're grateful enough to have secured as women on welfare; they stretch their budgets by feeding their children Kool-Aid and Kraft Dinner.

Coming through the house are Catholics from the West Indies who've "got caught" sleeping with men who, adamant to the point of violence, had forbidden them to use birth control and then abandoned them when they became pregnant, women who've lain mortified in hospital beds while nurses shout abuse at them, and women who, almost inevitably, contract an infection after an abortion even in an accredited hospital. ("I don't know what's going on in those hospitals but I have my suspicions," says Sharon. "But I put them on the shelf because if I start to think about it I'll go crazy.")

Women have come through the house who've started with drugs, fallen into prostitution and ended up in jail, and then have started the whole cycle over again. It works like this: they hit the streets, get involved in drugs, become addicted. It's very expensive. The best way to get quick cash is to hook without a pimp for as long as possible. They hook. A pimp moves in on them. Hooking is for real, now, and is dangerous and difficult work. They get high so they can do the hooking that they're doing to stay high. . . . It's a vicious circle broken only when they get busted and thrown in the tank for a few months. In jail, all they can think about is getting high when they're on the outside. They get out, they look for a fix, and it begins again.

They never get ahead. They never get out of debt. They wake up owing money to their pimp. On a week night, they're supposed to bring in three hundred dollars; if they make only two hundred and fifty, next night they have to bring in three hundred and fifty. They never make it up. On weekends it goes up to five hundred. The pimp doesn't care what they have to do to bring it in, whether it's ten blow-jobs at thirty dollars a blow or five of something fancier, just as long as they bring in the three hundred.

What the hooker gets in exchange is "protection". The pimp hires a young boy to take down licence numbers. Big deal. They get in the car and are never seen again – the pimp is going to go to the police? They take customers into some sleazy hotel on Carlton Street where the room is let twenty times a day and the sheets are never changed and somebody will come and check up on them if they're in there longer than half an hour. So what? They can be killed in the first five minutes. The pimp doesn't even put them up in rooms or apartments. He likes his girls to save him money by staying in hostels or sleeping in parks and abandoned houses. Sometimes a group of girls will take a room together which they pay for with the nickels and dimes the pimp gives back to them for the necessities of life (food, cigarettes, condoms). The pimp will make sure they have drugs of some sort, but nothing that will affect their performance; perhaps Black Beauties, an upper. The idea is for the girls to work, with minimal maintenance, until they drop. Then the pimp will get another string, from the next wave of lonely teenagers to drift into town. "We're talking," says Sharon, "about the lowest girls on the totem pole, disposable as Bic lighters."

Supper is served promptly at six, plates and cutlery and paper napkins having been laid out helter-skelter on a plain wooden table, and a big pot of chili placed at the elbow of the cook, who ladles it out with great solemnity. Girls stand up and reach over the width of the table to spear a bun and celery sticks or to seize the bowl of salad or a milk carton. They eat fast and without conversation, except for two girls who arrived just that morning at five o'clock (it's as though they haven't learned the rules yet) and who commiserate with each other about the early wake-up call, the friendlessness, the lack of dessert at supper. Half an hour later, those whose turn it is to do the evening chores (washing supper dishes, doing household laundry, collecting garbage, and cleaning bathrooms) are already at them, while a group of black girls is dancing in the dining room to the music coming from a blaster and making fun of the way white girls dance (ka*boom*, ka*boom*, with pelvic thrusts and giggles) and Sharon is back in her office, listening.

On the streets of Toronto, Cathy Newman, youth worker, walks up and down and talks to street kids, especially to girls, the runaways. The ones who have got away from "there" – the place where, under cloak of privacy, they were so often assaulted and disparaged – have come to ground on the street. Here Newman meets them and sees in them the effects of the sabotage they've experienced all their lives, undone by being female: "The weakness in being female and on the street is that girls have learned to be dependent; girls still tend to be attached to a guy and what he's up to." What he's up to: dealing, pimping. She runs the risks – she's his courier, his whore – and he gets the money, the leisure, the *respect*. "What's in it for her is that her dependency needs are met. Well, they're not really met, but she thinks she's nothing without a man." Sabotaged by femininity: wanting, needing a place – shelter, home – to make herself tidy, to have a bath. Betrayed by her own female organs: her uncared-for body, ministered to neither by lover nor by her own two hands, flares up in a fever and infection, bloats with pregnancy. The runaway girl is circumscribed even here on the street; even the street has its ways of cutting her down to size. In return, says Newman, she soon gets to be a lot smarter about life than nice, middle-class girls are: she's *not* a nice girl, wheedling goodies with the promise of sex down the line. She's a bad girl, bad-mouthed and in trouble, contemptuous of the men she deals with and willing to forgo some creature comforts, since to have them means always having to kiss ass. And yet, "they're also kids. They have their heart-throbs and they write his name on their running shoes, some guy who beats them up and lost his teeth last week in a brawl."

Newman has seen with her own eyes how more and more prostitutes are teenagers, fewer and fewer are in their twenties. It's a change from when she used to hang out in Yorkville in the sixties. A weekend hippie, she was nevertheless drawn to the street as a culture, a place to learn how to be a certain kind of human being: compassionate, co-operative, and unmaterialistic. Newman never hooked; she didn't need to. There was money around, from OFY and CYC and LIP, and from parents flush and friendly enough to send a cheque from time to time. All of that is gone, utterly. The grants, the cheap communes, the parents employed and vulnerable to extortion: "They're very interested in me being from the sixties," says Newman of her charges. "They ask a lot of questions about what it was like back then." Oh, the music, *great* music, and everybody was good friends, right? and the drugs were pure and the clothes were wild. Kids were special then, weren't they? Kids had power. Now the kids wait for Newman to do something. She had power then, she has it now. Them? Disqualified.

The first time Sandy ran away from home she was "almost fifteen" and fed up with her Christian parents' strictures concerning make-up and dating. She ran away for a few days to a friend's house. They found her there and brought her home. She turned fifteen; she was still not allowed to go anywhere, or, rather, not allowed to "hang out" anywhere. She hated her parents and was convinced they hated her. She ran away again, this time downtown, spending the day on the street and nights at the homes of buddies who would sneak her into the basement. She lasted a week – cold and hungry and sleepless – and then went home, agreeing to live with her grandmother, and to see a psychiatrist. The therapy was not a great success – she didn't want to talk, and the shrink didn't understand, and the whole exercise made her feel like her parents thought she was crazy – and she started showing up again downtown, mainly hanging out at McDonald's, cadging money for coffees and pills.

One night she took too many pills, couldn't walk or see straight, and passed out. When she came to, a friend told her that her dad was on his way to pick her up. She flipped out and ran down to the park to hide until the coast was clear; then, sneaking into her grandmother's house, she packed a suitcase and took off for a friend's house. Her parents, accompanied by a social worker, found her there and persuaded her to move into a group home. For seven weeks she lived in the home, partying and going AWOL, until she was placed with foster parents with whom she got along well enough for five months until they had a "big fight" and she was off again, followed by the cops, who told her she had a choice: a group home, or back to her parents. She said, forget it, she'd find a way to live on her own. She went to live in a house with three guys and one girl: it was a total party house, every night party, party, party, she had no money, none. But she was sixteen and not crawling back to Mum and Dad. An achievement of sorts.

And another: she was never busted. She was caught once shoplifting two candy bars and a tube of eyeliner – she was hungry, and needed eyeliner – but was merely driven to the police station in a cruiser and given a slap on the wrist and a probation officer. She found the whole experience deeply embarrassing and has been careful ever since with her petty thieving out of cars, her dealings with fences, her trading in drugs.

She knows other kids who are not nearly so lucky; they're in and out of the courts all the time, without a clue about what's going on except that they're standing up in a wood-panelled, hushed-up courtroom listening to someone read out the charges so fast he sounds like a chipmunk, something about jay-walking or glue-sniffing or being in possession or stealing clothes off a clothesline, and the lawyer is rattling on, the judge is nodding, there are words about the fifty-dollar fine they neglected to pay after their last appearance in court (that was fifty dollars they didn't have), about the fine option – working for a community program until the fine is paid off, which means getting up at seven in the morning and arriving at a particular place and staying there until the job is done, which means you might as well ask them to dance the Dance of the Sugar Plum Fairy – the judge asking them if they have anything to say . . . well, they just don't have a clue.

And another achievement: Sandy has never hooked. But her friend Debra has. Debra had problems in school and ran away. Hopped a bus and went east as far as the money would take her and got off. Met some women downtown who'd already been to prison, for shoplifting, and who told her what was what. Meaning, they introduced her to a guy whom she fell in love with, turned out he was a pimp. He put her on the street. Sandy thinks Debra was pretty stupid, working the street, giving all her money to her "boyfriend" so he would take her, in return, to Zeller's and "let" her buy a dress *with her own money*, big deal. And he beat her up. *She* works, uses up her body, burns herself out so he can get rich. If Sandy ever ended up on the street, it would have to be fifty-fifty with the guy, you'd better believe it.

Sometimes Sandy gets depressed, super-depressed, living on her own in the "party house", always wondering where the next meal is going to come from, the next gram of entertainment, how she's going to keep warm this winter and get a new pair of boots. To keep herself going she tells herself: You *wanted* to be independent. Now, you work hard and you'll make it. She will not allow herself to linger long over her regret at having run away from a place where all she had to worry about was school, where her meals were prepared for her, her laundry done, the utility bills miraculously taken care of. What she's most afraid of in her new life is that one day she'll look back on it and wonder what happened to her youth. On the other hand, she may have no money, but neither does she have a boss or a parent or a social worker telling her what to do. Sandy tells you she's free.

Do not deny Sandy the pride that comes from having managed to take care of herself. She and her street friends figure they know a thing or two about making it in back-alley society. They know how to panhandle and cut drugs and score a bed, how to get food and cigarettes and sex without paying for them, how to recognize who's "solid" and who's a "punk" (it's okay to scam a punk), and, when you're exhausted, famished, cold, sick, broke, pregnant, or just plain pissed off with the scene, how to rip something off a social service agency.

Normally, in good times, they wouldn't go near one of these places. Well, they might go for a free cup of coffee, to shoot a game of pool, meet a friend, but they wouldn't *ask* for anything. They know about social workers and shrinks and probation officers and counsellors – give them an inch and they take a goddamn mile. Go in for some advice about getting on welfare and you'll end up in some *course* or *program*, bam, just like that, your life all neatly structured and tied up for you. After all, *you* don't know what you're doing. Go in for some advice about the landlord who's just thrown you out into the street and they'll put you in one of these emergency shelters for women where there's nothing but crazy old bag-ladies shuffling around in oversize bedroom slippers, and a bunch of rules: wake-up calls, curfews, and, of course, a youth worker. Why do you think kids run away in the first place, except that some jerk in a suit has tried to lay down a bunch of rules and when you say fuck your rules, they put you on tranks and tell you you suffer from a "personality disorder"! So these agencies are just more of the same: lots of red tape and snoopy case-workers who think that if you've come into their office, you must be a basket case for sure, and who won't believe that, hey, everything's looking good, everything's okay.

Everything is most assuredly not okay, not when an emergency shelter for youth in Edmonton serves 20,000 meals a year, shelters 1400 clients over three years (twenty to fifty each night), and tries to figure out what to do next for the girl who wants to kill herself, the one whose mother never wants to see her again, and the one who needs surgery to restore the bone structure of her face after what her mother's boyfriend did to her with a base-

ball bat. Waiting-lists for the services provided by the
Ontario Association of Children's Mental Health Services
are growing longer by the day, and group homes like the
YWCA's STOP 86 are always full with the homeless and
penniless. Covenant House Under 21, run by the Catholic
Church, provides shelter, largely for juvenile prostitutes,
and a safe place to make the transition to straight society.
There are ingenious services, like the Beat the Street literacy program, a special project of Toronto's Frontier College for the numberless street kids who can't read ads or
street signs or fill out applications. Alcohol and drug de-
toxification centres. Birth control clinics. Native Friendship Centres. Sexual assault centres. Specialized Youth
Units in Canada Employment offices. Food banks and
advisory boards and liaison officers and "life skills" programs. And for those at the end of the line, who've been
through every conceivable institution – detention centres,
foster homes, youth assessment centres, group homes –
and who have once again been charged with glue-, Lysol-,
gasoline-, and disinfectant-sniffing, breaking and entering,
assault, prostitution, truancy, or vagrancy, these emergency shelters are residential holding tanks.

In Vancouver's Skid Row, the zone bisected by Main and
Hastings just a few blocks east of downtown, a girl's day
begins about four o'clock in the afternoon. She didn't,
after all, crash until the early hours of the morning. Leaving her hotel room, she'll check out the streets, see who's
around, see who's going in and out of which bars – there
are seven bars at her end of the strip – and who on the
street has money today: who's just been paid or cashed a
cheque. She'll check what kind of drugs are around and
what her friends are up to. By evening she will have found
someone to sit and drink with or to go visit friends with
and, if there's money around, to have a real party with,
drinking and sniffing and smoking. She grabs something

to eat wherever she can, a bowl of soup from the Chinese-Canadian café or from the pot on her hotplate in her room or, if she's desperate, from a food bank. If she runs into friends with money, they'll buy her a hotdog in the bar. By three or four in the morning, she's drunk and stoned and falling into bed. For the first few months on the strip, this routine seems pretty exciting, even supportive. The girl may not own much of anything, but what she does have a lot of is company.

At Hastings and Main, the girl is, more likely than not, native. This is her territory, claimed by earlier generations of native people who've left the reserves and come into the city to get ahead, only to be sabotaged by unemployment, the social services run-around, and a racism all the more profound for being deeply embedded within her own psyche, like the girl, half native, half Chinese, who called herself Chinese. There's only so much money on the reserve for training programs and higher education and so the girl quits the place, hitches a ride into town, and heads for Skid Row, because this is the area where kids from her band who have preceded her have ended up. She'll meet up with people she knows just hanging out downtown, share a hotel or motel room with one or two of them, and hit the streets.

What happens next is not encouraging. Upon presentation of her birth certificate and her social insurance number and some cockamamie story about being in an emergency situation, a girl can get money from an agency with which to rent a room or, if she agrees to live in a group home, she can score a monthly welfare cheque. Usually she lives in both places alternately, the street, the home, supplementing her income by drug-running for her boyfriend, by breaking into homes and selling a fur coat or some jewellery or a camera to any one of a number of guys happy to relieve her of "hot" items for a few bucks, or by aiding and abetting a gang of friends doing b & e's. Or by hooking. Why should she sweat a minimum-wage job in a dump somewhere when, for spreading her legs, she can make five hundred a week? Why hassle getting up in the mornings to go to school or work when you can party all night? And, if the landlord's coming around and the rent money has all been drunk up, hell, she just grabs her bag of clothing and bits of jewellery and make-up, some of her linen, and maybe the television set (whatever doesn't fit into the back of her friend's car is abandoned) and takes off for the next address, equally unfixed.

A hooker is not a prostitute. A prostitute is a professional, a full-time worker; a hooker hooks sporadically, for necessities, for family emergencies, for booze when the household runs dry. A mile away from the high-class white prostitutes working Granville and West Georgia, a hooker is a native girl turning tricks in Chinatown. The girl who's arrived in town meets a guy in a bar who invites her to a "tea party". She's impressed. The guy is a good-looker, talks tough, wears new clothes, has a place to stay, and, most impressive of all, is showing interest in her. She goes to the tea party and wakes up the next day with a needle in her arm. He's shot her up with a depressant and sends her, cooled out, out on the street. He'll take the money – he'll beat it out of her if he has to – but he'll offer in exchange a place to crash, and the circle of his acquaintances with whom to party, and, since she hasn't the first idea about how to do this for herself, he introduces her to tricks. Other hookers are freelance, picking up custom when the bars close or hustling for drinks inside the bars (single mothers with no extra money for entertainment exchanging a fuck in the alley behind the bar for a few beers) or screwing an old drunk and rolling him for his welfare cheque. They'll spend the money on junk food and pinball.

At two o'clock in the afternoon you see them on the street looking as if they just got out of bed and shuffling along with the slight sway of someone not quite sure of her footing, their complexions spongy and lacklustre, beyond the help of the purple lipstick smeared across their lips, their arms, disfigured with self-inflicted tattoos, hanging as though some essential muscular connection with the rest of their body had been severed. All too often they are ravaged by the perennial colds and malnutrition they succumb to, by the venereal disease and the do-it-yourself abortions they've toughed out. If they're wearing new runners, they just got their welfare cheque.

Eventually girls on the street will come to the attention of the police. It's not hard, considering the number of mishaps that can befall them, the variety of offences they are capable of committing: fraud, mischief, common assault, possession of narcotics, possession of stolen goods, attempted suicide, attempted murder, murder. At this point they will also come to the attention of Donna Hill, a member of Vancouver's native and police liaison committee, who's been on the street herself and who got bored waking up every day with nothing to do again between waking up and passing out drunk and who was angry because she knew she could function, and wasn't doing it. Convincing girls they *can* function too – can finish school or hold down a job or spend a day sober or take care of their kids – is what she's in place for, intercepting them at the point of their conflict with the police. She's there to help them through the system of police procedures, to attend their investigations, to speak for them if necessary. And, when all that is done, she takes it upon herself to get through to them, past the fog of their apparent indifference, their street shrewdness, their self-contemptuous slovenliness, to the heart of them, where they remember what it was they came to the city to do – make a life worth living. It outrages Donna Hill that no one, anywhere along the way of these girls' lives, has taught them, shown them, or told them how to take care of themselves by means of their own resources.

"What I'm saying is there is no accountability in the system at all; nobody has to account for anything they do. I can work with a street kid right now but I can't make her do a damn thing she doesn't want to do, and Welfare won't help me. Unless the kid says yes, I have to do something, this is what I want to do, show me how; and unless you support her continually, like a parent is supposed to, and be there for the ups and downs, give her a shoulder and a blanket, *and* be prepared to scold her, you can't do anything.

"We'll class anyone who's sixteen and younger on the street as a runaway because they do need specific protection. We drop them off at Emergency Services, but this little child, if she decides she doesn't want any of this bullshit, can just walk out the door, and we've lost her again. It happens all the time. We won't see her again until we're scraping her off the street or she's in a hospital."

This unaccountability, even among parents and children, is what Hill sees as condemning one generation after another to unrootedness and dispiritedness in the city. It is a process begun with the profound rupture between parents and children that the system of off-reserve residential schools represented in the life of the native people until only a few years ago: native children were taken from their families and placed in schools, often inaccessible to their relatives, where they were in effect raised by the school custodians. Such children became the mothers of the girls on the streets outside Donna Hills' office, mothers who did not in any crucial way raise their own children. Away from home, they never learned how; many eventually relinquished their responsibility as parents to social assistance agencies, so that many a girl has come to the streets from twenty, thirty different foster homes, wondering what it is so bad in herself that would have compelled her mother to give her up. (By the same token, kids who make contact again with their families and their band members very often blossom with the new pride of having relatives and an origin, a place and a people they have come from.) In turn, she has babies who are apprehended by the Ministry of Human Resources because, as Hill puts it, the mother "hasn't been looking after business". She parties every night, sometimes leaving the child alone, a parade of men clomp in and out of the house, she forgets to buy groceries. Not that she need keep up the Ministry's notion of "standards" – a bedroom for each child, a mummy at home baking cookies, a new winter coat each winter. Native standards, which is to say the standards achievable on $325 a month, are adequate: a place to sleep, eat, and be warm. But if the sixteen-year-old mothers screw up providing even this much, they lose their kids. They lose their kids all the time, for lack of what is known in the trade as "parenting skills": knowing which food is nutritious and how to prepare it, which clothing is protective, how to pay bills, how to get a babysitter and keep the landlord happy, how to choose trustworthy friends and how not to party, how to discipline children and give them attention. Her task is formidable: to be a mother while she herself is still so young, and working the streets for succour.

She's in grade eight, grade nine, and she's out. That's the most schooling she'll get. Either someone will take care of her on the reserve or she'll take care of herself on the street, running amok until she's twenty-three or twenty-four. At that point, she'll already have some kids of her own and be going one of several ways: on welfare but in stable housing; in an employment program; or dying, her children long gone from her into a foster home, and herself a casualty unclaimed by kith or kin.

At Edmonton's Bissell Centre in the heart of the inner city, Mary, the youth worker, knows that all she can do here is slap a Band-Aid on the festering wounds of her clients: she cannot restore them to wholeness. All she can do is refer them to other services, set up appointments for them, counsel them before a court appearance, get them a sandwich, a warm jacket, and find them a place for the night that isn't an abandoned house or plastic sheets and a park bench or a hole in the river bank. They come to the Centre because it's safe; Mary isn't going to call the cops or ask a girl a million questions about who the trick was who tried to rip her off and then threw her out of the car. In the teen drop-in room there's a pool table, a television set, a radio, and a telephone so they can phone up friends who are being held in the nearby Remand Centre. (They do not just walk over and visit in person because that would mean presenting ID, would mean being searched; half of them, half the time, are running around with warrants on them, and every cop knows who they are.) The drop-in centre has a hot meal program which, Mary acknowledges, is offered "basically as a bait": to draw kids in off the street so the staff can make contact with them. Sometimes it will be six months before a kid says anything more than "hi". But it has its moments, "like somebody who's only sworn at you for the last couple of years finally says 'thank you' when you give her a sandwich; for someone to say 'thank you' instead of 'gimme that fuckin' sandwich' is a major step." Mary has seen four or five people, in three years, get off the street. Four or five.

No wonder, then, that the need for services, no matter how disparaged by the clientele themselves, never lets up. It took a small lifetime for a girl to end up on the street; it won't be overnight that she finds her way back to home, school, friends, and safety.

Mary can see them coming. The girl's mother was on welfare – maybe had the kid just to get on it and never got off – and was partying day in, day out, so Social Services eventually took the child and put her in a foster home; mother went to court and got her back. This repeated itself until, by the time the girl was five years old, she was already screwed up, not eating right, not sleeping right, fidgeting and twitching. Later, in school, things started to build up: with no privacy at home (now her mother was pulling tricks at home for whisky money), no peace and quiet for studying, with the "social skills of a hamster", the girl began to fall apart, her grades collapsing, her attendance sporadic, her company dubious, and her pastimes increasingly self-destructive. In the end, inevitably, she was farmed out by an exasperated social worker to a detention home for kids under fifteen and then, later, when her activities had become flagrantly provocative, to a minimum-security detention centre. Having lost contact with her mother and her foster parents, released from detention with the clothes on her back, five bucks, and a "good luck, kid", she showed up on the drag, where no one asked her any questions: she blended right in, and didn't come out of the woodwork until, sick, cold, and hungry, she showed up at Mary's door in the Bissell Centre. She and a hundred others.

"When I first got here," says Mary, "I was really naive about this system and I thought, 'Oh, the poor little dears, look at them starving in the street.' But you start to see a definite pattern as to why they're here. You see that in a lot of cases it *is* their choice. A lot of them have been in foster homes but they've run from them because they had to be in at one o'clock on Saturday night or take out the garbage. So they take off from this place where they had clothes, three squares a day, a roof over their heads, and access to education – and at that point they've made a choice. They've decided they'd rather be down here with their boyfriends, sniffing glue.

"In a lot of ways it's secure down here: nobody really cares, nobody asks questions, nobody expects anything of them, and that corresponds to their opinion of themselves. How do you break through that? A lot of times you don't. Because it is that person's choice and that person's right to live as they see fit, and if they choose to stick a Talwin in their arm instead of going out for a steak, you can't take that choice from them."

She sounds more resigned than she feels, talks tougher too, in order to insulate herself from the despair and discouragement assailing her from the spectacle of everyday life on the drag. "A typical day for a kid on the street here: crashed out until lunch-time, get up, work Hope Mission or the Sally Ann for lunch. Then go see what you can freeload off the services around here – maybe free jeans at the Bissell store and groceries from the food bank – and that pretty well kills the day. When there's an evening drop-in here, that takes them to eight o'clock. At night they're in the bars or in somebody's house, partying, or pulling tricks." If they eat one square meal a day, it's because they've dropped in on the Centre; if they don't show up, God only knows what or how they're eating, or otherwise shoving into their bodies – a bag of chips, half a can of cold beans, a hit of Talwin (which costs fifteen dollars for a three-hour high), or snorts of glue or Lysol or inhalations of solvent – spending their welfare cheques every which way except on food and rest. At night high-tailing it to the bars to see what the dealers have for sale and then inviting every Tom, Dick, and Harry off the drag to party at their place, shooting up whatever is on hand. To this day, Mary doesn't know why they haven't died of malnutrition or been knocked over by a simple cold, their systems are so vulnerable. But a meal won't do what getting high can do: kill the sight and feel and thought of yourself doing what you're doing; it's easier to hook when you're stoned.

Get a job, someone is always telling them. *Look at all these want ads. Clean up your act and get a job.* Easier said than done. Most of them have been on the run at one time or another in their lives, from foster parents, from the police. They have the unkindest thoughts about people in authority, mixed with unalloyed awe of their power: we're talking about kids who won't even go to emergency wards of hospitals for fear of running into a cop, or to dental clinics for fear of having to give out name and address to a perfect stranger. But it's more complicated than this. It takes a certain kind of social skill – chutzpah, perhaps, or the gift of the gab and a conviction that your pain is not your fault – to be able to go up to a doctor and say, politely, reasonably, that you want help for the broken nose, the gonorrhea, the broken needle sticking out of your arm. We're talking about girls who would sooner wash their hair than their crotch, who even need to be told to wash their face too once in a while, and who haven't the first idea how to talk "nice". The question is not only who would hire her but how is she to begin to *imagine* herself walking into an employment office, blowing her own horn?

She'll tell you what she's worth: a hand job and ten bucks.

Unlike the kids who hang out at the Bissell Centre, a few blocks to the north of the Project office, the kids down-town in Edmonton do not belong to any identifiable com-munity: they do not come from an particular place, do not share relatives, do not make use of the services on a regu-lar or predictable basis. These are kids who have just hit the street from the suburbs, from small towns around the city, from detention centres, or who are weekend runa-ways, on the lam from parents who couldn't care less. That *their* community consists of other transients, hook-ers, druggies, pimps, drug dealers, and cops suits them just fine; they've had it up to here with social workers and probation officers and legal-aid workers, and all the rest of the conspiracy of do-gooders and mind-fuckers – *they'll* get their strokes from their buddies on the street. "Like-wise," says Brent MacKinnon, a youth worker from the Inner City Youth Project, "a lot of people aren't interested in working with kids who come in dirty with a negative attitude and who are working the street and involved with drug and alcohol abuse; their language is poor, they don't present themselves well, they're impatient. The kids will go into a reception office, the secretary will ask them to wait, they don't want to wait, they'll mouth off, the secre-tary gets uptight, calls the cops or somebody in, there's a confrontation, and the kid leaves and doesn't get the inter-view." You could write a book about why they're on the street. The point, however, is to get them off before it kills them.

They like to live in motels. In motels they don't have to clean up after themselves. They'll do whatever they have

to to come up with the dollars it costs to stay the night or
the week, but if they don't pull enough tricks or if they
spend the money on drugs or get ripped off, or if the
welfare cheque is long gone and they can't make the rent
payments, they'll crash at a friend's room or in a rooming
house or a flophouse, or they'll break into cars and abandoned homes. They say they want jobs, sure, but if the job
doesn't pay ten, twelve bucks an hour, forget it. Those
paid work-training government programs where they
place you in a hairdressing salon sweeping up garbage
from the floor? Get serious. There's a lot of money around
– check the cars, the condos, the boutiques downtown –
and they're going to get theirs. Meaning, if they're sixteen-year-old school drop-outs with crooked teeth, re-
cycled blue jeans, a nasty expression, and no fixed address, they're going to hook. Two or three times a week,
and they can make three hundred dollars. It never lasts, of
course. They're paying for motels and food on the run and
partying, and the boyfriend who hangs around between
appointments in jail.

It is the easiest way to make money. And at first it
seems there are no consequences. It isn't as though they
were hard-core prostitutes, understand: these kids are
mere "players", turning tricks to get by. "I need a place
to stay tonight – I'll turn a trick. I don't need a place –
so and so's invited me to crash with her a couple of days
– so I won't." Besides, they argue, it doesn't, deep down,
get to them; sex-for-sale doesn't "mean" anything to
them, so how can it do them any harm?

But it does, it does. They turn tricks to pay for drugs
(some of them have even been stoned since they were ten
years old, getting their first injection from their father or
brother fixing up in the kitchen), twenty and thirty dollars
a hit. Downtown, they're doing MDA and smoking dope;
closer to the east-side drag, it's glue and Ts and Rs, a
"highball" of downers (Talwin) and uppers (Ridlin) they
mix together and inject to get a buzz for a couple of hours.
There's nothing sacramental about this habit; it's pure

"get down, get wrecked, get bad, get crazy" until they can't even stand on the corners any more, their legs and feet – those pert little feet in the high-heeled shoes – are so full of needle holes. They're wasted. They've got bad skin and shadows around their eyes and they don't get enough sleep; and they stand on street corners in the middle of winter, in short jackets and thin skirts, trying to look foxy, but they're sniffling from never-ending colds, they've got gonorrhea, hepatitis, pelvic inflammatory disease, you name it.

Shelly Grover worked with them at Inner City Youth Project. Her personal beef was the guys who hang around them, the guys who say "I love you, we're gonna get married and have kids" – this is what they want to hear, to believe – "but right now I don't have a place to stay tonight, so get out there and do your thing and give me the money, sweetie." To Shelly, this is worse than pimping. Pimping is a business but this other thing is the cynical manipulation of unschooled emotions. No wonder, then, that for companionship two girls who work together on the street will often take a motel room and sleep together, sometimes sister-like and sometimes more intimately, for one night receiving the touch of someone who wants nothing back from them; as though to say to each other, "You just had to stand outside for three hours and you had to fuck a bunch of guys to get the money for this room, you're cold and you're lonely and so am I." For others, pregnancy represents the possibility of a genuine closeness with one other being and of getting off the street, but the reality is a letdown: their pregnant body and then their baby keep them from the company of their friends and boyfriends partying it up, and so they're back on the street, turning tricks, in their eighth and ninth month of pregnancy (some johns get off on that) or, post-natally, with the stitches still in from the episiotomy.

They get in deeper and deeper. They get busted, get a record, stay longer and longer out of school, becoming ever more unemployable; they lose their confidence, they get sick, burnt out, addicted. One day they wake up: they're twenty years old. Once upon a time, they were fourteen years old and down on the strip for the weekend, saying that whenever they wanted to, they could just walk away.

FOURTEEN

Nicole

"I want people to know who I was."

WE MET IN a little café near Pape and Danforth in Toronto's "Little Greece". She ordered only coffee and spoke, in a voice I could barely hear, into her lap. She'd been working at odd jobs since she was twelve, she whispered, because she's never wanted to rely on anybody, not on her family, not on her friends. "I hate to be dependent." She announced this with a sudden, audible ferocity that took me by surprise, lifting up her head so that her face was clear of her hair, and jangling the bangles on her arm. And then she subsided again. She grew up in Regent Park in public housing and has never gone very far away, even while living with her sister and her four-year-old niece. Of her father's life these last few years she has little idea, she does not spend much time with her mother, her friends are Blacks. At school they call her "wigger", for "white nigger". She does not seem to mind. She and her friends are "boogiers", which, I get the impression, is the only way to be when you're seventeen, hating school, loving reggae music and dance movies and old musicals on TV, hating everything that is depressing, such as newspapers, the news, and politics.

Nicole has always supported herself. This is her *leit-motif*: I don't want to depend on anyone.

They call it the ghetto of Toronto, where she grew up, at Dundas and Sumach, in a small three-storey, unprepossessing (she calls it ugly) grey apartment building in Regent Park, Canada's oldest and largest public housing complex. It houses 10,000 people, 35 per cent of whom are black, 40 per cent white, and the remainder Hispanic and Oriental, all of them needing liveable accommodation they cannot always afford to pay for themselves: they are single mothers on welfare, the unemployed, the incapacitated. It's divided informally into North Regent and South Regent; the former, says Nicole, is the more desirable place to live because the apartments have larger windows and balconies and all the rooms are laid out on the same floor; not uncoincidentally this is also where the white families live.

As though in compensation for the fact that they have not been provided with the fundamental wherewithal of security (a job with a living wage), the residents of Regent Park are the recipients of an extraordinary number and variety of services, among them a Boys' and Girls' Club, a health centre, an unemployment bureau, an adult recreation centre, two day-care centres, a Sole Support Mothers' Group, and a community centre still under construction in the summer of 1985, as well as an activist Tenants' Association and, for the last six years, a Teen Association.

The Association is open to all people aged thirteen to twenty-five who live within the east-west boundaries of River and Parliament, and the north-south boundaries of Gerrard and Shuter, which means some three thousand kids and young people who have need of their services and recreation: drug and pregnancy and employment counselling, recreational activities, and a Committee Against Police Harassment. (A report from the city's Office of the

Public Complaints Commissioner in 1985 identified issues
of concern to the Regent Park community, among them
that police use questioning, searches, and cautions of
young people "as a way of keeping track of things going
on in the community"; in 1984, for example, of the 961
"contacts" police had with Park residents younger than
sixteen, 166 were arrests and 388 were cautions.)

On Sackville, in what used to be a day-care centre, the
Teen Association sponsors dances, typically featuring
funk and reggae music. These are held in the South, which
means, in effect, that the white kids from the North don't
come. *Their* music is Heavy Metal. Too bad for them:
Karen St. Louis, one of the co-ordinators, points out that
these dances are just about the only event put on with the
black kids specifically in mind. "Why should the white
kids feel alienated," she asks, "when everything else is for
them?" Everything else being basketball and baseball
games and wrestling. ("Wrestling!" Karen slams her hand
down on the arm of the couch. "These kids watch *too
much* TV!") Cricket, the game of the West Indies, is not
offered. Neither are dress-making or cooking classes,
which would interest girls. What there is for girls to do is
to watch the guys play and to flirt with them from the
sidelines. "It makes me puke," says Karen, "the way girls
go all silly around boys in shorts."

This is where Nicole grew up. One senses that, at seventeen, she's outgrown the place but doesn't want to say so
out loud just yet because this is home, this is familiarity
and neighbourhood and memory, and you don't just
scrape that off your shoes like dried-up mud; who knows
whether anything like it will stick to you again? And so she
wanders around in the summertime, looking for action,
looking for friends, looking for the good old days when
kids would horse around together playing tag and piggy-
back and would go swimming and would wrestle, body
tumbling over body in the dusty grass. No one wants to

play any more; one of her old buddies is a dope dealer now and another is just recently a father, and everybody else just wants to sit around getting drunk in front of the TV, and even the old chicken 'n ribs hangout on Parliament is now a dope dealer's haven.

Nicole herself had a brilliant idea of something to do, a musical she created herself based on some Top Forty hits that tells the story of a young hooker, the barman who is in love with her, the bitch who's mean to her, and the pimp who controls her. But when she posted a notice in the Teen Association office, only three kids out of the whole Park signed up as interested in producing it. "Kids grow up too fast," Nicole complained to me. "They aren't into stuff like this any more." There are still some who walk down to the Eaton Centre with her, do a little break-dancing, and walk back, or drop in on her apartment with a pizza and some beer, but essentially she is alone, hating the thought of growing up, of not being able to run out of doors – down the dim corridor and out the dented doors – to play kick the can.

Having lived with her sister and baby niece for a year, in September she is back again living with her mum in the "ugly" apartment building in Regent Park North. She invites me there to visit one warm afternoon while her mother is out. The approach to the apartment is along low-ceilinged, linoleum-floored corridors whose walls seem to press inward, trapping the thick air pungent with a vinegary odour as though to mask the stink of something a good deal more disagreeable. When I walk into the apartment, Nicole complains of the new paint job, an unpleasant green that is already greasy and lacklustre. The drapes in the living room are drawn, the better to watch the show on the television set that dominates the room. At first she will not allow me into the kitchen but then changes her mind and ushers me in through the curtain hanging in the kitchen doorway and I see the naked bulb hanging from the ceiling, the laundry strung up on cords, and, on the scrap of a balcony, a great deal of rubbish in boxes and plastic bags. Her bedroom, though, is a space reclaimed from this oppressive meanness: bright-orange curtains and walls plastered floor to ceiling with pictures of Michael Jackson and photographs of her friends and relatives.

"They're trying to fix the Park up now, give it a good name," she says, on our way out of the building, "but when I was growing up it was terrible." She will explain what she means as we go on a tour of the Park, beginning in the North where she lives, walking past an ice rink and changing rooms, some sandboxes, a recreation centre run by City Parks and Recreation, and onto a knoll planted with a few spindly trees which Nicole calls a "forest". She points out to me how "boring" it is that every three-storey apartment block is laid out in exactly the same way; how are you supposed to tell which one is yours? We walk past the swimming pool where Nicole and her friends, late on hot summer nights, would go "pool-hopping" – scrambling over the chain-link fence and into the water – and past the baseball diamond where, when she was eleven, the black boys of South Regent clashed in a rumble with the white boys of the North. "It was like a war, about four hundred people mixing it up, people getting stabbed and shot, and the rest of us crowding around to watch." She describes this with relish, as though savouring an excitement that has never recurred.

The Boys' and Girls' Club houses the Teen Lounge in its basement; this is where Nicole used to hang out, in this room and corridor, with the pool table, the Ping-Pong table, the dysfunctional air-hockey table, and the piles of literature for the taking, untaken, about Sexuality and Relationships and Sexually-Transmitted Diseases. There is no one here. We carry on, walking along floors half covered in shredded linoleum, between the same contracted, greasy, dun-coloured walls, up the stairwells reeking of piss, kicking aside litter, and into the air outside, where Nicole turns sideways to me to ask, "Do you think this is like a ghetto?" From her tone it is clear she thinks so herself; what is not clear is whether this makes her angry.

Now we cross to the South, past the firehall, past the notorious Police Station 51 where, Nicole tells me, a man was once beaten to death for the crime of having been drunk. (In March 1983 a Regent Park resident died while in police custody. A coroner's inquest jury concluded that he had died as a result of having ingested a lethal combination of drugs, a conclusion that patently satisfied no one and was not, therefore, the one to enter Park folklore.) "If you talk back to the police, they chase you all around the Park, pick you up, take you over to Cherry Beach by the lake, beat you up, and leave you there." She says it with conviction. As we walk between high-rises, we have entered "Jamaican Jungle" proper, where, Nicole assures me gravely, two children have been kidnapped and found murdered, ten-year-old girls have been raped by fourteen-year-old boys at certain fire exits, and girls have been assaulted by other girls in the elevator "over some guy". This may be the Park but it isn't "hers": Nicole had wanted to be in the Teen Association fashion show but she was the only white who showed any interest; she dropped out, having been given very strong signals in any case that she wasn't nearly glamorous enough. Which is to say that she wasn't black.

As we approach her building and she points out which is her bedroom window, she tells me that last summer she was roused at three o'clock in the morning by a man's scream below her window. When she looked out she saw a man fleeing, another man pursuing, catching him, stabbing him, and kicking his fallen body before running away into the receding shadows of the morning. "It sounds like this is a terrible place where only bad things happen, but it was great to grow up here." She stands hugging herself, surveying the kingdom of childhood, and I understand that the reason she doesn't want to grow up is that she doesn't want to have to leave the Park. For all its nastiness, it is like a village, taking care of its own; "outside" all is phoniness (Nicole's word) and private ambition where people like Nicole are crumpled up and tossed away in bins.

A year earlier, saying it made her sick to live there any more, Nicole left her mother's apartment and went to live with her sister in an apartment at Bathurst and Adelaide, another world away. Her mother even said it was probably for the best; the truth was, she couldn't have kept her in any case. "I dominate my mother. She knows she can't tell me what to do, she never could. She's very childish. I have to treat her like I'm the mother. She would call me up to tell me she was depressed and was going to kill herself, and I would have to sit her down and tell her not to be stupid. She does it to get attention. I used to feel sorry for her, but now I've lost patience.

"Life isn't that bad. She's too self-pitying. She thinks we all took off and nobody loves her but I phoned her all the time. She says she's depressed and I tell her, well, she's sitting at home all day, she has no ambition. For a while she was going to some discussion group and really liked it. She said she was learning a lot. I could have real talks with her at that time. Then she dropped out and now she's depressed again. She complains about me, that I grew up too fast. She didn't want me to leave home. She says I'm too independent."

When she was a child, she loved her father. She'd wait for him to come home from work so that, little nurse that she was, she could put in the eye drops he needed against the glaucoma in his eye, and then talk to him about her day. He'd take her to the movies, his little girl, just the two of them. But then she grew up a bit and he began to behave badly, railing against her boyfriends and her friends. All her boyfriends, with one exception, were black and her friends were "different-cultured"; he was rude and uncivil to them all. She began to spend more time with them away from home than at home with Mum and Dad.

On her way home from partying, the closer she got to the apartment the more depressed she became. Finally, her dad threatened to kill her if he caught her walking around with a black boy and she believed him: she'd seen him smash the furniture, the dishes, her mother's rib cage, in a fury against his family. She wrote him a long letter disowning him as her father, the temerity of which enraged him further: "He didn't like that I fought back." Then, because she couldn't stand to be around him, she moved out. Over the next year she saw him but once. After he had gone too, she was free to move back. But that doesn't mean she feels she has a mother there.

"I had a boyfriend for four years. I met him in a club where I used to go with my friends to play cards. We couldn't keep our eyes off each other and two days later I started going out with him. He was cute, had a really nice smile. He likes to make jokes, fool around, cause trouble. We were supposed to get our money together and by next year move into the apartments across the street and get married in 1988. It didn't turn out. He broke up with me. I demanded my freedom: he's very possessive but I'm friendly towards people. I've got my girlfriends, my guy friends, and he didn't like that at all. I would go out with my friends and he would get mad and we wouldn't see each other and everyone would tell me stories about him and get me really upset. He denied everything. He said people just wanted us to break up. I believed him; he had no *time* to see anybody else, he was coming to my house every night. But it gets weird when people who don't even know each other are telling you the same thing about your boyfriend. He still denied it. But the more I heard about him, the angrier I got.

"I'm trying hard to forget him now. But, you know, we really loved each other. When we broke up, he cried on the phone."

She's had boyfriends since she was nine, holding hands while pedalling bicycles side by side around the Park. She'd like to be married by the time she's twenty-one, but the older she gets the more clearly she realizes it's not so much a husband she wants as babies. She'd have them even if she were single, she says, citing her sister and her cousins, all of whom have babies and no husbands, and who is to say their lives are so bad, women and children together, feeding and crooning and babbling together?

It's true that when her sister (actually her half-sister, the daughter of the man her mother lived with before living with Nicole's father) became pregnant, she "sort of" didn't want to have it and her mother didn't want her to have it, but Nicole made a great fuss: *she* wanted that baby! Nicole will admit that her sister grew up very fast, hanging out at bars at age fifteen, and that she'd probably have an abortion now; and that it isn't easy for her cousins, for the one who was deserted by her baby's father, and for the other who doesn't even know who the father is; and that you sometimes have to fight against your own kin for the right to keep your baby; and that you can be too young to have a baby (like her fourteen-year-old neighbour who's just given birth), too young even to be having sex, just like those people who work in birth control clinics, who give you looks of total disgust, think; and that just because you aren't rich and going to university doesn't mean you don't have plans that a baby would screw up (Nicole has lots of plans); but, damn it, Nicole wants her babies while she's young and she's not going to have an abortion just because of bad timing.

Why does everybody think that a teenage mother is a catastrophe? She can get quite worked up about this. Here is an extract from a paper she wrote for a sociology course in grade twelve:

Teenage pregnancy is known as a social problem but it
doesn't have to be a problem if people of society would open
up and communicate more with the younger generation and
stop seeing pregnancy as a negative thing. Teenage pregnancy
can be a happy experience if the teens were helped and given
love and support. . . .

"When I first found out I was pregnant it was no big deal

but now that it shows I finally realized that I'm having an actual real baby and I'm scared." This is a quote from a 16 year old friend of mine three weeks before she had her baby.

Nicole objects to the generalized statements made about pregnant teenagers: "If statements like these continue through society, the teenage parents will never feel good about themselves and they should. They shouldn't feel ashamed for being pregnant or for having mixed feelings about it. You will probably be scared, happy, and excited all at once."

Her feelings, too, would be mixed; babies, she has said on more than one occasion, are something she would consider having only if all her other plans fell apart. The very first thing she has to worry about is making money and saving some: her bank account fluctuates hopelessly. Before Christmas she had seven hundred dollars; now she has seventeen, having bought Christmas presents and new clothes and school lunches and – her extravagance – silver rings, at least one for each finger. She had tried, while at her sister's, to get on student welfare but she was given the royal runaround: the welfare people could never get hold of her mother to determine if she truly would not support her daughter. So it was more important than ever that she get a job.

Too shy actively to look for work, to answer classified ads and make appointments, she settled on an office job in a Yorkville restaurant where a cousin had earlier worked. She didn't even bother to ask what her wages would be; she'd find out from her first pay cheque! The work itself (a book-keeping job where she is responsible for counting out the cash for the waiters' floats and making sure the receipts are balanced) is "okay", but it is obvious from her diffidence that she is also thoroughly intimidated by this "high-class" establishment which serves "high-class" food to rich people – "I feel so inferior, I'm so afraid of making mistakes." For all that, she finds the food of the rich unappetizing (the sight of a shrimp makes her sick) and asked the cook for a hamburger for her first staff meal.

She was intimidated further when, expecting a Big Mac, she was served a huge plate including fancy salads and vegetables. She now takes her own lunch to work.

This is not where she wants to be five years from now. Nicole, a weak and lazy student by her own admission, hates school and has no plans for higher education. But she has dreams. She wants to be a professional actress, preferably in Hollywood. Even as a child she watched old movies on television and came to admire the work of Gene Kelly, Fred Astaire, and Ginger Rogers, who, compared to the mediocrities acting on television these days (showing themselves off in tight jeans and bathing suits with maybe one stupid line to say in the whole show), were *special*, were stars. She doesn't want to be a star, heaven forbid, just a "background singer and dancer" in musicals. She'd *love* to be in musicals; as a girl she sang and danced in talent shows and Boys' and Girls' Club shows and knows the joy of making rhythm and melody out of her own body. But the problem is, always has been, her crushing lack of confidence: a girlfriend tells her she should take singing lessons if she's at all serious about her dream but Nicole visibly recoils from the very idea of "pushing" herself in this way.

It is as though Nicole is always asking herself, Who the hell does she think she is to imagine herself on a stage under a spotlight like she was *somebody*? But that's not the end of it, because there is also a voice inside her which speaks, even as she sits curled up baby-like in the big chair in front of the TV, chewing her nails: "I don't want to die unknown. I want people to know who Nicole Paquette was."

FIFTEEN

Sexualities

"What are they getting out of it? They don't even get cuddled."

SHERRY: I love being a girl. I would never want to be a man. I love all the different hair styles girls can have.

JODI: I love perfume –

SHERRY: And make-up.

JODI: The greatest thing I love to do on the weekend is to spend an hour in the bathtub with a big loofah, get my skin soft, shave my legs and armpits and do my bikini area, give myself a facial and hair pack and then to make myself beautiful, put perfume and dusting powder on.

SHERRY: It's work but it's fun.

THERE WASN'T one of them who didn't enjoy her femaleness. I did not once hear that declamation familiar from the era of my own adolescence, delivered with exasperation or self-pity or regret, the irritated complaint of one who knows she has been cheated: "I wish I were a boy!"

Yet so many of them had been "tomboys", delightfully unaware of the soon-to-be inappropriateness of their behaviour, their enthusiasms, their looks, girls whose mothers let them run around the neighbourhood kicking balls and shooting pucks up and down the alleys and getting dusty and muddy, girls to whom it did not occur that their bodies were not instruments of their own agency. They look back on those child-selves and call themselves free spirits.

Then, at puberty, the great problematic begins. The girl's developing femaleness holds the promise of her ultimate value as a sexual partner (this is what her body is "for") and thus her entry into adult relationships. But it also exiles her forever from that society where there was no purchase in femininity, only the glory of being very young and uncontrollable.

And so the momentous physical changes of puberty are not in every case welcomed, even by those girls who will go on to enjoy this newly gendered self. "I really wanted to start getting my period because I thought then I'd be a Woman! But when I did get it I was scared and then I started hating it, it was such a big hassle and so yucky." Suddenly the procedures of her body become the subject of intense and intimate conversation *out of men's hearing* and the object of considerable scrutiny by mothers and gynecologists, not to mention horny young men in the hallways. Suddenly her body is no longer at her own disposal but has become a zone where others have competing interests – parents and boyfriends and social workers and ad agencies – and a territory liable to a whole series of catastrophes: diseases, pregnancy, rape, abortion. Her self-consciousness is acute; she has become a new person, one she will spend a lifetime trying to appease – the woman who has stepped outside her own body and reviews it "objectively" and who finds it wanting. She will never know again, in other words, the girl-child's blissful indifference to her own attractiveness.

Lucky the girl, then, who has come to terms with her woman-self, who, in the words of one sixteen-year-old, has always "been proud of my sex" and continues to be so and who realizes "there is more than one way to be feminine." There *are* teenage girls who firmly believe you do not have to be all girlish and cutesy and helpless to be "feminine". There are girls who revel in their femininity to please themselves, who enjoy wearing soft and loose clothing and bangles and scarves and musk oils for the sheer sensuousness of them, who love the feel of their own skin and the reassuring sway of their unbound breasts, without reference to the response of male companions. There are those who can even mock their younger selves who had not yet escaped the indoctrination of the media's view of femininity: "I shaved my legs, I shaved my armpits every day. I had an obsession with shaving. I wore lots of make-up 'artistically' done, jewellery, fishnet stockings, corsets. I plucked my eyebrows, I gave myself facials, I spent money on moisturizers. I wore high-heeled boots in the winter! I was thirteen." And who, as lesbians, need no convincing of a "female power" that has nothing to do with conventional sexual allure. Some girls feel it is an advantage to be female, to be free of the awesome pressure that bears on males to be "money-makers" and to win at everything, to be free "to expand our lives intellectually and emotionally" while men who want both are seen as "wimpy". Girls have the chance to do all those "fun" things, like doing up their hair and buying shoes and looking for the perfume that expresses their personality, and kissing and hugging their best friends – boys can't do that.

For all this freely assumed femininity, though, for all the gladness in one's God-given body and the rituals that celebrate one's sexual function, there is the tyranny of the sexual marketplace where femininity is largely constructed.

In the fall of 1985, for instance, a high school newspaper ran a helpful list of what was in fashion that season for girls: a "soft new difference" (feathered cuts and super-soft curls) in short haircuts and new hair colours (cherry, auburn, and copper); two "important shapes" in clothing – long and narrow, big and loose – and lots of bright colours, used to make "bold statements"; "big accessories like wide belts and mesh scarves and wooden beads; and the "healthy" look in make-up: gold and taupe eyeshadows, brown eyeliners, copper-coloured translucent blushers, and clear lip-gloss. A story running concurrently in the *Edmonton Journal* about teenage fashion noted that modelling and "self-improvement" classes are popular with many girls who lack the self-confidence to make their own choice of "looks": "We find the things that teens like best about our courses," said one director of a model agency, "are the make-up lessons because there's always such an immediate improvement." Pastel colours were advised. "You just want to see a soft blush and soft lips with soft eyes all of the same intensity."

All such counsel is couched in terms of promotion of the individual's peculiar attractiveness – "wear things that you are comfortable with, that show what you like and who you really are" – but such rhetoric is disingenuous. Neither the fashion industry nor certainly the girls themselves believe for a minute that "style" and "allure" are as you make them, that a woman is somehow in the position of defining her own appeal. Almost every girl I spoke with was acutely aware of what was currently fashionable and of the details that defined each separate "look", of where to shop for each, of the "statement" being made by other girls who were either ahead of the fashion times ("trendsetters") or behind ("bags") or in parody of them ("sluts").

It is also reassuring, I suppose, at a time in one's life when idiosyncrasy is rewarded by humiliation and exclusion, to be directed and told about the presentable, the permissible, the desirable as reproduced by one's peers. But the underlying current of anxiety is unmistakable – the fear that you will make a wrong decision about your haircut or choice of handbag or cut of jeans and incur the mocking judgement of friends. Or the fear that, just when you think you can relax (you *are* trendy, you *are* pretty), a new trend comes along, a new "look", a new set of must-do's and how-to's, and the cycle of insecurity and pitiless self-appraisal begins again. The images in the media, for example, are remorseless and relentless in their message that (in the words of Sheila Kitzinger, author of *Women's Experience of Sex*)[1] "you are deceiving yourself . . . if you think that what you are is good enough." Here, for example, are some of the contents of *Mademoiselle* magazine (an American fashion and beauty magazine for young women) in December 1986. An article: "Save Your Skin!" Several diets: for example, the Day-After Diet. Instructions about how to correct the problems of smeared mascara, dandruff, and "pre-menstrual bloat"; a column: "Help For Hassled Hair: Is your hair worst during winter?" A fashion feature about make-up "mistakes": "What went wrong tonight?"; a list of "what will help" if you suffer from chapped lips and split nails. Not to mention alarmist ads that promise the reader "cleaner days" with a certain sanitary napkin and advise her how to "stop a wrinkle from happening", and suggestive ads that promise sexual success with an anointed perfume.

All of which is taken very much to heart by millions of girls who dare not trust the authority of their own brief experience (childhood) of being at home in their own bodies, but look instead to the arbiters and monitors of femininity in the media, in the shops, in the eyes of men, to be confirmed there as "sufficiently" feminine. The confirmation, of course, can be withdrawn at any time; one has only to gain five pounds, be afflicted with "thunder thighs" and sagging breasts, or stain one's panties, to lose approval and be banished from this place where men find women pleasing. Or so girls fear. There is really only one way out of this arbitrariness: "I want to die young," said Jodi. "That way I will never not be pretty."

SHERRY: The pressure on girls these days is on losing weight. All the commercials on TV for diet pills and NutraSweet! It puts a lot of pressure on *me*. I wish I was thin. I'm on and off diets all the time. It runs in my family. There isn't one person on my mum's side who's thin. Even on my dad's side, everybody's got big thighs. It sure isn't considered ideal *these* days.

JODI: It has to do with the athletic picture of a beautiful body being lithe and supple, that looks like it can jump around and be real sportsy. This is the age of health, and excess fat is not healthy. But you have nicely shaped legs, a nice waist. You're just *bigger*. I wish I had bigger hips and chest.

The body is *the* zone of female anxiety: so many things can "be" or "go" wrong with it. The size of the head relative to the neck, the tautness of the throat, the slope of the shoulders, the fullness and pertness of the breasts, the narrowness of the torso, the boyishness of the buttocks, the length and firmness of the thighs and the slenderness of the calf, the length and arch of the foot – any one of these concerns may have been the cause of months, even years, of anguish to women for whom, regardless of their active accomplishments and successes as people in the world, the sine qua non of their female worthiness rests in the approximation of their body to the current feminine ideal. Since the teenage girl has had little chance yet to know herself as an agent in the world, her sense of accomplishment and success rests perforce on who she *is*; and who she *is* – as she is reminded everywhere – is her sexuality, her body. Unlike boys, for whom the body is an instrument of activity, of *doing*, girls merely inhabit their bodies; a girl *is* beautiful, *is* sexy. And so, except for the exceptional figure of the athlete or the dancer, a girl's only mode of activity through her body is on the body itself – to change it. And these days the principal form this activity takes is to diet.

"I love food with a passion. I could eat all day, but I gain weight really fast. I hate it. I'm really concerned with my weight because I *love* slim: it's so nice to look at." By "slim", girls do not mean the merely healthy body in correct ratio of weight to build; increasingly they mean the prepubertal body, the female body without breasts or hips or menstruation, even. Whether this is a symptom of overwhelming anxiety concerning the adult female sexual state or an oblique rebellion against our cultural norms of female maturity or an absurd punishment inflicted on the self for being "bad" or "unworthy", the fact is that inordinate numbers of adolescent girls, in the midst of middle-class plenty, are close to starving themselves by denying themselves the food they need. *This* is their accomplishment, to have become as thin as possible. It may be that they do this to satisfy in the only way they know how the need to control or make an impact on or protest their environment. But this "tyranny of thin" also coincides with the increasingly popular male fantasy of the girl-child as sexual object and with the "flight" in this fantasy from marriage and child-rearing into the denuded sex act, endlessly repeated without consequence. In the words of a high school counsellor, "This is what is attractive to men – a body that has no child-bearing qualities. At its extreme, once a girl loses enough body fat she stops menstruating. At that point she is truly a sex object: she can't get pregnant."

At that point also one is talking about anorexia nervosa, an eating disorder which, according to Dr. Sujatha Lena at Ottawa's Eastern Ontario Children's Hospital,[2] has doubled among teenage girls over the last ten years and now affects one in a hundred. In effect, anorectics go on a "hunger strike" which, if unchecked, could lead to permanent physical damage, sterility, and even death. An associated disorder, bulimia, characterized by cycles of bingeing and vomiting, may afflict as many as sixty thousand Canadian girls and women, according to a Toronto psychiatrist, Dr. David Garner.[3] He has also found that 70 to 80 per cent of adolescent females feel that they are fat.

Carla was thirteen when, distressed by the possibility that her family might move to Calgary, and obsessed in any case with the fact that she was always a "little fatter, maybe by ten pounds" than everyone else in her family, especially her mother, she started taking pills – Anacin, Tylenol, 222s – to "relax". She discovered that by taking pills a handful at a time and getting sick – waking up sweating and shaking in the middle of the night, suffering headaches and ringing in her ears – she lost her appetite. Terrific. After two weeks of this regimen, she lost five pounds. That was easy; she tried for five more, and so on. Under her parents' watchful eyes she couldn't stop eating altogether, but she'd restrict herself to a salad or a bowl of soup a day (one hundred calories at most, she calculates) and put herself on a furious program of exercise, three hours a day of jogging, bike-riding, and sit-ups. Food became her obsession, her "enemy": she would chew a cookie just to get the taste of it, then spit it out. She would go on binges, eat a carton of ice cream, throw it up, eat another one, and so on, until her throat bled and her rib-cage ached from the repeated vomitings; when sticking her fingers down her throat didn't work, she swallowed mouthwash. At night she would sometimes dream of food, waken in horror (had she only dreamt eating?), and go straight to the bathroom to throw up. She was down to eighty-two pounds. She spent all of grade eight, it seems to her now, hallucinating and fainting. But whenever someone told her, admonishingly, that she was "too thin", she was happy.

"A lot of guys don't like it," she acknowledges. "They don't like skin and bones, but I kind of like it. I hate fat. And if hips and breasts disappear too, that's fine with me."

Carla rejected all medical intervention. She liked the idea of herself as independent and knowing what she was doing. She cured herself of anorexia by going on a pro-longed binge and not bothering to throw up. She went back up to one hundred and fourteen pounds – nine pounds heavier than her mother on her wedding day – and was told how much better she looked. Everyone was happy for her. But Carla became depressed, started swallowing tranquillizers, and a few months later tried to commit suicide. Since then she hasn't had the nerve to step on a scale once: even now that she's cured, she still wishes at times that she *looked* anorectic.

Adherence to the feminine ideal is not, then, without its costs and penalties. As she grows older, a girl will, it is hoped, acquire the self-confidence born of experience – a confidence that she relies on ephemeral "femininity" to deliver in her adolescence. But should she be unlucky – should she find herself consigned to the social oblivion of divorce or a dead-end job or genteel poverty – "femininity" will once again provide the means by which she may survive the sexual struggle of the fittest. But the cultivation of this sort of femininity, as American writer Susan Brownmiller points out in her *Femininity*,[4] results in a woman's accepting restrictions on her behaviour and gestures; it shrinks her ambition and dissipates her time in narcissistic self-examination: men like feminine women, is she feminine enough?

JODI: A man's hands turn me on.

SHERRY: I look at the face first, the eyes, and then the hair. I like really blond or black hair. I even like bald men. I think it's so sexy. I like the way men walk. Oh yeah. And the arms. I like big arms – so they can lift me up!

JODI: I like to watch my boyfriend walk. Very tall and straight, one arm swinging.

SHERRY: Not like Ken, always slouched over. He's so skinny and scrawny you get the impression he *crawls*.

JODI: I liked the way Michael walked. He kind of bounced.

SHERRY: He has good posture.

JODI: He's just not very manly.

SHERRY: I always prefer a man to be my height or taller. I could never go out with someone shorter. And it's important how they dress.

JODI: *Tight* levis and big sweaters.

SHERRY: Jeans.

JODI: Faded, tight. Not baggies unless they're stylish. Dress pants with suspenders. But guys look best in jeans. They've got such nice bums.

SHERRY: If they wear GWG, forget it.

JODI: Or designer jeans. They make the bums look round and gross, like women's bums.

It is the conceit of every adult generation that the younger generation is sexier. Adults are always convinced that young people, whose sexuality is not circumscribed by marriage and child-rearing, are potential if not actual sexual anarchists, screwing each other incessantly without regard to the standards and regulations of institutionalized sexual intercourse. There may be an element of adult wishful thinking in this – involving the adult's own fantasy of unflagging randiness – but, given the punitive, contemptuous, and patronizing tone of so much adult commentary on teenage sexuality, it is much more likely that adults project onto their children their *fear* of this still-unfettered sexuality.

In point of fact, they need not fear so much. In spite of sensational, and superficial, evidence to the contrary, this generation of teenage girls seems cast in the same mould as their parents and condemned to relive their sexual sorrows. It is not sexual liberation that they have inherited from the great post-war experiments of their parents but sexual atomization: in the Land of Sex, each is on her own to make her way through the mine-fields of penalties and pleasures.

A national survey conducted out of the University of Lethbridge[5] in 1984 indicated that 74 per cent of the high school and university women surveyed felt that sex without or before marriage is acceptable "if they felt strong affection for their partner." (80 per cent of males agreed.) Withdraw "affection" from the scenario, however, and the percentage of women still approving of premarital sex plummets to 6 per cent (yet the equivalent male response is as high as 42 per cent). With such a discrepancy in attitude between boys and girls concerning the meaning of unaffectionate sex, it comes as no surprise to learn that girls still experience the situation in which intense pressure is brought to bear upon their reluctance and scepticism until such time as they either simply "give in" or fall in love. (According to a 1975 study by University of Alberta sociologist Charles Hobart,[6] in which university students were asked to "justify" their first sexual experience, "males were twice as likely as females to give as a reason the strength of their sexual drive than saying it was an expression of love for their partner. For women the most important reason was that sex was a natural expression of their love." Plus ça change . . .) And the pressures are varied and manifold, not least because, for all the rhetoric of female sexual emancipation, the assumption still holds that sex is something a girl "has" which a boy "gets", and that it is up to her whether the transfer is made.

Reasons that girls give for having sexual intercourse even though they do not feel like it (from *Medical Aspects of Human Sexuality*, 1984)[7] are predictable: Not to hurt the boy's feelings. Not to be thought of as a prude. Afraid of losing boyfriend. Sense of being obligated. To show love or give reassurance. Being high on drugs or alcohol. Being in a group where everyone else is doing it. And so on. Anecdotally, I have been told that, as though cynically aware of girls' sexual "psychology", boys will demand sex using the classic argument that "if you truly love me like you say, you'll do it." (This is the male counterpart of the fifties' woman's line: "If you truly loved me, you wouldn't ask me to do it!") Clearly it becomes harder and harder, in dating situations where the couple goes to a movie or watches a home video, for the girl to find the grounds to resist acting out the sexual scenario just witnessed on the screen as "normal". What *would* her grounds be? Theoretically, she need not fear pregnancy, or loss of reputation, since "everybody" is doing it; by her own admission sex is not a bad thing if she cares for the boy, and "nobody" believes in waiting for the wedding night any more; and what has "waiting for Mr. Right" got to do with it any more – if a girl is horny, why shouldn't she get laid, too?

There *are* virgins in high schools, lots of them, boys and girls; this should not be obscured by the fact that there are also many, younger and younger, who are sexually active. There *are* girls who find their reasons to say "no" and will not be budged. The girl who simply doesn't trust "high school boys" not to use her and dump her (bragging about it in the locker room), the girl who, although not necessarily waiting for the "right" guy, is waiting for the "right" moment, the girl whose ego won't let her lose her virginity to someone who would not stick around if there were "consequences", and the girl who herself is simply not ready: she cannot yet "imagine" herself doing this amazing, strange, awesome thing called sex.

"I've heard grade eleven girls talk about their friends sleeping with their boyfriends," nineteen-year-old Mandy told me. "It shocked me. I know it's going on but when I think back to me being in grade eleven I think, oh my God. Sex is a *huge* commitment to being together. It doesn't have to lead to marriage but I'd like to know it's going to last a while, that I won't sleep with someone and then have it pulled out from under me. There was one girl in my class who slept with her boyfriend after a month, and that really shocked a lot of people. That was really too soon. To me a relationship doesn't mean just going out for dinner and to the movies and you talk to each other on the phone. I've had lots of those relationships. But you really have to know a person and how he feels about things, about sex for instance. It's such a big decision to make when you're only fifteen. I'm having a hard enough time dealing with it, and I'm nineteen and in love."

Are teenagers having more sex than ever before? It depends on what is meant by sex: a study in Saskatchewan in 1980[8] found that 75 per cent of fifteen- to nineteen-year-olds had engaged in "light petting" (above the waist), and 63 per cent in "heavy petting" (below the waist), and, among virgins, one-third had already experienced oral sex. Girls masturbate. Girls have sexual fantasies. But even among those who have experienced sexual intercourse, it is infrequent: among high school students in Calgary,[9] for instance, 60 per cent of the non-virgins had sex less than once a month. Society's overwhelming preoccupation with heterosexual intercourse obscures the variety of ways (some delightful, some not) by which the body finds its satisfaction.

LYNN: I like men's bodies. Oh yeah. They're *hard*.

SHERRY: They're strong. The manliness.

JODI: And where you touch a man it always seems warm.

LYNN: That's how they think of women.

JODI: I used to like hairy bodies. But Karl is very smooth, very muscular, soft too, with dark olive skin, and I think that's wonderful.

SHERRY: That's because you think *he's* wonderful.

JODI: I like running my lips over his forehead. I like his muscular thighs. I like thighs. I like Karl's naked bum. Nice and firm. . . . What I hate is when a guy worries if he's "big" enough.

LYNN AND SHERRY (in unison): Oh yeah.

JODI: Like, who cares?

LYNN: They're still concerned about that, oh God, yes.

JODI: It's insecurity. The big bulge in the pants. That's what *they* like. I actually prefer men with a small penis because I'm so small myself. It's just as silly as me being worried about my flat chest. I joke about it but I like being flat-chested. It seems thinner. It seems sexier. More sensitive. It's like my trademark. I don't mind what size my breasts are as long as they're nicely shaped. And if it makes a difference to a guy, then I think he's being stupid. There's no point in getting involved with him.

The New Year's party, you name it, it happened. Sharon was there. She saw. Everybody was loaded, and when a girl is drunk, she just can't say "no". So three guys jump one girl and they're doing every possible combination, and over in the corner is a couple doing "69", and in the bathroom a bunch of guys were busy whacking off together in the bathtub – was that gross! – and that's why Sharon likes to keep her wits about her at those parties: she wants to be able to *remember* what she did, and, besides, she's got some class; she'll wait until she gets home to do "it".

Penny had a boyfriend and he was really sweet and she loved him as a person but the trouble was he was so, so *masculine*. If she had never slept with him she could have gone on just loving him, but she did go to bed with him and it was awful, terrible; he took off his clothes and there he was, furry and male. He smelled male, he tasted male, he felt male, and he just turned her right off and she couldn't even explain it, not even to herself. Luckily, she then met a much more "androgynous" man, a transsexual in fact, and they went to a bar for a drink and back to his room and they made love all night. She needed it so badly. He took her coat from her shoulders, unbuttoned her shirt, dropped that too, took her in his arms and just held her, and she began to cry and he held her and held her and he started crying and they both cried and made love and laughed and made tea, and it was really beautiful.

Lana had been going with Vic for several months and without even discussing it with anyone, thinking it all through in her own head, she decided he would be her first lover. She *cared* for him and she was ready. She went to a birth control clinic and got the pill, because she wasn't going to take any chances whatever, and they went to his place, and it was very beautiful. Vic was very thoughtful, he took his time, she took her time, it wasn't *casual* sex after all, there was a lot of feeling between them. But a few weeks later she broke off with him. It seemed he didn't understand that just because she had made love with him once or twice she didn't want to do it *all* the time. There were times, a lot of times, when she just didn't want to be close to him in that way and there was nothing she could do about it. If she doesn't want it, she doesn't want it. Sorry.

All right, it was six o'clock in the morning and Mo had been out all night with her girlfriend and here was her mother shrieking at here, WHERE THE HELL HAVE YOU BEEN? and all Mo wanted was to get some sleep. Hey, Mum, I'm all cried out and fucked out and messed out, I've got a sore brain and sore thighs and I don't want to

talk, okay? Just leave me alone. DON'T YOU THINK I UN-
DERSTAND, DON'T YOU THINK YOU CAN TALK TO ME? No, I
can't. You *won't* understand. . . . Okay. I've fallen in love
with Tracy. Shriek, gasp, wail. YOU'RE NOT GAY! YOU LIKE
BOYS! And then, just as Mo feared, it was off to the shrink.

SHERRY: I've never had a guy ask me if I've come.

JODI: I've always had them ask me that.

LYNN: I ask them, too. I can't always tell.

JODI: Karl gets upset. He doesn't understand that it isn't important to me. So he doesn't ask any more. I think if men
are concerned whether you're enjoying it too, that's nice.

LYNN: I hate it if they ask only because *they* can only feel
good if you do. They want to *make* you come. Well, it hasn't
happened to me yet. I haven't had an orgasm while making
love.

SHERRY: Me neither. And not even by myself.

LYNN: Orgasm through intercourse still perplexes me a bit.

JODI: Is it normal if you don't have them through intercourse? Because I have them only one way. . . . What position should you be in?

SHERRY: Lorraine was telling us – this is her new thing with
Don – that you have to get on top.

JODI: On top I can't even have one. I had one once, but only
once. It was just a little jolt. I thought it was mostly mental.
What I don't understand is women who've never had an orgasm and who go to bed with someone they don't care
about. What are they getting out of it? They don't even get
cuddled.

LYNN: Probably just for the feeling of being attractive.

SHERRY: I did it once. What I got out of it was . . . power.
"Thank you. Good-bye!"

JODI: I got good sex out of it.

LYNN: But did you have an orgasm?

JODI: No. I think women can enjoy just fucking, but it's not
something that's going to make them feel good about themselves.

LYNN: For guys it seems a more exterior thing. They can put
it in but *you're* taking them *in* to you, you know?

There is a subtext in these conversations, aching and wistful and perplexed: how, in all the varieties of groping and handling, heaving and stroking, sweating and straining, coming and not coming, is a girl to find her pleasure? It may be, as some argue, that from the female point of view heterosexual intercourse is structurally incapable of satisfying women (if satisfaction is understood to mean orgasm), and the girls who make love for the cuddling and the caresses are simply making the best of an inalterably poor situation. Less radically, we can argue that it is a matter of education – of girls and boys – so that the mysteries of pleasure may be unveiled as matters of technique. There *are* things to be learned: how to masturbate, how to ask for what you want, how to relax and take your time, how to find ways of pleasuring other than intercourse, and so on. At this point it becomes depressing to realize that for all the publicity of the "sexual revolution", the advice of sexologists and porn publishers, and even the broadsides from the women's movement over the last twenty years, a girl can still be paralysed in bed with her lover for fear that her need for clitoral stimulation label her as frigid. Or that seventeen-year-olds who have been sexually active since they were fourteen still need to be informed of the most elementary conclusions of sex research. Or that boys, from most accounts, are the same boorish and greedy and clumsy lovers their fathers were, in spite of thirty years of the Playboy Philosophy.

What is essential is that a girl not be harassed into sex she does not want, for if there is anything that the stories tell us it is not that girls are having "too much" sex but that they are having sex before they are ready, with too little arousal, and for all the wrong reasons. I have heard them tell me that they get "nothing" out of it, that it's "awful", that they don't like it, but it's what their boyfriend "expects" from them. (The girl who lies down on the couch, pulls down her jeans, and opens her legs, all the while smoking a cigarette, so her date can "get his rocks off" and then take her to a movie.) They feign orgasm.

They say it was "good" because that's what the boy wants to hear and they're afraid of what he might do if they tell the truth: he might leave.

As for her own pleasure, whoever said that that is what sex is *for*?

SHERRY: A slut is someone who can have sex and it doesn't mean a thing to her.

JODI: Also, it's the way she dresses and carries herself: Fuck me, fuck me! Like Lorraine, who's nice to me but she's a slut. Last night she was here with her boyfriend and let him caress her while she was staring at Karl.

LYNN: That's what I figure a slut is: hurting your boyfriend.

JODI: She was wearing leotards and a camisole and she kept leaning over the table – she's quite well-built – and rubbing herself against Karl. It was making me sick. I told her to get her hands off him. That's what I call sleazy. . . . And Ilse, she'll go to bed with anything that moves.

SHERRY: She likes the look.

JODI: Tight pants and looking dirty. Lots of make-up.

LYNN: She gets up on the dance floor and dances by herself.

JODI: She could have an orgasm if the wind blew. She doesn't care what the guys look like either. She once seriously asked me if I'd mind if she went to bed with Karl. "There's nothing wrong with it, you know," she said. "Love doesn't mean possession." That's gross. Her family is ultra-suburban tacky. She was a head for a long time. Now she's a punker, probably to get more sex.

LYNN: From the guys' point of view, they sleep with a girl, they get a pat on the back. They brag about all the girls they sleep with. But the girl who sleeps with them is a slut!

If the "double standard" of sexual morality is still operative in adolescent sexual negotiations, it is in part due to the fact that girls police each other: they monitor each other's behaviour with a pitiless scrutiny and have the power, within their own cliques, to expel or exclude those who have broken the sexual code. In spite of their parents' worst dreams, this is not a sexual culture in which "anything goes"; the line drawn between "good" and "bad" girls may not be drawn precisely where adults would wish it to be, but it is drawn.

Twenty years ago, "nice" girls did not have sex; nice girls were virgins, and it is questionable just how many would allow even heavy petting. Today, "nice" girls may very well be having sex – virginity no longer seems to be the point. The point is the conditions under which sex takes place, and here it becomes a question of whether girls have simply accepted the culturally based moral judgement that "virtue" is a function of *female* sexuality or have appropriated it in order to defend themselves the best they can from the lawless rapacity they sense is brewing in boys' culture. Girls are in no position to redefine the terms of morality; the least they can do is try to manipulate those terms to their own advantage.

Thus, the designation "slut". A slut is a girl who goes to bed with a guy she has no feelings for. (Note that it is not a question of the *boy's* feelings. It is universally assumed that boys will screw anybody who lets them, irrespective of their own feelings about their partner, since the sex act itself is deemed to have an inherent value in male culture.) She is making love to a "body", not a "person". She has no self-respect: boys talk about her in the cruellest way and she doesn't seem to care. She has no standards, she'll even come on to her friends' boyfriends.

The way to have a sex life, then, without being designated a slut, is to make love only with someone you are going out with, someone with whom it is generally acknowledged you are in a relationship, even though this "relationship" may last no longer than a month. The point is that this shows that you are discriminating, you are protected against your partner's locker-room gossip (if you're a "slut", what would that say about his taste in girlfriends?), and, by "belonging" to someone, you have spared yourself the opprobrium reserved for girls who think they can screw whomever and whenever they like and get away with it. But it is more complicated than this: the point of reserving sex for "meaningful relationships" is that, as Lana put it, "it's well known that sex is much more enjoyable when you're in love with the person." The redeeming power of love: when Jodi met Mick, she was not a virgin, but he was her first great love, and so making love with him was like "losing my virginity all over again". Girls insist on the emotional surround of sex because this is their own best chance to feel secure, relaxed, and aroused. Pity the poor slut, then, who is guaranteed none of this.

The distinction between "nice" girls and "sluts" has also a class component. It is no accident that the sluttish "look" bears a strong resemblance to the look favoured by working-class girls. If proletarians are thought to be "sexier", "randier", "earthier" than middle-class women and their costumes correspondingly more enticing, then by distancing herself from the "slut", the "nice" girl reasserts her superior class position: "*I'm* not one of *them*!" The slut, or the working-class girl, is seen as someone who does not care about the consequences of her own actions ("It's no big deal if a slut gets pregnant") and who has no definition except as a sexual object ("She's on the pill – she must be sleeping around"). The truth of the matter, of course, is that an unwanted pregnancy for a working-class girl is a crisis that cannot be so discreetly "taken care of" as for a middle-class girl. Her attitude to contraception is likely to be excruciatingly ambivalent: unlike middle-class girls, whose sexual reputations are mitigated by their families' education and status, nothing stands between a working-class girl on the pill and her reputation. An Ottawa high school teacher observed this: "I see a very heavy judgemental attitude on the part of middle-class girls towards the 'other' sort of girl. They're looking after themselves and their friends, and there isn't a lot of sympathy or sisterhood outside their little circles." The sexual code: class and gender policing.

In a culture where the sexual double standard still regulates sexual morality, where there are two "kinds" of women (the one you screw and the one you marry), where shame and mystification and anxiety attach to sexuality, its deepest impulses embedded in pornography, and where girls must deny, most importantly to themselves, the goad of their own desire, it is hard for girls not to be hurt by sex. Their code, most especially to sleep only with someone they care for, can moderate the hurt. But there is no absolute protection except, I suppose, in cloistered chastity in an all-female family. Otherwise, the varieties of pain are legion: the street kid with her pimp and her habit; the battered girlfriend; the lesbian hissed and spat at by schoolmates, hounded by her parents, and threatened by her lover; the school slut, humiliated and ridiculed. And the diseased, the pregnant, and the aborted.

In 1983 there were more than 8500 reported cases of gonorrhea in Canadian adolescents. The incidence of this disease, and chlamydia infection, in the fifteen- to nineteen-year-olds is second only to that of the rate among twenty- to twenty-five-year-olds. In a ten-year period (1970–80), the number of hospital admissions for pelvic inflammatory disease, a leading cause of infertility, not to mention of acute disability, in women, increased in fifteen- to nineteen-year-old women by 46 per cent. Physicians register their concern about the increased risk of cervical cancer in the sexually active teenager. In other words, according to the Canadian Pediatric Society, sexually transmitted diseases have reached "epidemic proportions among teenagers, and there is reason to be gravely concerned about the long-term medical consequences of early sexual activity. Physical characteristics notwithstanding, it would seem that the fourteen-, fifteen-, sixteen-year-old female body, for all its seductive representation in the media, is not ready for sustained sexual intercourse.

It can, however, be impregnated. In 1983, more than 16,500 babies were born in Canada to single mothers aged fifteen to nineteen (up from 9600 in 1974, and to be compared to the 21,500 babies born to unmarried twenty- to twenty-four-year-olds). From a peak rate in 1975, however, when one in eight Canadian babies was born to a teenager, the rate of teenage pregnancy is dropping, by 11 per cent from 1976 to 1981. To the extent that many of these pregnancies were unwanted, this is good news. But there is a difference, of course, between an unwanted and an unplanned pregnancy: increasingly, the unplanned pregnancy is nevertheless welcomed, or accepted. According to one study, among girls not using contraception fewer than one per cent said they wanted to become pregnant; but another study, asking adolescent girls what they would do if they became pregnant by accident, revealed that about one-half would want to keep the child.

Whether or not this represents a social trauma depends on the extent to which social institutions are prepared to assist a young, dependent mother. But for the pregnant girl herself, no matter what her decision concerning the baby proves to be, the situation is perilous. In the vast majority of cases, the father takes no responsibility; "I've been working for eighteen years," one school counsellor told me, "and I've seen only two boys stay in a relationship after pregnancy." The girl is at the mercy of her family for support. In school, her "condition" marks her as a slut or a fool, and few pregnant teenagers stay on to complete their education. Their awareness of what they will be up against as uneducated, unskilled, sole-support parents is limited, to say the least. Their loneliness, in a life lived apart from the society of their peers, is staggering.

LYNN: When I decided I was going to be sexually active, I told a friend. We have the same doctor and she told him and he said, "Get her in here!" I got pamphlets on all the different methods of birth control.

JODI: IUDs are scary things.

LYNN: So is the pill.

JODI: The first pill I was on I had like morning sickness. I'd get up in the morning and feel nauseated and I'd vomit. I was really irritable and my breasts would be sore. But with this new pill I don't get any side effects. Well, some breakthrough bleeding, but you can have that even without the pill.

LYNN: I get yeast infections.

JODI: A friend's mother had an IUD; it tore her uterus. My mother had hers put in backwards and she started hemorrhaging. They're constantly trying to improve the pill, though. I hope they come up with a men's pill soon.

LYNN: My boyfriend was always good about that. He would always ask if I was on birth control.

JODI: I've never been in the situation where I'm already in bed with somebody and *then* they ask if I'm using anything. When I go to bed with somebody, they already know that. They know enough about me. When I was having problems with the pill and wanted to go off it, Mick was really great about it. He could see the side effects and he didn't want that happening to me. He told me to give my system a rest and bought safes.

Why, if a girl does not want to become pregnant, does she not use contraception? Why, according to research, are only one-third of teenagers using contraception when they first have intercourse, when they reportedly are not having sex to get pregnant? Why do fewer than twenty per cent of girls planning to have intercourse obtain the pill beforehand, while the rest wait six months or longer into a sexual relationship to get a prescription? (Clearly, being "on the pill" is not a motive but rather a consequence of sexual activity!) In my own conversations with girls, I did not meet one who didn't think it "stupid" to make love without "taking all precautions". Who, then are all the "stupid" teenagers who have manifestly not taken precautions?

First, we should leave aside the question of the availability of information about contraception. Even armed with information, the girl may decide that, for all the times she's going to be in bed with someone (adolescent intercourse is infrequent and sporadic), it simply isn't worth the risk to her body to be on the pill or to have an IUD inserted. It is severely embarrassing to her to purchase condoms, and in any case their use requires her lover's co-operation. (A study of abortion patients in 1977[10] found that the most common reason for stopping the use of condoms was that the partner objected to using them.) Successful use of the diaphragm or cervical cap requires that a girl not be squeamish about touching her own genitals. As for the rhythm method, not all adolescent menstrual cycles are so regular that the period of ovulation can be accurately determined. When even adult women have grave misgivings about the method of contraception they employ and risk the consequences of contraceptive failure, it is clearly idiotic to label a teenage girl's lack of precaution some kind of perversity.

But it is not, of course, simply a question of technology. The inhibitions surrounding a girl's consideration of the question are very strong. When her female dignity is at stake, when her reputation as a "good" girl is in the hands of the boys she knows, when her own guilt about even *thinking* about doing this dirty and dangerous thing called sex is overwhelming, where is the fifteen- or sixteen-year-old with the poise and self-confidence to announce herself – by outfitting herself with contraceptives – interested in sex? After all, if she's using birth control she must be *planning* to have sex, and if she's planning it, who's to say, now that she's safe and won't get "caught", that she won't fuck every Tom, Dick, and Harry who comes her way? The only acceptable attitude to sexual intercourse is to be in love, to be so overwhelmed by your own feeling and the imperatives of desire that, in spite of your best intentions, you go all the way. Later, maybe, you can pick up the pill; if you're lucky, you can get it without an internal exam and a whole bunch of questions about your personal life, you can hide it without your mother finding it, and you can take it without your boyfriend freaking out: "Hey, what kind of girl are you, anyway?"

LYNN: I know a girl who's pregnant. She's not having an abortion because she's more than three months pregnant.

SHERRY (scornfully): How can you not notice you're not having your period for three months?

LYNN: She thought she couldn't get pregnant. She'd had a miscarriage once.

JODI: I know somebody who had an abortion. It didn't mean anything to her at all. It was like going in for a Pap smear. She's not a very nice person anyway. She's in the trendy scene, hanging out with weird hairdressers. Venereal disease and rock'n'roll. She didn't seem to care. It seemed she *wanted* to get pregnant. She was nineteen but dumb.

LYNN: If it were me, I'd probably get an abortion.

JODI: I'd get one too, but it would be traumatic.

LYNN: I wouldn't get pregnant in the first place. People get pregnant because they don't know enough about birth control or don't care.

Consider: if, on the one hand, girls are reluctant to use birth control in any systematic way, yet do not want to get pregnant, and, on the other hand, only some twenty-eight per cent are prepared to get an abortion to terminate an unwanted pregnancy, what is one to conclude but that the great majority of teenage pregnancies which are carried to term involve duress or protest? Or, put another way, between her ambivalence about contraceptive use and her misgivings about abortion, a girl is immobilized.

In the first place, if she lives in rural Canada or in the North or at any distance from a hospital with an abortion committee or on Prince Edward Island, and if she's in no position to fly herself down to the metropolitan centres or to Detroit or Seattle, she will have no alternative but to bear the child: she will have been effectively denied access to an abortion. In the second place, unless she's a middle-class girl bent on going to university, for whom early motherhood would represent the scuttling of her ambitions, the pregnant girl's "right" to an abortion is a less than meaningful option: the decisive alternative to motherhood is what, exactly? Compared to the other jobs available to her, parenting could be a pleasure. In the third place, emotions among her friends, not to mention her parents, run high on the subject of abortion. In spite of the fact that the large majority of young women in high school and university, some seventy-five per cent, believe that the decision to have an abortion is a private one, it would appear[11] that many would not countenance that decision. (Only seven per cent of boys, asked if they would go along with a girlfriend's decision to have an abortion, said they would.) Girls who have had abortions have been openly attacked as "baby-killers" by their own classmates, and those who identify themselves as "pro-choice" on the question have been summarily dismissed as "pro-abortion". Besides this psychological terrorism inflicted by the group, there is the inner violence of her own conflicting emotions; she desperately does not want to be a mother – does not even want to give her body over for nine months to a child she has no intention of raising – and yet is sentimentally overpowered by the imagery of Madonna-like mothers and their cherubic infants deployed by the anti-abortionists and by her own susceptibility to appeals to her maternal "instinct", by her conviction that no matter how necessary the act of abortion is, it remains nevertheless the extinguishing of a life which, had it been brought to term, might have been a thing that was all hers, to have and to hold, to defend and cuddle and nurture. As against this – a *baby* – how can a girl with no strong sense yet of the shape and demands and commands of her own life choose herself? She cannot choose, and is immobilized.

LYNN: They should have people coming into the schools to talk about birth control. We get big talks about *shoplifting*, for heaven's sake, but they won't come in to talk about birth control. In junior high they talk about adolescence and the birds and the bees and a guy comes in and talks about the concentration camps. Why can't they make the same sort of speeches about birth control?

SHERRY: I learned everything from friends.

JODI: I had a friend who thought the idea of breast-feeding was disgusting. She didn't know that's what breasts are for. So my mother explained everything.

When an adolescent girl does not know what breasts are for, thinks she cannot become pregnant if she doesn't have an orgasm, worries about being "frigid", and finds it much too embarrassing to visit a family-planning clinic, then, clearly, her society has failed dismally to provide a sex education that is not, in every sense, shameful. For all the hyped-up sexuality pervasive in our culture, we seem unable to pass on to the developing generation an appreciation of what is about to happen to them – the blooming beauty of their bodies, the bitter-sweet ache of the flesh, and the vertiginous somersaulting of emotions – probably because we do not, in our heart of hearts, believe in it. What we *do* seem to believe is that the female body is the site of corruption (moral and physical), that love-making is a version of sexual assault (this holds as true for its romantic as for its pornographic depictions), and that one nevertheless has the obligation, as a citizen of free-wheeling, raunchy capitalism, to consume as much sex as possible without undue wear and tear to the soul. These are our teachings, and we get the students we deserve.

But teenagers themselves protest against this state of affairs. In a recent national survey[12] of 33,111 students aged nine, twelve, and fifteen, 40 per cent of the grade ten students reported that they had learned about sex from friends (with 26 per cent learning from parents and another 26 per cent from school). A Gallup poll[13] commissioned by the Planned Parenthood Federation of Canada in 1985 found that 91 per cent of respondents felt that parents should discuss the "facts of life" with their children. Given the gap between those children desiring such conversation and the number of parents willing to take it up, it is not surprising that, according to an Alberta survey[14] of 3000 grade ten and twelve students in 1986, students rate "sexuality" as a much more important course of study – if they could get it! – than "religion". Yet in all of Canada, fewer than fifty per cent of schools have sex education programs of any sort. When we know that in Newfoundland,[15] for example, pregnancy is the single most frequent reason why girls leave school before graduation, and we also know, from international data, that those countries with the most readily available contraceptive services and the most formal and informal sex education programs have the *lowest* rates of adolescent pregnancy, abortion, and child-bearing, then to withhold sex education from teenagers is a form of generational sadism. And not far removed from the homily that bad girls get what they deserve.

Lana gets her ideas about romance from the songs of Joni Mitchell and James Taylor and about sex from the novels of Judith Krantz and Harold Robbins. She knows that they are "trash" novels but they are also frank, blunt, candid – and they speak informatively of the sex act in a way which she is hard-pressed to hear anywhere else, unless it's in the books her parents keep in their bedroom, *The Joy of Sex*, for example. Mandy, who reads a lot and who has the good fortune to live with open-minded parents, considers herself well-informed on the subject of sex and is even prepared to discuss "facts" with her school friends (although not intimate details). In knowing superiority, they all got a good laugh out of the story about the girl who jumped up and down with great vigour in an effort to bring on her period. But then Mandy and her friends *need* to be well-informed: as she points out, *they're* going to have careers. Nicole, who was so street-wise, knew the pill worked but until recently had no idea how, and Christine has been amazed to learn (peals of laughter) that boys have feelings.

SHERRY: Oh yeah, I've seen pornography. I've been with friends when they've rented porno movies like *Deep Throat*. I think pornography is sick.

JODI: But that's not violent. I saw the most violent pornographic film – a naked woman was being dragged around on the ground by a horse, then she was raped by a gang of men, and by the end she really liked it. I saw this at a guy's birthday party. I was only fourteen and I was really offended by it. I saw a *Playboy* in Karl's room and I got really furious at him. He said it was "art".

SHERRY: When I saw *Deep Throat* I couldn't understand how the women, and the men too, could make these films. It was really sick. How do people like that have the right to live?

JODI: Well, I wouldn't go that far. I just don't understand how people can get turned on by them. Some women have the desire to be dominated, and that's all porn is. A lot of my girlfriends have talked about how they like it when the guy gets mad at them. Lorraine was saying that, when her boyfriend is standing there and yelling at her, all she wants to do is pull down his pants and give him a blow job.

SHERRY: I think porn should be banned.

JODI: Some of the rock videos are really disgusting, like that stupid Devo video, "Whip It", with a man whipping off this woman's clothing.

SHERRY: A lot of the Heavy Metal videos show girls in bikinis.

JODI: Censors really have their heads in the clouds when they ban images of people making love to each other but not pictures of people killing each other.

It has been argued that pornography should be allowed to circulate as a kind of informal sex education for the young; indeed, it seems already to function that way, if a recent study by a Toronto psychologist[16] is to be believed. He found that "young people" between the ages of twelve and seventeen are the "primary consumers" of pornography in Canada, and that thirty-seven per cent of them watch sexually explicit videos at least once a month. The study does not say how many of these consumers are girls; we can assume that some are, even though many more girls than boys would support the banning of pornographic materials, according to Bibby and Posterski's study.[17] When a girl finds her boyfriend's anger at her arousing and wants to fellate him, we can then assume that some girls are even acquiring a sex education from porn videos, just as their distributors argue. Some sex, some education.

With the arrival of the adolescent as a participant in our social chronology, adults have been terrorized by the phenomenon of a creature who is neither sexually innocent (child) nor sexually regulated (adult), but who hovers shimmeringly, tantalizingly, in that zone where sexuality is enjoyed for its own sake, and threatens to challenge the authority of marriage, family, monogamy. The dissemination of the ideology of romantic love among the middle classes and then the working classes met that challenge: the agonies of the ripening flesh were conceptualized as the harbingers of "true love", the most exalted expression of which was the marriage between passionate lovers who would remain forever true to each other. Thus potentially disorderly adolescent sexuality was rerouted into adult stability: young people were taught that one falls in love, one goes steady, one becomes engaged and then married. Adolescent sexual feelings, ardour, and love, far from being disruptive of the social order, became included in the process of the domestication of desire.

Whenever this domestication may be said to have happened, the last thirty years in North America have witnessed its re-barbarization, or so popular analysis would have us believe. Thanks to the widespread influence of the mass media (movies, television, and advertising), "sex is transformed,"[18] as one critic put it, "from a dark and profound adult mystery to a product that is available to everyone – let us say, like mouthwash."

During the sixties, however, traditional authority was questioned and challenged, youth proclaimed its intellectual and emotional autonomy, "instant gratification" of desire became a categorical imperative, and all the institutions of middle-class respectability were held up to disrepute: sobriety, marriage, monogamy, and the missionary position. Adolescent sexuality was no longer on the route to anywhere but its own self-determined satisfaction.

For a few breathless moments it seemed that all of bourgeois culture had been successfully contested, including its sexual institutions. But it is becoming more and more untenable to argue that anything very revolutionary has happened to the adolescent experience of sexuality. As we have seen, distressingly little has changed for today's teenage girls, or little enough to alter the social and economic context of their experience. They may take the pill, but it could make them ill, and they may obtain an abortion, but only if they're lucky or very sure of themselves. They may have babies outside of marriage, but only at the price of their pauperization. They may consume pornography, but at the risk of a certain debasement of the spirit. They may screw whoever and whenever they like – and join the ancient sorority of sluts.

In a mass culture that celebrates at the discotheque and the singles bar the spontaneous sexual union of strangers (in the words of Canadian writer Stuart Ewen)[19] – people who have not seen each other before and will never see each other again – and that postulates the glamorous single woman – well-dressed, employed, interested in kinky underwear, on the pill, and sexually available – as the ideal sexual partner for the "new" man who will not be "tied down", what is to be the teenage girl's sexual experience? What will she come to know herself to be? Ahead of her lie years of paying for her own drinks and giving head for free, years of men on the bar stool and herself in the mirror of the ladies' room looking back out at a woman-child on her own.

SIXTEEN

Frankie

"Call us on Tuesday."

"HERE," SHE says, proffering a brown paper bag at ten in the morning, "have some lunch." We are bouncing on the back seat of the Kipling bus north to Albion and Martingrove, and "lunch" is an apple, an orange, and a banana. I take the apple.

It's likely that Frankie hasn't even had breakfast. When I called for her at nine o'clock at the group home, she wasn't ready; there's always somebody, the housemistress explained with obvious dissatisfaction, who can't get herself going in the morning. I catch a glimpse of Frankie, towel wrapped around her head, dashing out of the main-floor bathroom. Later, she will explain to me that because the other girls sleeping in her room were so "hyper" – so yakkety-yak and giggle giggle – she couldn't fall asleep; in the morning she couldn't wake up. We stroll down Spadina towards the subway station, Frankie swinging the paper bag. We are going to a Canada Employment Centre an hour's ride away so she can look for a job in a part of the city where she wants to live and work.

As far as I'm concerned, bouncing along in the Kipling bus, we've come to the edge of the known world, but Frankie prefers it here, miles from downtown, because it's "quieter". Even as she speaks, huge truck-beds and buses and diesel-engined semi-trailers gear down, roaring through the intersection. But it's near here where she grew up, from the age of six, with her mother.

Mother. The heartless one. Gave birth to her near Montego Bay, Jamaica, on her own father's yam "plantation" and four years later took off for Canada. Two years motherless (fatherless since the age of six weeks), the daughter waited for the summons to the home in Toronto, to the mother who, "because of" the child, was scrubbing floors and who, only by heroic effort, secured a proper job. By the time Frankie showed up in Toronto, her mother was working as a claims officer for the Workers' Compensation Board. Mother is a really smart person.

Mother, furious. Coming home from work, finding some laundry undone, clobbers Frankie. Frankie is afraid of her: Mother is always clobbering her. When she clobbered her finally with a tin can, leaving a nasty gash, Frankie was not even brave enough to tell the school nurse what had happened. "Oh! A bowl fell out of the cupboard and hit me on the head." Disbelieving, the nurse called in the vice-principal, who called the cops and the Children's Aid and whisked her off to hospital for stitches. "Oh no, oh no," thought Frankie. "What have I done?" Mother, furious, took her home from the hospital, only to be visited by two policemen that very night: Did Frankie, thirteen years old, want to charge Mother with assault? "No." And they went away.

Then the torment began. Being locked inside the apartment. Click, door opens, she goes to school; she comes home, the door closes, click. In the summer, she does not go out. Mother calls from work to make sure she's still there. Where else on earth would she be? Watching from the window how kids play in the park, she finally decides, the hell with this, and breaks out. Running, running, on the grass, around and around the park, and then, realizing she will be beaten on her return, she runs away. Through the streets until three a.m. Children's Aid finds her.

Mother, they tell her, doesn't want her back.

You could hear a pin drop in the Rexdale Employment Centre. Standing in clumps at the notice boards, people study the help-wanted cards with grave deliberation (as though the one phone number, here, will produce a destiny different from that one, there) and then sit and wait very quietly. Everything is padded, muffled; even, from all appearance, the anxiety.

Clerical Jobs. A word-processor operator, must be fluently bilingual, etc. Frankie can't speak French and doesn't type "all those words per minute". Anyway, she prefers a weekly to a monthly pay cheque: you don't have so much time to lose track of it. *Sales.* "I ain't gonna sell nothing." *Cashiers.* "I don't operate machines." Not only that, she doesn't have grade twelve (but she's lied about this before and not been found out), she doesn't have much work experience (customer service at The Brick, food prep at McDonald's, chambermaid at Howard Johnson's), and has no car or driver's licence.

Dining Room Service. Fast-food preparer, $4 an hour. Reliable, courteous, friendly. Enjoys working with public. Reads, writes, spells English. No experience required. Duties: preparing food in the kitchen area of a fast-food restaurant. Frankie writes down the phone number. *Kitchen Help.* She writes this down too. $5 an hour, M-F 7–3. Physically fit, neat, clean, willing to train. Duties: some heavy lifting of bags up to 50 pounds, peeling vegetables, general clean-up.

The fast-food restaurant is McDonald's; Frankie scratches it off her list. The "kitchen help", it would appear, is supposed to be male: the fifty pounds required to lift have suddenly become sixty, as Frankie speaks with the employer on the phone. When she tries to get his

address, he hangs up. There is one more place to try: the
Constellation Hotel needs a room-cleaner. We head off on
a bus, and another bus.

For six months, living as a ward of Children's Aid, living
in a group home with a bunch of crazy kids. Willie, handsome at fourteen, with a moustache, a dope dealer. Mau-
reen, fifteen, a prostitute, and Ken, at sixteen a heroin
addict. Ronnie with the angelic face, a dope fiend. Dope
and sex and hi-jinks, yes, they were all each other's
friends, even when the boys ambushed Frankie in the
basement, gagged and tied her up, and left her there. Fooling around. Whenever they wanted to get out of the home,
simple: they kicked out the screen window and dropped
down to the roof below and from there to the pavement.
And away to the park, for a couple of tokes and a couple
of beers. Those were good times. Mother thinks the group
home ruined Frankie – she gained weight, she learned to
smoke, she did some drugs – but really she was a good
girl. Even after nine months living with her crazy, burned-
out friends, even after getting charged with car theft (it
wasn't her fault!) and being fined twenty dollars, even at
age fourteen, Frankie was still a virgin.

   In her mother's home again, nothing changed. Except
now Frankie is "ruined" and "bad". The social worker,
another "Jamaican bitch", sides with Mother, and Frankie keeps running away. Three days before her birthday
she is broke, calls up Mother's boyfriend from a pay
phone, says she'd like some money to party. He says sure,
meet him on Queen Street. She's under sixteen and on the
run. She gets off two stops before Queen and walks to the
corner, looks around, sees nothing suspicious, walks into
the restaurant – and a guy grabs her, asking her, his snout
in her face, if she's Frankie T. She says No, and, even if
she was, who wants to know? He's a detective and he puts
her in a detention centre. The next day Mother picks her
up, drives her out to the airport, and puts her on a plane.

One-way ticket to Jamaica. If she ever tries to get in touch with her Toronto friends, there'll be no ticket back.

Frankie's been looking for work for weeks, ever since she got laid off from The Brick, and has had only two interviews: at Lickin' Chicken as kitchen help on the midnight shift (she turned this down) and on a switchboard for a courier company. She was qualified, she *knows* she was; they gave her a spelling test of street names and she got them all right, but the guy said, "Call us on Tuesday," and when she did he said the job was filled. In fact, as she pointed out to me on the Employment Centre board, the job was still posted. Could it be, she only half wonders, that they didn't want to hire a Black?

So it's back to the hotels and the application forms for chambermaid, a job she'd rather not have to do. Well, the Bristol Place would be okay – beautiful men who drive beautiful cars go in and out of the lobby doors – but the dolly you have to push around loaded with sheets and towels and cleaning fluids and ashtrays and mops is very heavy and you're expected – can you believe this? – to clean seventeen rooms a day. But she'll do it again. Just to get some money, get established; and then to think of upgrading herself.

Jamaica, again. At first hating it, the food smells, the mosquitoes, the kids running after her, calling her "Miss Frankie", like she was some kind of *tourist*. At times she lived with her grandfather, at other times with friends, and sometimes alone, loving to hike through the "plantation" at dawn to watch from a plateau the sun come up over the green island and the village awaking below. She dropped out of school. In Jamaica you have to pay to go to high school, and for the bus trips and the lunches and the uniform, and Mother said she couldn't afford to keep her.

Learning Jamaica. Learning Rasta. The men in dread-

locks became her first friends there and taught her how to
toke properly. Learning weed and enjoying the smoke,
God knows. Under their tutelage she became an expert
marijuana grower and struggled to understand what she
calls their "rebellion" – the holy weed, the Ethiopian
church and redemption, the stories of David and Solo-
mon, black men. . . .

Learning men. She had boyfriends, oh yeah, oh yeah.
Three. An English chef. A student, tall and beautiful. And
Les. Half Chinese, half Indian Les, tall and tanned and
rich: his father owned many head of cattle and thousands
of acres of sugarcane. But Frankie was too "dark" for the
liking of Les's mother, and so she sneaked out to see him,
leaving behind, under her bed-covering, plumped-up pillows in the shape of her sleeping body. . . . She was
caught, and Grandfather locked the door to keep her in at
nights.

When she was seventeen, in 1983, Mother came to Jamaica and took her back to Toronto.

The personnel manager at the Holiday Inn is off for lunch,
but from a small table outside her door Frankie helps
herself to an application form. She fills it out while drinking coffee in the employees' canteen and while I take measure of the fact that, having inquired of a busboy in the
corridor where the cafeteria is, we were directed here,
behind the Staff Only door. Muzak, microwave ovens, free
coffee in a pot.

At the brand-new Venture Inn we sit awhile in the
wicker chairs in the lobby, admiring the airiness and the
pastel prettiness of the interior. Frankie is filling out another application. Says she wouldn't mind working here at
all. Finally we arrive at the Constellation Hotel, where she
is expected; again an application form. She waits, and is
interviewed, and waits some more. The interview, to my
mind, was very brief. To Frankie, it was to the point: her
job history. The pleasant young personnel manager comes

out of her office to tell Frankie that she's passing on her application to the chef and if she's heard nothing by next Tuesday. . . . Yeah, says Frankie to me, aboard the bouncing bus back to the subway station, personnel managers look down their nose at you. It's part of their job, didn't you know?

Life with Mother at seventeen: stupid rules. No phone calls in, period. No going out, period, unless to go shopping with Mother. Out at nights? Only dogs and prostitutes run at night, says Mother. All evil things are on the loose at night. . . . The things that made Mother mad: the way Frankie cooked, the clothes she wore – jeans and runners and big shirts. A bum, Mother called her. Screamed at her for cutting her hair. Threw out the make-up Frankie hid in the pockets of her purse. There was no understanding her; there was no conversing without arguing. Frankie would march off to her room, shut the door, and read. This only made Mother madder. But Mother wasn't beating her any more. Back from Jamaica, Frankie stood up for her rights. Mother yelled a lot but Frankie never yelled back. Just stated her case and walked calmly to her room and shut the door.

She was back at school and failing. She quit to work at The Brick. And here she met Alan, a salesman. Now the real trouble began, for Alan would phone her at home in the evenings and Mother grew very suspicious: Who's that keeps calling?

At Christmas in 1983 Frankie left home for good. She was seventeen. At first she lived with Alan, but then found her own apartment. She was getting a weekly pay cheque and feeling good, in control of things, even to the point of telling Alan, no, she was not interested in getting pregnant. It pissed him off, her taking the pill. Guess he wanted to prove his manhood, like all those Jamaican creeps who hang around the black girls at the group home: get them pregnant and then split. No thanks. Frankie doesn't want babies now. She hasn't finished school, she hasn't *seen* anything yet, *been* anyone yet.

Then crisis. Frankie was laid off. She had exactly one week's pay cheque and some holiday pay, enough for one month's rent, but that was all, until she could collect UIC. She asked her landlady if she'd take half the rent until she had more money together. Nothing doing. Frankie came back from a weekend at Alan's and found the locks on her apartment door changed. She turned around and went back to Alan's, leaving behind, locked inside the apartment, all her precious things: a small television set, some gorgeous shoes, her teddy bears, her teapots, and her books. She had to leave her books behind.

Man, she was not getting along with Alan. Walked out on him at one in the morning with nothing but the clothes on her back and some quarters in her pocket. From a pay phone she called the women's hostels; all filled, and her down to her last quarter. She would *not* go back to Alan's to use his phone. "What are you? Some kind of bum? Hostel? Only lazy bums need hostels." And so on. One last call. There's a bed in a group home off Spadina. She caught the last bus to Kipling station, waited and waited for the train to Jane. Waited and waited again for the bus to Davenport, getting off and wandering lost, heartsick, and in tears, trying to find her way. She found it, and was home again, in her fashion.

It grew on her, this house with the musty basement and the bathtub to share with nine others. The furniture was rather shabby but the food was good, and so what if she owned precisely nothing. She had a place to hang out free of charge – the TV in the basement, the radio in the dining room, the paperback novels at her bed – and some people who attached themselves to her. Her problems were the least of them in that house. Here were pregnant girls who didn't know who or where the father was. Boyfriend is beating them. Pill-poppers. Girls who've slept in stairwells for nights on end. Most of them think they've got Prince Charming for a boyfriend, but you can tell from what the girls themselves say that really they're just assholes. Like one girl has a guy who won't work, won't go to school, won't leave his mama's home. Another girl is pregnant, the boyfriend is in the States; according to her, he's working there, so why doesn't he help her out, huh? A black girl's pregnant, the father is Italian. No way is his family going to let them marry, so here she is, weeping and wringing her hands, asking Frankie, should she get an abortion? Sometimes Frankie would just like some space, some privacy. Sometimes she'd just like to be able to lock herself up in her own room.

She won't be staying in touch with her old friends. She needs what a social worker once referred to as a "role model", and the old friends have no motivation. Just sitting around, collecting welfare and doing drugs – grass and acid and free-base cocaine – and selling drugs and hitting Frankie for some dollars when she got her pay cheque. But when she was down and out, where were they? At the dance halls, that's where, and the pool halls and the pinball arcades. She still thinks about Alan. She got up the courage three weeks ago to call him, but all he had to say was, "If you call here again and my new woman answers and you give her a hard time, I'm going to call the cops!" She did call again and he answered and she couldn't say a word. She just hung up. . . . She's not going to stoop that low again.

Sitting at a picnic table behind the house, jabbing her bare toes into the long grass and laughing low, slow, throaty laughs, it's the future she wants to talk about. Get a job and get out of here. Back into an apartment of her own with her teapots and her books. Finish school. Maybe work *and* go to school at nights. Pondering what she wants to be: a lawyer, a cop, an accountant.

She wants to travel. She wants her own bed.

SEVENTEEN

Jobs

*"A counsellor told me that, five years ago, a teenager
would have to make fifty or sixty contacts before
getting a job; nowadays it's more like one hundred
and eighty or two hundred."*

"OF THE EIGHT female full-time workers, two worked as
waitresses, two as babysitters, two as sales clerks, one
as a hairdresser, and one did crafts. Of the three who
worked part-time, two were babysitters and one was a
cashier." The figures refer to the teenage girls interviewed
for the 1985 report from the Canadian Advisory Council
on the Status of Women, "What Will Tomorrow Bring?":
They are nothing if not banal. Of course, the reality of
girls working is also banal: the work they do is low in
status, badly paid, taken for granted, and mainly without
possibility for advancement.

There are the occasional exceptions. One girl is a model
and earns professional fees as she's shepherded around by
a watchful mother from client to client. Another works in
her boyfriend's motorcycle repair shop as the accountant,
sales manager, and clerk. A third – alert, cheerful, bright,
ambitious – is hired on as a page in the provincial legisla-
ture. A girl whose father is a CN employee puts the pressure on him to get her a brakeman's job.

But the girl who works at the window of a take-out

restaurant for four dollars an hour and who has no idea if she's entitled to benefits as a part-time worker; the girl feeling lucky to get $4.50 an hour in the jean boutique; the girl hired on at the movie theatre because the owner applied to a subsidized "hire a student" government program – these are the dime-a-dozen cases, the typical cases.

Charlene and Donna, seventeen and eighteen years old respectively, are good friends who both work at the quintessential teenage job: at a fast-food joint. Both have just finished high school in Vancouver and are not quite sure what to do next and when to start: their final grades were not brilliant. They both live at home to save money. Donna would like to get into theatre; she's a cook in a Boston Pizza restaurant. Charlene would like to be a travel agent; she's a cashier at Kentucky Fried Chicken. Both feel they are lucky to be employed at all. Donna filled out thirty job applications before she was hired on as a pizza cook; she was hired, not for her experience, which was limited to waitressing a few weeks at a burger joint for $3.05 an hour, but because of her "enthusiasm". Charlene, who hired on at Kentucky Fried Chicken just by walking down Richmond's main drag and asking for work, had no work experience except babysitting.

Charlene has been at this job since grade eleven, when she worked thirty hours a week from 5 p.m. to 11:30 p.m. every night for three dollars an hour for the first month; this was raised to $3.65 after a month on the job, to $4.45 after three months, and to $6.00 after six months. She thinks she's being overpaid – her job, called Customer Service, is to take orders and ring them up – because she does a lot of sitting around. This may be true, Donna points out, but the reason she's sitting around is that she knows her job so well she can do it virtually without thinking about it; she's *earned* that six bucks. Put it that way and Charlene agrees: damn right.

"A lot of people have told me I'm the fastest drive-through. Some people don't have my memory. The most orders we can have at one time is three, but you should see some orders – fifty million things. I don't write it down. That's why I can run it through so fast. I demand they pack my orders fast. You can pack a full meal – chicken, fries, salad, and a biscuit – and have them out of there in one minute. I *love* seeing the expression on people's faces: 'My order's ready?!' "

Donna's starting wage is four dollars; she makes the dough, slices the green pepper, tomatoes, and onions, grates the cheese, and makes the sauces from scratch. Some days she doesn't sit down once between nine in the morning and five in the afternoon: she doesn't eat, doesn't take a coffee break, doesn't even go to the bathroom, she's so busy, running herself off her feet. The other staff members tell her to take it easy, but if she does sit down, she fears she'll never get her jobs done in time. Maybe when she's more experienced she'll be faster.

Their jobs are fraught with hazards and perils. Charlene buys her own (expensive) leather work-shoes, because she's seen what hot oil spilled on canvas sneakers can do to your feet; Donna has burned her hands on hot cooking pots and cut her fingers on the meat-slicer. The possibility that a plainclothes company inspector may come in to order a chicken sandwich in which Charlene has failed to lay the lettuce "just the right way" makes her exceedingly nervous, while Donna is still apt to burst into tears in chagrin at not having enough time to get everything done. But Charlene's harshest feelings are reserved for the "ass-hole" customers, the drunks, for instance, and the guys "in jean jackets and greasy hair down their necks and a joint hanging out of their mouths" who like to spray ketchup at each other and tear up the lunch boxes, yuk, yuk. Donna quit her old job at the burger joint because of a manager who persistently fondled her bum but whom she feared to confront – "I was really wimpy" – because he was so important and the other female staff chose simply to avoid him as best they could: "That's the way it works," they said. Charlene has put up with a manager who makes lewd references and little jokes about taking a shower with her – "How about it, huh? Huh?" – but she has not chosen to make a complaint: "Maybe *they'll* complain to the top manager and my side of the story won't sound good enough."

It would be reasonable to assume that, given the degree of their dissatisfaction and distress at their jobs, Donna and Charlene would welcome the change to belong to a union. Charlene indeed is a member of the Food and Service Workers of Canada, one of a small minority of fast-food workers to be organized, and is appreciative of the fact that, thanks to the union, she's earning more than the industry minimum. Beyond that, however, she expresses absolutely no sentiment of solidarity with her co-workers or with the notion of a workers' collective: if the union called a strike, *she'd* go to work, *she'd* cross the picket line. Donna, not unionized, is more thoughtful: "A friend of mine works in a movie theatre and makes $6.50 an hour – doing what? I *sweat* when I work. It doesn't seem fair."

If their working lives were only drudgery, of course, Charlene and Donna would be simple wage slaves. But they are able to extract something for themselves in the exchange of wage and labour: for Donna it's the pleasure of hearing that someone really enjoyed the pizza, the one that *she* cooked, and for Charlene it's the customer who drives away smiling, laughing at her joke, saying he's coming back with some friends, she's such a good waitress.

In April 1986, 795,000 Canadians between the ages of fifteen and nineteen were employed. (In 1982, this figure was 817,000; the decline reflects the crisis of unemployment in this age group as elsewhere.) Unsurprisingly, teenagers are generally employed in trades, which include jobs in boutiques in shopping malls, and services, which include fast-food restaurants. The Canadian Advisory Council on the Status of Women report, cited earlier, stated that teenagers (of both sexes) who came from "lower SES [socio-economic status] families" were *less* likely than middle-class kids to be working part-time while attending school. This is an unexpected finding until one realizes that, in the retail and service sectors, the pressure to present an inoffensive corporate image is intense on the employees ("Be neat, clean, and conservative", in the words of an Ontario Youth Secretariat job-finding guide) and only the blandest-looking of "nice kids" need apply.

Although some teenagers, usually working-class, work to help out their families, most teenagers work in order to pay for the satisfaction of their own desires – for something as vague as their own "independence" or something as vivid and concrete as "a red Mustang just like the one my girlfriend has." They save for summer holidays and for Christmas presents, they want their own money for clothes and cosmetics, they like to be able to pay for movies and video games and snacks, even on a date; they have acquired expensive tastes: drugs, imported vodka, designer jeans, fifty-dollar haircuts. In fact, a January 1986 American marketing survey[1] estimated that U.S. teenagers spend $30 billion a year on items of their own choosing.

If they work for pay, they also pay for working: their school grades drop as they discover they must choose between a placement on the night shift and homework, and, in fear of being laid off, they choose the night shift and fall asleep at school. To make up enough hours on the job, they cut classes and miss exams and try to do their homework on the bus to school. They don't seem to be at all impressed or depressed by the fact that they are usually paid only a minimum wage and have no idea what they're entitled to in the way of benefits, or that they are ignorant of the protection available to them under the law and of the means to qualify for unemployment insurance; to their minds, in spite of the gross exploitation and manipulation of their situation by employers and advertisers, "kids who don't work are spoiled, middle-class jerks." The *wanting* to have things, the *need* to work, said one high school principal in Edmonton,[2] "makes these kids as intense at age sixteen as a guy of thirty carrying two mortgages."

Vivian needed money. She needed clothes: her mum would only buy her the bare necessities and Vivian was tired of wearing T-shirts until they shredded and sneakers until they got holes. So, at sixteen, she has her first paying job, at McDonald's, and brings home thirty to one hundred and fifty dollars every two weeks, depending on how many hours she's worked. In six months she's made nine hundred dollars and has one hundred in savings to show for it, plus some clothes, a couple of purses, lots of shoes, and the memory of a bunch of lunches she's treated her girlfriends to. Her parents are not thrilled. They don't like the way she can say to them, when she's brought home another pair of shoes, "It's *my* money and I can buy what I want." This independence scares them to death; next thing they know, she'll be buying cigarettes and gadding about all hours of the night, paying for her own taxi fares.

She's on crew at McDonald's. Three dollars an hour. When you're sixteen and non-unionized, what can you expect? If you question the arrangement, you can get into trouble. The staff still tells the story of the guy, a couple of years ago, who was "talking union" and got fired – the subject has never come up since. Vivian might be getting a raise one of these months, to $3.30. There's no point in quitting; if you quit and then want to come back on, you start all over again at the minimum.

When McDonald's hired her, they asked her: What job do you want? She said, Window! because that's the job where you meet people. She didn't want Grill, because that's where you have to worry about ugly burns from the fryer, and your hair gets all gross from the steam, and the hats they have to wear are real stupid, and she didn't want Lobby, where you do the degrading jobs like mopping the floor and taking out the garbage. The place has one hundred and fifty employees, full- and part-time, and there's more guys than girls doing Grill and more girls than guys doing Window. Of course, no one ever discusses wages, but Vivian doesn't think the boys get paid more than the girls. Well, the starting wage is the same, but it's true that if you work in the kitchen where the boys are, you learn a lot more skills – you learn how to do fish fillets and McChickens and dress the Macs and work the grease vats – than if you're at Window, where there are only two or three things you have to learn. Vivian supposes this means boys get their raises faster than the girls.

These are Vivian's duties: she checks to see that all orders have been taken, that the plastic cups and lids are stocked up at the counter, that salt and sugar containers are full, that everything the customer can see is clean; she makes coffee and fries and ice cubes. It can get very busy, because no food may sit around prepared longer than ten minutes: that's company policy. "There's lots of throwing out" and starting over again. Vivian timed herself once on her stopwatch: a minute and a half to take an order – Big Mac, a Coke, fries, and a sundae – and serve it. That was under perfect conditions: no interference. But she loses time when customers make trouble for her, like the lady who ordered a turnover and was staring right at it while Vivian packaged it and then said she hadn't ordered it at all! When Vivian argued, the lady said she was rude and called the manager; Vivian was not pleased. This was a mark against her, because of course she was in the wrong.

She is constantly being tested. Her raise depends on her performance, and crew trainers put her through tests. The Service Test, for example. There are Six Steps in servicing a customer: greeting the customer; taking the order; stating the price; receiving the order from the kitchen in a certain sequence so none of it gets cold; presenting the order and taking payment; saying "Have a nice day!" You can screw up in a hundred ways. You can forget to "suggest" the customer also order fries or a dessert, you can forget to say the price, or you may look uncertain about how much change to give, or put too much or not enough ice into the cold drinks, or even make the sundaes too big or slop ice cream over the cone. You don't exactly *fail* these tests, but when they do a follow-up on you – where you start at 100 per cent and lose points for every mistake – and you only score 50 per cent and your service tests weren't perfect either, well, don't expect much of a raise.

It isn't that Vivian exactly feels *spied* on all the time. Usually she knows who's doing the testing – other crew members. She accepts the criticism as their way of helping her do better, and now she does the same with the new crew hired on since she began. The important thing is to get along.

Vivian is proud to be a McDonald's worker. (If she had power to make changes, though, she'd go for it: increase the wages, and change the nylon uniform which gives her blisters when she works under the heat lamp.) It makes her mad – sad, even – when people dump on McDonald's, calling it a junk-food joint. Okay, so it's not gourmet; it's bread and meat and lettuce and tomato. But when she was a kid she used to love to come to McDonald's, and now just the idea that she's actually *working* there, serving the food she loves, well, it's just too wonderful.

"Age: 18. Sex: F. Source of income at referral: nil. Last job: waitress. # weeks of employment: 60. Reason for termination: fired. Living situation: unstable. Education (grade completed): 9. Barriers to employment: lacks work experience; lacks direction; motivational problems; lack of self-discipline; history of poor attendance; history of poor punctuality; poor relationship with authority; emotional; poor attention span; housing; life-style; lacks appropriate coping skills; self-esteem; dependent on others."

"Age: 18. Sex: F. Source of income at referral: social assistance. Living situation: stable. Native status: native. Education (grade completed): 7. Last job: waitress. # weeks employment: 12. Reason for termination: personality conflict. Barriers to employment: grade level; drugs and/or alcohol; lack of self-discipline; history of poor attendance; unrealistic goals; racial/ethnic."

"Age: 19. Sex: F. Referred by: Rape Relief. Living situation: stable. Education (grade completed): 12. Last job: cashier. # weeks employment: 78. Reason for termination: not enough hours. Barriers to employment: lacks work experience; emotional; low frustration tolerance; medical; lacks appropriate coping skills; self-esteem; dependent on others; family problems."

The bare bones of biography: the computer print-out from a government-funded youth employment program. It may be filled in with details of a girl who hates school and heads for the street, another who is trapped at home with a predatory father and a case of shattered self-confidence; a girl, drunk and stoned, "forgetting" to show up for the five-o'clock shift, sulking, screaming even, at the supervisor who points this out; another, daydreaming of the movie director who will set eyes on her and take her away from this place, for there is no way she will (can?) change her own life, she whose hands sweat and heart races at the very thought of having to quit this lousy little job, open up the newspaper, circle the ads, and start all over again, Please, mister, can I have a job? ("Get outta here.")

In April 1986, there were 169,000 unemployed Canadians between the ages of fifteen and nineteen (17.5 per cent of the labour force in that age group). Add those who have given up looking for work or who are underemployed (working part-time but wishing full-time employment), and the rate of youth unemployment is closer to 26.5 per cent, according to a study by the Social Planning Council of Metro Toronto released in 1985.

The figures – roughly a quarter of a million unemployed teenagers – symbolically represent an emotional prostration – anger, depression, despair – that afflicts people who might reasonably expect to be getting on with their lives, testing their intellectual and social prowess, and learning how to take care of themselves. Instead, they are thwarted in this development, this growing up, by uncontrollable events: the collapse of a local economy, the worsening of international trade relations, the freeze on social service budgets, the over-enrolment in colleges and trade schools, and so on. And, when they realize that against such overwhelming odds they can offer only their pitiable eagerness to work (but no record of what they are capable of, and little experience of their own authority or awareness of their personal attractiveness), then the slide from eagerness and resolution to resentment, frustration, loneliness, and helplessness seems almost inevitable. Savings have run out, one more application has been filed away, the parents have been nagging and goading, the Canada Employment officer was rude and unsympathetic, the future – of the whole world! – looks grim and bleak, what the hell is the use of anything: they flop down in front of the television set and do not move for months.

She started life as the daughter of café owners in a northern British Columbia town, a role in which she learned to work, and work hard (as soon as she could get her head over the countertop), grilling hamburgers, washing dishes, washing the floor, and standing up to drunks, refusing them credit. When she was older, her parents gave her a bit of an allowance; she saved it, allowing herself to spend money only on fashion magazines; something to take her away from the town. She had a plan; she was going to be a make-up artist.

She graduated from high school and a day later left for Vancouver. She lived for a while in a house in a seedy area in the east end and shopped around for a place to study. She chose a six-month course at a "fashion school" which cost her seven hundred dollars to study, two nights a week for two hours each night, basic glamour make-up and theatre and special-effects make-up. She paid for her own supplies and, because the school did not provide models, she was forced to drag in friends to practise on. When she completed the course, she had in mind to "get into" clothes, design, putting looks together – a kind of consultant for models, say.

She started with the department stores and with the specialty make-up shops but discovered that every other fashion and make-up graduate had put an application in ahead of hers. CBC had ceased hiring after suffering budget cuts; stage actors, too poor to hire professionals, were doing their own make-up.

She began to read Help Wanted ads and to look for Help Wanted signs in store windows and to check out the listings at the Canada Employment centres. The competition was formidable, even for the scrappiest little job. When interviewed, she was rarely asked about her education; what employers wanted to know was how long she was planning to stay in the job. Tricky question. If a job is paying four dollars an hour, are you going to say you'll stay forever? She learned to agree to everything, just to get her foot in the door, to smile agreeably, wear a non-descript feminine suit, and present a padded résumé; she guessed she was getting the hang of it when, of the fifty people who applied for a sales job at a bulk-foods grocery, the boss picked her.

She had a job for two months filling ice-cream cones for four dollars an hour from five in the afternoon until midnight. They had promised her full-time work, but who was going to buy ice cream in the winter? She got a job in a muffin bakery but was fired after two weeks when a crazy customer threw a tray at her, causing "negative attention" to be drawn to the bakery. Then she became a chocolate-maker, a job she loved because it was a kind of craft, hand-dipping the individual chocolates, with no one giving her orders; over an eight-hour period she could make four or five hundred. She started at four dollars an hour and was up to five dollars when she was laid off after Valentine's Day. For three months she held down a job at a clothing boutique in a mall. There were two conditions of employment: that she not discuss wages with the other salespeople, and not sit down in the showroom – it doesn't look good from the point of view of the customers. ("After hours of standing, tagging clothes, you get a little tired – but sit down and you get suspended.") She's not a pushy person, she was not going to sell a customer something that was unflattering, she tried to make genuine suggestions, and so she'd sell only sixty or seventy dollars' worth of merchandise a day, compared with other clerks who were regularly selling several hundred dollars' worth. She was "terminated", never having earned more than $3.65 an hour. For $4.50 an hour she made sandwiches at the bulk-foods store, but, rent being what it is on fashionable Granville Island, the shop went belly-up and she was out of work again.

Between jobs, she's been out of work for weeks, even months. She tries to keep her depression, her fatigue, her fluttering panic under control: she adds the latest job to her résumé, cranks up her smile, and hits the pavement one more time.

She shares an apartment and pays $210 a month plus utilities; rarely eating out and eating no meat, she spends $150 a month on food. She buys clothes at second-hand shops, goes to the art gallery, and buys the occasional record for entertainment. She doesn't drink, she doesn't own a car. She owns a futon, some clothes, some dishes, books and records, and some shelving. It can all fit in the back of a Volkswagen. She's saved not a cent. She lives, she says, below the poverty line.

The only time she had some spare cash was after an accident when a drunk driver knocked her down and broke her collarbone, and the Insurance Corporation of British Columbia paid her victim's compensation.

She's walking a line, between being "incredibly materialistic", not wanting anything in life but money and goods, and being defeated, taking a job at Jean Junction and asking no more for anything. Between jobs, her morale is low, flat, beaten. To be nineteen and to feel you are of no value to anyone or anything, to feel you are "scarcely human": how did this happen to her?

As of August 1985, there were 24,000 people aged fifteen to twenty-four in the Greater Vancouver area looking for work; all the youth employment agencies in the area together service about one thousand a year. Of these, the YMCA Job Generation program had serviced to that date one hundred and thirty-five, "graduated" one hundred and six, and found jobs for ninety-one, at a cost of about two thousand dollars a client on a three-month-long program. This is the proverbial finger-in-the-dyke, but for every young person matched up with an employer, there is, presumably, one less biography of despair.

In despair they arrive at the office on Davie: if they *do* know how to look for work, *do* know what they want to do, and have a respectable appearance, the co-ordinator, Niall Trainer, can do nothing for them. His mandate is to assist the people, fifteen to twenty-five years of age, who have been either out of school or unemployed for the last six months and who are unlikely to find a job without help. (In September 1986, the unemployment rate in Metro Vancouver among fifteen- to twenty-four-year-olds was 14.3 per cent.)

Thirty-three per cent of the clients are female, reflecting the fact that, in absolute terms, there are fewer unemployed women than men in that age group: in British Columbia, the male-dominated industrial jobs are vanishing, while service and retail jobs ("the pink collar ghetto") are relatively plentiful. But the despair of that 33 per cent is real, vivid, unarguable. Young single mothers, for example, who haven't worked for a while, relying on social assistance, have a hard time taking themselves seriously as potential employees; even when they do, they find it hard to work evenings, and must deal with employers suspicious of their parental obligations: is she going to be late to work because she has to drop the kid off at day care first? Will she miss work because the kid is sick? Young women who've been on the street are reluctant to break with their street friends, not to mention with drugs and alcohol. They're unfit, suffering from malnutrition (not eating complete proteins for days in a row), lack of exercise, and alcohol and nicotine addiction, and are almost incapable of withstanding even a mildly strenuous eight-hour-a-day job. They have achieved, on average, a grade ten education but read at a grade six or grade seven level.

"We ask our clients," says Trainer, "to develop three goals: for today, for a year from now, for three years from now. We help them develop a career plan so that they can see dishwashing, for example, as a stepping-stone. Otherwise, they just job-hop from one low-income, high-frustration job to another." Indeed. As Trainer himself points out, the jobs his clients are being offered are "low-skill entry-level positions", positions vacant as a result of jobs changing hands, workers job-hopping in a vain effort to find some satisfaction. But a girl starting out as a clerk in a boutique can aspire to be a supervisor, say, and then to study design at night school and look around for a job in a higher-class store. Or, if she is a waitress, she can hope to be promoted to cashier and then to manager. Or, as a secretary, she can desire to be an even better one. On the other hand, there are young women who want only to work as a salesperson in a budget-clothing department "forever and ever" because they want never to have to look for a job again.

"I try not to get people terribly excited about their job possibilities," Trainer continues. "You do them a disservice getting them excited about very unexciting jobs. Well, welcome to the real world!" Trainer's "optimistic" scenario for them comes as no surprise, then: marriage to good husbands. He has no doubt that this would be a "better life" for them than what awaits them in the work force.

Fran arrived at the office of John Duggan at Vancouver's Specialized Youth Unit (a Canada Employment Centre),

referred by a group home in which she was living, seeking
refuge from the street. She was a prostitute wanting to
give up the life, had gone off drugs, and was wanting to
work with kids. Or animals. Or as a hairdresser. The standard catalogue. She had no job experience, no skills, only
a grade nine education and a grade four literacy level. But
this much she had going for her: she had the idea she
could do something. Her social worker knew of a day-care
centre that was willing to take her on if they didn't have to
pay her the going rate, and so Duggan drew up a Career
Access contract according to which the Specialized Youth
Unit would pay 85 per cent of Fran's wages for thirteen
weeks, 50 per cent for twenty-six weeks, and 25 per cent
for the final thirteen weeks. In return, the employer agreed
to train Fran. It is doubtful, said Duggan, that Fran
would have been hired except under such an arrangement:
Fran is an example of the "employment-disadvantaged".

SYU is a "pre-employment" program, meaning that it is
concerned to provide clients just as much with skills and
resources as with a job referral or placement. The target
group is fifteen- to nineteen-year-olds with no more than a
grade ten education who have been out of school at least
six months. They need all the help they can get, from bus
fare and clothing vouchers to a sense of outrage about
their condition. Duggan says "kids this young are not
angry about their unemployment, they accept it as a condition of their life." They do get upset about specific outrages, like being cheated on their wages, but on the whole
Duggan finds them "unaware of the world around them
and their rights." He's particularly aware of girls' passivity, their opting for only the most traditional work, their
inhibition in telling you what they mean when they say, "I
can't get a job because I can't do anything." Duggan sees
in all of them a kind of delayed adolescence in which the
young person still expects "instant action" in response to a
demand loudly enough pressed: "They see the world as
'solid state' – push a button and something instantly
comes on." They are, at the same time, curiously unenter-

prising, reluctant to go "all the way" out to Richmond, for example, to get a job; some of them, born and raised in the east end, have never been to Point Grey, only a few miles away.

The first time Lara came to SYU she was fifteen; she was living on the street, and was a drug addict, and a social worker brought her in. She submitted to an interview and then vanished. She turned up again when she was seventeen. She had gone back to school and called SYU on her own; she wanted to come in, she said, to talk about "career planning". Accordingly, the staff gave her a battery of aptitude and interests tests, but Lara was left dissatisfied: nothing was suggested to her that deeply interested her or offered the potential of a "decent" salary (i.e., one starting at $11,000) or could be pursued with only a grade twelve education. She tentatively selected the interest category "Dressmaking, Tailoring, and Hairdressing", a selection which, in the case of hairdressing, shows a certain unawareness, Duggan thinks, of the work world: hairdressing is an occupation in which she could expect to be on her feet all day for little money but much abuse from customers.

A few months later, Lara received her grade twelve equivalency, which would have admitted her to a vocational school (but not to a college), but she decided that what she really wanted was to get a job straight away. Basically, says Duggan, she wants a job that pays "a lot" of money (say, six dollars an hour) without her having to go to school. The SYU staff consulted her test results again: Lara had consistently focussed on production rather than office work, and on creative rather than routine work, an uncommon combination in a world of mass production. Her first job was tagging clothes for a merchandise display. Her second was with a jeweller who was willing to pay a little more than minimum wage to get a white-skinned employee. The employee, however, had to agree to take only five minutes on her coffee break. She agreed. She lasted a month.

Chalk it up to experience. That's how Duggan would like to see it: the opportunity for a kid to be "exposed" to more of the world, to expand her sense of what is possible for her to do. Never mind that the projections regarding youth employment are "terrifying" and that what waits for her out there in the world of work is a kick in the head. For a couple of years at least, when she's nineteen, twenty years old, she will have the chance to believe she's found the work worthy of her. For a couple of years.

It is not an edifying account, this narrative of young people, out of school, out of work, without the motivation or discipline ascribed to middle-class success stories. The narrative sweeps on to include kids with learning disabilities who can't read, have only visual memory, cannot remember oral instructions, cannot file alphabetically, kids who need constant supervision on the job or who, after repeated rejections in numberless personnel offices, simply take no more chances, no more risks, feeling safe only at home in front of the television set and drawing welfare. There are the kids who refuse on principle – and who would gainsay them? – to take on boring work performed by interchangeable labourers, and the kids the governments do not know what to do with except to pass them on to employers (who are willing enough to augment their profits with labour subsidized by the state) and hope that nobody will notice, once the subsidies and grants have run out, that what we have here is a group of people who will spend half their lives unemployed: they will never have work, or none by which they can measure their humanity. The question, "And what do *you* do?" will strike them as completely inane.

In the black-and-white photograph Xeroxed onto the second page of the newsletter, Wendy stands clutching herself at the elbows and wearing a big grin. The photograph is labelled "Career Start's New Office Assistant" and her comments run alongside: "I think Career Start is a very helpful programme. I have been here quite a while and I have seen a lot of people get jobs. . . . It is nice that people care about the job problems the youth have and that they are willing to help." Wendy is sixteen and her grin is a brave one.

She was living away from home and looking fruitlessly for work when her parents phoned to tell her about Career Start, sponsored by Vancouver Community College and financed federally through Canada Employment, whose target group is those who have dropped out of school, and have become bored with watching the soaps and lying on the beach, and who are looking for work without much hope of finding it.

The first couple of weeks Wendy was tested to find out what academic level she was at and what sort of character she had. She learned that her math was grade nine, her English grade twelve, and her self-confidence nil. She had to answer, for example, the question "Do you have any friends?", which she found perplexing: when she's depressed (and she was depressed in those days) she feels she has no friends at all. "Do you lie?" Do they mean is she a compulsive liar, or someone who just tells little white lies once in a while? "Do you steal?" Do they mean a car, or bubblegum? She didn't pay too much attention to these questions, being more concerned to upgrade her academic qualifications. It was a matter of some jubilation to her to discover that, on a computer, she *could* do math.

She began a systematic job search. It was part of the program, four hours a day for four weeks. Usually people have found jobs at the end of six weeks; Wendy looked for four months.

"You go every morning, punch in, phone a certain number of business numbers every day. Then you've got to go 'cold calling', which is just going around to places asking them if they have a job, except you've got to go through a routine: 'Hi, my name is Wendy and I'm good at this and this and I want a job.' I never did that. I'd just go in and ask, pretty quiet, if they had any job openings at the moment, and they'd say no, and I'd leave them a copy of my résumé. It had *nothing* on it except this one job I had for a year in a fast-food joint and some babysitting. I was looking for a job in a clothing store and I was called for an interview exactly once. They phoned me back to tell me the job had been taken. Then I started phoning around pet stores and finally even babysitting jobs, but that's too little money, about two dollars an hour. I had maybe two interviews in all. Nobody would even call me back: that was really depressing.

"A counsellor told me that, five years ago, a teenager would have to make fifty or sixty contacts before getting a job; nowadays it's more like one hundred and eighty to two hundred. They told me I was having trouble because I'm only sixteen, and I don't have experience, so they knew it was going to be hard for me. But they also told me what I had going for myself: 'You've got a nice personality and you work hard and you've got to make them understand you can do it.' Which is what I've been concentrating on. But I'm shy.

"At first I was very enthusiastic and made a lot of phone calls, but then I got totally depressed very quickly. After the first month or two I thought I'd had enough of it and I started saying I'd made phone calls I never did and I just sat there, doodling. I was really bored; looking for a job is boring. I don't know why I stuck it out. I kept telling myself this was the only way I was going to find a job so I just had to stick it out. And I did."

Finally, the College itself hired her for two months as office assistant. Her job was simple – answering the phone and doing some typing and filing for the secretary. When she took over the secretarial duties herself, she was given a raise to $4.65 an hour. It barely covered her expenses but she was grateful enough for it: the job gave her something to put on her résumé. And it gave her the patina of someone who is used to work, or, as Wendy put it, "I talk better, more confident, even though I'm not." As a result she landed another job for a month, taking telephone orders and typing a newsletter and some correspondence and filing for a cosmetics manufacturer who hired her at six hundred dollars for the month even though she was only sixteen and didn't have grade twelve or much of a typing speed. So Wendy is grateful all over again and enjoying the feeling of actually *doing* something and having a routine.

"I don't eat breakfast [or lunch or dinner]; I just snack. My stomach's shrunk, so when I do eat something I get a stomach-ache. I get a half-hour for lunch. And quit at five. They're supposed to give me a coffee break but I didn't say anything about not getting it because I'd rather have the money. They don't pay you for lunch break. I walk down to a pay phone at every lunch break and phone my boyfriend and then have a few cigarettes. I suppose I'm bored, but I make myself say I'm not. The people here are really nice to me."

At the end of the month, however, she'll be laid off. She knew that when she took the job. What she is dreading ahead of her is not the impossibility of living on three hundred and fifty dollars a month from Unemployment Insurance but the probability of having to go back to Career Start and begin the job search all over again. Seven months' looking for a one-month-long job: it exhausts her just to think of it.

There are several ways by which a teenage girl lives in poverty: she shares a household with impoverished adults; she lives on the street; she works for a subsistence wage; she lives on student welfare. But there is only one way by which she lives in affluence: she lives with or is supported by well-to-do adults. She may not perceive herself as exceptional – "I've never thought of myself as all that rich," says Teddy, who lives in an enormous house, has the use of her parents' condo in the mountains, and drives her own little red car – but, outside her own circle of friends, she is the school's "richie". She may take care not to flaunt her privilege – to keep her fur coat in the closet and go to school in the same duffel coat and Roots shoes as her buddies wear, and to get a summer job alongside everyone else in the mall, but she doesn't fool anyone. Maybe she shops in Thrifty's, too, but she'll buy for one hundred dollars the jacket that the next girl must wait for to go on sale for fifty. "You can always tell who's got money," says Barbara, who works in a laundry on weekends to pay her own way. "I don't know how – maybe the way a girl acts, the group she hangs around with, her ten different pairs of shoes, her designer hairstyle, her gold bracelets, take a look at them: real gold."

By contrast, the "working poor", the young women with menial office jobs who bring home two hundred and seventy dollars every two weeks, got there on their own. They spend one hundred and sixty-five or two hundred dollars on rent, they pay utilities and telephone, twenty dollars a month on a bus pass, thirty to fifty dollars on clothes out of every cheque ("I used to wear a jean jacket, a black T-shirt, and jeans all the time," says Wendy, "but then I found out guys don't like girls who dress like that, so now I actually wear dresses"), and hardly anything at all on food. Partying is expensive. They buy a litre of rye and drink it at home. What a drag, to be sixteen and worrying about the frigging utilities bill!

Fifty per cent of Canadian teenagers get an allowance,[3] about half of whom are on a "weekly dole" of six to ten dollars. If they're living at home and spending their nights doing homework, this might just do them. But once they start doing drugs and partying, they need a whole lot more: in two months one girl's bank account went from two hundred dollars to nothing as she withdrew a few bucks at a time to buy grams. If they have the misfortune to live in a group home on a five-dollar-a-week allowance, they can buy themselves two packs of cigarettes. Big deal. In a situation like that, it's easy to see why a girl would go back hooking.

Penny lives alone and goes to school; her parents send

her four hundred dollars a month. She pays one hundred and fifty dollars for a room above a pizza restaurant, forty dollars on a Metropass to travel about Toronto, one hundred on groceries. She regularly runs out of money before the end of the month. The first time it happened she grew dizzy and tremulous from lack of food and took to her bed with her stuffed animals, driving herself a little mad by holding her face above the heating duct and breathing in the odours from the pizza ovens below. She's more resigned now: "Living alone was my choice and I did what I wanted to do, and even if it's hard it was the right thing to do." In any case, she's not one to compare her difficulties with the pain of those hopelessly impoverished, like the school friend whose parents simply didn't have the money to provide their child with lunch, or the people Penny reads about who do not eat for weeks, people who *die* from not eating. To make herself feel better, she will sometimes borrow the money to go into a nice café and have a pot of tea just to make believe she can afford it.

Live band playing tonight, show starts at nine o'clock, it's going to be a big crowd, jumping and hollering. To top it off it's Hallowe'en, people are going to be a little crazy, heck, it's crazy already, look at the way the waitresses are dressed: Rosie's wearing pyjamas and dangling a teddy bear, and Lisa's in a leopard-skin lycra suit stretched over her pregnant belly, with a black nose and whiskers painted on her cheeks, and Joan's come as a slice of cherry pie – that's what she says – in a red shirt, red stockings, red shoes, her shoulders draped with fabric she explains is the "crust" of the pie, but she looks like nothing so much as a giant used sanitary napkin, says Lisa.

Quiet time. Twenty minutes to sit around the brown Formica table and have a drink, grab something to eat – hot roast beef with chips and gravy – on which, as staff, they get a discount of – wait for it – ten per cent. The owners of this place live up on the second floor (two brothers and their aged father) and take an active interest in the way the place is run. Nudge nudge, wink wink. The doddering old father comes down to have a look every day and cop a feel from the waitresses. Cute. Joan says, no sweat, nah, it's not sexual harassment, it's just his thing, and "if you glare at him he won't do it more than a couple of times" and then will move on to the next girl. The other thing about the management is they don't believe in raises: Rosie's been working here for three years and she's *still* making only four twenty-five an hour. Now do you under-stand why waitresses depend on tips? Once, for a few weeks, she made a lot more, the time that management got the bright idea that all the waitresses should wear corsets and garter belts. Wow – she took home a hundred dollars *every day*. Hot money for a nineteen-year-old. But now she's back to scooping dimes and quarters out of the spilled beer and peanut shells.

Rosie's been working since she was fourteen. Her father pissed his money away, her mother, remarrying, told her to move out. Rosie left school in grade eleven and began her working woman's career: a month as a bank teller (until she was held up and robbed); several months in a boutique until she was transferred to a mall in the suburbs of the unemployed and saw her commission plummet to nothing; a few weeks at a leather-goods store until the manager fired her because the manager's ex-boyfriend fancied her; and now this bar.

Not to worry. Rosie's got smarts. She took film and stage courses at a modelling agency and she's going to make it in show business. Don't laugh. Rosie isn't laughing.

EIGHTEEN

Marta

"No one should lead anybody else, but still you should take care of each other."

IN HER PARENTS' none-too-spacious three-bedroom home she has been given the smallest bedroom but she occupies it to maximum effect, and to walk into it is to enter her entire world in miniature. Nothing that is important about Marta, and to her, is missing here. To begin with, the faces of several formidable characters bear down from posters hung on the walls – the androgynous rocker Annie Lennox and computerized renditions of Einstein and the Mona Lisa and of The Who, tough guys from an earlier era – beside an Ontario Science Centre poster (she's good in science in school), The Artist as a Young Machine. This eclecticism of taste is repeated in the found objects on her shelves: a globe, a roll of red toilet paper, a "punk rock" (a rock adorned with a fringe of synthetic fur), a handful of seashells, a Chilean bark painting, a small mirror emblazoned with Led Zeppelin decals, a set of poster paints, a pair of glacier glasses (originally designed for the benefit of mountain-climbers, now in vogue with break-dancers), and a button collection. The collection speaks worlds, as it is intended to: buttons flogging rock groups and their concerts; anti-nuke buttons; "Smash 'H' Block" (from Northern Ireland); "Chile – 10

Years of Resistance"; "To Remember Is To End All War";
"Waddle You Do Without Me?" (Wildlife Artists Inc.
1977). If you follow her into the crawlspace under her
bunk bed, you enter the "Oriental Room", a cranny decorated with odds and ends of chinoiserie: landscape pictures crafted from reeds, a fan, Chinese stamps. But here
Marta also keeps her Asterix comic books, an old encyclopedia, a Spanish edition of Dante's *Inferno*, and, holy
of holies, her sketchpads.

There were girls like this in my high school twenty-five
years ago. They were a year or two older than I and
remote and a little strange, but in a way that I found
deeply alluring: they were artists. They wore dark clothes
and masked their knowing gaze with dark glasses and
disdained the company of someone like me (prudish, a
brown-noser, the president of the United Nations Club,
for heaven's sake), preferring that of boys like themselves,
unkempt and sullen, with whom they read books by Law-
rence Ferlinghetti and listened to music by Dave Brubeck
and sipped tiny cups of bitter coffee at the jazz club by the
railroad tracks. They were, in a word, original. There can
be no more admirable accomplishment at sixteen or seventeen years of age than to be one of a kind.

Marta is an original. She goes to see *The Rocky Horror
Picture Show* at midnights and watches French films on
television and reads George Orwell and Arthur C. Clarke
and admires the Dead Kennedys, the Kinks, and Pink
Floyd, and spends her allowance and babysitting money
on fantasy comic books from specialty shops. She goes to
a French-immersion high school and takes biology notes
in French and enjoys just sitting around with the biology
teacher yakking about art and science and politics. She
also likes to hang out with her friends in the computer
room at lunch-time, devising video games and discussing
just how bad the rock videos can get on MTV.

Needless to say, her friends (all boys, since Marta does
not talk to girls) are originals like her. They are the
school's intellectuals: when they get together they talk

about math. They discuss world affairs, a subject in which each of them has a stake – Sammy is a Sikh, Sean is Irish, Austin is from Trinidad, Ernesto is Argentinian, and Marta, well, Marta was born in Talca, Chile, in 1968 – and their voices around the computer console, *their* computers, can rise and ring with indignation and distress as they review current events: the assassination of Indira Gandhi, the post-Falklands restoration of Argentinian democracy, the IRA, abortion. About these friends Marta has said, "They don't like authority very much, but they won't admit they're anarchists either."

Marta is an anarchist, which to her means "no one should lead anybody else, but still you should take care of each other." She tries to practise this credo at school, helping out students who ask her questions. "What's a byte?" one will ask, and Marta will explain. She never *tells* people how they should do their assignments; she tries to show them how they can get it done their own way. One girl in the computing class was willing to pay her to do the assignment, but instead Marta gave her the basics of her program and suggested she elaborate on it herself. "I'd rather be behind the lines than up front, telling people what to do," she says. She's a good student, she's no troublemaker, but she does admit to having a great urge to paint graffiti all over the school, NAZI PUNKS FUNK OFF!, for instance, on the pukey-green walls of the washrooms.

Her political vision is almost as old as she is: as a child she was taken by her parents to meetings of the Young Socialists in the basement of a left-wing bookstore, from which she retains a strange memory of a crudely animated film about the history of the world as narrated by the rat-inhabitant of a slum. And a memory of herself at six, seated at the very front of an audience listening to a feminist speaker, and making a drawing. She drew a picture of a woman kicking a man, then turned around in her seat and showed it to the crowd. She was a big hit. At eight she announced to her religion teacher ("the guy was a total nut, as far as I was concerned") that she was an atheist

and would no longer come to his class. This provoked
quite a to-do at the Catholic school, eventually involving a
lawyer engaged by her father to make Marta's case. The
argument was, in any case, superfluous as far a Marta was
concerned: she would simply "not stand for" the assumption there was a God. She had tried out a line of questioning on several believers, stumping them each time: "Who
created you?" "My mother." "Who created your
mother?" "My grandmother." And so on, back to Adam
and Eve, who had been created by God. "And who created God?" No answer. Aha. But this was only her trump
card. She had already been scandalized to learn of the
corruption of the Church during the period of the great
crusades; who was to say the corruption was not persis-
tent and actual? She had watched evangelists on television
and coverage of the mass suicides at Georgetown,
Guyana, and had been profoundly depressed.

It is in libertarian politics, not theology, that she
grounds her sense of optimism about the future, although,
to tell the truth, she seems more often aroused to anger
and scorn than to cheerfulness. Ever since she learned
about former president Richard Nixon's foreign policy in
Cambodia and about the murder of four students in a
subsequent anti-war protest at Kent State University in
1969, she has thought of the United States government as
"disgraceful", and when she studied in grade ten the history of Quebec, up to and including the October Crisis
and the War Measures Act, she found herself arguing on
behalf of the FLQ: "I don't sympathize with the FLQ as
terrorists, but I do sympathize with riots and demonstrations, because when your rights are taken away the way
they were by the War Measures Act, well, that reminded
me of Chile: I can't stand repression." President Reagan
horrifes her – he is a "war-monger" – in inverse ratio to
her admiration of the Sandinista revolutionaries in Nicaragua, men and women who "stood up for themselves"
and rid themselves of a savage, American-supported regime. She calls all these ideas a "socialist attitude", care-

fully pointing out it is not "communist", for communist systems, like the western imperialist ones, are "disgraceful", having perverted the original revolutionary idea. She readily admits that, on the whole, her politics are a bit of a hodge-podge, derived from a variety of unassimilated sources: her parents, her "hippie" neighbours in the housing co-op, a newsletter from a Latin American solidarity committee, leaflets from anti-nuke marches, songs by Pink Floyd and the Dead Kennedys, and Charles Dickens' *A Tale of Two Cities*.

But there is one source of her ideas which is pristine and unconfused: her birthplace. Although her parents emigrated to Canada before the election of Salvador Allende and the subsequent military coup, they have maintained contact with their relatives and, more to the point, have cultivated a Chilean "consciousness" in their home in Canada: they speak Spanish to each other and to their children, they spend whole weekends listening to their taped collection of Chilean music, they are unabashedly "progressive" politically, and they look forward to the day when their people will be liberated from the curse of the Pinochet regime. It is obvious that this upbringing has shaped Marta's mind and heart – most particularly her rage against oppressors – but she is by no means her parents' clone. She speaks English, and even French, more fluently than Spanish, having a vocabulary in both as complex as her thinking, and is, she confesses, becoming bored with 1940s Chilean folk songs every weekend – and, I suspect, a little embarrassed by her mother's mispronunciations in English (she works as a nursing aide) and her father's inclination to wink and whistle at women in the street.

But in early 1984 she travelled with her mother to Chile and experienced there a clarity of identification that has never deserted her. She was prepared for her relatives' poverty – her parents had been sending them her own cast-off clothing – and even for the token signs of resistance to the junta (she had seen the newsreels), the graffiti

on pock-marked walls, "Muerte a Pinochet!" She easily
fell into the Hispanic atmosphere, the expressiveness of
her companions and the irrepressible conversation of
everyone around her (on every topic except politics) and
the appreciative whistling from boys in the street, "Oh, la
bonita!" But there were other aspects of Chilean life that
took her by surprise – her cousins' preoccupation with
North American clothing fashions and the new dance
steps (they'd all seen *Flashdance*), the way they coveted
her Police T-shirt, the familiarity with American rock
music, especially with Pink Floyd, whose film, *The Wall*,
had just played, the availability of Clash posters in the
shops, and even posters of the Chilean singer Victor Jarra,
who had been murdered by the junta. There were those
that disturbed her beyond reckoning. It was simply not
safe to be in the streets at night (she had noted the groups
of soldiers, the army trucks hurtling out of side streets)
and so she did not go out, and it was not wise to speak out
loud about politics (her uncle warned her not even to
mention to anyone outside the family that she studies
karate, it being considered a "weapon" by the military
authorities). Relatively well educated, but only intermittently employed, her relatives complained bitterly about
the vulgarity of the official media: the two television channels, for instance, the one broadcasting masses, the other
every move of Pinochet. She had brought along a copy of
Orwell's *1984* and, having read it through, her aunts told
her that that is what it is like, life in Santiago. Marta
could not get used to the ants in the cupboards, the cockroaches on the walls, the fleas in the furniture; to the
beggars; to the thousands of "merchants", men, women,
and children selling pathetic little collections of popsicles,
plastic combs, nail files, bits of cheese, from blankets laid
out on the sidewalk.

No, she would not want to live there. But, when it came
to her leave-taking, "everyone was crying their heads off,"
and she did too, for her cousins, for the benighted Chilean
people, for the *idea* of that country which, although it is

not, she says, her "homeland" any more, did give her birth, and is dying.

Marta wrote this for English class and received seventy-five per cent:

. . . The seventies came with new bands such as Deep Purple, Ted Nugent, Bad Company, and Rush, all of them quite similar to Zeppelin according to rhythms and guitar solos, while the punk revolution was enforced by the Clash, the Dead Kennedys, the Monks, Iggy Pop (who is considered as the Godfather of punk) and Generation X, who all were apparently out to destroy the political/religious/financial structure, teddy boys and Heavy Metal itself, which tended to lean on sex, male stuff, motorcycles and Satanism.

The difference of these two musical ideas is evident in the lyrics; it's hard to find similarities between "the tune will come to you at last/when all is one and one is all/to be a rock and not a roll" and "I am emperor Ronald Reagan/Born again with facistic cravings/Still you made me president.". . .

Marta takes her music very seriously indeed. She always has done. Her first passion, as a pre-schooler, was the music of the Beatles, which she heard for the first time while watching *Sesame Street* on television: a little girl with braids sang "Lucy in the Sky with Diamonds", accompanied by monsters, and a distressed muppet, answering a phone, sang "Help". She began to listen to AM radio, waiting for the Beatles songs. Having no idea how to go about buying records, she contented herself with taping songs direct from the radio onto a primitive cassette recorder and became an early fan of Kiss (she does not readily admit to this now) and Fleetwood Mac and Queen and Pink Floyd (especially their song "We Don't Need No Education"). When, in grade six, she figured out how to buy records, she went a little crazy, buying K-Tel specials, *Goofy Treats*, for example, featuring "Ahab the Arab" and "Purple People Eater". At sixteen, however, she's

settled down with the Dead Kennedys and Police and
Jefferson Airplane: "It's important that songs have something to say."

This is true even when Marta is fooling around, which
she does, playing air guitar with her older brother, Jaime,
for co-op festivities, for the Coalition for Nuclear Disarmament, for a day-care centre. Marta is always the lead
singer. In a big white shirt, loose black tie, and dark
glasses, her high-boned, dusky face almost boyish beneath
her black cropped hair, she jumps and rolls about and
dashes around and screeches and hollers out the songs –
"The caretaker was crucified for sleeping at his post/Re-
fusing to be pacified . . .", "If we can share this night-
mare/Then we can dream/Spiritus mundi" – like a holy
roller in a church of her own.

When she listens to songs, images come swirling into
her head, whole imagined worlds sometimes; songs have
"correspondences" with images. She imagines "Amazing
Journey" from The Who's *Tommy* as a dove flying
around. She draws, too, from her dreams: a cosmic mo-
torcyclist, a figure radiating an aura, images provoked, for
all she knows, from some buried memory of a song heard
in babyhood.

It all converges: the Arthur C. Clarke novels and the
Greek and Babylonian myths she was "hooked on" as a
child and the "Avengers" comic books, the reveries by the
stereo speakers, the recollected dreams and the sketchpads, the pile of sketchpads in her sanctuary under the
bed. Marta is always drawing. Marta pulls out her pad
and opens her box of pencils, or inserts the Micro-Illus-
trator program disc into the Apple II Plus, and draws and
draws and draws. She designs posters for friends' election
campaigns at school and satirical sketches for the school
paper and has even drawn illustrations for articles in a
now-folded ecology magazine. She has never had any formal art education, having been made to feel uncomfortable at art gallery classes and in art classes at school about
drawing so much more expertly than her classmates. But

her father encourages her, making canvasses for her and giving up his own time on the computer so that she can fool around.

It was comic books that got her going. She was five when she bought her very first one, an "Avengers" issue with one of the first appearances of Altron-5, an indestructible robot. She wasn't yet collecting comics – "I didn't know the system and I didn't treat the books very well, kind of scrunched them up" – but in 1977, at age nine, she picked up "X-Men" and was hooked. She wanted to know what happened next, and so bought issue after issue (the series is now a collector's item). She was, in fact, paying more attention to her comic books than to her homework, but she had her reasons: she was fascinated by the drawing – the detail of the machinery and weaponry and costume – especially the European style of sci-fi illustration, a non-idealized, non-heroic depiction of the humans, reserving for the creatures from outer space a nobility of demeanour and bearing.

To her sketchpads she committed her first renderings of the figures and tableaux inspired from her reading: the heads of Medusa and Perseus, the body of Pegasus in full flight, a helmet, a lyre, a bunch of grapes. Then came the supermen and superwomen, Goliath and Dark Star and the Vanisher, who had the ability to teleport himself, and the Avengers, masters of the powers of meditation and the martial arts. And the most awesome, the most tormented of them all, Phoenix.

Marta tells the story: "In all of comicdom, the most powerful is Phoenix, whose strengths are telekinesis and telepathy. She started off as Jean Gray, an ordinary girl from the suburbs of America. She became a member of the X-Men, all mutants. At the time, she was considered pretty weak as compared to all the other members. Later, on a shuttle craft, she was attacked by cosmic rays and died. But just before she left her body she made contact with this universal force called Phoenix and she became one with it and reborn. Still Jean Gray but more complex.

She kept on growing in power, but some villains took advantage of her and changed her point of view and she became Dark Phoenix, the evil version, and schizophrenic. She could change plants into crystal. On her first appearance as Dark Phoenix she took off to another galaxy and consumed the sun, which destroyed all the worlds around it. And she couldn't care less how many people died because of it. Eventually, to save the universe, she committed suicide."

There is no denying the admiration for this woman vibrating in Marta's voice as she tells the story, or the pleasure she took, with her pencils, in drawing the flood of black hair whirling around Phoenix's head, the arm thrust out in command, the strapping thighs bearing her down the galactic path to her own destruction.

If one must be female, this is the kind to be. Marta was a tomboy and has always hung out with boys rather than girls. She's not interested in make-up and never wears dresses, although her mother has been suggesting, rather ominously, that she might look good in a skirt. She has also been wondering, out loud and rather wistfully, if any of Marta's friends could turn into a boyfriend one of these days. Marta is in no hurry. The boy would have to be very special: good-looking, dark-haired (a Hispanic would be all right, an Oriental even better), unsexist, anarchist, and sharing her taste in music ("it goes with one's philosophy of life"). He could be religious as long as he didn't try to convert her.

She hasn't ever met such a person. So what? Did Dark Phoenix marry?

NINETEEN

Computers

"What are computers for?"

IT IS THE wish of Kim's father that his daughter become a computer systems analyst (he himself is one) and so she has enrolled in Computer Sciences 20 and sits at her appointed place, one of a class of twenty-two, in front of an Apple. With great application she chews a wad of gum and shuffles her shoes while the teacher admonishes them not to fool around. He knows that many of his students, especially the East Indians and Orientals, are here only because their parents insist on it, and that others are here because of the "gee whiz" factor which has made facility with the personal computer the *sine qua non* of middle-class self-esteem. On the other hand, he has had to keep out the "hackers", those boys who think the class is an entertainment, to be used to make up and play their own computer games or to invade others' programs and files. This inspires the teacher's admonitory anecdotes about a young woman waiting for a kidney transplant whose medical files were "wiped out" when some smart-ass hacker at the university broke into the University Hospital computer. Kim chews gum and shuffles her shoes. The teacher tells another story, about a girl (it's always a girl) who comes into her first computing class, enters "What is your name?" and, when the computer answers "Unknown command", gets mad. Ha ha. Finally the teacher gives the class their data-processing assignment: to make a program that will provide information regarding sales discounts. Unspeakably bored, Kim surreptitiously slips in a friend's disc and plays games instead. "It's a machine," she will explain to me later. "I want to deal with *people*. I'd be a much better social worker than systems analyst. Ugh."

I was to hear this time and again. Computers are boring. They are boring because they require that you think a certain way (usually described as "logical") and no other, as Nina discovered when she "missed steps, jumped over things" that the computer can't jump. "I just don't have the brain for that. I couldn't comprehend a lot of things I was doing *because* it was so logical." Sharon was made to study computers in grade seven – "like, if *this*, then *that*, then that, for this, next that" – and has hated the machine ever since. Computers are boring because, as Carla asked, "What are they *for*?" Oh, it's obvious enough, because everyone is talking about it all the time, that the computer is here to stay, doing marvellous things behind the scenes at banks and airports and so on, but for what interests a sixteen-year-old girl – her friends and her music and her poetry collection – what good is a computer anyway? Jodi gets depressed just being in the same room with a computer, not to mention in the company of a computer enthusiast who doesn't really want to be with you anyway: he wants to be up in his study, hacking away. Jodi says that computers are making people "boring and unsociable": "My boyfriend's old girlfriend *builds* computers. . . . She's a very boring person."

If only it could just be left at that, with computers humming away in the background while they themselves got on with the important things. But many girls are anxious about the potential power of the computer over their lives. Carla frets that she won't be able to find a job that a computer couldn't do just as well, and Nina is scared that the new technology is "going to hit us like another Renaissance" and leave her behind in the dust of history because she *will not* learn, and Sharon, who feels she's living in the "wrong age" anyway, ruefully expects to die an "unnatural death" thanks to a computer malfunction.

In 1985 it was estimated (by the Pepper Wood El-Hi Report on Computers in Canadian Education)[1] that, by the end of the 1985–86 school year, there would be 120,000 microcomputers in elementary and high school. While educators all seem agreed that "computer literacy" is the goal of this impressive investment, there is no agreement concerning the definition of "literacy"; it ranges from "a degree of programming skill" down to "knowing where the on-off switch is". In the literature, however, there is agreement that, no matter the degree of the technology's accessibility, girls avoid computer "literacy" as though it were a kind of social disease. They are not found, for instance, playing in the video arcades; if they are present at all, they are standing at their boyfriend's elbow, gasping in admiration as he demolishes the electronic enemy. Nor do they show up in the same numbers as boys in the computer clubs in school and in the computing sciences classes. Because computing is associated with math and because computer science teachers often double as math teachers and are usually male, "computer avoidance" may in fact be descended from math avoidance. But they do fill up the "data processing" classes, banging away on the electronic keyboards like the generation of girls before them at IBM Selectrics and the one before that hammering at Underwoods. This is another way of saying that girls do not have an independent and instrumental relationship to the computer (there is nothing they want to *do* with it), and will learn to use it only as this era's version of the typewriter: a means to getting an office job. If this is "computer avoidance", then, it means that one way or another girls have "learned" that as far as computers are concerned this is still a man's world.

Consider the advertising. Sitting in respectful contemplation of a Commodore 64 computer and its software (a science program on the screen) are a father, a mother, a son. The boy is in the centre, hands on the keyboard. The father has an arm around him, and, in his hand, the user manual. In relationship to the computer, the mother is doing precisely nothing. In another Commodore 64 ad, for home computer systems, four men are portrayed using the system to compose a song, design graphics, compute calculations, and "scheme"; a woman is shown using hers – in the kitchen.

Consider the associations attaching to computers. Computers are "about" math and machinery and logic, all of these predefined as hostile to femininity. Males much more often than females are seen using a computer, whether in advertising, in workplaces, or at home, and using it authoritatively and creatively. The extreme of this is the "hacker", the amoral free spirit who pirates software, unlocks telephone lines, and overloads time-sharing systems, a thoroughly modern hooligan. There is the student who aggressively "takes over" the machine, and time, in the computer club and feels no compunction about reaching over to press the keys of a computer at which a girl is working; and there's the solitary kid who can spend hours by himself in front of a screen never thinking he's missing a thing by confining his communing to a "dialogue" with a word-processing program. These are all stereotypical male roles, played out in a masculine culture which American psychologist Sara Kiesler, writing in *Psychology Today*,[2] described as "a world of electronic poolrooms and sportsfields, of circuits and machines, of street-corner society transplanted to a terminal room."

Girls' culture is not like this. Girls' culture is intensely verbal, the preferred activity being to hang out together and yak, and is based on a diversity of interests (clothes, movies, hobbies, romance) that obviously cannot be satisfied by means of single-minded devotion to a computer terminal. At this point in her social and sexual development, a girl is acutely aware of the penalties imposed on girls who are "aggressive" and "competitive" and "brainy", and so will hold back from taking over a machine from a boy, or from competing with him in a game for fear of winning, will "give up" in the face of a technical difficulty, pleading feminine incompetence, will think twice about jeopardizing her social standing by choosing programming proficiency over hanging out with her friends, and will even, according to a report by Canadian writer Heather Menzies,[3] *underestimate* her abilities in such male-oriented disciplines as math, and fail, much more than boys, to match her scholastic achievement with her IQ.

Consider the software. The cursor on the screen is referred to as "he" by the teacher, and "characters" are often identifiably male. Packaging displays male athletes, male warriors, male pirates, while the games and programs themselves are overwhelmingly masculine in tone and assumption: games of combat and assault, aggressive and destructive challenges, tableaux of explosions and collisions, and general mayhem. These are programs setting spatial tasks, but programs for writing, music, and art are far less available. In an American study[4] noting software preference, it was learned that girls prefer fantasy games, "word-oriented rewards" (as opposed to graphics-oriented), and completion tasks (where the object is to finish something); unsurprisingly, then Pac-Man is the only arcade game equally popular among girls and boys for the simple reason that it is a completion task and does not involve blowing anything up.

In response to the seemingly overwhelming disadvantage experienced by girls in school in relation to computer science, the Toronto Board of Education Committee on Sex Equity and Computers has put forward a series of draft recommendations that include: "encourage staff to ask girls to transport and set up computers in rooms and to demonstrate software"; "encourage promising Grade 9 mathematics students to take Computer Studies"; "set aside one or two after-school or lunch periods per week for girls only"; "encourage students to discuss their work together"; "use word processing in all classes involving writing"; "hold father/daughter, mother/daughter computer evenings at school".

All such proposals assume, not without evidence, that unless girls quickly achieve "equity" in the computer science classroom, they will be superseded in the workplace by better-prepared male colleagues. Numerous studies have identified "trends" in the patterns of female employment: the separation of women into a secondary work force where they work at only a few different jobs, and the concentration of women in clerical work, which leaves them particularly vulnerable to the automation (i.e. computerization) of the workplace, especially the office. In *Women and the Chip*, Heather Menzies wrote that the million or so women actively seeking work could be unemployed all over again by 1990, an unemployment related not so much to lack of jobs as to lack of appropriate skills to go along with the new type of work. Since a large proportion of the new jobs being created is in computer-related fields, such as systems analysis and design and programming, and since the office of the future is undergoing radical change from hierarchical work relations to a more collegial model, from "passive" clerical support work to "dynamic" computer communications, and from dull, routinized work to work requiring more science and computing skills, then girls in school had best prepare themselves for these changes *now*, while they still have the opportunity to acquire more skills and a self-image that is assertive and forward-looking. It has even been argued that girls are potentially *better* computer programmers because of their well-known attentiveness to detail, their willingness to take time over painstaking work, and their neatness in laying out a program.

"If computers are the answer," said Ingrid Wellmeier of the Toronto-based New Technology Working Group, "what is the question?" It is precisely the failure of the computer aficionados to ask some basic questions about the whys and wherefores of the new technology that upsets the sceptics. MIT's computer science teacher Joseph Weizenbaum[5] is not the only – but perhaps the wittiest – observer to have noted the relationship between the arrival of personal-computer ads in all media, with the consequent generation of acute anxiety among middle-class parents lest their children be labelled "illiterate", and the need, among hundreds of high-tech companies, to sell their product. As Weizenbaum put it, "computer literacy is basically a disease that was invented when it became necessary to market the cure." What has been lost amid the hype and hysteria is any sense of what constitutes real literacy, i.e., mastery of one's own language, the ability to speak and write clearly and precisely, which is to say the ability to think clearly.

"Computer literacy" guarantees none of this, only that a student will be able to manipulate a certain kind of machine. As an education consultant, Gail Posen worries that not only are children failing to learn to read and write with any kind of flair or confidence, but they lose the chance to learn to relate socially with ease and to stand up for themselves and make demands of their environment by being hooked up earlier and earlier to a computer. Because you are "making" a computer do what you "tell" it to do (this notion bears some examination), there is the illusion of control. But in fact there is no possibility to intervene in the program and ask *who* conceived of this technology, who designed it, how it was introduced and why, and whether it should continue to be used.

Parental anxiety regarding children's computer literacy, and the number of programs and courses and the sums of money invested in alleviating this anxiety, obscure the extent to which it is a middle-class event. After doing a survey of all United States schools in 1983, Quality Education data[6] reported that the 12,000 wealthiest schools are four times likelier to have microcomputers than the 12,000 poorest schools; and that, among junior high students, fewer than 17 per cent of the students from rural and ghetto areas reported use of school computer equipment, whereas 32 per cent of the thirteen-year-olds in "urban/rich" areas reported such use.

Aside from the obvious economic inequity between the household that can afford to buy video equipment to "fool around" with and the household that cannot, there is the subtler disenfranchisement inherent in the failure to fulfil the original mandate of a school system – a basic mastery of English, oral and written, and of math, and a nodding acquaintance with history and geography – on behalf of its working-class students. These remain *the* tools of economic and social survival and even advancement. While the school system may be counting on the parents of middle-class children to provide them these basics while the school itself devotes its energy to "computer literacy", no such environmental pedagogy assists the working-class kid. By knowing how to key in data but not how to write two sentences in logical sequence, the working-class girl is no further ahead of the game. The "system" may very well require more and more engineers and mathematicians and systems analysts, but it won't be her it will draft. The computer, far from disrupting class relations, reinforces them by rendering the "problem" as one of machine power beyond social control and the "solution" as amenable only to the individual application of "literacy", in which, of course, not all are equally adept. All the rest of us are asked only to adjust.

Simon Fraser University computing sciences teacher Margaret Lowe Benston, in writing about "The Myth of Computer Literacy",[7] warns against wholly believing the new "dogma" that a New Information Age is upon us, that we all, but especially women, must learn the new computer languages, and that anyone who questions the dissemination of computer systems is a neo-Luddite. Unfortunately, as Benston points out, the issue is not nearly so simple. The computerized workplace, for instance, far from being a liberated zone of "dynamic" and "collegial" relations, is experienced by bank tellers, airline reservation agents, check-out clerks, and telephone operators as a nightmarish locale where they are served a long list of boring and repetitive tasks which are then speeded up. Worse, the employees operating the computers are kept under close supervision and even surveillance so that they are measured quantitatively rather than qualitatively in their performance, lose rather than acquire skills (a computer program, not a typist, centres the page), are isolated from their co-workers by being tied to their screens, and must deal with a hostile and uncomprehending public when the computer "goes down."

It may very well be that the new jobs being created are in the heavily computerized service sector, especially in the fast-food industry, where even now the cashier does not need to know how to ring up sums but need only push the button that says "double cheeseburger" or that simply shows an *image* of a double cheeseburger, eliminating the need not only for "computer literacy", but for literacy altogether. But such jobs, along with automated office jobs, require only a minimal technical skill. These are what Gail Posen of the New Technology Working Group calls "part-time junk jobs – it's phoney to say this is the big opportunity for the future." After all, as the Canada Employment ad in the subway car said, a good typist can become a good word processor in an hour. If that's true, just how demanding and challenging and financially rewarding could such a job be? A woman working at a word processor does not have to program her own machine; she has only to use it, a skill she can pick up on her own from a manual or in one semester's instruction in school. In fact, unlike the old secretarial skills, which were not easily transferable (how many managers could do shorthand?), word processing and data processing are easily enough learned that there is pressure in some offices to dispense with secretarial staff altogether and have middle managers key in their own memos and correspondence. Clerical staff would be retained only for data entry, as this is, far and away, the most boring task.

It is a myth, then, that simple computer literacy is the key to the mass entry of women into "high tech" employment; it is the key, rather, to continued ghettoization. The truly challenging jobs with the financial reward are in computer engineering and systems design, male-dominated disciplines that remain closed to most women in the same way and for the same reasons that engineering and physics are. To render them accessible to women will require a strategy and effort vastly more radical than the simple demand for more computer literacy courses for schoolgirls. In any case, historically there has been very little correlation between higher education or retraining and women's job mobility; statistics have consistently showed that, for all their superior education, many female workers earn less than male colleagues at the same level.

It is therefore stretching things somewhat to argue that computers represent a revolutionary break with western print culture and that girls will thereby become beneficiaries of a new order. Computers are no more than state-of-the-art tools of our current social and economic practice and, from a girl's point of view, are already comfortably installed in its sex-biassed traditions. Why *should* she study Computer Science 30? It will only, in the end, be used against her.

TWENTY

Nina

*"I want to be a business executive and an
artsy-fartsy dance teacher and a designer and a
lawyer. I wish I could be twenty-five forever, so
I could do them all."*

MAKING my way through clutches of dance students
tittering in the corridor and pairs of parents whisk-
ing children in and out of doors and instructors leaning in
open doorways smoking cigarettes (dancers smoke so as
not to eat) and dancers massaging their swaddled legs, I
am trying to find Nina's ballet class. I poke my head into a
classroom where a dozen girls are performing warm-up
exercises on the floor. They lie on their backs, their heads
towards the far wall, and raise and bend their legs in one
stretch after another. From my vantage point I see the
sharp arch of their pelvic bones and the flat, muscled
plane of their bellies and the slight swell of their little
breasts. They are all fifteen and sixteen years old, and the
power of their girls' beauty (a femaleness still unconsum-
mated, still unaware of what is to become of it) is stun-
ning.

I slip away to the gym, which, by means of barres and
full-length mirrors, has become Studio One of the Edmonton School of Ballet. There is a man at the piano, and
a male instructor, one male student, and thirteen girls,

some of them remarkably large-bottomed. I recognize Nina: tall and slender, wasp-waisted, hipless, her hair tied up and pinned and flattened down. She is lifting her leg high, higher, and looking very concentrated and very, very feminine. I am seduced again by ballerinas, even these would-be ones, these less-than-swanlike ones, who, driven by their private fantasy, sacrifice their leisure time to come here and lift high, higher, higher, to the tinkly tune of a school gym piano and the raspy drill of an aging danseur, transforming the utter mediocrity of the scene into one of incipient grace. "You don't *extend* yourselves," the instructor chides them, "as if you're wondering if your body can last. It *can* be extended. Now is the moment when you can let things happen. So, get the legs up there, hold them, go beyond what you've done before." This isn't quite Nina's problem. She will explain to me later that, although she has a lot of extension, she doesn't know how to control it. She hasn't got enough stomach muscle. After ten years of ballet, she's just learning now to use her muscles.

Here is another mystery: If dance is not a recreation and it is not an exercise or an entertainment, if it is not even one's job, what is it? What is Nina doing, Tuesday nights at jazz dance class, Mondays and Thursdays at Ukrainian dance class, Wednesdays and Saturdays at ballet school, sweating and leaping and twisting and panting, her whole being focussed on points of her complaining flesh, if she is not exercising or amusing herself? She is not at all sure she wants to be a professional dancer, is not sure she's good enough. Why is she doing this? She's been dancing since she was five: an instructor in a children's movement class put on a Cat Stevens record and away she went, spinning around the room, arms in a graceful arc above her head, feeling like a flower twirled on its stem. After seeing a ballet, the notion of loveliness became specific: it was a ballerina with her leg raised in the air. Fragility and delicacy. Maybe the paradox is why Nina dances: through muscled exertion to create, to be, this delicacy poised on space.

But her forte, she says, is lyrical jazz. I'm not sure that what I'm seeing one evening at the Dance Art Academy is lyrical; it certainly isn't ballet. But Nina is in her element. This is an all-girl class and here they are, just before class begins, wrapped up in layers of woollies and T-shirts and socks, flopped like rag dolls on the floor or over the furniture, sharing a cigarette and a can of Diet Pepsi, sitting in each other's lap and fiddling with each other's hair-do, exchanging information about coats on sale, and teasing some hapless, blushing girl about her boyfriend. The instructor, big and bossy with a benevolent-looking face and several earrings up and down her left ear, takes them through a warm-up. Nina rises slowly on her toes, twists her torso with great deliberation, raises her arms and holds them there; she doesn't wobble. From the p.a. comes a blast of disco music. They slide, in mock sultriness, around the room to the beat of "Sex Shooter", then practise striding across the floor and spinning on one foot. From one corner to another, over and over, they leap in grand jetés and tumble over in cartwheels, until one girl – everyone stops to applaud her – can do it without her hands touching the floor.

Nina likes to dance to music that pushes her body, which means almost any music except Heavy Metal and funk at the local discos. She goes with girlfriends; they go to dance, to get rid of some energy. She'll get up on the floor by herself if she has to. She liked the movie *Flashdance*, and had no problems with the bar scenes, because all of it, from the ascetic ballet routines to the lascivious thrust and bounce of the go-go dance, is *dancing*, is a woman in love with throwing her body around.

On a Monday night at the Ukrainian National Federation Hall, Nina practises with Cherymshyna, the "farm team", as it were, for the Cheremosh Dancers, one of Edmonton's most polished Ukrainian dance troupes, a

team its instructor thinks is a "gold mine" of fine young
dancers. Since I was a girl, clattering around on the stage
in the church basement in a makeshift costume in time to
music wafting in from the wings off a portable record-
player, Ukrainian dancing has entered the realm of high
seriousness. I note in the hall the vestiges of the old days –
the pink and white crepe-paper streamers hanging from
the ceiling from a Saturday-night wedding, and the iconic
portraits of poets Ivan Franko and Taras Shevchenko
supervising the hall. But in so many other respects what is
going on here has left the world of the community hall
behind. The instructor has studied in Kiev and speaks of
the need to "stylize" Ukrainian dancing ("Once you put
folk-dance on a stage, you can't dance like villagers any
more, like old 'babas' who can't lift their legs") and to
study the Polish, Russian, Byelorussian, and Hungarian
variations. The students, a large number of them at least,
have studied ballet, and undisciplined jumping and kicking will not do any more; and even the apparently Ukrainian folk steps have fancy French names. So these Ukrainian dancers show up for class in the tights and leotards
and sweat-bands and leg-warmers acquired for their ballet
and aerobics classes, and they line up at barres and practise *fouettés* and the instructor bawls out at them, "Lean
away, *croisée*, lean over, *croisée* front!" and "Okay,
stretch" and they drop to the floor in splits and yoga
postures. Nina looks grimly out from under her bangs at
her reflection in the mirrors. She is magnificent: she kicks
higher than anyone else, keeps her torso straighter, and
handles her limbs like so much spaghetti. After the break,
the practice is given over entirely to the "hopak", a spir-
ited Cossack dance, and the dancers pull out all the stops,
and it all comes back to me in an exhilarating rush: the
urgent, strident music, the pandemonium of whirling and
stampeding bodies, the braggadocio of the male dancers'
leaps and struts and stomps.

Nina dances in Cherymshyna not simply because it's
fun and exciting but also because she is of Ukrainian

origin, and when she's up on stage in her embroidered costume and red boots, gliding gracefully through the steps and gestures of a "haivka", she gets a "certain feeling" from the realization that her ancestors had once upon a time danced like this, too. Her statement is simple: I'm a Ukrainian and I'm proud of it. Not for her the diffidence and the identity crises of the first and second generations. "If I was denied something on the basis I am a Ukrainian, I wouldn't be ashamed, I'd be *angry*." She doesn't speak the language (although she studies it, with indifferent results, in her school) and she bakes untraditional shortbread for Christmas and her family doesn't make a point of going to church, but she's Ukrainian all the same. Every time she takes her place in Cherymshyna, pointed toe tapping to the beat, ribbons flying about her head, she proves it.

Ballet is the basic dance; from it comes all Nina needs for her other dancing: control, balance, a sense of timing, line, strength, and (this will come up again and again in talking with Nina) self-discipline. It is a punishing exercise; Nina does not think the body was meant to do splits in mid-air or to walk on bent toes. But after ten years of dancing ballet, it's hard to pin down what's "natural" in dance: for a ballet student, walking with a 180-degree turn-out is natural, and when dancing a simple "kolomayka" (a circle dance) Nina will instinctively "pull-up" into a ballet posture. Even though ballet is a two-hundred-year-old form, its rules and techniques long established, and allows for self-expression only in the subtleties of a prescribed movement, Nina none the less feels just as creative in her ballet as in her jazz dance class. "When I'm dancing in front of the mirror, certain movements just lift me in a certain way. I *feel* sadness or happiness. How do you explain why an arm curved in a certain way can break your heart?"

Jazz is more brutal, she says, meaning it seems more uncontrolled than ballet: you can throw your legs around and have a good time. It takes the same basic movements and exaggerates them or modifies them according to its own aesthetic; so, for example, an arm can be bent at the elbow and a leg at the knee, violating the *curve* of ballet, or a dancer is asked to bend way back from the waist or to land on her foot from a high kick. It's demanding, but for Nina there is a "letting go" in it that frees her up from mere technique and into self-assertion. "I'm more sure of myself," she says. "Who I am gets better expressed in jazz dance – that part of me that is searching and striving. It demands that I go into myself to find out what I'm feeling and then to show that in my movements."

Ukrainian dancing is not about self-expression; it is the expression of an ethnic group, and when one dances it one is taking one's place within the collective choreography of generations of people who kicked up their heels; one honours them by recapitulating the gesture. What is required here of the dancer is stamina: incessant hopping and, one after the other, sixty-four jumping twirls. If you've taken ten years of ballet, you can do it, and keep going. But the really wonderful thing about Ukrainian dancing is you can do it just to have a good time. In the middle of a party you can form a circle and start high-stepping it, clapping, shouting, grabbing somebody around the waist, and spinning away. And you don't, not really, have to worry about your technique.

But Ukrainian dancing, because of its very rootedness in a peasant culture, is uncritically reflective of sexist values in that culture, a characteristic that enrages Nina. Prancing prettily as decorative background while the male dancers do their star turns – all those Cossack splits in the air that bring the house down – is not the kind of dancing that demands to be taken seriously. While she acknowledges that "there's not much that you can do with girls' dancing" in folk-dancing, still it must be possible to design a dance that would express femininity more imaginatively than does the trite and predictable "flirtation dance" – the girls seeming to offer themselves to the boys and then fleeing, twittering like so many chicks in the barnyard. "In a lot of our movements we're supposed to be admiring the men. Like in the 'hopak'. The men come running out doing those big cabrioles and we're supposed to stand in a line in the back going 'oooh'. I hate it."

In ballet the ballerina is often the centre of attention, but her role is all too often as a "catch for some prince" and her physicality is contained within sensually innocent romance. Still, it is possible to break these conventions, as in a *pas de deux* (choreographed by the daughter of the renowned Cuban dancer Alicia Alonso) Nina once saw performed by students at the Banff Centre. It was called "Passion" and *she* was seducing *him*. "Even though the man was lifting her, she was the controller. She was aggressive and sexy, saying to him, 'Here's my body.' It was really neat."

But it is her jazz class that epitomizes female free-spiritedness. Not only is it an all-female group where the absence of males means the girls are free to "talk about sex during the exercises and not be embarrassed", it is a kind of dancing that deliberately celebrates the raunchy. This is *not* tits-and-ass dancing, Nina emphasizes, this is sexy dancing *for its own sake*. Here the body – its hips and thighs and buttocks and breasts – is an instrument of self-absorbed delight, and unfettered movement is its own reward.

When I first met Nina she was suffering from "burn-out" as a dancer, skipping classes and giving in to weariness, fearing she had lost her "motivation". It didn't last long, but as long as it lasted she wondered what she was doing as a dancer. She has no intention of being a professional dancer – she wants to be a lawyer, an interior decorator, a movie producer! – although she daydreams occasionally of dancing with a company in New York and living in jaunty poverty in a little flat all by herself. Her ambivalence leaves her vulnerable to her father's reproaches: if she's not going to be a professional, or even get a degree in fine arts or, heaven forbid, make money at it, what the hell is she going to all these damn classes for? She tries to explain that dancing makes her the person she is, and, anyway, she can't just do homework all the time. Would he prefer her to watch TV and turn into a bum?

She has her reasons. Dancing is about learning to discipline yourself (learning to concentrate on one thing and getting it done), a lesson she applies to schoolwork with impressive results. It has taught her how to manage her time (besides all her classes she works part-time at a day-care centre) and to communicate without words, especially across that gulf between stage and darkened audience: "When I watch a great dancer, the hair stands up on the back of my neck and I know she's made me feel what she's feeling. That's what I want to be able to do" She keeps on wondering, then, if she dances to please an audience or to please herself. But when she tells me that she dances to feel good, and she'll never forget how good that feels, she's answered her own question.

Nina is long-limbed and moves with a gravity somehow at odds with the bright girlishness of her face and voice, as though the girl within had found herself resident in a self-assured body while waiting to grow up. She comes into my home in a cloud of scarves and long brown hair and crisp October air, and claps her hands in exclamation at the "cuteness" of my single woman's rooms (they are small and chock-a-block with pictures, books, papers, and mementoes). We talk about living single, and I sense behind her airy femininity and laughing enthusiasm a robust purposefulness which, although still without an ultimate goal, nevertheless is directed firmly away from the trivial and jejune.

She does not suffer silliness gladly. At school, for instance, she has few friends, for she finds her peers to be generally shallow and unambitious, with no desire to do anything but have a good time. Their daily round, as she sees it, is to go to school (mainly to socialize), come back home, watch TV, and, on weekends, to party. She feels sorry for them, that they should find satisfaction in such inanity. *She* goes to school to work, to study, and to get good grades, and her idea of an evening well spent is to meet a friend in an espresso bar and have a good talk.

Just once, earlier this year in grade eleven, she discovered a rebellious streak in herself. Not that she did anything so drastic as skip classes, but for a whole week she sat slumped at her desk, arms folded over her chest, refusing to learn anything: she was fed up learning what she didn't want to. The rebellion was over when she realized the boycott was "unproductive", and now she's very clear about what school is for: to learn self-discipline. She does not, for instance, *have* to go to every math class – "it's easy and I get high marks" – but she goes in order to learn, along with algebra, something that will be valuable in her future working life. "When I finish school, it will help me go to work every morning even when I don't feel like it. I won't phone in sick; I'll *go*. That's what I'm getting out of school: to get my ass in gear and work." She rejects the argument that what she's preparing herself for is "being a good little worker and listening to your boss and getting your pay cheque": that's the most boring kind of life imaginable, just as skipping school to sit at home watching soap operas and eating chocolate bars is boring. She commits herself to self-discipline and diligence for her own sake, so that, looking back on the years of effort, she will be able to see what she is capable of, what she has accomplished, and what she has to look forward to, now that she's that much smarter.

But if schooling were only an abstemious drill – just as, if dancing were only a means to keep the body in shape – she would not be so engaged. There is more to be gained from intellectual work than just study habits: there's what she calls the "wow!" of coming to *know* something, the measurement of a circle, for instance, which is stimulating. There's no *reason* to learn many things, she admits, but it's just so "neat" to know them – "it's really neat to

know that inside your brain is a little molecule called DNA"
– and "exciting" to fill up your head where before there
was only great ignorance: "I *love* Social Studies 20. I'm
learning how the Middle Ages were schizophrenic, they
lost so many writings, the art was so expressionless, and
the Renaissance comes all of a sudden, and Classical art
and literature are reborn . . . and I think that's so *fantastic*!" Her eyes light up and her body leans forward and her
arms weave about in the air between us and I think she is
about to do a little dance. Learning something, and dancing something, converge: "It really feels good."

Nina will not be deterred. From what, she has not yet
quite formulated: "I don't know. I don't know what I'm
going to do and it's getting close and I have to decide."
She will eventually go to university, but first she wants a
break, perhaps to travel around the world. Or to teach
dancing, even though the hours she would have to keep
would be bad and the money not much, but having her
own business would be an enormous plus, to be her own
boss and set her own schedule and not have to answer to
anyone. On the other hand, law has always interested her:
all those people who need defending from the cold, callous
prosecutor, or, from the other side, all those crazed men
who attack children who must be punished. She loves art,
and design magazines, and furniture stores. One afternoon she took her boyfriend shopping for plants and pillows and lamps for his apartment, and it was the most fun
thing she'd ever done. "In grade nine they told us to
decide what we were going to do in life because we had to
plan our high school courses to accommodate that. Yuck.
Forget it. I want to be a business executive *and* an artsy-
fartsy dance teacher *and* a designer *and* a lawyer. I wish I
could be twenty-five forever, so I could do them all."

She will not be deterred. She learned that about herself
last summer when, at sixteen, she studied ballet at the
Banff School of Fine Arts. It was the best summer of her

life. She took the bus down from Edmonton, butterflies in her stomach, still surprised she'd made it through the auditions, and settled into a room with two other girls: together they were known as the Terrible Trio, an epithet, to be honest, more applicable to Shannon and Jane than to Nina. Shannon, Nina says laughingly and affectionately, was the perfect American sweetheart. "She'd see a nice car, she'd say, 'Oh, I love that car! I want to make love to that car!' Or she'd see a man on a motorcycle and she'd say, 'Oh, I want that guy so much!'" They'd go out dancing together at the local discos down the hill and Shannon, of course, would invite a whole soccer team to their table and Jane fell head over heels in love with one perfect blond, tanned specimen and they were both so giggly and spinny and melodramatic that Nina laughed and laughed. Sat back, watched her friends, danced and laughed, and was in bed by eleven.

Nina met a lot of guys and was attracted to none of them. She was glad. Jane was in love and Shannon was having one fling after another and boys came and went, easy come, easy go ("Oh, what am I going to do?" wailed Shannon. "I'll never see him again!"), and Nina watched and listened and commiserated, with no problems of her own. She was friends with them all and was happy to leave it at that. "I'm so glad I didn't have a fling." She didn't, she explains matter-of-factly, see any reason for having one. Her classes came first. The technique. The drill.

TWENTY-ONE

Cultures

"More fun than a human being should be allowed to have"

WHEN THEY were not at school and not at work, here, from a swift survey of details culled over a six-month period, is what they were doing: they watched television – *Hill Street Blues, Three's Company, The A-Team, Fame*, the soaps, hockey games, football games, Much-Music, and, one lone interviewee, *Sixty Minutes*. They went to the movies: *Purple Rain, Ghostbusters, Indiana Jones, Gremlins*, and *The Breakfast Club*. They read a handful of books – a Harlequin romance, some sci-fi, horror stories, *Valley of the Dolls*, and *Mistral's Daughter* – and flipped through some magazines: *Seventeen, Teen, Vogue, True Story, People*, and *Chatelaine*. They listened constantly either to the radio (FM heavy rock or FM pop) or to their Walkmans, to Michael Jackson, Madonna, Huey Lewis and the News, Billy Joel, Jane Siberry, Twisted Sister, and Corey Hart. Some of them kicked or swatted a ball around on soccer and tennis and ball teams, two lifted weights, one went rollerskating, another swimming, and several rode their bikes. Occasionally they visited friends at home or attended private parties, but far more popular were the "video dances" at school (a DJ, a big screen, and rock videos to dance to). They also patronized certain disco bars downtown and certain franchised restaurants (most especially the mall McDonald's). They loved to go shopping or at least to go window-shopping in the malls, and they spent their money in franchised shops such as Mariposa and L.A. Express and Fairweather's, and on drugstore cosmetics, cassettes, records, the occasional video rental, the occasional concert ticket, and on bus fare, school lunches, and cigarettes. Finally, with whatever time was left over from these occupations they did a bit of housework, their homework, and had a chat with their parents as they gulped down some orange juice on their way out the door in the morning.

Some of these details are perfectly stereotypical, just what you would expect to hear of teenagers. They are not, as a rule, a very literate group, or, rather, not much interested in reading anything that isn't "mindless" (their own word) and easily consumed. Yet they are impressively articulate in the sense that they are never at a loss for words, an aurally related skill that was undoubtedly learned in childhood at the knees of the television set. By the time they are fifteen or sixteen years old, however, television has become a much less important pastime, for the good reason that it is something you do in the company of parents and younger siblings (dire tedium), and, as they will tell you themselves, it is so boring. When a girl wants to have fun, she goes *out*.

She goes to the mall. After the last class in the morning, after the last class of the day, she goes to the shopping mall. She goes there to see her friends, the same people she's seen in school and hung out with the day before, to be with them on her *own* time, to sit around a small table in McDonald's sharing a paper plate of French fries and a large Diet Coke, keeping one eye on who is coming and going. She goes to the mall so as not to go straight home, so that for an hour or so she's got some time that belongs neither to the school administration nor to her parents nor to an employer. She goes there on weekends, too, to walk up and down in front of the shops comparing notes with a friend about what's cool and what's not, and what would look best on her. She goes to the movies in the mall; she prefers them to TV: going to a movie is something you do with friends, away from the house. And she drops in on a video arcade and looks for Help Wanted signs in the boutique and restaurant windows. The mall is her community centre, with the advantage over the original that its patrons, except for her friends, are anonymous.

She goes to the bars and the discos. She will go to the one or two that suit her taste in music and men; even here, into the supposedly adult environment of booze and one-night stands, high school culture has spilled over, for there are Heavy Metal and biker bars out in the east-end working-class taverns, without any "stupid" dress codes (you can wear your sneakers). There are franchised "family" restaurants out on the airport strip where you have to eat something if you want to drink, but where you will always run into somebody you know from the preppie brigade. And there are ultra-chic discos downtown servicing mainly single office workers, male and female, and specializing in synthesizer pop. Take your pick.

At half past nine on a Thursday night no one is on the dance floor but the place is filling up. Girls come in in twos and threes, stand up against a brass rail along a side wall, protectively light up cigarettes, and engage each other in animated conversation. At the same time, eyes darting about, they are checking out the scene, evaluating the desirability of the men leaning on their elbows at the bar or critically assessing the looks of any new woman who enters the bar. They have come to dance, and when they do it is not so much to *be* with a partner as to display themselves and to see who else is around (with that gaze peculiar to dancing couples who don't care about each other, eyes directed at some indeterminate spot several metres away in the crowd). They have come, probably, to "tease", to dance and flirt and dance, and then go home, alone. Alongside the slinky office girls, the teenaged girls, in simple pants and baggy shirts, clutching enormous handbags, look somehow outclassed, even by the decor: track lighting, designer wallpaper, furnishings in grey and purple, and waitresses in bright-blue sleeveless shifts slit at the back and belted twice around the hip.

Here are two girlfriends, one rather fatter than the other, absently chewing gum, and there is the willowy WASP princess floating on the dance floor just out of arm's reach of her partner, a conventioneer in a grey business suit; here is the (modified) punk couple, he with a dangling diamond earring and she with a quasi-Mohawk, and over there, dancing in a minimalist style (slow pivot on one spot, arms flopping from the elbows), is a very cool black woman in a calf-length black skirt, gaze directed well past the sweating, jerking body of her frantic partner. There are no "older" women here. Only the young and the very young.

A Friday night at Goose Loonies, "Party and Playhouse", at an unlikely location among warehouses and railroad tracks. This month, at least, Goose Loonies is all the rage among teenagers and it is difficult to get a seat after eight o'clock. It is, without argument, a very amusing club. ("Girls Just Want To Have FUN. Mondays at Goose Loonies are LADIES NITE!! Every Monday is your chance to win a $750 ring from Jason's West Edmonton Mall. Mr. Physique Contests – Guess What – It's Not Immoral, Illegal or Fattening!!") It is also – and this may be the secret of its success – a club where the amusement is very carefully *managed*; Goose Loonies is run by the owners and managers of that other emporium of consumerist fantasy, West Edmonton Mall. Every night of the month is accounted for, whether it's a "lip-sync" competition, free pizza and hot rum specials on Tuesdays, or Hawaiian Nite on a Thursday, or Stanley Cup Dreaming and Shopsy's Hot Dogs ("More Fun Than a Human Being Should Be

Allowed to Have!!") on Saturdays; nor is any moment of the time you spend inside left to chance as dozens of bar employees are deployed upon one entertainment after another. Tables are visited in quick succession by a young man in a tuxedo who plays magical tricks with red balls, by a hunk in a football uniform who hands out Kiss Coupons ("Good for one kiss in the corner in the dark. Redeemable from any participating human being.") and by a fellow in a white fright wig who rolls around on a unicycle. Periodically a "fog" puffs out over the dance floor and confetti spills from the heavens, blue lights descend from the gear-works in the high-tech ceiling, turning and blinking like a kind of periscope upside-down in a sea of cigarette smoke, and small video monitors, placed strategically throughout the bar so the patrons can watch – themselves! – flash the bar specials for the night. Angel, a house dancer, in zany striped socks and a brief skirt, dances her heart out on the floor. The floor clears, the couples withdraw; Angel, after all, is an entertainment.

Everyone is having so much fun! Whole tablefuls of middle-aged couples, dressed as for a cruise, celebrate a birthday. Boys lean against a pillar watching Angel, indifferent to the phalanxes of single girls eyeing them up and down. ("They're all dressed to the nines," one boy complains. "They stand around in their groups and all they want is sex, sex, sex.") Fun. It would, of course, be perceived as anti-social in the extreme to want just one quiet, unprogrammed moment by yourself. Or perhaps, to the people who run this place and to its patrons, that possibility is simply unimaginable. When has the generation baby-sat by television ever been alone?

She parties. She gets together with some friends, some music, some booze, and sometimes some dope, and parties. She has a birthday party for herself: puts up some rock posters (removed from her bedroom) on the basement walls, borrows her brother's stereo, cooks up some curried chicken, and asks her mother to pick up the pop and beer. It's mostly girlfriends she invites; they can bring their boyfriends or even their brothers, she doesn't care. As far as she's concerned, "they're coming here for fun, not for boys."

She'll be playing Trivial Pursuit on a Friday night with a bunch of friends from school and they'll start arguing with each other about abortion and Reagan and computers, but before anybody can take offence someone calls up and wants to know who wants to go to a movie or maybe dancing at CJs and they all pile into her car; she likes to drive, she likes to feel in control. They'll drink, sometimes. If she's driving, she won't.

She goes over to her boyfriend's house, the only place in town where she can party without being hassled by parents, teachers, and cops. She's got snapshots of the best parties. Here's Steve with his bottle of Southern Comfort and his arm around Jill with her bottle of beer, Molson's Ex (is there any other kind?). Here they are sitting around her boyfriend's kitchen table playing Rock Trivia for drinks; if you can't answer a question, you take a drink. Here's Steve sharing his potato chips with his dog and here's Barney putting peanuts in Jill's beer when she isn't looking. Hilarious.

She's invited to a biker party. Well, not exactly invited. She'd been drinking and dancing at one of the biker bars and at the end of the last set the band invited everybody left in the bar to a party. So she went. Downtown somewhere, in a scrummy apartment. First thing she saw was a big fat biker in a black leather jacket and bandanna; she asked him if he could open her beer with his teeth, but instead he used the knife in his belt. No, she wasn't scared. Was there some reason she should be? She sat around looking at centrefolds from *Easy Rider* magazine, airbrush drawings of guys on their Harleys. Really nice. She'd buy a drawing like that for herself if it wasn't for the biker chicks flashing their tits in the same pictures: people would think she was weird. She wandered back into the kitchen and looked at some snapshots on the bulletin board: three guys standing naked on top of a Winnebago. Pretty funny. That was about it: people wandering around drinking beer, chicks in black leather jackets and low-cut shirts with their big boobs hanging out, and some guy in nylon break-dance pants (who let *him* in?) playing with a toy truck. She got home at half past five in the morning. Her dad was really mad.

She went to a party at Marcia's. It was a very good party. Everybody was in a partying mood, there was lots of music, booze, mainly beer booted from somebody's older brother (she was drinking Irish Cream; she'll drink whatever she can get her hands on). They were hot-knifing hashish in the kitchen. (Hot-knifing: turn the stove burner on to maximum, stick the tip of a kitchen knife onto it until it turns red, drop a piece of hash onto the blade, stick the whole thing into a plastic cup, and breathe in the smoke.) There were even a couple of fights. Marcia's parents didn't seem to mind about the holes in the wall and the beer on the floor and the stereo speaker blown. It was a good party.

Legally, of course, none of them is supposed to be drinking or doping, but, as a 1986 national survey[1] of 33,111 Canadian students aged nine, twelve, and fifteen discovered, two-thirds of the fifteen-year-olds drink alcohol at least once a month and forty per cent at least twice a month, and one-third report consuming five or more drinks at a sitting. One in five uses marijuana or hashish at least once a month; twenty per cent say there is no harm in occasional use. In the course of my interviews, I only once heard a censorious thought expressed regarding booze and dope consumption; if anything, their use at parties is considered a normal and useful way of "getting loose". Procuring liquor is not much of a problem: you can get an older friend to buy it, you can steal from your parents' supply, or you can inform some desk person at the Motor Vehicles Branch that you've lost your ID, and, flashing an

older friend's birth certificate, get a whole new fake ID
with your picture on it, just like that.

She does them both, booze and dope. She smokes a little
bit every day, and twice a week she drinks a forty-ouncer
with some friends – it never lasts longer than a couple of
hours because they just drink until it's gone. She'd rather
drink at home with her boyfriend because she can drink
until she passes out and not have to worry about where
she's going to wake up. She never smokes home-grown,
preferring Cambodian at ten dollars a gram (that's about
four joints) every second day. She used to do a lot of acid
when she was younger (she's now sixteen) and she popped
a lot of pills, anything to get a buzz; occasionally she'll
still do MDA – at eighty dollars a gram – but she never buys
it off the street.

She had a group of friends, of varying backgrounds,
sexuality, and experience, who loved each other very intensely. Some were fifteen-year-olds, others were in their
mid-twenties, and a couple were dealers who would show
up with samples from a new shipment and invite everyone
to try some. They started off with small amounts but
ended up doing "massive amounts" – three grams of hash
a day just by herself and the occasional acid and coke –
until she finally had to call it quits. She had other things
to do in life besides get stoned, but it was great while it
lasted.

She hung around with twelfth-graders; on weekends
they'd smoke up. Marijuana, hashish, that was okay. But
she didn't like being around people who were doing coke
and pills. She had a friend who did 'luudes. She told her
she'd be her friend again once she quit the stuff. Nobody
can push *her* into coke or 'luudes. She knows just how far
to go.

If she wants to buy dope real bad, she can always get
the money. Say, Mom, I need some money for lunch, I

have to buy a book for English. . . . Five bucks here, ten bucks there, it adds up.

The students of SEED alternative school took their play to the Sears Collegiate Drama Festival in February 1985, a play they were very proud to have written in large part themselves. Called *Addicts* (Setting: here, Time: now), it was in turns a funny, a touching, a silly, a deeply felt production. And it was here, in the course of songs and choruses and skits and monologues about addictions, that I finally heard teenagers themselves speak critically about their own relationship to drugs and booze, a criticism all the more surprising considering its source: a bunch of punkers.

Out comes the Chorus to a gasp of admiration from the student audience: kids dressed entirely in black, some with spiked hair, black lips, kohled eyes, one with green hair, one with fuchsia, another with a skunk-like stripe, in combat boots, in black tights, skinny legs emerging from under an enormous jacket. Three girls step forward to recite, punk-style, Hamlet's Soliloquy, ingesting, toking, snorting, shooting their drug of choice while intoning the famous lines with a languorous delivery sinister (pale faces, black eyes) in its insouciance. Between scenes played straight from Eugene O'Neill and Sam Shepard and Jean-Paul Sartre, illustrating one kind of "addiction" or another (dependency, sex, despair), the students' own skits spoke of their own concerns: the graphic representation of a heroin addict shooting up (another gasp from the audience), and two girls, one mimicking the mirror reflection of the other, "hooked" on make-up, a scene of such frantic insecurity that a third actress, unable to bear it, confronts them: "Erase your face?! What's the matter, can't you stand yourself?"

For all the punkishness of the play's style and mood, however, for all the outrageousness of its content and its self-conscious hyperbole, here was a series of statements decidedly "adult" in their morality. Consider the heroin addict shaking and trembling and hallucinating about his mama, the opium addict scarcely sensible of the absence of his wife whom he has murdered, the jealous and possessive lovers consumed by bad faith: what are these if not conventional morality fables, even from the mouths of adolescents, cautioning us that an obsession with drugs, sex, beauty, and time will ruin us, our lives will fall apart, our brains will rot, and our very memories will betray us? How do sixteen- and seventeen-year-olds know this, except through grown-ups' conventional wisdom?

She was a TV addict when she was a kid but now she's sick of it. Traded in the TV for a ghetto-blaster, and now her idea of heaven is to get stoned and listen to her tapes. They call her a "stoner": a Heavy Metal person and/or one who does dope. Usually they're one and the same. Okay, so she's a stoner. She *hates* Boy George. A fag like that should be stomped out of existence. Rush is her idea of real music. Listen to their song, "The Enemy Within" – it's part of a Trilogy of Fear, and it's all about the fears you carry inside you, about how you're afraid of things you don't understand and that's why some people want to censor books and stuff like that. Rush put *thought* into their songs. Have you ever listened to the words to "2112"? It's about a guy who lives in the future. He finds an electric guitar and, although a priest tells him to leave it alone, he dreams about what it would have been like to be alive in "that" world, which is her world. It's about a guy dreaming about what it would be like to be free. Another song, "Subdivisions", is about cities and suburbs and how there's no place there for the misfit or the dreamer. . . . A lot of people hate this music, they say it's violent. But *their* music isn't anything at all. Listen to Duran Duran: garbage of the year. Or Wham. Bubblegum music.

In another world altogether, a group of grade thirteen private-school girls pooled their money and bought themselves a blaster too. It caused them some difficulties, as no one could agree on the music that should be played on the common machine. There were a couple of radicals who favoured Echo and the Bunnyman and The Cure, and one girl who liked Heavy Metal ("she was from Scarborough"), and one who listened only to Mozart. At one time everyone could agree on Bronski Beat, the gay band from England, but it was overplayed and became insufferable. Basically, the group loves bouncy music that you can dance to – their Grad theme song is "The Wild Life" by Bananarama, a really "up" song – rather than music with deep meanings, whose words you have to listen to. These girls just want to dance.

It has been estimated that teenagers spend six hours a day listening to music – on their radios, stereos, blasters, Walkmans, and car radios. Nothing remotely approaches it, not even boy-girl relationships, as a source of enjoyment. According to Bibby and Posterski's survey,[2] some ninety per cent of teens say they listen to music "very often". But they are not all listening to the same music; there is no single music which "defines" the teenage experience in the 1980s, as one could have said about Elvis Presley in the 1950s and the Beatles in the 1960s.

This would seem to indicate that today's music does not provide what could be called a unified generational experience, that teenagers do not experience the music of their favourite groups as the expression of a collective activity that distinguishes their generation from the preceding one. In the fall of 1984, for example, three of the five best-selling record albums listed by an Edmonton rock radio station were the work of musicians in their late thirties and their forties (Bruce Springsteen, David Bowie, and Tina Turner), which is tantamount to pointing out that teenagers enjoy their parents' music. When I queried one grade twelve student about this, she was unruffled: she likes Elvis, The Who, and the Beatles, she explained, because it's *good* music and nothing since the sixties has surpassed it.

This, of course, is more complicated than individual taste. Youth of the 1960s experienced their music *together*, in the collective activities of what was known as the counter-culture: in the anti-war movement, the student rights movement, the struggles against established sexual codes, the clandestine consumption of drugs, and the dissemination of rhetoric attacking the corruption of The System – not to mention concerts, festivals, and be-ins. By gathering in a political as well as a musical culture, the youth of the sixties shared in a generational consciousness that affected their experience of fun, sex, and rebelliousness. As the English rock critic Simon Frith wrote in *Sound Effects*,[3] leisure itself was politicized.

Teenagers in the 1980s, by contrast, seem to have fallen back into privacy, where the enjoyment of music is a matter of individual taste and the perennial concerns of adolescence – getting sex, good times, and independence – are resolved privately. Rock commentators who grew up in the 1960s seem to find this discouraging, if not offensive, pointing to the apathy regarding social issues and the fascination with high-tech environments, and the withdrawal into "alternative worlds" that the new music represents. If the best that it can do, in the face of global catastrophe, is to intone the pseudo-profundity and utter naivety of Culture Club's "War, war is stupid, And people are stupid", then 1980s rock is truly bankrupt as a culture of adolescent resistance to adult perfidy. Styles of consuming music, then, reflect the almost complete incapacity of our culture to deal with the general crises such as unemployment and militarism except in the most reactionary way. Thus students, panicking about an uncertain future, commit themselves to the personal solution of grades and career preparation, and youth culture, fragmented among "taste publics", withdraws into private conventions around drugs and sex, and the relief of anxiety in partying. (Relax!)

There has been, however, one particular collective experience which belongs not to the culture of the 1960s but to its aftermath in the 1970s: the women's liberation movement. Looking at the rock modes of the 1980s, it is impossible not to wonder how the messages of feminism – an ideology whose basic tenets have filtered down through all social cells to the point where they have been appropriated even by distillers' advertisements – have penetrated rock culture. One can ask, for instance, how rock in the 1980s projects masculinity and femininity to the teenage girls and boys, who spend six hours a day listening to it.

In *Esquire* magazine in 1984, the American journalist Bob Greene[4] revealed the alarming responses to a Texas radio station's promotion of an upcoming concert by the Heavy Metal band Motley Crue. The station invited listeners to mail in their answers to the question, "What would you do to meet the Crue?" Winners would be given tickets to the show. Here are some of the answers: "When I see them I'd get on my hands and knees and give them my body and even tear my clothes off if I had to" (a fifteen-year-old girl). "I would even get fucked by the ugliest, fattest, most disgusting guy in the world to meet them" (a fifteen-year-old girl). "I'd leave my tits to Motley Crue" (a thirteen-year-old girl). Greene spoke with some of them, following up on their responses. One did not know where her ideas came from: "They just came out." Another thought that rock groups had the right to be treated "like God", which is to say approached by naked women crawling on their hands and knees. A third said she'd be "crazy" not to agree to a gang-bang with the whole band if that's what they wanted. And a fourth said that what turned her on was the fact they looked like "women-lovers".

Women-lovers. A guy wrapped in black leather projects unadulterated masculinity; the unadulterated male desires the female; therefore, Heavy Metal is "about" loving women. It is not difficult to understand the logic, given the ambiguity of the sexuality projected by other male icons of rock and of the object of their erotic suggestion, and the refusal of punk rock artists to play sexual games at all.

Heavy Metal, it seems, is the only rock style that does not equivocate about the content of masculinity and femininity, does not experiment in that purplish zone of unisex where the separate appeals of male and female sexuality overlap. When a girl, drawn to Heavy Metal's unregenerate heterosexuality, imagines herself in that scenario of leather, studs, chains, hair, and sweat, it is not surprising that she has no materials for her imagination other than the conventional ones of male power and female submission. That is what "love" is, and there is nothing present in Heavy Metal to contradict this.

And yet it is not quite so simple. This "message" coexists with a series of others, apparently contradictory. The muscled, humping, leather-bound, bespiked, and bestudded male whipping females into a frenzy of masochistic lust also wears the signs of other identities. Twisted Sister's lead singer, for example, carries around a small suitcase filled with rouges, lipsticks, nail polishes, and eyeshadows, and the members of Judas Priest (hairy chests bared between industrial-strength zippers) wear their hair long and thick and wavy, for all the world like the mannequins in shampoo ads. Motley Crue wear thigh-high leather boots with stiletto heels, a style usually associated with female sadism. It is as though, having established their masculine credentials by playing very loud, very hard rock, they are now free to play around at the edges of that identity without raising questions about the sincerity of their masculinity. It also represents – as does the more experimental androgynous esthetic of New Wave and Prince – the appropriation of "femininity" from female culture by male artists. What is left of it for female musicians themselves to express?

Women growing up in the 1960s found plenty of ammunition that suited their own purposes in the counter-culture, especially in rock music. Taboos that had served to confine women's sexuality within chastity and monogamy fell away and women could get up and rock and roll for the sheer sensual joy of it. They could act on their passions

without cloaking them in demands for marriage and organize their own adventures "on the road" miles away from
home. And they could do all this to the tunes of female
rock stars such as Janis Joplin, Grace Slick, and Mama
Cass, who could shake, rattle, and roll with the best of
them.

Not all of this has been lost to the reaction of the 1980s;
indeed, much has been constructed since. It remains true,
of course, that rock is a male-dominated business (men
monopolize the recording studios, the airwaves, the music
press, the clubs) in which it is difficult for women to intervene, except as singers of others' songs, as celebrities or
sex symbols, and as groupies. Difficult, but not impossible. In fact, an astonishing number of female artists have
recently come to the fore of rock, each with her own
unmistakable character and style. It is no longer true that
women musicians have only the two roles to play, virgin
or whore. They can be middle-aged (Tina Turner), wacky
(Cyndi Lauper), hard-core (Joan Jett), ugly (Annie Lennox), trashy (the Go-Gos), vampish (Madonna), intellectual (Jane Siberry), uproarious (Sheila E.), weird (K.D.
Lang), and self-absorbed (Luba). They can wear all
manner of garment, from brides' dresses to flea-market
specials to leopard-skin jumpsuits, and play all sorts of
instruments – guitar, synthesizer, drums. They do not, of
course, sing with one voice; female speech in rock is diverse. But there does seem to be a consensus in their lyrics
and presentation: being nice never got a girl anywhere.
The 1960s social project may have collapsed, but the
1970s feminist agenda remains in place, and with it a
whole new possibility of female uppityness.

Many teenage girls admire Madonna (the bleach-
blonde hoyden with the come-hither eyes and lips), finding
her "interesting", "not dumb", and "not afraid to be exactly as she wants to be". They find her intriguing enough
to imitate, ratting their hair to look the way hers does,
slinging chains and crucifixes around their necks, and bar-
ing their midriffs between the lines of a corset and a hip-

hugger miniskirt. Madonna is *not* the girl-next-door, that much is obvious, but whether she is more than a fifties-clone calendar girl, updated with fishnet T-shirt and black rubber bracelets, is a matter of some debate.

The popular press has dubbed her the "Marilyn Monroe of the Eighties" (even Holly Brubach, writing in *Vogue* magazine,[5] takes this seriously enough to compare the sex appeal of the two, concluding that Monroe put hers at the service of "love", while Madonna's is at the service of "power and money", but it is not clear which we are to find the more endearing). It is not a particularly helpful juxtaposition, in spite of Madonna's conscious echoing of Monroe's "Diamonds Are a Girl's Best Friend" in her own "Material Girl". For the one woman was as immobilized by her sexuality (passive, displayed, adored, haunted) as the other is the impresario of it (arrogant, elusive, self-sufficient, irreverent). A number of critics, looking for the New Woman in rock, are dismayed by Madonna's references to a pre-feminist femininity which teases and seduces, inveigles and manipulates, and reduces female character to sex appeal; they decry the famous bare tummy, the pouting baby-doll expression, the lingerie-cum-daywear, the outrageous messages of her songs: "feels so good inside" ("Like a Virgin") and "the boy with the cold, hard cash is always Mr. Right" ("Material Girl"); they accuse her of pandering to male erotic fantasies and vamping her way to the top.

In her own defence, Madonna has complained[6] that when a *male* singer acts out his sexuality (his horniness, his desirability), he is seen as an "honest, sensual human being", but *her* overt sexuality is seen as demeaning. She has a right to complain, for the accusation is rooted in our profound mistrust of a female sexuality that is not contained and disciplined by marriage and motherhood, as Madonna's most assuredly is not. Female sexuality, unlike male, has never been accepted as an end in itself; Madonna comes close to flaunting hers as a self-enclosed system. But there's more to her: her mischievous theatri-

cality. It is impossible that a woman who straps her notorious Boy-Toy buckle over a white tulle skirt, who dresses
up like a bride to writhe about on the floor, incongruously
taking on a sex kitten's snarl, can be doing anything but
sending up the conventions of femininity. It is only *because* the sexual codes of the fifties have been superseded
by a feminist ethic that an artist like Madonna is now free
to appropriate them for her own use, in the service of an
idiosyncratic vision, and to send them out again as a joke.

Jodi put on a cassette containing some sixty rock videos
recorded over the last six months. She's watched them
often enough to recognize within a second the good ones
and the bad ones. So she fast-forwards a lot, which in
itself produces an interesting effect: a great many blips
and bleeps, rapid-firing colours, and, on the rewind, fragments of a baseball game coming in from the channel.
This is her music: British New Wave. At first the images
are fresh and startling – faces are routinely distorted, dis-
embodied arms wave from out of a floor, a body lies in a
morgue, a montage of news clips flashes by to subliminal
effect – but eventually the lack of any obvious or even
punning relationship of image to lyric becomes tiresome:
one wishes the producer and the artist had resisted such
gratuitous effect and got on with the point. But this
doesn't bother Jodi; she says there *is* no point. Her taste
in men – in British New Wave men – strikes me as similarly indefensible: she actually fancies these "androgynous" (her word) lead singers with their skinny bodies and
floppy postures, their hair stuck together in bits, their ill-
fitting clothes assembled from a second-hand shop. They
remind me, all too distastefully, of the teenage boys of my
youth, with the brush cuts, the pants too short for their
legs, the bobbing Adam's apple; we called them jerks. But
Jodi swoons.

One can tune in and tune out of rock videos at one's
discretion, which is largely the point. There is no story as

such; they do not cumulatively have a point or "get any-where". But that is in the nature of the medium. One does not "read" them in the sense of beginning at their begin-ning and ending with a cathartic resolution. Teenagers don't read much in any case; their consumption of rock videos, therefore, does no particular violence to their no-tion of literacy. They flip on the switch, get a diet pop from the fridge, call a friend on the phone, dance around the room, paint their fingernails, all while "watching" TV. One cannot read a book this way. The new phenomenon, the rock video, would seem to be just another kind of radio.

It is easy to decry rock video, to see in it only the latest gimmick in marketing, and therefore a fad manipulated from corporate headquarters. While it has served to bring to public attention certain artists who would earlier have been confined to local or cult popularity (Jane Siberry is an example), it has also inflated the reputations of others whose videos are rather more interesting than the music, which, though ostensibly the "reason" for the video, has become background. Rock critics have deplored the rock video as "heartless" and "asphyxiating" the imagination,[7] since it manufactures mass images for the viewer, thereby relieving her of the chore of constructing her own. Femi-nist critics have expressed alarm at the images of female sexual display (Madonna's breasts and buttocks thrust at the camera) and sexual violence (Duran Duran's "Hun-gry Like a Wolf", in which the Great White Hunter stalks his naked Third World prey, a black woman, and rapes her).

In fact, rock video images generally are of such stagger-ing banality that the principal crime may be that, far from representing any revolutionary development in pop cul-ture, they are merely insipid. Rock star is surrounded by bathing beauties, rock star drives big car, groupies grovel at rock star's boots. Some arty slow motion. A computer graphic. People in masks. A crucifixion scene, a swastika. Lots of dry-ice fog. All that money ($1.1 million for four-

teen minutes of Michael Jackson, for instance), all that
equipment, all that talent – and this is all that artists can
come up with?

Yet all is not lost, according to others. The medium that
peddles the semi-pornographic also broadcasts the fresh
and cheeky images of women partying together (Lauper's
"Girls Just Want to Have Fun") and uniting to overpower
a pimp (Pat Benetar's "Love Is a Battlefield") and stepping out from their dead-end jobs to parade together
(Donna Summers' "She Works Hard For Her Money"),
thus demonstrating the medium's capacity to represent
the optimistic as well as the surreal or brutal image. In any
case, according to a University of Tennessee study[8] of
sixty-two MTV videos in the fall of 1985, although almost
sixty per cent of the videos under review contained sex
and/or violence, the content was "understated, relying on
innuendo through clothing, suggestiveness and light physical contact." The most common image, in fact, was "special effects" – unusual camera angles, special lighting, fog
– as though the sheer newfangledness of the process, its
gadgetry and gimmickry, were its most innovative component.

As for Jodi, bouncing around the living room on her
way out to meet her boyfriend at an underground gay
club, fast-forwarding past China Crisis to get to the Talking Heads while waving her left hand in the air to dry the
fingernail polish, she can take it or leave it.

A girl's bedroom: it is in the basement, off the family
room; or on the second floor next to the bathroom; or in
the smallest room of the house. The bed is covered with an
afghan made by her granny or a patchwork quilt made by
her great-grandmother, and supports her menagerie of
stuffed animals (a pink elephant, a penguin, a Care Bear).
Posters festoon the walls, turning the little room into a
kind of grotto where images of the beloved are hung for
contemplation: Van Halen, Tom Selleck, Michael Jack-

son, Jim Morrison, The Who. There are other images,
mementoes of peak moments: posters from the movies, a
boyfriend's photograph, a girlfriend's (taken in a photo
booth in the bus station), a group picture taken at summer
camp. Here is her ghetto-blaster and her Walkman and
her collection of tapes. Her reading material: a pile of
fashion magazines, an old encyclopedia, *The Godfather,
Who Has Seen the Wind*, and Heavy Metal comic books.
Clothes spill out over the broadloom and the furniture
(inherited from Dad after his remarriage) and are flung
over the dressing table, knocking over the bottles of nail
polish and of Blue Grass and Baby Soft, tubes of styling
gel, and lip-slickers. Poised unmolested on a shelf is her
special collection – of beer cans arranged in an awesome
pyramid; of buttons (The Clash 1984 Now; Who Knows,
Who Cares, Why Bother); of porcelain figurines; of seashells – and the souvenirs of past pleasures: the plastic
horn from the Grey Cup game, the Outstanding Female
Athlete trophy, the key-chain from Maui, and the ticket
stubs from the David Bowie concert inside a brass frame.
She apologizes for the mess but you realize that's just
another way of saying she's not quite sure she should have
let you come in here: this is private space.

A girl's leisure starts here, within the walls of her own
bedroom. If she has a telephone extension, this is where
she'll talk to her friends, at great length, and, if they visit,
where she'll invite them to sit (lie or flop) and drink diet
pop and listen to the tape she just bought, and give counsel regarding a certain pair of pants and a pair of boots.
Here is where she composes poems in the journal she
secretes beneath the mattress, and writes letters on the
Garfield stationery, and makes pencil sketches of her cat
sunning in the window. She practises on the clarinet and
knits a sweater and reads a love story here. And, all by
herself, with her pitiless eye, she examines herself – her
nose, her chin, her profile, her hairline, her breasts, her
bum, her knees – in the mirror by the closet, clothes off,
clothes on.

She has little to do with the rest of the house. She will do a bit of housework or join the family to watch *Dallas* or to play a video game, she'll join them for meals when she's hungry (not necessarily routinely) or to give an account of herself when asked. But mainly she's in her own room, door shut. Or "out".

Three recent separate studies of girls' leisure give three slightly different pictures. Bibby and Posterski's extensive survey of Canadian high school students[9] asked the question of their informants "How often do you . . . ?", and organized the data according to gender. The five most popular leisure activities among the girls were, in descending order: listening to music, daydreaming about the future, dancing, sitting and thinking, and watching television. (Among boys: listening to music, watching television, following sports, playing team sports, and participating in non-team sports.) A study commissioned by the Canadian Advisory Council on the Status of Women, "A Study of the Aspirations of Adolescent Women", reported in 1985 that, among the 122 girls surveyed, watching television was the single most frequent leisure activity, followed by "socializing" (both at home and away from home), sports, reading, and listening to music. A 1983 paper by M. Ann Hall at the University of Alberta, "Patterns of Girls' Leisure and the Social Construction of Femininity", based on data collected from 150 teenage girls, found that "beyond any question" the most time during an average week was spent on simply "talking with family and friends" (including on the telephone); at nineteen hours per week this was more than twice as much time as on any single one of the other most popular activities: watching television, listening to music, going out, and playing sports. (When a girl had a boyfriend, she spent as much time with him as in listening to music.)

There are some discrepancies, then, among these reports. Just how popular is television? How many sports *do* girls play? How often do girls get out of the house? Furthermore, it is impossible to know, from these reports, how different the leisure activities would be for a girl in a working-class family or in a household suffering unemployment, a girl in charge of a number of siblings, a girl in a single-parent family, an immigrant or a Catholic or a Moslem girl, or a girl in a small town. Nor do we know how they finance their leisure: from their own earnings, an allowance, a special bonus? But we can begin, nevertheless, to put together an account of the particular subculture that teenage girls inhabit.

In contrast to boys' leisure activities, for instance, girls' are remarkably inactive, consuming many more hours in passively "daydreaming" or "thinking" and far fewer in athletics than boys'. But that is only to say that girls are not physically active; there is a great deal going on mentally and emotionally in their other pastimes: window-shopping, socializing, talking, visiting, reflecting, analysing, even daydreaming together with friends and alone. Nor are these "passive" activities devoid of pointed purpose: a great deal of time is spent in shopping for and buying and applying the accoutrements of femininity – clothes and cosmetics – so that in a very material sense "leisure" is usefully employed in keeping up with the current codes of femininity and attractiveness. This is all the more true of the time girls spend together: it is only apparently purposeless, for the gossip, and the idle chitchat, function as a means of transmitting information. This is how they find out what's done and what's not done, what their "reputation" is worth, and what their peers are up to. Considering how important this information is to the status and self-esteem of a girl, and to her chances then of securing her "career" in a relationship, all these apparently leisurely activities – making-up, shopping, primping in the bathroom, exchanging fashion notes, gossiping on the telephone – are in fact "work". If a heterosexual relationship (preferably but not necessarily marriage) is to be her future (pre)occupation, then "her leisure before marriage is her work," writes Simon Frith.[10] And since so much of this takes place at home, in her bedroom even, the place of leisure – the home, as it is used by men after work – is transformed for her into another workplace.

This is another great distinction between boys' and girls' leisure: to pursue leisure, boys *leave* the home, go out onto the street and into public places – roads, street corners, staircases, subway stations, arcades, bars. None of these is available as leisure space to most girls. Girls are under much greater supervision than their brothers, they are expected to do more housework, they have less disposable cash, and they are all too aware of the physical danger they run in being out at night in "male" territory. All of these factors conspire to confine girls and their culture[11] indoors. In light of this, it is interesting to consider the shopping mall as an increasingly popular leisure space for girls. It is away from home but, because it is enclosed, is patrolled, is frequented by families, is indeed *private* property, it has none of the ambiguous connotations of "the street". In the same way, perhaps, that boys have staked out the pinball and video arcade, girls have claimed the mall fast-food restaurant: there they sit, sipping Coke, giggling, flirting, just out of the reach of Mum and Dad.

From *High School Trend* newspaper, October, 1984:

"T.J. Michaelson, Go!" The rally call sounded out from the enthusiastic crowd stuffed into the stands surrounding the T.J. Michaelson Composite High School playing field. Today, on this sweltering autumn day, the first game of the year for the senior football team had begun. Some, however, did not go to the game. A.J. Kroft sat in the computer processing room, tapping away on his latest program. Beside him was his life-long friend, Julius Carter, reading out the copy of the program that A.J. had written out the night before. (From "The Conspiracy of A.J. Kroft")

"Oh, Peter," Jennifer half cried. "It is the most beautiful thing I have ever gotten. In fact this is the first time I ever re-

ceived a flower from a guy." "I guess you haven't known any decent guys. Because if you did they would know that a girl like you deserves to have flowers thrown at your feet," Peter said charmingly. Jennifer looked up into his face and sweetly smiled as she waited for the surprise. Peter opened his bag lunch and pulled out a single pink rose and handed it to her.
(From "Wild Rose Composite High: A Soap Opera")

It has been argued that girls' own culture is a histori- cally recent phenomenon because girls have only recently had a "youth" – that period of transition between child- hood and adulthood when the young person lives indepen- dently of parents and before marriage. Until romantic love became the norm and women were allowed to choose their husbands, girls simply had no youth: at puberty they were removed from their fathers' home to their husbands'. Boys, with a long tradition of living away from home to find work, have had an adolescence, and a culture to ac- company it, for a much longer time.

This would suggest, then, that teenage girls have a short cultural memory of *being* female teenagers and, compared to males, a very short time in which to construct the culture that corresponds to their experience. What has tended to happen, to fill the absence, is that they consume "youth culture" (read male) as though it were their own, a process that can only be profoundly contradictory.

The "meaning" of youth culture – that it is spontane- ous, pleasure-seeking, anarchic, unconventional, risk-tak- ing – has been unavailable to girls, except to those who don't give a damn about their "deviancy". For most, how- ever, there has simply been no way to participate in teen- age culture except through some kind of denial or tran- scendence of gender. How, for instance, is a girl to participate in the anti-romantic ethic of teenage culture, with its emphasis on impulsive, uncommitted, earthy sex, when it is she who takes all the risks; when it is she who becomes sexually devalued, pregnant, impoverished? How is she to celebrate the "liberating" effects of drugs and booze when her common sense tells her that a drunk girl is in sexual and moral danger? How, even, is she to "identify" with motorcycles, electric guitars, and video war games, when each of these has been layered with meanings of masculine prowess that include her only as the *object* of need and fantasy? If teenage culture is all about escape and flight from bourgeois conventions and domestication and predictability, then girls are immediately at a disadvantage. As British writer Angela McRobbie argues:[12] "it is monstrously more difficult for women to escape (even temporarily) and these symbolic flights have often been at the expense of women (especially mothers) and girls. The lads may get by with – and get off on – each other alone on the streets but they [do] not eat, sleep, or make love there." It is still women who feed men, keep house for them, raise their children, all of which ties them to the home and to all the conventions of relationship and security and family that the rebellious male despises. How, then, does a girl enter a culture that is predicated, in its deepest impulse, on a revolt against women?

She retreats into "girl culture", that culture of feminine practice, best friends, and romance fantasy, where she is safe from marauding teenage males and where – especially for the working-class girl with nothing but unemployment or boring, ghettoized work ahead of her – she prepares herself for the marriage that, sooner or later, the boys will contract when they grow up and settle down. *Her* culture provides her no access to the escapes from traditional sex roles except at the risk of "failing" as a woman, and she has no unambiguous means of experimenting with independence and defiance and sex. Until girls collectively accumulate experience of their youthfulness outside the female norms of domesticity, the claim that "girls just want to have fun" will remain a utopian slogan shouted at the future.

TWENTY-TWO

Myra

*"The teacher asked me if I wanted to change
the system and I said, 'Yes.'"*

I WASN'T prepared for Myra's house: a shabby duplex
abutting the railroad tracks at the top end of Palmerston Avenue in Toronto, desperately in need of a coat of
paint. Inside, the floors were half exposed under torn linoleum covering; the furniture was, at best, second-hand, at
worst, retrieved from cast-offs left out for the garbage
truck. Up on the second floor, where two rabbits and a cat
about to give birth had their home, was Myra's room. It
was, as she had warned me, a mess: a small, unmade bed,
a floor strewn with clothes and papers, a windowsill losing
its paint. I knew that her father was a nuclear physicist,
her mother a librarian, but this house had absolutely none
of the customary trappings and accoutrements of the genteel intelligentsia. I was nonplussed. But what Myra's
room did have, on the walls, was fabric art from Kenya
and Botswana, anti-apartheid and anti-nuke posters, and I
understood: Myra and her parents don't give a damn
about gentility.

I begin to take the measure of this girl when she tells me
that she deliberately transferred out of City alternative
school (where she had very much enjoyed the political life)
into Oakwood Collegiate – a "mixed" school of Italians

and Blacks and Orientals as well as Anglos, of working-class and middle-class students – in order to mix things up a bit for herself. It was as if life had got too easy at City: the teachers were "progressive", the administration accommodating (they let you put up posters), the students informed. Never mind that "it was all just talk"; at least she wasn't a freak there. But at Oakwood, ah, that's a challenge. It's not that the students are apathetic exactly, it's that they want to have fun; and Myra, with all her peace and feminist and anti-apartheid buttons up and down her chest, her hand waving in class to say something about Reagan's policy in Nicaragua, her locker door decorated with postcards that say "Protest and Survive", isn't fun. Kids have come up to her, a little curiously, and asked her what this or that button "stands for" and she's explained and they've said, "Oh," and drifted off. She has a postcard in the locker that is a photograph of Rosa Parks, and the girl at the next locker asked her who that was and Myra explained that Rosa Parks was a black woman in Mississippi who in 1954 refused to go to the back of the bus and so started the whole civil rights movement in the United States, and the girl said, "Oh." It's almost a relief, then, when the jerk in English class teases her about the cruise missile tests, saying it's the "best thing" that's happened in Canada for a long time; it gives Myra a chance to argue.

She's taking her time. She moved to Oakwood in grade twelve and it's not easy to build networks of friends among people who have had their friends since at least grade ten. Fortunately, the teachers at Oakwood are more progressive than the students and she's had some good talks with them. With their support, and the interest of some eight other students, she's thinking of organizing a club where she could talk about all the issues that stir her up. If she had the power, she'd make all the teachers raise these issues in class – peace, South Africa, Central America – and damn the curriculum!

There are army cadets at Oakwood and they call her

"pinko", "Commie", and "weird", grimacing at her as if she had a disease: hang around Myra and you'll get weird too. Her French teacher is a reactionary, likes to bait her: "The Catholic school system would never allow homosexuals to teach there." So, of course Myra has to say something – "Heterosexuality is being *forced* on homosexuals. Why can't they just be different?" – and the teacher ever since has been picking on her and sending her down to the office if she's one minute late to class.

Why does Myra bother? Why, some would ask, does she set herself up for this kind of petty harassment when she knows she's not going to change anybody's mind? The answer is, in part, that she cannot help herself. She cannot remember a time when she did not have these ideas, and when the world did not sound just as it does now: groaning with the sufferings of the oppressed. By grade six, in fact, her ideas were in place. They were in the music she had always heard – Pete Seeger, Phil Oakes, Arlo Guthrie – and in the long and impassioned discussions of her parents and their friends (her father has been active in a Toronto anti-apartheid group) and in her own childhood adventures in Africa, where her parents had lived from time to time. It was, she says of her eleven-year-old self, a "classic case of having beliefs but not knowing why". That nuclear power was bad, the bomb was bad (she was just about to learn about disarmament), the American government was bad, and, since the Americans said the Russians were bad, the Russians were good. She did her own reading of newspapers and left-wing and feminist magazines and literature handed out at demonstrations, and her beliefs became more sophisticated. But she's still learning. At seventeen, Myra is still learning.

Yet, for all her engagement and her certitude, a delicate melancholia wafts off Myra as though, yes, she will do as she does, she could not do anything else, but she would wish it otherwise. She would wish, of course, that oppression and pain and dying were overcome, but, short of that, she would wish that she had company. The company of her generation. She's had teachers who grew up in the sixties and when she listens to them talk about how wonderful those years were, she thinks she and her eight friends are "nothing". Back then they had the feeling that they could change things, you could have an idea and go out there and *do* it, and it didn't matter if there was a lot of resistance or one crisis after another – the Cuban missile crisis, the King and Kennedy assassinations, the war in Vietnam – because there were thousands and thousands of you, all young, and people paid attention – the media, governments! – and were even a little bit afraid, and you didn't feel that you were the only freak.

Intrigued, I ask for another interview a few days later. She whisks the laundry off the sofa at my arrival. Stan Rogers is on the record player and new-born kittens mew under the armchair in which Myra sits, cross-legged, in blue jeans and sweater, poised and still, and looking at me gravely, expectantly; there is absolutely nothing about her at this moment that is adolescent. As we talk, though, I sense her preoccupation and her distraction and she seems somehow less generous with her words than when we first talked, as though it was just too much work to answer in full. But when I stop the tape and suggest we continue some other time, she says, "No, no, let's carry on," and when we get to the end she tells me she has never talked so much all at once.

Myra was born in Kenya, where her father was teaching physics at the university in Nairobi while her mother taught chemistry. She has no memories of this. Two years later the family was in Cuba, where her parents worked with cuso (Canadian University Service Overseas) for three years. About this she remembers going to a Cuban kindergarten and speaking nothing but Spanish, even at home; on their return to Canada, where Myra was put into grade one, she forgot it completely. A year later they were in Lusaka, in Zambia, where her father was working

at the university. Her parents split up and her father went
to Botswana, the children flying to visit him from time to
time, blissfully unaware of the wars raging beneath their
plane in Zimbabwe (then Rhodesia) and Namibia. She
lived two and a half years with her mother and brothers in
Lusaka, going to an English-speaking local school, and it
was here, one suspects, that Myra's politics began to take
shape. They had servants, a husband and wife, who lived
back of them, and in school she knew she was being
treated differently because she was white: black pupils
who made spelling mistakes were whacked across the
knuckles but Myra was never touched. Neither, for that
matter, would anyone play with her. She began to read a
lot.

Her parents reconciled and the family returned to Toronto, bought the house on Palmerston, and put Myra in
a multicultural neighbourhood school; her best friends
were Chinese and Korean. Over the next few years, Myra's feelings became ideas. The memories of Botswana
and Zambia propelled her into anti-apartheid activity; her
experience as the privileged untouchable and the family's
adoption of a black child made her "anti-racist". She
thinks Castro is "neat" – she's heard he goes out to cut
sugarcane alongside his people – and calls herself a socialist. She hates being whistled at in the street, and identifies
with feminism. And so on. A thick, gamy stew of argument and discussions; questions; reading, listening, and
talking, talking. "I remember that in grade ten the family
was around the supper table having a discussion about
South Africa and suddenly all this stuff I didn't even
know came out of me."

At school they call her a Commie weirdo but they
haven't got it right. She's a socialist, not a Communist.
Communism she's rejected on the grounds that it hasn't
"worked" anywhere, but socialism represents all the ideas
that she finds exciting, whether it's equal opportunity for
women, support for unions, pro-choice campaigns, a
crackdown on pornography, and bringing hate-mongers

like Keegstra and Zundel to trial, or spreading "nuclear disarmament, anti-imperialist ideas, ideas of freedom and revolution" around the world. Socialism *is* the people of Nicaragua rising up to throw off Somoza and now the "contras", socialism *is* feeding starving Ethiopians, socialism *is* the riots in Soweto.

When she talks about these things, Myra does not flap her arms around and shriek and pound tables; she remains as poised and still as ever, but the melancholy lifts and from the bright, widening light in her eyes you can tell that Myra's *feeling* about something is inseparable from the idea of the thing itself. Back in the sixties, someone once said he was a revolutionary because it was the only life worth living. Myra is a paraphrase of that statement. This is *her* life, sitting cross-legged amid the laundry, and the smeared and dusty blues records on the floor, with anti-imperialist posters tacked up on shredding wallpaper, at her elbow leaflets to be handed out on street corners, in her head the speech she wants to make to the friend who doesn't want to boycott Eaton's – this is hers, and this is the way she wants to live it.

"I had to give a three-minute presentation in French class on the topic 'Is your generation conservative or revolutionary?' I said they are basically conservative because they don't want to change the system. They don't protest nuclear arms, they don't protest militarism, they don't question how this country is governed. And then I said that what youth wants today is financial security, and that when they take a job they don't think about the conditions they are taking the job under. There's quite a lot of anti-union sentiment in the school, even though they're working-class kids. I ended it off by saying youth don't think about stuff that doesn't directly affect them. The teacher asked me if I wanted to change the system and I said, 'Yes.' She asked me if I wanted it to be a Communist system and I said, 'Not really, socialism would do fine.'"

She loves this story: her father's grandparents were radicals, Jewish radicals in Poland. They moved to the States.

Great-grandfather was an atheist, an anarchist who knew
Emma Goldman. She came around on Friday nights, and
on Saturdays they handed out anarchist leaflets together.
For doing just this he was finally arrested and threatened
with deportation, but Great-grandmother bribed the
prison guard and off they fled to Canada. Their grandson,
Myra's father, married a gentile from Philadelphia. His
grandfather didn't care but his father did, and disinherited
him. Eventually the family was reconciled; it's not the sort
of family not to heal itself. There's a photograph taken
just after the war of a family get-together in honour of
some European relatives who had survived the camps.
There they stand, the two survivors, beside a table full of
food, looking bewildered. They're all right now.

Her father's Jewish origins and the family stories – had
her grandparents stayed on in Poland they would have
been murdered and she, Myra, would not be here – led
Myra to choose to be Jewish too. And ever since his
mother died, her father has begun to take his Jewishness
rather more seriously. The family celebrates Sabbath every Friday night and Hanukkah and Passover, but, for all
her self-identified Jewishness, Myra has a hard time singing the hymns. "I may be Jewish but not that kind of
Jewish! Maybe Emma Goldman-Jewish." Which means
she can be proud of the Passover celebration, a festival
commemorating the liberation of a people from bondage.
This is not religion, she protests; this is politics.

Besides home, the other place where she can do politics
is, of course, the school. She thought she had about eight
interested students lined up for an anti-apartheid club, but
it turned out to be three students and four teachers. But
she's not giving up. Whenever she gets the chance, she
talks her ideas up, spreads the word, and keeps in touch
with people who, if not exactly kindred spirits, respect her
and take her seriously.

And isn't that worth something? One has the impression that, for Myra, the grudging respect of an Oakwood
Collegiate senior is worth twice the calculated sophistica-

tion and tolerance of a City hipster. City kids are so cool, everything's *okay*, no problem, live and let live (City kids are liberals): how do you get a grip on people like that? She went back there for a visit not too long ago and felt slightly uncomfortable for the first time: everybody was the same sort of person, worldly-wise and pretending to care about the world. Well, at Oakwood they don't pretend. They're very up front about what they care about, namely make-up, VCRs, and cars, they're crude about sex and race and don't apologize, and they manifestly do not think that "everything" is okay; punk, for instance, is not okay, nor, in spite of their own working-class background, are unions. Myra finds all this rather annoying but at the same time more "real", more "direct". Nobody's pretending to be anything they're not. Neither is Myra. She doesn't have television at home and doesn't pretend to know what they're talking about at school when they talk about *Miami Vice*, and she doesn't go to blockbuster movies, so she hasn't a clue about what's so exciting about Rob Lowe, and she listens to records more than to radio, so *her* idea of a hot act is the now-dead Stan Rogers. ("Who," asks Myra, "is Wham?")

But, funny thing, some of the kids think she's all right anyway. They pick her up in one girl's father's car and go driving around on a Saturday night, *cruising* is what they're doing (can you imagine Myra cruising?), whistling and smacking their lips at cute boys on the street, stopping at a shop to buy rum balls (Myra eating rum balls?), and maybe staying up all night at somebody's house, yakking and laughing and watching TV. (Myra likes *Love Boat*!). It's all so out of character, and, once in a while, so much fun.

Five years from now, Myra says without hesitation, she wants to be working in a developing, socialist Third World country, doing whatever it is they need from her.

Five months later, Myra was in grade thirteen, still at Oakwood, and studying math, Spanish, two history courses, French, English, and biology. She was leaving her academic options "wide open" so that she can go in any one of several directions when the time comes to go to university. That won't be for a few years; first she wants to spend some time in Africa.

After taking a two-week training course, she had a job over the summer in a "progressive" day-care centre, hired on as a summer student on a government grant. She loved it. It was a co-operative day-care, it was vegetarian, it was pro-union; unfortunately, as a government placement, she could not join the union, nor could she be paid for overtime. She didn't mind. She loved being there, she loved the kids and her co-workers, with whom she had a lot in common.

Alas, the society of her schoolmates is as elusive as ever. She suffered a setback in being assigned a locker in a part of the school away from her friends of last year; she has to begin again with new companions. She had the good fortune to make friends with a girl at the day-care centre who also studies at Oakwood. With this girl, and a girl from grade ten, she's started up a group called Youth Against Apartheid, which is part of a city-wide grouping called the Anti-Apartheid Coalition of Toronto. Myra is very excited about the possibilities: with South Africa daily in the news, she expects that the twenty (twenty!) who showed up at the first three meetings will rapidly expand. The plan is, with the endorsement of the Race Relations Department of the Board of Education, to go into schools and make presentations in classes and assemblies that will educate the student body in the issues facing South Africa. The need to educate is fundamental: only five students in Myra's English class knew what "apartheid" means.

By contrast, the peace movement is dead for her. She'll go on marches still and sell buttons and take an Oakwood banner to show the colours but – deep sigh – there is no *energy* there any more. Myra has energy. She has commitment, resolution, hope. One way or another, South

Africa has been in her consciousness since the first day it glimmered. She knows what she has to do.

We've been talking or whispering loudly at a carrel in the library during lunch hour. I want to take her picture. We dash out a minute before the bell, I pose her under a tree. Now I have the picture. Back straight, shoulders back, gaze direct, smile conspiratorial. There are a lot of good causes out there. Myra should be a happy woman.

TWENTY-THREE

Politics

"Nobody my age is doing anything interesting – or is ever going to."

T HE SCHOOL cop thinks this is a "super generation" coming along in the eighties, especially the girls, girls not looking to stay at home to rear children and look after hubby, girls "looking to pull their own load", girls who "aren't asking for any favours along the way". This is, he says, a generation with an agenda for a society that could use some shaking up. But there are few others who would agree, least of all the teenagers themselves. The hundredth time I listened to a teenage girl name as her favorite musicians the Rolling Stones, Tina Turner, Jim Morrison, Jimi Hendrix – people either dead or old enough to be her parents – I challenged her: "That's *my* music; what about *your* music, the statements *your* music has to make?" She replied: "There's nothing else in music to be interested in. Nothing's happening. Nobody my age is doing anything interesting, or is ever going to."

For all its illiteracy, the generation seems to have an awareness of where and how it fits in the successive generations of post-war adolescents, namely in relation to the sixties generation of hippies and anti-war protesters. Some teenagers feel that the sixties "rebels" made a mess of things – family life, child-rearing, work discipline all trampled on and abused, befouled – which the eighties people have now to clean up; hence the renewed commitment to pre-hippie values of monogamy and the sanctity of the nuclear family, to steady employment, to fitness, even as the world is falling down around their ears under the blows of social, economic, and ecological catastrophe. Others regard their parents' youth as somehow more innocent and luckier than their own: "When my mum was younger, she loved being a kid. Back then in the sixties you didn't have as many problems as today, with AIDS for example. Everything is so synthesized now; there are chemicals everywhere." One very thoughtful girl speculated that the way the children of ex-rebels rebel against their parents is to party and get drunk and not give a good goddamn about anything larger than their own inconsequential lives. A sixteen-year-old, active in the peace movement in Toronto, has no patience with her peers. "People say that youth today is growing up under the threat of dying at thirty. I disagree with that. It's ridiculous. I mean, if I was a kid who thought I wasn't going to make it to thirty, I'd kill myself right now. What's the point? And a lot of the time kids think of political activity as an adult thing. It's okay to run around the city scrawling 'Anarchy' on walls, but to join the NDP, say, is seen as somehow collaborating with adults. And the way they deal with their oppression as students – going into class and clicking their binders as a way of getting back at an awful teacher – is so degrading and mindless."

A girl from Gimli, Manitoba, says she cannot imagine any of her friends sitting around talking about "deep intellectual" things like what a jerk Ronald Reagan is ("I'll be voting for the Rhinos," she says, "to repeal the law of gravity!"), and a girl from a reputedly progressive alternative school complained of having to sit and listen to a "bunch of speakers" who had been invited into the school to talk about Nicaragua "and we just sat there and they just talked and talked, and it was really boring." So, although it may be disappointing, it is not altogether surprising to learn from Bibby and Posterski's survey[1] that "most young people endorse the political, economic, legal and gender status quo" in Canada, registering strong approval of the "work ethic", the nuclear family, the police forces, and the inherent justice of "the system", and disapproval of trade unions, women in politics, and "disrespectful youth", which is what they themselves might be expected to be. In Bibby and Posterski's sober analysis, the kind of people this era seems to be producing "lack imagination and creativity and seem to be oriented toward finding out what is expected of them and doing that. . . . They lack a sense of self; they have nothing to say." (And we get, perhaps, the kind of adolescents we deserve.)

If this is true, it may be that it has something to do with their having been, in a sense, "struck dumb" by the terror of nuclear holocaust. Although the sixties generation was the first to have been born into a world already armed with nuclear weapons, it is the eighties generation that seems to have accepted it as an irreversible fait accompli: generation-long Ban the Bomb activity has demonstrably failed to halt the escalation of nuclear terror; more of the same is seen to be likewise ineffectual. In a 1984 study of 1011 students from grades six to thirteen in Toronto,[2] "war and peace" ranked as the "major worry" in fifty-one per cent of the cases. Two years later, another study in Ontario,[3] based on the views of 45,000 secondary school students, found that, although half "often worry" about the possibility of nuclear war, "very few" were prepared to do anything about preventing one. In June 1985, at a high school in St. Albert, Alberta,[4] a representative of Physicians For Social Responsibility presented a film, *Living in the Shadow of Nuclear Threat*, to a steadily decreasing audience of students. According to the newspaper reporter who was there, "feelings of frustration, despair, depression and hopelessness" overcame the (mainly female) audience who remained to talk with the doctor. "If you think about it all the time, you get depressed," said one girl. "I want to have kids but . . ." said another, trailing off in tears.

"I saw a movie once that made me real scared of nuclear war but my parents told me that there was nothing we could do about it. We'd just live our lives and let those people play their war games. It freaks me out. I don't believe I can change what there already is; what can *I* do to change the fact that we've already got enough weapons to blow ourselves up several times?"

Three of them, Sharon, Tina, and Brigitte, sat together in a living room and talked about death. Their own death, in a nuclear war. Every night, lying in bed before falling asleep, Sharon thinks about it: she is obsessed by the notion that she will not die a natural death, will not live to be a "little old feeble woman" being administered the last rites in her own bed, but will be "vapourized", turned into a shadow in the heat and light of nuclear Armageddon. Tina thinks of death as an "altered state" of being, an adventure, something new and, yes, scary, "like any other major changes in your life, like moving out of home"; it is immaterial how this transition is effected, violently or otherwise. Brigitte feels no such equanimity, is outraged by the "senile old men" who have the power to order our lives and deaths and who won't be around to do penance for the consequences of their belligerent hubris: "It's our elders who started this!" Yes, says Sharon, it only takes "one weird person" to push the button. No matter how many anti-nuke demonstrations parade up and down the streets of the continent, it only takes one finger, one button.

Even those teenagers who have paid dues to an anti-war organization, have answered the call and gone to meetings and leafleted parades and worn their protest badges into the hostile environs of their own schools, have often given up in discouragement, alienated as much by the procedures of the organization as by the indifference or despair

of their peers. One girl complained to me of the lack of
"community" among the activists, of the anger and frustration and "bitchiness" that took the place of any real
compassion for the victims of a nuclear war as month
after month of thankless political labour took their toll;
and another withdrew from a youth-for-peace group when
she realized that the activists had only the foggiest idea of
how "the system" stacked against them actually works –
what was important, it seemed, was just to let off steam:
"It was emotionally charged without a lot of direction and
substance, and I found that that was draining." Although
the support of sympathetic adults is important, a teenage
activist in the peace movement is relegated to the margins
of the group of which adults are seen to be in charge and
in control of the agenda. "It's adults who are organizing
and writing up the leaflets and doing all the important
work. All I had to do was walk in, take a bunch of leaflets,
and walk out."

Ruth's friends called her a "peace freak", as though she
was doing this just because it was *trendy*, but she had been
there when there were only twelve, fifteen people outside
the United States consulate, years before it was "correct"
to be there, and she had the right to take herself seriously.
She'd been to all the meetings and listened to the intermi-
nable discussions, the "what-iffing" and "supposing" and
"how-abouting", the "hierarchical bullshitting" about
who was going to be head marshal and second marshal
and squad leaders on the march; she'd learned to shrug it
off that no one there was the least bit interested in what
she had to say about anything: she was just a kid. But
some things you don't shrug off. She had finally been
appointed a marshal at a rally and she asked for the gay
men's contingent: these guys were into *enjoying* themselves at rallies, they brought tapes and blasters and
danced down the street, they were cool. But when she
joined them, marshal's band around her arm, one of them
turned to her, curled his lip, and snarled, "What are *you*
doing here, you little cunt?" And that was it. Ruth hasn't

been to a march since. She says now that the issue of peace is "too important" to trust to organizations.

Nina went through her "rebellious" stage in grade ten. She hated the "establishment", raged at her parents for their failure to have banned the bomb, and felt enormously sorry for herself and her friends: "What kind of future do we have, tell us! *Look* what you're leaving us!" There are still times, two years later, when she'd like to move to Vancouver, live on the beach, braid flowers, and smoke pot – "Like what's the point of doing anything else?" – but usually she is more optimistic than that fantasy implies. She does have hope, she swears she does, just wait until she can vote and have a say in politics. If she sat at home brooding, she would, of course, fall into despair, but instead she keeps herself busy "developing *me*" and strengthening her character, her intelligence, her resolve. Oh, she has hope, she really, really does! She's pretty sure she'll live to see thirty, yeah, she thinks so.

Punk politics. On a Saturday night at the Spartan Men's Club in the city's northeast working-class district near the CN railway lines, the punk band SNFU plays its last local gig before packing it in for Los Angeles and the big time. No one is dancing. Everyone is pressed up against the stage, prodded and shoved together by the crowd behind, or they have taken the stage themselves: one guy is jumping up and down and banging his head with his own fist, others go flying out over the audience in a belly-flop from the lip of the stage and every now and then a boy crawls up from the audience and flings himself onto the stage floor, rolling about and kicking his legs in spastic frenzy. The band, grimacing, yowling, are wet with sweat from their furious exertion at their instruments; their words are indistinguishable – the music is so loud that the separate notes blur into reverberation.

I am standing in the wings, looking out onto the crowd. There are a few shaved heads and sculpted spiky coiffures, there is a lot of dark eye make-up on boys and girls, but most people look slovenly and tattered and faintly menacing in oversize shirts, torn T-shirts, stained and bespattered denim jackets, studded bracelets, and combat boots. I see Solidarnosc logos on T-shirts, an anarchist sticker on a guitar, Dead Kennedys and Amnesty International buttons on collars. It's as warm as a steam bath in the club and all the lights are down, increasing the already gloomy aspect of a crowd dressed almost entirely in black. (I am reminded of the Beat style of the fifties, black-clothed bohemians in contemptuous withdrawal from that other era of the Bomb, the Cold War, and the Grey-Flannel Suit.) When the set is finished and the lights go up, I also see a lot of rubbish and beer bottles on the floor and the faces of very young people who have suddenly taken on the appearance of celebrants at a rather cheerless costume party. The boy next to me, wearing a bicycle chain around his neck and a black kerchief tied in four knots around his head, explains that everyone is wearing black because "there's nothing in life worth celebrating."

This was touching, if a little melodramatic, and I was impressed. Of all the adolescent subcultures I had come across, punk was the only one seriously to engage the world around it, not only to refuse agreement with "adult" values and assumptions but to argue with them. The boy in the kerchief was right: the point of punk was precisely not to celebrate but to dissent.

And so, in punk literature and magazines and songs and posters, "the system" is under attack for its violence and militarism, its sexism and racism, and its class warfare. The punk idealist is called on to turn away from "greed and selfishness" and to find creative ways to "break the back of the system."

Many take this to heart. Disdaining consumer goods, they dress in cast-offs and hand-me-downs; scorning conventions of taste, they wear outrageous hair-dos and make-up. Many are vegetarian and anti-booze and anti-drugs. Their bands record on independent labels and dis-

tribute the records themselves, and sing discordantly and
savagely that "the USA is killing kids/protecting their best
interests/revolution is o.k./if you're fascist and pro-USA"
(in the words of Edmonton's Down Syndrome).

Punk is not endearing. It is the descendant of every
preceding youth movement of the last two hundred years
that has taken for its program the disparagement of the
status quo, which is to say of the achievements of the
parents' generation. They "dump" all over them and try, if
they are creative and inspired, to imagine a new world cast
in their own image: peace-loving, democratic, "free".

But punk, inevitably co-opted by the media, advertisers, and trend-setters *as style*, has been trivialized to the
point of innocuousness, so that it becomes possible for a
kid to sport a Mohawk hairdo as a *sufficient* demonstration of her/his "uniqueness".

To the extent that it is a subculture of machismo, punk
is also limited in its potential to politicize girls. The combat boots and studs and chains, the pushing and ganging
and stomping, the all-male bands, the maniacally aggressive music, the violent imagery (a dead body in a noose on
a gig poster) – none of this appeals to very many females.
Or is that to put it the wrong way about? Girls, maybe,
should get tough.

It's an on-going debate. If girls were as assertive and
sure of themselves as boys, they wouldn't be such push-
overs. On the other hand, that's why the world is so
screwed-up – suffering from an excess of aggressiveness.
For all its rhetorical feminism, punk has not resolved this
contradiction.

A diminutive sixteen-year-old figure in a woollen jacket,
pleated plaid skirt, and beret, she was waiting for me at
the turnstiles in the St. Clair subway station at lunch-time.
We wheeled out together into the street past Harvey's
(full), Pizza Hut (line-up), a sandwich deli (full), and
settled on La Maison, a bistro in pink and grey. Her face

is fine and narrow, her skin clear, her hair cut short and blunt, and her ears pierced through with tiny blue earrings. She knows exactly how to handle herself in a restaurant, and when she speaks to me, clearly, readily, helpfully, it is obvious she knows how to handle adults. With admirable forthrightness she tells me the salient facts about her public life: she is a feminist, a peace activist, and a conscious, though not religious, Jew. She orders a pasta salad and chocolate mousse cake and a glass of water. I pay.

In grade six she had her first sexist teacher ("Which girl is going to bring me a cup of coffee?"), in grade seven she studied the history of the suffrage movement (and realized that women have not always had the vote), in grade eight she learned that there was no guarantee of equal pay for equal work. In grade nine, wearing regulation T-shirt and panty-like red gym pants, she ran around the track to the hoots of boys – "Shake your ass, baby!" – and vowed never to be humiliated like that again.

Sarah is now in grade eleven in an alternative school. Grade ten at North Toronto Collegiate had been unendurable: social life appeared to be organized around cliques formed back in junior high school through the country-club circuit, style was unrelievedly preppie, and the atmosphere, when not hostile to Sarah's concerns, was indifferent. She always wore a variety of buttons that proclaimed her view of things (pro-choice, anti-apartheid, anti-nuke, pro-whale) and acquired a reputation: "Oh, oh, here comes Sarah!" It was no good, for instance, her trying to organize a boycott of Nestlé's products in the school; she'd plop herself down in front of someone who had just bought a Nestlé instant pudding in the cafeteria and challenge her or him: "Do you know what you're eating? Do you know about the boycott? No? Well!" And she was off, urgent, pressing, *serious*. Those she didn't scare off she merely bored.

A political life is more easily pursued at the alternative school. Certainly the teachers (graduates of the sixties, for the most part) are supportive, especially the female staff. The big event of the year is International Women's Day in March. Sarah had first celebrated it in grade eight: Joyce Wieland the artist, Abby Hoffman the athlete, Mary O'Brian the philosopher, came to the school, *everybody* from the school showed up, there was a potluck lunch, a dinner – it was a big deal. Still inspired by that day, Sarah has made it her business to organize IWD this year at school.

A group of twelve joined her committee. That was the high point. At the end, it was clear that only three had really had their hearts in it. Everyone agreed that inviting speakers to the school was a good idea, but no one wanted to do the phoning, pleading bashfulness on the phone. The committee argued over the speakers' list and then began avoiding Sarah in the halls, sure she was going to grab them for a task. Finally, just before the big day itself, someone showed up at the committee meeting complaining that to have a *women's* day discriminated against the boys; it should be a *people's* day. Sarah was fit to be tied.

Sarah wants feminism to arouse and enrage and exhilarate people just as it has done her, but what she experiences is a student population politely, and indifferently, taking their seats in the auditorium because they have to: at an alternative school, the celebration of IWD is *policy*. Well, that's why they're there, and not at North Toronto. Still, she wishes they came out of commitment, out of passion.

There are days when even Sarah has a hard time keeping her spirits up. She did her duty and joined the big IWD march downtown on March 8, but for the first time she did not try to round up a bunch of her friends to come along: she could no longer convince herself, let alone others, that "the more you march and physically exhaust yourself, the more you are doing." The last anti-cruise march she had been on was very disappointing; the impassioned and infuriated crowds of months ago had dwindled to a handful of earnest souls making exactly the same speeches as the time before. "It was so boring." To think she could have gone to a movie instead.

There has not been a time, in the lifetime of a teenage girl in the eighties, when there has not been a women's movement. She has no knowledge of a world without feminism, and so, while she may reject for herself the "label" feminist, it is impossible for her not to be informed by feminism: it is in the air. Whence the familiar, and maddening, assertion: "I'm not a feminist but . . ." as in the example that Sarah gives of the Miss Teen Canada finalists who, wanting to be doctors and lawyers, to travel, to be educated, are *not* feminists, oh heavens no, they *like* boys, they *want* to be married.

Ruth does not call herself a feminist. She wants to get along with everybody, and in her view feminists just do a lot of bitching. What she hears in them is a great anger towards men and not the compassion that Ruth thinks is necessary if you're ever to understand why, for instance, women stay with men who beat them. And Ruth shies away from any claim that women, en masse, can be helped, can be "liberated". "If I can't keep my own life in control, I can't do anything for other people. Fuck saving the world; I'm losing *me*."

There was a time, a couple of years ago, when Joanne called herself a feminist: it meant she hated men. She was reading Germaine Greer and Kate Millett and Simone de Beauvoir and she was in a black fury of resentment which she didn't "snap out of" until her boyfriend told her not to be so stupid: her feelings, vented on half the human race, weren't getting her anywhere. She pulled back from them and says now that she could never just cut men out of her life: "They're different from women and I like that difference."

Mandy distinguishes between a "feminist" and a woman who is "liberated", the former being unattractively aggressive and hostile to men, the latter being attractively pleased with her femaleness. "I think what a liberated woman really is is someone who understands that for now this is a male-dominated world and accommodates herself to that fact." It does not mean she is without "goals" or the desire to "expand" herself; it does mean that, contrary to feminist argument, this goal and this expansion could be satisfied in marriage and motherhood.

These girls sound sure of themselves. Most others, about feminism, are ambivalent. Their instincts are feminist, but intellectually they hesitate to make a commitment: commitment is not without its risk.

It begins with the grievances of everyday life, the "little things" that rankle all the same: "It's just not fair!" That brothers are allowed to stay out later, and don't have to make their beds, and are lent the family car more readily. That teachers pay more attention to the boys than to the girls in class, support boys' rather than girls' applications for scholarships, praise a boy's progress in art class but do not seem to notice the girls', and, in a creative-writing class, accept a boy's short story about futuristic warfare but reject a girl's poem about menstruation as "inappropriate". That the aptitude-testing computer program in the guidance counsellor's office asks as its first question: Are you a boy or a girl?

The grievances become more complex and interrelated. A girl who wants to "make something of myself" does not "see" herself as a wife and mother; her own mother, married to an alcoholic, had done "everything" in the family. Another grudgingly accepts that she will have to add on housekeeping and child care to her paid work: who else is going to do it? "We girls," said Nina, "have to work harder for whatever we want to do. We've got to prove ourselves all the time." It's not fair! The way boys think that they're so superior, that girls are going to fall all over them, that they can pick and choose, and so you've got to be thin and pretty and flattering; the way boys are so *in charge* all the time, you can see it, the way they sit in their desks and laugh and don't give a damn about their homework; they're so cool, *they* don't have to get all worked up emotionally to make a point: they're listened to *all the time*! Sexuality, when it is mentioned, is assumed to be the girls' responsibility (it's all about menstruation and pregnancy and the pill). The teenager who discovers that she desires other women more than she wants to be with boys, who falls in love with another girl and wants to tell everybody about it, who wants to kiss and cuddle and hold hands in the bleachers, also discovers she is no longer considered "cute" or even sexy; she is a monster.

As for the girl who identifies herself as a feminist, she may find that among her peers, she is ridiculed (the girl wears a "Stop Sexual Harassment" button, the boy responds, "Hey, why stop it when we can start it?") or resented (at SEED school a course in women's studies was open only to girls, a fact described as "counter-sexist" by the boys) or, among older feminists, patronized: how can someone so young know her own mind? Her taste in music is regretted, her company unwelcome at the bars, her sexual preference made light of ("baby dyke!"), and her naivety assumed. Hey, it's not fair.

"By feminist I mean being able to make choices, to decide for yourself what you want to do. The thing about a lot of teenagers is that they'll support equality for women, but they just don't define it as feminism."

A whole bunch of them got together with me in a living room to talk about the idea of equality between males and females. Nadine opened it up by pointing out the difference between equality in a man-made world where priorities are still determined by men, and equality in a world "*we* want". The significance of even discussing it as a notion, a "concept", said Tina, is that "if you have to say that you have it, then you don't really have it." Equality is *active* and equality is its own justification. That's all very well, interjected Sharon, but "some things can't be equal" – at which point Nadine, anticipating her line of argument, pointed out that "you can be different but still equal." "As, for example," Sharon pressed on, "in sports." "Aha!" said Brigitte, "but that's because the standards are set by males! Why can't a woman be a construction worker? Because the guys won't let you in, that's why." "Or a truck mechanic," added Alexa, "even when she can do the work." "All the same," Sharon insisted, "you don't see too many women with the body-build to play football." Tina, disagreeing that equality is a state in which men and women do the same things (who in her right mind *wants* to play football?), said it's all about "the things you do, I might not want to do," and Nadine, summing up, said equality is "being judged as a person." Now that's fair.

CARLA: I guess we've turned into liberated women, slightly.

SHARON: Yeah, I'm a liberated woman but I need a guy who's in charge.

CARLA: Half and half.

SHARON: I think most girls are like us, basically. Deep down inside.

Deep down inside they're young women struggling for a female pride that does not have to pay what they see as the penalty of feminism: separation from the solace of male company. Aside from the young lesbians who've come out and the girls whose friendships with each other are their first loyalty, they are for the most part still too inexperienced to know and trust and count on the nourishing company of women. Feminism, they fear, will set them adrift in a social and emotional landscape where there are only women and where the closest relationship is only friendship. And yet they are adamant about their own worth. "I guess I'm liberated," says Arden. "I'm not pushy about it but I don't take shit." In the "I guess" lie the tentativeness, the hedging of bets, of a young woman fearful of the perceived contradiction of her desires: to dispose of herself as she sees fit, *and* to be lovable. So Arden could never "wait on a guy" like her mother waits on her father, like women wait on the "jerks" on television shows; so Arden greatly admires a teacher who calls herself "Ms." and another who didn't change her name at marriage; but, on the other hand, Arden never pays her own way on a date – a guy likes to feel he can pay for things.

George's mother works all day, her husband cooks dinner, the kids clean up: George calls her a feminist even though "she doesn't go out and protest." By the same token, George is a feminist: she disagrees "totally" with a state of affairs in which an employer can decide not to hire women for certain jobs, say, but, on the other hand, George thinks it's "fine" if a woman wants to stay at home to take care of her kids, and she herself won't apologize for enjoying cooking for her boyfriend "even if some feminists say you shouldn't do that."

Many girls told me that they've never "felt" discriminated against, at least not in any "major" way. But . . . in their anxiety to dissociate themselves from the feminist "man-haters" and in their eagerness to sympathize with boys – pointing out that boys aren't permitted to be "soft and gentle", that there's too much "blaming" of men, too much sexual stereotyping even on the part of feminists, that men *have* made progress in their attitudes to women – I sensed a kind of nervousness, a placatory shuck-and-jive of young women afraid of male disapproval of their "temerity", and seeking to reassure the males around them that their need and desire to possess themselves has nothing to do with being angry or vengeful or perverse. Has nothing to do, that is, with "feminism".

NINA: "I haven't been put down because I'm female. If something like that had happened, I would have remembered."

Amnesia. How, after fifteen years of a women's movement naming the "putdowns" and hurts and injuries and assaults (physical, emotional, economic), and worse, that women endure, can a girl not "remember" her own pain? The question suggests its own answer: the act of remembering is an act of historical consciousness not fully available to a sixteen-year-old. But neither, it seems, is it "available" in the social and intellectual life around the girl. If, for example, she does not read feminist texts (and few do), her perception of feminism is limited to the message of mass media, popular culture, and hearsay, which are distorted and trivialized.

"I'm not a feminist, because I don't hate men and because I like to wear make-up and have a man open the door for me." I heard this a hundred times in the course of my conversations. This, then (just as popular critics have always charged), is what the women's movement boils down to in the minds of teenage girls: feminism is the ideology espoused by unattractive women who want all of womankind to live the same joyless lives they do. In other words, it is a kind of crusade of sexual losers against the lucky. Clearly, the pleasure and exuberance and wonder feminists feel in their communal and collective activity have not penetrated the mass media. But, as Susan Brownmiller charges in her book *Femininity*,[5] it is also true that the women's movement, in the manner of all "grim moralists", has often simply fulminated against the fraudulent use of make-up, sexy clothing, deodorants and scents, and so on, as the "self-enslavement" of women as sex objects. This is not something that a teenage girl, coming into her own as a sexual being, wants to hear; neither is it something she can *use*, so long as her chance to live the "good life" still depends largely on her ability to attract a sex and marriage partner. Similarly, the ability of a young woman to inspire chivalrous or gentlemanly behaviour towards her is important as long as the alternative – violence – remains a threatening possibility in their encounter, and as long as "gentlemanliness" remains a signal that a woman whose car door is opened for her (cigarette lit, coat helped on) is a lady. The woman who does not wear make-up and who opens her own door is, then, that rare creature who needs neither the approval nor the protection of men. She is not likely to be sixteen years old. As necessary as the revelation of sexual violence has been, it is too much to ask an adolescent girl to take up the task of redefining sex, romance, and intimacy when she is at a point in her life where she wants to believe in the loving-kindness of male desire and the innocence of her own.

As for the attack on the "feminine mystique" – the "femininity" that required women to stay at home as wives and mothers – the issue has been decided. "Independence," writes Sharon Thompson,[6] "appears inescapable." Grown up, girls *will* be working for a living, will be single or divorced, will be heads of families. But this seems hardly to be liberating. The single woman, treading the circuit between office, singles bar, and bachelor apartment, is seen as merely lonely. The career woman, bereft of networks, vulnerable to harassment and exploitation, under hostile or sceptical male surveillance, is seen as profoundly on her own. The superwoman, managing career and family life, is all too often burned-out, exhausted, at the end of her tether.

None of this is likely to convert masses of girls to militant feminism. For now, feminists must content themselves with the observation that it isn't always important what a girl *says* about feminists and feminism – they must look at what she *does*. Wherever and whenever she conspires to make a life organized around female friendship, intellectual curiosity, useful work, and affection, there she is feminism's daughter.

I was at SEED school and we women were sitting in the library, talking about growing up female. Penny remembered her dream:

"I had it last year. I'd been thinking about nuclear war, hunger, famine, pain, death. I went into myself like a recluse for two months. Ate very little, smoked like a fiend, wrote. Wrote and wrote and thought and thought; I was really tortured. The day it ended was the night I had the dream. All the women who had ever lived and would

ever live were in it. They were personified in one woman
and she was talking to me. She had beautiful hair and it
was down over her face and she was naked and she was
huddled in a heap. She was every emotion: she was crying,
she was laughing, she was tortured, she was exultant, she
was free, she was incarcerated. And she was saying, 'You
can't let the children die in vain, you can't let our lives, our
deaths, the children we've not had, the children we have
had, you can't let it all be in vain. Dance with us? Dance
with us?' I started to cry in my dream. 'Yes, I'll dance with
you.' The woman looked up at me. She was radiantly
beautiful. Then I really freaked out because she was me.
She had my face. . . . That's when I decided to be a
feminist."

TWENTY-FOUR

Eva

"I'm gonna go for it."

NOTES FROM the first meeting, over coffee in the school cafeteria. Eva is tall and blonde. She smiles beautifully, even with a mouth full of braces. She has a high, thin, girlish voice which she says she hates. She is in grade twelve for the second time, trying now for her senior matriculation. She'd like to go to "university", to study psychology, although it is not clear whether she distinguishes between university as such and all post-secondary schooling. She's eighteen years old and has been living on her own since she was sixteen, when she left home in the middle of her grade ten year. Not wanting to quit school but feeling "directionless", she spent grade eleven taking "piddly courses". Now she's directed again: her favourite school day is Thursday, when she studies biology, social studies, physics, chemistry, and math. Until she was eighteen, she was supported by child welfare; at eighteen, she transferred to a high school maintenance grant of $347 a month. She has a part-time job at a fast-food drive-in. Her boyfriend, who lives with his parents, has dropped out of school and works at an auto-body garage for $4.50 an hour.

Eva's parents are divorced. She is taking care of herself. I explain that this is why I want to keep on talking with her: to learn how she has managed this. I will, in fact, see Eva off and on for the next year and a half. Of all my interviewees, she is the only one to keep in touch with me, phoning me every few months to keep me up to date with her situation. As it turns out, her situation is always changing; a new address and phone number, a new boyfriend, a job lost, a job found. As for her schooling, that changes too.

The abiding condition of her education, as of her whole life at this point, is that she is on her own, to make it or be defeated by it. No one is propping her up, encouraging and congratulating her, reminding her of the reason she is there – to finish, to get on with a life better than her parents'. Granted, no one is there to witness her discouragement, either, the times she's late for classes – there's no one to nag her to get her ass out the door – and the times she skips out of them to go strolling downtown or back to her apartment to watch the soaps, or to chide her for her undistinguished grades, to point out that a mere pass mark, while it may make her "happy", will not get her into university. What's the sense of trying to dream, asks Eva rhetorically, as though to excuse her lack of application by appealing to the hint of absurdity in what she is trying to do: get into university, a place no one she knows has ever been. In fact she *does* dream, but it is the great loneliness of dreaming alone that gets her down, and the tremendous effort of setting her own challenges without benefit of admirers (except for her boyfriend, Ray, who is proud of her determination) that wearies her.

Her mother had raised her and her brother on welfare. It was a very hard life for them all, and Eva has sworn she will raise children who have "everything". To get ahead, however, you must either be well connected or educated, and since Eva has no connections, she must be educated as far as she can go. Otherwise – she can see this very clearly – some "dinky little restaurant" is going to claim her, that and her love life and the soaps, and she will be lost. So she bends her head to the books again, although she does not like to read or write, and repeats to herself like a mantra that *everybody* has brains and should make the effort to use them – there are an awful lot of lazy people in this world, her boyfriend being one of them – and what is life about except to take some risks *just in case* you get lucky and win your dream? It's all out there, she argues, but you must go after it: "I'm gonna go for it," she assures me.

As it turned out, she didn't even finish the semester. She quit school in early January, not bothering to write the exams, and got a job washing dishes in the bus depot café downtown. She explained that she had had no choice: Student Financial Services had promised her nothing, and in the meantime Ray had expensive car insurance to pay and couldn't cover her if student aid didn't come through and working part-time would be no help at all and, besides, she was just really tired of school. Not that anybody cared, really: her mother was utterly indifferent to her decision, and her father, inordinately influenced by his lackadaisical girlfriend, said "whatever makes you happy". But Eva knew in her heart of hearts that she had done a cowardly thing. "I'll go back to school," she told me. "I'll do correspondence and night classes. This is only temporary. Honest." Perhaps she convinced herself, if not me.

Notes from our second meeting, while Eva was still at school. A third of her Biology 30 class is peopled by immigrant Chinese students; the brightest student, Eva tells me, is a Chinese boy. She give me her notebook to look through. The teacher has written on the top sheet of the first quiz: "A good start! (20/28). Try and get to class by 8:20, okay?" Eva's average in Physics 20 is 54, up from 30 in Physics 10. She is very pleased with herself and determined not to slacken. She seems to me, at least, to speak with impressive confidence as she explains the results of last week's experiment in the lab to determine "the least amount of force required to move along an object at a constant speed."

I go with her to Social Studies 30, where the teacher introduces a film about the Warsaw Ghetto by warning the class they are about to see scenes of considerable horror and that previous classes have been so upset they have thrown up. He pauses, then continues rather diffidently, saying that, to tell the truth, students of the last few years have not had this reaction at all, that they wonder what he was making such a fuss about, they've seen much worse on TV. Today they are, in fact, unmoved by the film, whispering to each other throughout – one girl takes this opportunity to do her nails in the flickering light of the ghoulish images coming off the screen – and asking no questions at the conclusion except to inquire, "What was the Holocaust anyway?" Eva, with whom I leave the classroom, says only that "it was kind of awful", meaning the pictures of corpses, dead from starvation, being tipped head first down a chute into a burial pit, their limbs folded in upon themselves as though pleated.

We go for lunch in the cafeteria, where she points out some of the girls she took Beauty Culture with the year before. She is contemptuous of them all. She draws my attention to one girl, a smashing brunette, all curls and eyelashes and fingernails, in tight jeans and stiletto heels, who "dresses like a hooker and has no brains". But Eva herself is wearing an equally tight pair of jeans that zip along the crotch and up the bum and a tight-fitting sweater that shows her broad shoulders and slender torso and full bust to best advantage, although she seems utterly unconscious of this. Her remark that the girls had all "put me down" for taking her studies so seriously indicates that she is not so much contemptuous as estranged: yet clearly it would not occur to Eva to seek out the company of the middle-class lovelies in the academic stream.

I buy her lunch – a hot dog, fries and gravy, chocolate milk, and a bismarck – and, having sensed her lack of

interest in conversation about the Second World War, I
switch subjects. She chatters on amiably and freely about
her family. Her parents separated when she was very
young and her brother still an infant; the children were
put into foster care until the mother retrieved them some
time later and raised them as best she could, on welfare
and meagre employment as a Girl Friday. But the divorce
embittered her mother – she tried to "poison" her children's minds against their father – and her poverty
shamed and enraged her. Eva admits that, when her father re-established contact with his children and treated
them to their first trip away from home, not to mention to
"lots of food" on weekends, she was very much impressed
by his largesse, and disgusted by the meanness of her
mother's life. Her mother "abused" her and Eva went
again to live in a foster home when she was thirteen. A few
months later she went to live with her father and for three
years did not see her mother. When she did see her again,
her mother had become "grey and fat"; she was "unrecog-
nizable". When I suggest to Eva that her mother's life had
been hard, she retorts that she'd "made it hard for herself". Her father, a carpenter, had rebuilt his life; her
mother had given in to despondency and regret. That this
might have had something to do with the hardship of
raising children in poverty – the father meantime had
girlfriends – does not seem to have occurred to Eva. She
frankly admits that she "idolizes" her father. Why, then, I
want to know but do not ask, did she then, in the middle
of the night and with nowhere to go, leave her father's
house?

After leaving her father and "bounding around all over
the place", Eva settled in at the downtown YWCA for several months and began the process of having herself declared a ward of the government. It was hellish. It meant
several court appearances and hearing her parents declare,
from his and her corner, that, yes, they yielded their child

to the care of the government. It was what Eva wanted to hear – that she was no runaway, that she would not be returned to her parents' care – but it broke her heart all the same. She then had her choice of fates: to go into a detention home, to become a foster child, or to enter the government's Support Independent Living program. She had already lived as a foster child and had heard nothing to recommend detention centres, and she thought, I *want* to make it by myself and piss on everybody who wants to screw up my life. She chose SIL.

The program meant that someone handled her money for her, paid her rent and utilities, told her about garage sales and birth control, asked for a copy of her house key and made checks on her living quarters, looking for evidence of dope and alcohol and overnight guests, and told her not to party. (Ray, however, was not a casual boyfriend, and they could not stop Eva from seeing him.) Eva wondered how this kind of supervision was supposed to teach her to live independently, but it did keep the wolf from the door for two years. At eighteen she was out of the program and "free".

"Free" meant trying to live without financial aid from her parents, without social assistance, and without a room-mate (she had a room-mate once, a fat girl who ate more than her share). It meant taking the fast-food job, trying to save money from one-hundred-dollar pay cheques to make ends meet between school maintenance grants, budgeting forty dollars a week for food, two hundred a month for rent, nothing for clothes or entertainment (Eva neither drinks nor smokes), borrowing old furniture from an aunt, a used vacuum-cleaner from her father, and then blowing all her savings on a telephone call to a girlfriend who'd moved to Newfoundland.

For the longest time it drove her crazy to be alone. That's why she picked up a cat from the animal shelter. When she acquired a second-hand television set, she'd turn it on just to have the comforting buzz of human voices in the background. She admits she'd rather watch

TV than clean house (in fact, she keeps her apartment very tidy) or cook meals. She's not much of a cook, she says, and can't see the need to make "a big fuss" over a solitary meal, but she likes to bake. When she feels restless or melancholy or unnerved, she bakes cookies, putting all her "loving care" into a batter of chocolate chips and walnuts, and eating the whole batch herself.

Eva is poor but she doesn't like to think of it that way. She has little money but she's "rich" for all that. Friends come to visit, they look around her apartment, they're impressed: "Where did you get all this?" they ask. Hey, thinks Eva, I *do* have something here. I have a home.

Notes about Eva's Christmas. When I arrived at her apartment in mid-afternoon early in January, she was still in her nightie (she'd decided not to go to school that day) and was taking down her Christmas tree, an activity that did not, this time, make her feel sad: her Christmas had been "boring". On Christmas Eve, she and Ray had gone over to her mother's for dinner, but her mother seemed to have forgotten the invitation and served up only cheese and crackers and desultory conversation. This was not festive. On Christmas Day, invited to Ray's parents' home, she fought with Ray about his refusal to dress up for the occasion. *She* had dressed up and she wanted to be there with him as a couple. But his insistence on dressing casually along with the rest of his family signified to Eva that his loyalty, after all, lay with them and not with her.

She now sits cross-legged on the floor amid the disorder of the tree and its trimmings. This, and the great pile of yellowing, unread newspapers by the front door, and the tone of her voice, disgruntled still, are the only signs of disharmony in her rooms. Unless one includes the photograph on top of the television which prefigures her complaint: she is posed in a studio, in a long pink dress, with Ray at her side. She tells me he was "falling down drunk" and indeed he does look rather unsteady, atilt, with a long red nose. Eva is smiling in a tight-lipped way and she's holding her crossed arms at the elbows. This was supposed to be *her* big night (she was finishing grade eleven) and he had ruined it. Telling me all this, she is indignant all over again.

Just before Christmas, Eva quit her job at the fast-food drive-in. There had been little enough money in it and less satisfaction; she felt that she'd been given no credit for her work, for the times she'd worked the counter window, freezing in short sleeves, and in the kitchen, cleaning out the big frying vats, and at the electronic till, being timed and given shit for chatting with the customers – customers *like* you to talk to them – even when there was no line-up. There was no "personal relationship" whatever with the other girls who worked there, some of whom had been there for years and had the attitude that they knew the score much better than she did and could throw their weight around, bossing her and checking up on her. The final indignity was the matter of her pay cheque. This had been her first real job, and when she received her first cheque she looked at the pay stub and saw "a whole bunch of little columns" of figures, for all the world as if it was an official document, and she thought, "Wow, this is the real world!" There was nothing in the columns, however, about contributions to UIC. When she challenged the supervisor about this, it was explained to her that she wasn't working sufficient hours over a year to qualify for, and could not therefore contribute to, unemployment insurance benefits. So there it was: her first real job, which, should she lose it, would not entitle her to the dignity of UIC (money she had *earned*) but would press her into the disgrace of welfare. It really pissed her off.

It took her six weeks to get the job at the bus station café washing dishes at minimum wage. "It's crazy out there," she explained, meaning the unemployment rate among people like herself – high-school drop-outs. For

$3.80 an hour she's on her feet for eight hours, tired already after six, and trying not to be overwhelmed by the fact that she's working so hard for so little. She and Ray are talking about his moving in with her so he can help with the rent.

Notes after a Tupperware party. Over a supper she had prepared for me one evening after an interview (Campbell's cream of mushroom soup – her favourite – and an onion omelette served between slices of white bread and margarine), Eva told me about a friend of hers, Trish, who was planning to work in the evenings selling Tupperware as a means of keeping herself occupied while her fiancé worked at two jobs, day and night. Trish is seventeen, the fiancé nineteen, and they plan to marry in the summer. I wondered aloud why young people are in such a rush to get married, to which Eva replied, rather primly, that this is what you *do*, after going together for a while; the alternative, of course, is to break up. Nevertheless, in Eva's opinion this is an ill-fated union: the boy is Chinese, Trish is not, and his parents are evidently hostile to the match. Trish assumes that she will "work things out" after the wedding, which Eva thinks is very ill-considered: you've got to work these things out *before* getting all tied up in marriage.

Some weeks later, Eva phoned to invite me to one of Trish's Tupperware parties which she was hosting at her own apartment. I noted that she had rearranged her furniture and that all the photographs of Ray were gone. In their place was a large colour portrait of a baby she referred to during the evening as Billy. I had no idea who had produced this baby, but as the evening progressed and several comments were made about a "Mike" – as in "You should meet Mike. He likes the Rolling Stones, too" – I concluded that Eva had a new boyfriend with a baby.

There were six of us at the party, including Eva and Trish: Connie from down the block, a grade eleven stu-

dent; Maxine from across the lane, a woman in her
twenties who'd spent the winter selling Avon products
door-to-door and who was now preparing to move up to
the Yukon to work as a camp cook; and Eva's mother, a
soft, plump woman who sat quietly in a corner chair and
smiled agreeably from time to time.

This was, Trish explained as she took the floor, only her
second presentation and she apologized for not having all
the answers to our questions about the products at hand,
for not having a very large sample display, and for trip-
ping – she was wearing high-heeled shoes – over what she
did have, arrayed mainly on the floor. I discovered that a
Tupperware party is only ultimately about selling bowls
and picnic sets: there were games to play first. With paper
and pens provided by Tupperware (which we were obliged
to relinquish at the end of the games) we wrote answers to
trick questions from Trish: How many species of animals
did Moses take on board the Ark? Can a man living in
Montreal be buried in Calgary? We were next asked, going around the circle, to think of a "positive" adjective,
beginning with the same letter as our first name, to describe ourselves, as in "terrific Trish" and "marvellous
Myrna". I had brought a square, which Eva passed
around along with a plateful of doughnuts provided by
Trish: Eva said that if we didn't eat the doughnuts Trish
would kill us. We ate. And Trish began her presentation.

She invited us to consider the virtues of the product:
how well the lids seal, how attractive the colours are, the
handiness of the shapes (separate containers for bacon,
ice-cream cones, frozen patties), and the variety of sizes
(all in metric dimensions, to the consternation of the
group). And she invited us to look through the catalogue.
For almost an hour we all rather gravely examined this
catalogue (with a view to buying something out of defer-
ence to our hostess, but without spending a lot of money)
and wandered in and out of conversations about Avon
colognes, the price of assorted nuts at different department stores, the creepiness of the boarding house next

door to Eva, the price of paperback novels. I ended by ordering $18.75 worth of Tupperware; I imagined the others ordered roughly the same amount. At twenty-five per cent of sales, Trish's commission for her evening's work would have been about twenty-five dollars.

I chatted briefly with Eva at her front door as I left. It seems she was fired from her job at the bus station café, had broken off with Ray and returned his ring, and had fallen in love with Mike.

Not long after, I heard that Trish had broken off her engagement to the Chinese fiancé and was no longer selling Tupperware.

The year that Eva studied Beauty Culture she did not yet have Ray's ring upon her finger and so was obliged to listen to the other girls in the class, each with her "rock" on her left hand, yakking about their rings, their boyfriends, their spats. It made her sick. She thought that what these girls needed most was to grow up. But when she received a ring herself, she understood the implications. It wasn't exactly an engagement ring, it was a "promise" ring, one that is a commitment to be monogamous – if you will, an intensified version of going steady. She wore it on her left hand and began thinking of putting some of her savings, over the next few years, into a special "wedding account". Alerted by her friend Trish she knew there would be considerable expense involved: the marriage licence, the invitations, the engraved matchbooks, the guestbook. She *would* marry Ray, eventually.

As a kind of intermediate arrangement, he moved in with her. At first he had resisted the proposal, being more than content to live at home, cared for by a doting mother. But when Eva pointed out that his share of the rent would be less than what he was paying his parents for room and board and that she was prepared to write him out receipts for income tax purposes, he succumbed. At first Eva was thrilled: to have Ray around at night made her feel secure, to have him around in the day made the apartment feel like a real home. But his presence also rankled. She resented having to clear out a couple of drawers in her dresser for him and she took exception to the way he shopped for groceries, going out on the spur of the moment to the neighbourhood all-nighter to pick up this and that, fish sticks and Kraft Dinners and tons of goodies for his own lunches, instead of going once a week to do a big shopping at Superstore the way normal couples do.

Eva took a book out from the library, *How to Live With a Man*, and discovered there the name of her malaise: a feeling that your Territory is being Invaded. Worse, Ray had a bad attitude towards life: he wanted everything *now*, disdaining the effort required to start in one place, even in a boring part of town at a boring job, and work towards a goal. He wanted to live in the country, he said, on an acreage. "Oh, sure," said Eva, "we've got all sorts of money to be buying acreages." He went to a psychic who told him that he'd have his own company in five years and that he was going to marry, then divorce, Eva. Thanks a lot, that's just what she needed to hear.

Ray was her first love; she'd written flirtatious little notes to him in grade nine and then dated and fallen in love with him. Everything she did with him was for the first time and this bond, this memory of his presence and of his attendance upon her, was the glue that kept her stuck to him, even when they broke up from time to time and Eva had her "wild times", being set up with guys and teasing them outrageously, but never in fact going to bed with any of them. Ray was her first lover, although she had not at first let him even touch her, wanting companionship, not sex. She had promised herself that eighteen would be a "nice age" at which to lose her virginity. She dropped this down to sixteen, but she was in fact only fourteen when, frightened by his interest in another girl, she decided to sleep with him to "keep" him. She wishes she had waited: in her younger, more naive days, she had thought that sex was essential to love. She had misunderstood; now she knows it's the other way around.

She talks with Trish about sex. Trish used to sleep with her fiancé, an act of homage not to sex but to the relationship: what she got out of it was the post-coital cuddling. When Eva was fourteen, sixteen, she wasn't at all horny, but Ray wanted to screw three and four times a day. It drove her crazy. Even now, among the younger girls and boys, she can see that to be a "good lay" is an important component of a girl's reputation, but not so much of a lay that she gives it away freely. The trick still is to play hard to get, a kind of theatre or posturing which prolongs what Eva calls the "romantic process" whereby a boy learns to woo the girl he will possess.

Ray is a small man, and quiet. Eva guesses that choosing him to be her man was her way of expressing her individuality: since no one, least of all her parents, could picture her happy in a marriage with a guy like Ray, it just proves that no one really knew her as well as they thought they did.

And then it was all over, the ring packed away in a box at the back of the dresser drawer and a "fifth anniversary" present, a bronze figurine of an embracing couple, returned. There was no single, apocalyptic moment of rupture, just a dawning realization that there must be more to a relationship, to a *marriage*, than the kind of emotional mediocrity of her alliance with Ray, more than this sitting around together on weekends doing "dink shit" while girlfriends were spurned, waiting around for him while he went out, at a snap of the fingers, with his buddies, more than being loyal to the idea of their love, the "major accomplishment" of Eva's life, this *nostalgia* for a fourteen-year-old's daydreams.

Besides, she had met Mike, a twenty-four-year-old would-be disc jockey, and had begun an affair with him as she sensed Ray's waning commitment. They had one last conversation and she told him about Mike, that she was "seeing" him; it was her way of signalling that if Ray wanted her back he would have to fight for her. Ray had nothing to say.

Eva is in love with Mike. But she's no fool. She looks at this guy's life, a man on welfare suing for custody of an infant son from a wife to whom he had been married less than a year, and wonders if he'll be able to pull himself together, if she'll be saddled with an "instant family", if Mike will tear himself away from his child long enough to remember Eva, an eighteen-year-old with little time to burn. But he looks like a fighter, she says, and she's willing to invest. "Okay, I'll give my heart to him and I'll see what he does with it."

Notes after a conversation in Eva's new home. She has moved in with Mike, to a pleasant apartment in a new, working-class suburb of the city, miles from anywhere except a shopping mall. The quarters are tidy and homey; as Eva prepares me tea (she offers a wide assortment), I sense her pleasure in acting as mistress of this domestic terrain. She's changed the colour of her hair to a startling chestnut brown and to me it looks like a wig, unexpected against the peachy blondeness of her skin. But she's fetching for all that, dressed as usual in a skimpy tank-top and shorts and going barefoot; she has long, shapely, baby-smooth legs. We join Mike in the living room, one wall of which is taken up with a stereo system, records, and tapes, evidence of his coming this far, if no further, in his dream to be a disc jockey. We talk about the weekend they have just spent with little Billy and all his year-and-a-half-year-old's accomplishments, and then I ask Eva why she lost the job at the bus station café. The official reasons were that she had been rude to customers, difficult to get along with among the staff, and inefficient in handling cash, all of which she hotly contests: "I was a good little worker! I was working eight hours a day, nine days in a row. I thought I might even have a chance to be Employee of the

Month. When the boss put me on the till, he said it was because I had a nice smile and the café needed that. Then he fired me. Scum won't even give me a reference."

Mike says the real reason she was fired was the fact that her three-month probation period was up, and if she was kept on, her pay would have to rise. The cheapest manoeuvre for the owner is to fire her and take on a new girl for the same three-month period. Eva hadn't thought of this, that it might not have been her fault at all that she was fired. But will she fight it? "Who would believe me?"

Now she is looking around for another restaurant job and has enrolled in night school to get her Biology 30 and Chemistry 30. It is the first time since she quit school eight months ago that she's mentioned her educational plans to me. Perhaps the fear that some "dinky restaurant" will claim her, entrap her, is closing in?

She invites me to look around the apartment, and we end by sitting on the bed looking at her photograph albums. She points out her father with his girlfriends, with Eva the fifteen-year-old, the sixteen-year-old. He has a ruddy, roughened face, like that of a prairie farmer, squared off. He's broadly built and looks uncomfortable in a suit and tie. Eva lingers over these pictures, betraying nothing in her voice or her posture of the emotional furor that had driven her out of this home to try to make her own.

As domesticated as she now seems, her relationship with Mike is problematic. She has discovered she'd rather go out at nights to see a movie than stay at home babysitting. Time enough for that with her own kids one of these days. She recalls, with retrospective fondness and pleasure, the weeks and weeks she had all by herself in her own apartment, accountable to no one. To think, she laughs, she once thought she was lonely there.

We had talked for hours over the months. She was so open, almost ingenuously open, and talked as though all reminiscences and all confessions were equally weighted – a story about a favoured puppy dog and one about her sex life were equally part of a burgeoning autobiography. And so one night when we were talking for the third or fourth time about her family, and I was slowly, and with great anxiety, getting the drift of her conversation, of where she was headed in this story, she moved straight as a beam into the heart of it and out again, as though *all* memory were auspicious, and this particular memory no more than any other.

She was two years old when her parents' marriage fell apart and she's been wondering ever since, because no one will tell her, why it happened. She remembers being left by her mother at a babysitter's one week when her father was out of town and, when her mother failed to return to claim her, being taken away by a social worker some days later and put into a foster home. Her father, back in town, rescued her. The next time it happened, her father was once again out of town and her mother "forgot" her at the babysitter's but showed up a couple of days late, acting as if nothing had happened. Eva was happy to see her, but confused. She guesses now that her mother out of loneliness had taken a boyfriend. Eva could have lived with this if it had not been for the beatings. At one and a half she had broken her leg in what her mother called "a silly accident". It was another, unforgettable beating at age thirteen that had sent her out of her mother's home and into her father's.

Her father, a complex, demanding, inscrutable man, was someone she wanted very much to please. After all, he had rescued her when she was abandoned and now offered her his home, a sanctuary from poverty and beatings. He had wanted her to be a boy and she worked as diligently as she could at his side, pleased and proud the day she could flex her arm and say to him, "Here, feel this!" But she was thirteen, fourteen, and wanting also to be a girl. This he didn't know how to teach her, or at least not the things she wanted to know: how much make-up to put on, what kind of clothes to buy, how to handle a boy on a date. What he did know to teach her, and did, was sex.

She was turning into a woman, anybody could see that, but she was so much still a little girl inside; he blocked that out. What he saw was a daughter who could be his housekeeper, his girlfriend, his lover. He took her as them all.

He taught her how to French-kiss. She'd be cooking supper and he'd come up behind her and grab her breasts and she'd swat him but he'd just laugh: "What's the matter? Aren't you horny?" Or: "You like it. You know you do." She thought this was normal, it was a loving father-daughter relationship, almost a romance – she who had grown up fatherless was now a father's beloved. The hurt she felt when he brought home his girlfriends was palpable, girlfriends he took into the bedroom (*their* bed!) while she had stayed up late watching movies so that when he came home she could tell him how much she had missed him. She hated these girlfriends.

Then she met Ray and the relief of being able to be in his company (not having to be hush-hush about fooling around with him) and to receive from him not lust but affection was so overwhelming that she began to avoid her father, dreading his embrace. He reacted like a jealous lover, drawing up a list of draconian regulations concerning her behaviour about the house (ladylike language at all times; keep kitchen and family room clean; no boyfriend in house without presence of parent), whacking her around so that she went to school with blackened eyes behind sunglasses, even, so help her God, arranging to be discovered by Eva one day after school in bed with her best girlfriend. The last straw came the evening that Ray showed up at the house to invite her to a party and her father, lying, said she was busy. She heard him say that. She had a fit. She said she was going to the party no matter what, and he said if she did she might as well pack her bags and leave. Which is what she did.

And that was the story. And she was finished with it

and on to others, about girlfriends and pay cheques and phone bills, about Christmases at home with Dad and about Dad's support for her education, and Dad this and Dad that (in the background, like an uninvited guest, her mother, the timid, shy, resourceless, unpitied mother). Her hand rested on the photo album, his face looking back at us, communicating nothing, and hers next to his, the amorous daughter, that much is obvious, but nothing else. I would never have guessed.

Just a couple of weeks ago she called me from a pay phone. She's left Mike, moved into another basement apartment, had her phone cut off for lack of payment, and found some work as a data-entry clerk in a prestigious law firm. But this is not all. There's an ebullience and even a kind of throaty assurance in her voice that I haven't heard before as she tells me she's been accepted, not into university, but into a community college out of town. She is beside herself with excitement and misgiving, hardly able to believe her dream is about to come true. If she doesn't blow it.

Bon voyage, Eva. Go for it.

TWENTY-FIVE

Futures

"I'm not counting on being married. You can't count on anything."

WITH A HANDFUL of exceptions, each girl had a scenario of her future, some more remote than others. Nina had just finished reading *The Agony and the Ecstasy*, a fictionalized account of the life of Michelangelo, and had decided then and there to put aside university studies in favour of a few years of travel, while Arden, dreaming of the good life in a big beach-side house in the company of a large dog and a blond hunk ("we'd go skinny-dipping, watch the stars at night"), had determined that the only means to this end – "not having to work nine to five" – was to become a rock star. Donna, temporarily cooking pizzas for a living, wants to be a theatre director, and her friend Charlene, ringing up fried-chicken sales, is studying to be a travel agent. Inspired by an accountant who spoke at her school's Career Day, Teddy is thinking of becoming an accountant, advising small businesses in their financial decisions, and Mandy, who knows herself to be a confident and capable person, sees herself, rather vaguely, as an "executive". Barbara has no business sense whatever, she claims, and so plans not to own a big beauty salon but to work in one in New York; Sherry counts on inheriting her grandmother's shop and opening up an electrolysis studio as well. Torn between wanting to be "rich and famous" *and* a writer, Jodi dreams of being both at once: a rich and famous writer. Roxanne would like to work with "troubled teenagers" as a social worker (she has her own values "pretty straight" and can put that to use on their behalf) or as a police officer, blazing a trail for other women in the police force who want to get out from behind their desks. Wendy simply wants to straighten out her life: by the time she's twenty-one, she wants to have quit doing drugs, wants a steady boyfriend, a nice apartment, a car, a cat, and a job, but *which* job?

Some thrash about among several possibilities, none of them sure. Wendy wants to be a dance teacher, an actress, a lawyer, a dress designer, a boutique owner. Sharon's plans change whimsically, according to what her esteemed older brother wants to do: when he wanted to be a doctor, she wanted to go into medicine; when he dreamed of being a professional hockey player, she decided to study physical education. Carla would love to travel and study "other cultures" – as her admired aunt, the wife of an oil company executive, apparently does – or, perhaps, she would live in New York as a writer, "analysing life". Others simply feel nervous, casting about for the occupation that will keep them employed forever – law? nuclear physics? professional photography? – and, at the very least, assured of a standard of living no lower than that of their parents.

They say they don't have to be rich to be happy. One girl would settle for $1600 a month in take-home pay, enough, that is, to assure her her independence from creditors, parents, and husband. Another, growing up in a "government house", wants enough money to buy a home, a car, and a fridgeful of groceries every week. Nina says that, if she were working at something that made her happy, she could lower her standard of living – "I have no problem eating ordinary bread instead of crumpets, you know what I mean?" – but, on the other hand, wonders how long she'd be willing to forgo luxuries like travelling, and a "really, really nice home", either an old, renovated one or a very modern penthouse in the middle of the city, or "lying in a bathtub full of perfume". Because she's never lived on her own, Jodi can't say how much money is enough – how much do utilities cost? car insurance? a microwave oven? – but, in spite of her artistic ambitions, she has a horror of the life of typical artists, a hand-to-mouth existence eked out between gigs: "Money can't buy happiness, but it helps." Sherry has her own "happiness list" already drawn up: a house with a garden, a stereo system, a waterbed, a well-stocked bar, and lots and lots of clothes and make-up.

It came as a shock to all of them to learn that, in spite of their ambitions and requirements, they would earn, on average, sixty-four per cent of what their male counterparts – same ambitions, same requirements – will earn. This "wage gap", and the equally devastating statistics regarding "job ghettoes" (the concentration of female employees in clerical, service, and sales jobs) and female pauperization (in 1983 one in five Canadian women had incomes below the poverty line), was a revelation to them. Clearly, neither at home nor at school has anyone enlightened them about the economic structures that will shape their futures. To give parents and teachers the benefit of the doubt, it can be argued that no girl, dreaming of achievement and fortune, should be discouraged. But we will surely pay the price of educating and employing young women whose naivety about the way the world still works – "I have enough confidence in my abilities that I'll be able to overcome whatever difficulties will face me," to quote one – can easily collapse into cynicism, demoralization, and self-reproach if they haven't been given the tools to analyse what they're up against as female workers, and at least a hint about what is to be done to rectify economic injustice.

Multiply by a hundred thousand times, though, Nina's reaction to information about the wage gap, and one may detect the possibility of a generation prepared to fight for itself: "I didn't realize . . . I mean, I thought we had progressed from that! I was talking to two guys at school and even they said that females at our school have much more brain power, that we're better students, and . . . oh God, this male-female thing and money – it makes me want to deny my femininity. It makes me want to put down 'M' instead of 'F' on job applications. It really does. I shouldn't have to do that! I should say, 'Yes, I am female, and I can do as much as or more than a male and I'm worth it!' "

To achieve their personal ambitions, girls are increasingly committed to post-secondary education; in the last fifteen years, women's enrolment in Canadian universities has nearly doubled. This is most dramatically represented by their presence (in 1983) in medical schools (42 per cent of enrolment), law schools (44 per cent), and business and commerce faculties (43 per cent), professional areas until very recently dominated overwhelmingly by men. Of course, the telling statistic will be the defeminization of those occupational sectors historically reserved *for* women, but in the meantime, despite the discouraging statistics on female faculty,[1] the fact that girls want to study engineering, counselling, law, computer graphics, psychology, mathematics, and creative writing is an encouraging development as long as a higher education continues to provide women access to privileged work.[2]

Not everyone who has the desire to be educated, however, will be fulfilled: only about 15 per cent of all high school students in Canada actually attend a university, even though, at age fifteen, 65 per cent expect to do so. The gap between those percentages may be accounted for in part by the difference between Mandy and Jean, for example: Jean has been waiting on tables for two years to put together the money to get into an art school and build a portfolio that will dazzle the admissions committee; Mandy, whose businessman father could "pull strings" for her at one or two universities, has applied to McGill,

Queen's, and Toronto, and is spending the summer twiddling her thumbs, waiting to see who will have her.

If one asks what is the young woman's *probable* future, as
compared to the one she so buoyantly imagines and plots
for herself, the answers, extrapolated from current trends,
are discouraging and worrying. At the same time, the data
stand in stark relief against stereotypical beliefs concerning the woman worker and her work; the *reality* of her
situation, no matter what she may believe personally to be
her case, may have the effect of mobilizing her sense of
injury.

A woman who is now entering the work force for the
first time will work on average only four years less than
her hypothetical mate. She cannot count on being
"looked after" by a working spouse while she keeps house:
three out of four Canadian women either never marry or
lose their mates through separation, divorce, or death.
Even in families with children under six years of age, 48
per cent of mothers work outside the home; it is estimated
that by the year 2000, 47 per cent of the labour force will
be female.[3] (In Quebec, for example, in 1983 that proportion was already 40 per cent.)

For all their increased economic activity, though, wom-
en's situation within the labour force has if anything wor-
sened over the last decade. The sudden arrival of educated,
middle-class women to positions of apparent influence and
power, as managers and business people and executives,
obscures the fact that more and more women are stuck in
clerical and service jobs: ten years ago, some 66 per cent of
working women held such jobs, today more than 75 per
cent do. Where women are unionized, as waitresses for example, the hourly wage can be at least a dollar more than
that of a non-unionized worker (but still less than the unionized male waiter); but, as of 1982, women constituted only
32.3 per cent of Canadian union members.[4] Yet the stereotypical union member – the white, male industrial worker –

on whose behalf union militancy has been deployed to win gains for the "family breadwinner" has been superseded by events: the family depends almost as a matter of course on the incomes of two breadwinners, and even more frequently on that of a mother alone.

Now that the initial hullabaloo about the computerization of the work force has subsided, some observers fear that microtechnology is not necessarily a liberating technology as far as women's work is concerned. In fact, as Heather Menzies has observed in *Women and the Chip*,[5] women are uniquely vulnerable to automation as telephone switchboards, banking machines, cash registers, and keyboards – all traditional sites of women's employment – become automated. In fact, she estimates that by 1990 up to one million women in Canada could be made redundant by technological innovation in the workplace, especially the office, rendered "paperless". Technology, Canadian labour historian Elaine Bernard reminds us,[6] is a *system*, not just individual machines working in isolation from a social and economic context. The invention of the typewriter and the consequent "feminization" of office work did not radically alter the status of women in the society as a whole; if anything, it drew women out of their homes only to reconfirm them, at the desk, as handmaidens of male bosses.

As long as clerical work, computerized or otherwise, is identified as women's work and therefore devalued, a wage gap of 15 per cent to 20 per cent – after number of hours worked, educational background, labour force experience, and level and rate of unionization are taken into account – will continue to exist.[7] This discrepancy is the essence of discrimination, for it is not the job itself but the fact that a *woman* is performing it that renders it of less worth to an employer.

If teenage girls have received even a whiff of these developments – of the wage gap, the job ghetto, the automation of tasks – their ambivalence about the possibility of achieving happiness through paid work alone, without the consolation of family life, is not altogether surprising. I spoke to no one who wanted to be a full-time housekeeper – an "interesting life" was frequently juxtaposed to "just a housewife". But, with a handful of exceptions, neither did anyone envisage herself with equanimity as a thirty-year-old spinster, watering her plants and feeding her cat in a bachelor apartment after a long day over the word processor. Almost everyone imagined some kind of combination of "career" and "family", usually with the career in place before the marriage and children would be considered – "Who knows, maybe I'll have a husband and three kids running around. But first I have to have a career. Men will always be around, they're not going anywhere. . . ." – and, in most cases, with time off to rear the children full-time until they're in school. None of them anticipated any difficulty moving in and out of the labour force without penalty according to their own schedule, and none of them felt that their decision to work was related in any way to the ability of their future partner to support them. (According to Bibby and Posterski's survey,[8] only five per cent of the girls surveyed agreed that "married women should not work if their husbands are capable of supporting them.") They saw themselves in much the same way as young males do: as citizens who would pursue some form of higher education, get a good job, and settle down and raise a family.

CARLA: I don't want to get married.

SHARON: I'd like to get married.

CARLA: No way. I like being by myself and I can't see myself living with a *guy*. Travelling around the world – now *that's* interesting. Freedom. Having kids, sure, but I don't want to get married.

SHARON: I'd love to get married.

CARLA: The excitement dies out in the first five years.

SHARON: But I get bored of boy-hopping. I'm dead serious. I've always dreamed of marrying a gorgeous guy and just

settling down –
CARLA: And living happily ever after. Fairy tale.
SHARON: Not "settling down". There's no way I'm going to
be a housewife. We're going to have a maid.

The surveys and statistics paint a broad picture of the
teenage girl as a romantic: one who hopes and expects to
get married, live monogamously, raise her children with
the co-operation of a loving and helpful mate, and enjoy
the benefits of a middle-class or even an upper-middle-
class income, earned in the first place by the husband-
professional, and in the second by the wife, who will re-
enter her profession after the birth of her children. The
romantic does not envisage divorce, unemployment, or
poverty in her scenario, does not see a husband who will
refuse to do housework, a day-care centre with a two-year
waiting list, or an employer who does not promote married women. But of course they are romantics: the data
concerning marriage breakdown, the crisis in child care,
the economic recession and so on, do not prevail against
the iconography of our mass culture, namely the representation of the white, middle-class family unit, with a mum
increasingly represented by a woman who is at once a
glamorous career woman and a gourmet cook. If one
seeks social integration, connection with men and children, so the icon argues, this is the means. All other forms
of relationship are risky. It is implicit that the person most
at risk outside the parameters of the romantic ideal is the
woman.

But I did not speak with any girl who was not in the
process of revising the ideal, adjusting it to suit her own
needs and to reflect the crude realities of heterosexual
relations in the society around her. Girls who have been
warned by their mothers not to marry "too young" take
the admonishment very seriously, observing in their own
mothers' early marriages the squandering of girlhood
dreams and the trauma of being naive about men, of having married the wrong man. These are girls determined to

"play the field" before marrying, in the process learning not only about men in general and a man in particular (that he is or is not a good listener, has a sense of humour, is good with children) but about themselves as well, developing themselves in relation to what they know, understand, and like about other people. As tentative and apologetic (as though she were being too daring, speaking out of turn) as Nina is, this is her argument: "During their twenties, people really find themselves, they find what they want to do, where to focus their efforts. But if they get married instead – maybe this is a closed-minded view? – I think it's kind of limited. Maybe this is selfish but I want to spend time on *me*, I want to develop *me* instead of having to think about marriage and someone else. There's nothing wrong with that, I don't think." Of course she's defensive: the feminine ideal has consistently proposed female "unselfishness", female service, and female self-effacement. It takes an extraordinary sixteen-year-old courage to contradict that ideal, which promises, remember, female happiness in exchange.

But everywhere I heard girls doing just that, more or less decisively. Girls who are adamant about earning their own keep ("the idea of a wife leeching off her husband totally repulses me") and assuring egalitarian marital relations by paying their fair share of the rent, so to speak ("if you go into a relationship being self-supporting, I think it can work out"). They are determined to avoid the "incredibly stupid" fate of being stuck at home with babies while the husband has the "interesting" life and the wife begs for pin money ("I would never get myself into a situation like that"). Everywhere I met girls who hate "macho men", rude, obnoxious jerks, and other assholes who expect you to wait on them, clean up after them, cook for their buddies, and let them go off, no questions asked, on fishing weekends while you spend yours doing laundry and babysitting. While no girl actively *plans* for divorce, perhaps even keeps the spectre at bay by daydreaming ("so I'm going to get married and have children, I'm going to travel, I'm going to live with someone really understanding – it sounds like out of a storybook, doesn't it?"), neither does she totally discount the possibility (if not the probability) of living alone: "I'm not *counting* on being married; you can't count on anything." They all know someone who's raised her kids by herself (staying unmarried is so "iffy"), or who's left a marriage, childless (the gay divorcee in the Ozzy Osborne T-shirt), or who's waited until her thirties or later to settle down. Or who has never married. And none of them, contrary to prediction, is a basket case.

In fact, to my own astonishment, I heard repeatedly from girls that raising children was a far more important goal than being married, and if they had to do it husband-less, they would do it. Barbara: "There's nobody I've met I could imagine marrying. I'm too picky. I'd rather have a kid than a husband, anyway. If I had a choice, I'd have the kid." This is extremely put, of course, but many, many girls feel sufficiently strongly about being mothers that they are prepared to raise children without the assistance of a mate; in fact, it is as though the decision to marry (finding the "right" guy) were independent of the decision to bear children, as though the very definition of "family" were being adjusted to account for the possible absence of the father.

It has dawned on these girls, however, that although they may not be in any position to be full-time mothers, neither will they be able to raise children completely with-out assistance; they talk, then, of making sure they have the money to hire a nanny or to place their children in care. One girl who had worked in a day-care centre saw at first hand just how demanding child care is – "the mothers were at work or at school all day long and then they came to take care of their squalling kid and had an exam to study for the next day; they did everything I did in a day *plus* took care of the child – they didn't stop working until they fell asleep!" – and everyone was agreed that single mothers need help. But there was considerable ambivalence about the appropriateness and benefit of day care in providing that help. While some of the girls, who had themselves been placed in care as children or had been reared by only one parent or by grandparents and did not feel that they had been harmed by the experience, argued that children have lots of "fun" in day-care centres and learn many useful things and that mothers deserve a break from constant attendance on a child, most other would-be mothers had deep reservations about this form of child care, not necessarily because non-parental care is damaging as such but because it is so difficult to secure *good* professional care, one where a child is instructed imaginatively and is unreservedly loved. A situation, in other words, that would replicate the "ideal" family if only there were time and money enough. Some girls insist, of course, that this really is the best way to mother – to be at home with young children, watching their every step, rejoicing in their every accomplishment – but even though they did appreciate just how much *work* is involved, none spoke of mothering as their prospective *job*. Child-rearing was seen as a "rewarding", "challenging", "beautiful" interlude in one's work life, as though work were defined only in terms of the paid labour force, all else being a kind of recreation. Jodi: "You spend so much of your life in a routine at school and at work that taking care of children would be a refreshing break. I think women are lucky to have that."

According to the data reported by the Canadian Advisory Council on the Status of Women, what female adolescents "want most in the future" is marriage and family (45.4 per cent) and a good job (26.1 per cent), almost the exact reverse of boys' aspirations. It is misleading not to separate marriage from family (particularly since boys are not registering a similar commitment to family life), but even so there are more than fifty per cent of girls who would *not* place this as the most important part of their future. To be sure, reacting to the popularized "feminist"

argument that women who want to be "just" wives and
mothers are inadequate human beings, some girls insist
there is nothing "wrong" with being at home with children and they would in fact be "proud" to be such a
mother, and more than compensated by a child's delight
in being alive ("I want some child to say to me, 'Gee,
Mum, thanks for having me!'; that would make me feel
good, that I'd done something for this person"). Others,
however, remain ambivalent. They are fearful of the pain
of childbirth and of the ravages to the body; they are torn
between two scenarios – the freewheeling childless woman
guaranteed promotions and vacations, and the Betty
Crocker mother surrounded in her bungalow by adorable
children and appreciative spouse – and are in a quandary
about how best to arrange their working and their mothering lives. "It's kind of a vicious circle: if you take off too
much time to have children, it's hard to get back in to the
labour force, but if you wait too long to have children . . .
they say that after thirty-five it's kind of dangerous. So,
between twenty and thirty you have to do everything! The
whole thing seems overpowering to me sometimes."

There are also those few who do not want to be mothers, who have "read" the signals of a social transformation
and have determined that the message is: you don't *have*
to have kids, you don't *have* to have a husband, you don't
have to sacrifice yourself, you can do what you want to.
Implicit in this refusal to mother is the acknowledgement
that, cut it whichever way you like, the main burden of
child-rearing is the mother's. It is women's lives that have
been most deeply affected by the decision to have a family,
implicating men hardly at all: according to the most recent American information, the time that husbands devote to family tasks has increased six per cent in the last
twenty years, and this in spite of the fact that these same
twenty years have seen the massive employment of women
outside the home. The decision to have children irrespective of marriage may not be such a radical one after all;

even if a woman has a husband, for all the work he does around the house he may as well not be there at all.

This generation of teenagers is frequently berated for exhibiting a lack of vision and nerve in its contemplation of its future, or those aspects of it that are within its control. In a report in the Montreal *Gazette*, for example, in May 1985, concerning the aspirations of Montreal high school students, teachers and counsellors deplored the "tunnel vision" of teenagers who, as early as grade nine, are choosing courses that will determine their careers as adults. Apparently they feel the pressure before they graduate to have picked their vocation, a vocation determined not so much by what they enjoy or are good at, but by the likelihood of finding a job in it. "What I find depressing," said a counsellor at Dawson College, "is the lack of optimism." What is depressing to a counsellor to contemplate must be oppressive for the student herself or himself: it is the teenager who is confronted with the youth unemployment rate, the shrinking of the funding of the social sector, the de-industrialization of the Canadian economy. Young people are not so much reactionary, then, as reacting to circumstances beyond their control, and making whatever choices they can to mitigate the dismal effects.

Bibby and Posterski found[9] that the "major personal concern" of young people is what they're going to do when they finish school and that this concern is "equally felt by females". Girls as well as boys take the measure of their surroundings, calculate the capacity of the environment to fulfil their ambitions, and shape their expectations accordingly. It does no good to berate girls for their disappointing failure to imagine themselves en masse as Ph.D. candidates, as doctors and lawyers and prime ministers, to commit themselves to uninterrupted employment and job mobility, and to match their expectations to their desires, if the situation for girls is such that they can do nothing else. Why is it, for instance, that studies have suggested that as girls approach the end of their high school educatin they actually *lower* their educational aspirations? The answer must be that they have already accepted that they will be doing "women's work".

The results were published in 1980 of a survey[10] of a thousand Ontario secondary school girls who had been asked two questions: What is the occupation or career you would most like to have if there were nothing to limit or prevent you? What occupation do you actually expect to have in the future? While 60 per cent *aspired* to "upper class" occupations, only 40 per cent *expected* to gain them. Only 5 per cent aspired to "lower class" occupations, but 10 percent expected to have one. For example, while a girl might aspire to be a lawyer, she expects to be a legal secretary; she aspires to be a doctor but expects to be a nurse. Given the gender division of labour and the ghettoization of women's work, this discrepancy between aspiration and expectation should not be startling. Neither should it be, perhaps, an entirely gloomy affair that girls still tend to identify with "traditional" women's work, this being work that, for all its low status and recompense, continues to be valued by women because it allows for "contact with people" rather than with "things" or "ideas". Girls, it has been shown, want "interesting" work rather than prestigious or powerful positions. The social "crime", then, is not so much that girls should hold these values as that they should be economically penalized for them.

Similarly, when the most common scenario a girl proposes for her adult life is to marry, have children, and work outside the home only after all the children are in school, it's no use lamenting her lack of initiative and boldness of enterprise. A major Statistics Canada study[11] on family histories, released in September 1985, showed that women respondents were three times more likely than men to experience major career breaks and interruptions (because of the demands on their time of child care, marriage, and lay-off, in that order). Younger women between the ages of eighteen and twenty-nine are "only" twice as likely as men in their age group to be interrupted in their work lives. "The exigencies of marriage, pregnancy and childcare had a major impact on the continuity of work for a large majority of women," the report said, "but almost no impact for men." Almost no men reported that being married or having a child was a factor in their loss of job continuity; rather, men were affected by lay-off, return to school, or illness. None of this is surprising. When employers, indeed society as a whole, continue to assume that women, even working women, are situated in the first place *in the family*; when public opinion believes at one and the same time in "equal opportunity for women" and yet in the supreme importance of mothers' presence at home with preschoolers; when fifty per cent of surveyed teenage boys[12] (in Halifax, Vancouver, Montreal, Toronto, and Winnipeg) believe child care is first of all a woman's responsibility and *none* would drop out of the work force to raise his own children; when girls themselves believe it is not in the nature of masculinity to be able to handle babies or push a mop around; then girls are being only realistic to assume that they will have to quit work to raise babies. It is hardly surprising that they are not up to the task of confronting the whole structure of the male-dominated family and its accompanying ideology regarding a woman's "place".

From the 1984 yearbook of the private girls' school Havergal College, a random reading of the fate of the class of '82 reveals that Havergal old girls are studying economics, commerce, sciences, math, geography, and biology at Queen's, Western, McGill, Toronto and Harvard universities – "South of the border Jeanne Des Brissay continues to enjoy Harvard and American life. She invites anyone in the neighbourhood of Boston to visit and enjoy her delicious chocolate chip cookies" – and are involved in sorority life, the rowing team, and the campus Tory club, and holiday in Greece and Cuba.

What is true for women as a whole, however, is mitigated by class. Although a majority of girls aspire to post-secondary education, those from wealthier, better-educated, and professional families are likelier not only to make this choice but to carry it through: their parents pay for their education, whereas a working-class girl is often obliged to take a job to finance her higher education or to contribute to the family itself. The Canadian Advisory Council on the Status of Women report shows that fully 82 per cent of girls with professional working mothers planned to go to university, but only 21 per cent of daughters of mothers who worked as manual labourers intended to do so. The girls I spoke with who had uncommon ambitions for themselves were as likely to be negatively influenced by their mothers' situation as inspired by it: "I admire my mother as a person but she just got married and had children and that's exactly what I *don't* want to do." Or: "My mother works at the blood bank as a lab technician and that doesn't interest me at all." Or; "Definitely my life is going to be different than my mother's. I'll make a point of it. I wouldn't want her job – personnel manager – I want a better education, I'll treat my children better, I'll never leave them." As for the mother who wants her daughter just to be "happy" at whatever she chooses to do, one is forced to ask if such lackadaisical standards woul be applied to a *son's* aspirations.

At the other end of the scale are the street kids, who, according to those who work with them, are doomed either to perpetual fantasy about making a million dollars from prostitution, quitting the life and going to live in a big house by the ocean, or to resignation to the fate of all people such as themselves: They're going to get the shit kicked out of them just for being around. A youth worker, speculating on their probable future, five years on, sees them "still here, doing the same thing, unless the government takes some responsibility for the fact that ten blocks away from the politicians' limousines are kids stealing a can of beans."

Between the princesses and the hookers are the daughters of the working class, girls who plan, like most others, to work outside the home. They will do so not as a matter of course, of personal fulfilment, or of "liberation", but as auxiliary labour to their primary responsibility to keep house and raise children. These are the girls who drive some feminists crazy: they "prefer" housework to paid work ("it's easier"), rationalize their lack of choice ("a woman's place is in the home"), exalt their husbands' work, and dedicate themselves to the provisioning of male comfort, aspire to "traditional" jobs without prospect of advancement, and assume the lion's share of child care even when they are at work. Paradoxically, all this selflessness just diminishes their domestic power; their unpaid work within the home carries no monetary reward, and their paid work outside is seen by their employer, and by themselves, as an extension of housework and thus secondary.

Their thinking is not entirely irrational. As Vancouver sociologist Jane Gaskell has said,[13] "the real world is traditional and they've resigned themselves to it. It's not just that they don't plan or are unrealistic. It's just that planning in an unequal labour market means traditional choices." They plan to be secretaries because clerical jobs are available, they expect to do the housework because men will not help, and they plan to drop out of the labour force to raise children because alternative child care is expensive, and it's the absence of their husband's income that would be most keenly felt by the family. They "know" that life as a housewife is not glamorous or exciting but they do not see a way they can avoid it if they want a family life.

But at the heart of a working-class girl's ambivalence about work in the labour force is surely the historical fact that women of her class have *always* worked outside the home. Since the demise of the cottage industries, they have slogged and sweated and moiled at labour in sweat-shops, mines, and clangorous and suffocating mills, labour that has only recently and only partially been dignified with trade union membership and has produced no tradition of female artisanship. As the American sociologist Gisela Konopka has written:[14] "The working girl, therefore, comes from a tradition . . . of exploitation. She could not consider work a privilege or a right to fight for. Her goal for centuries has been to get out of it as quickly as possible." No wonder, then, that such a girl's love-life, her dreams of romance, her anticipation of marriage and children in her early twenties, override the prospect of work outside the home; when such work promises so little of what is valuable to her – security, relationship, self-esteem – then love and marriage and family must provide all.

But this too may be changing. In her own research, Jane Gaskell has noted that more and more working-class girls are reconsidering the supposed advantages in the "traditional" set-up, which is not so traditional in the working class after all, as we have seen. They are looking hard at the alleged disadvantages of paid work, and are almost as enthusiastic as their middle-class sisters about moving into jobs after schooling. In spite of the prospect of ill-paying, low-level, and boring work, they observe that waged work of any kind provides an independence and status – not to mention money – unavailable to the housekeeper and mother. "They are treated as responsible adults," Gaskell writes,[15] "and paid a wage, signalling that they are competent to perform a task that is of real value to someone else." Waged work is grown-ups' work, and which adolescent girl does not want to be part of the culture of the adult, self-supporting, self-disposing, and self-knowing?

Perhaps it is only in retrospect that adolescence, that time of a woman's life between childhood dependence and adult responsibility, seems precious. To the girl living it through, that time is charged with anxiety, ambivalence, and misgivings, not to mention powerlessness and constraint. But from a long view it represents that time in female lives when each girl stands at the brink of momentous possibility: the chance to live in her own singular way the whole marvellous drama of a human life.

The fact that most will be doomed to something considerably more constricted – by ill-health or poverty, by sexual violence, by dashed hopes and thwarted ambitions, by discrimination and hostility and their own propensity to sell themselves short – should alert us to the price we ask these girls to pay in "growing up". What *is* it about female growing up that diminishes, instead of dilating, their potential? The answer to that, of course, is in the whole of female history at least since the Industrial Revolution, and each girl, as she steps giddily into the open spaces of her maturity, has as much chance of replaying that history of loss, waste, and pain as she has of living the prototypical life of liberation.

Two things would help her realize her possibilities: democratic and non-sexist social and economic institutions; and her own conviction (let her be given space and autonomy enough!) that she can be and do more than she was ever allowed to imagine. Let her imagine herself bold and clever and sovereign. Let her imagine herself a woman.

Acknowledgements

This book was made possible through the financial support of the Alberta Foundation for the Literary Arts and the Canadian Research Institute for the Advancement of Women. For support beyond the call of duty, my warm thanks to June Callwood and Merna Summers; Candas Jane Dorsey; and Raymond Wintonyk at Hunky Dory Enterprises. And to all those who talked to me, especially the girls, my heartfelt thanks for the conversation.

Notes

INTRODUCTION
[1]Sheila Kitzinger quoted in the *Edmonton Journal*, October 15, 1985.
[2]Simon Frith, *Sound Effects: Youth, Leisure, and the Politics of Rock 'n Roll* (London: Constable, 1983), p. 201.
[3]Patricia Meyer Spacks, *The Adolescent Idea: Myths of Youth and the Adult Imagination* (New York: Basic Books, 1981), p. 292.

THREE: BEST FRIENDS
[1]"friends had replaced parents": See Reginald W. Bibby and Donald C. Posterski, *The Emerging Generation: An Inside Look at Canada's Teenagers* (Toronto: Irwin, 1985), p. 30.

FIVE: SCHOOLS
[1]"unofficial school": See Sandra Kessler et al., *Ockers and Disco-Maniacs*, Inner City Education Centre pamphlet (Stanmore, Australia, 1982).
[2]"multiculturalism of teenagers": See Leah Steele, "Preppies to Punkers: A Guide to High School Life", *Herizons*, January-February 1985.

SEVEN: CLASSROOMS
[1]On the science education of women, see Joan Scott, "Is

415

There a Problem?", *Who Turns the Wheel?* (Science Education of Women in Canada Workshop, Science Council of Canada), January 1982.

[2]On girls' math and science avoidance, see "Sex-Related Difference in Mathematics Participation and Achievement: A Review of Related Research", *Mathematics: The Invisible Filter* (Math Department, Toronto Board of Education), 1983 (no author).

[3]On the University of Winnipeg study, see Carol Hurst, "Mathophobia", *Herizons*, January-February 1985.

[4]On gender differences in mathematical ability, see "Sex-Related Difference in Mathematics Participation and Achievement: A Review of Related Research".

[5]"research indicates that 'teachers praise boys more than girls'": See Myra and David Sadker, "Sexism in the Classroom of the '80s", *Psychology Today*, March 1985.

[6]On the American research study reported in 1974, see "Sex-Related Difference in Mathematics Participation and Achievement: A Review of Related Research".

[7]On motivation research, see Edward L. Deci, "The Well-Tempered Classroom", *Psychology Today*, March 1985.

[8]"a Canadian study has underscored": See Margot Charlebois, "Le monde des sciences et de technologie a-t-il un sexe?", *Canadian Women's Studies*, Summer 1984.

[9]For ratios of women teachers to female students and for girls in co-education schools, see Scott, "Is There a Problem?"

[10]Maureen Baker, *What Will Tomorrow Bring?* . . . (Ottawa: Canadian Advisory Council on the Status of Women, 1985), p. 21.

[11]On working-class girls' self-image, see Gisela Konopka, *The Adolescent Girl in Conflict* (Englewood Cliffs: Prentice-Hall, 1966), pp. 105-6.

[12]On girls' resistance to school, see Kessler et al., "Ockers and Disco-Maniacs", p.4.

NINE: BOYS
[1]Edward S. Herold, *Sexual Behavior of Canadian Young*

People (Toronto: Fitzhenry and Whiteside, 1984), pp. 64-5.

[2]Sharon Thompson, "The Search for Tomorrow", *Pleasure and Danger: Exploring Female Sexuality* (Boston: Routledge and Kegan Paul, 1984), p. 364.

[3]Ann Douglas, "Soft-Porn Culture", *The New Republic*, August 30, 1980.

[4]Janice Radway, *Reading the Romance: Women, Patriarchy, and Popular Literature* (Chapel Hill: University of North Carolina Press, 1984), p. 215.

[5]Angela Miles, "Confessions of a Harlequin Reader: Romance and the Fantasy of Male Mothering", unpublished paper.

[6]Angela McRobbie and Trisha McCabe, *Feminism for Girls: An Adventure Story* (London: Routledge and Kegan Paul), p. 165.

[7]"the primary vocation for girls who live dangerously": See Thompson, "The Search for Tomorrow", p. 354.

[8]"not a single shred of solid documentation": See Patricia Gibson, "Under His Thumb", *Healthsharing*, Summer 1984.

[9]"Why is this happening to teenagers?": See Patricia Gibson and Sarah Crichton, "The Riddle of Dating Violence", *Seventeen*, August 1982.

ELEVEN: FAMILIES

[1]On stress in children of divorced parents, see David Elkind, "All Grown Up and No Place to Go", *ATA Magazine*, May 1983.

[2]On children's reactions to divorce, see Margaret Krikke Webber, "Children and Divorce: The School's Role", *ATA Magazine*, May 1983.

[3]Germaine Greer, *Sex and Destiny: The Politics of Human Fertility* (London: Picador, 1985), p. 241.

[4]Elliot Leyton, *The Myth of Delinquency* (Toronto: McClelland and Stewart, 1979), pp. 191-2.

[5]Sgt. Gordon Howland, quoted in the *Edmonton Journal*, "Assault Figures Shock Police", October 3, 1985.

[6]*Sexual Offences Against Children* (Ottawa: Committee

on Sexual Offences Against Children, 1984) p. 175.

[7]For statistics on suicide, see Bibby and Posterski, *The Emerging Generation*, pp. 69-70, and the Montreal *Gazette*, May 18, 1985.

[8]Dave Taylor, producer, *Walking in the Rain* (Toronto: CHUM Ltd., 1985).

[9]For "Diane's" story, see Brenda Rabkin, *Growing Up Dead* (Toronto: McClelland and Stewart, 1979), p. 22.

[10]For the incest victim's story, see Taylor, *Walking in the Rain*.

[11]Neil Postman, *The Disappearance of Childhood* (New York: Dell Publishing, 1982), p. 138.

[12]Herbert Hendin quoted in Rabkin, *Growing Up Dead*, p. 52.

[13]Greer, *Sex and Destiny*, p. 241.

FIFTEEN: SEXUALITIES

[1]Sheila Kitzinger quoted in the *Edmonton Journal*, October 15, 1985.

[2]Dr. Sujatha Lena quoted in the Toronto *Globe and Mail*, September 11, 1985.

[3]Dr. David Garner quoted in the Toronto *Globe and Mail*, September 27, 1985.

[4]Susan Brownmiller, *Femininity* (New York: Fawcett Columbine, 1984), p. 221.

[5]For the University of Lethbridge survey, see Herold, *Sexual Behavior of Canadian Young People*, pp. 4-11.

[6]For the Hobart study, see ibid., p. 19.

[7]"How Adolescents Can Deal With Pressures to Engage in Sex", *Medical Aspects of Human Sexuality*, June 1984.

[8]For the Saskatchewan study, see Herold, *Sexual Behavior of Canadian Young People*, p. 26.

[9]For the Calgary study, see ibid., p. 17.

[10]For the abortion patients study, see ibid., p. 80.

[11]On attitudes to abortion, see ibid., p. 117, and Baker, *What Will Tomorrow Bring?*, p. 128.

[12]For the national survey results, see the Toronto *Globe and Mail*, February 7, 1986.

[13]For the Gallup poll results, see the *Edmonton Journal*, October 1, 1985.

[14]For the Alberta survey, see the *Edmonton Journal*, February 11, 1985.

[15]For the Newfoundland statistics, see the *Edmonton Journal*, October 1, 1985.

[16]On pornography consumption among teenagers, see the Toronto *Globe and Mail*, March 11, 1986.

[17]Bibby and Posterski, *The Emerging Generation*, p. 88.

[18]"Sex is transformed": See Postman, *The Disappearance of Childhood*, p. 137.

[19]Stuart Ewen quoted in Varda Burstyn, *Public Sex* (Toronto: CBC Ideas transcript, 1984).

SEVENTEEN: JOBS

[1]For the U.S. marketing survey, see the *Edmonton Journal*, January 14, 1986.

[2]High school principal quoted in the Toronto *Globe and Mail*, April 22, 1982.

[3]On teenagers' allowances, see Bibby and Posterski, *The Emerging Generation*, p. 58.

NINETEEN: COMPUTERS

[1]For the Pepper Wood El-Hi Report, see the Toronto *Globe and Mail*, March 1, 1985.

[2]Sarah Kiesler, "Second Class Citizens?", *Psychology Today*, March 1983.

[3]Heather Menzies, "Computer Technology and the Education of Female Students", an information paper for the Canadian Teachers' Federation, no date.

[4]For the American study, see Glenn Fisher, "Access to Computers", *The Computing Teacher*, April 1984.

[5]Weizenbaum quoted in "Two Minutes with Mr. Chips", *Boston Magazine*, May 1985, no author.

[6]For Quality Education data, see Ronald E. Anderson et

al., "Inequities in Opportunities for Computer Literacy", *The Computing Teacher*, April 1984.
[7]Margaret Lowe Benston, "The Myth of Computer Literacy", *Canadian Women's Studies*, Summer 1984.

TWENTY-ONE: CULTURES
[1]For national survey results, see the Toronto *Globe and Mail*, February 7, 1986.
[2]Bibby and Posterski, *The Emerging Generation*, p. 33.
[3]Frith, *Sound Effects*, p. 195.
[4]Bob Greene, "Words of Love", *Esquire*, May 1984.
[5]Holly Brubach, "Women in Rock", *Vogue*, August 1985.
[6]Madonna quoted in "Rock's New Women", *Newsweek*, March 4, 1985.
[7]Richard Goldstein, "Tube Rock: How Music Video is Changing Music", *The Village Voice*, September 17, 1985.
[8]For the University of Tennessee study, see the *Edmonton Journal*, September 5, 1985.
[9]Bibby and Posterski, *The Emerging Generation*, p. 40.
[10]Frith, *Sound Effects*, p. 228.
[11]For a discussion of girls' subculture, see Angela McRobbie and Jenny Garber, "Girls and Subcultures", *Resistance Through Ritual*, eds. S. Hall and T. Jefferson (CCCS, London: Hutchinson, 1975); Angela McRobbie, "Settling Accounts with Subcultures: A Feminist Critique", SCREEN *Education*, Spring 1980; Angela McRobbie, "Working Class Girls and the Culture of Femininity", *Women Take Issue: Aspects of Women's Subordination* (CCCS, London: Hutchinson, 1978); Mike Brake, "The Invisible Girl: The Culture of Femininity vs. Masculinism", *The Sociology of Youth Culture and Youth Subcultures: Sex and Drugs and Rock 'n Roll?* (London: Routledge and Kegan Paul, 1980).
[12]McRobbie, "Settling Accounts with Subcultures".

TWENTY-THREE: POLITICS
[1]Bibby and Posterski, *The Emerging Generation*, pp. 142-3; p. 26.

²For the Toronto 1984 study, see the Toronto *Globe and Mail*, December 18, 1984.

³For the Ontario 1986 study, see the Toronto *Globe and Mail*, May 28, 1986.

⁴For the St. Albert event, see the *Edmonton Journal*, June 7, 1985.

⁵Brownmiller, *Femininity*, p. 160.

⁶Thompson, "The Search for Tomorrow", p. 359.

TWENTY-FIVE: FUTURES

¹For statistics on female faculty, see *Economic Equality for Women: A Progress Report*, Government of Canada, 1985.

²On students in university, see Bibby and Posterski, *The Emerging Generation*, p. 160.

³On women in the work force, see "Women and Work" fact sheet, Canadian Advisory Council on the Status of Women, no date.

⁴On women and unions, see "Working Together: Women and Unions" fact sheet, Canadian Advisory Council on the Status of Women, no date.

⁵Heather Menzies, "Cinderella Meets Mr. Byte", *Le temps d'y voir* (MontreaL: Guérin, 1986), p. 111.

⁶Elaine Bernard, "Science, Technology and Progress: Lessons from the History of the Typewriter", *Canadian Women's Studies*, Summer 1984.

⁷On the wage gap, see Michael Ornstein, "Equality in the Workplace/Gender Wage Differentials in Canada" (Ottawa: Women's Bureau, Labour Canada, 1982).

⁸Bibby and Posterski, *The Emerging Generation*, p. 164.

⁹Ibid., p. 57.

¹⁰For the Ontario secondary school survey, see Avis Glaze, "Ontario Girls' Career Aspirations and Expectations", *Orbit 53*, June 1980.

¹¹For the Statistics Canada study, see the Toronto *Globe and Mail*, September 5, 1985.

¹²For the teenage boys' survey, see the *Toronto Star*, November 6, 1984.

[13]Konopka, *The Adolescent Girl in Conflict*, p. 73.
[14]Gaskell quoted in the *Edmonton Journal*, November 13, 1985.
[15]Jane Gaskell, "The Reproduction of Family Life", *British Journal of Sociology of Education*, vol. 4, no. 1, 1983.

If You Enjoyed *This* Book ...
NEW TITLES FROM M&S PAPERBACKS